MW01147748

UNIVERSITY OF NOTRE DAME

Liturgical Studies

Liturgical Studies

THE BIBLE AND THE LITURGY

BY

JEAN DANIÉLOU, S.J.

UNIVERSITY OF NOTRE DAME PRESS

NOTRE DAME, INDIANA

IMPRIMI POTEST: Theodore J. Mehling, C.S.C., Provincial

NIHIL OBSTAT: Eugene P. Burke, C.S.C., Censor Deputatus

IMPRIMATUR: ✠ Leo A. Pursley, D.D., L. L.D., Apostolic Administrator,
Diocese of Fort Wayne

June. 12, 1956

The original version of this work was published in 1951 by
Les Editions du Cerf, in Paris, under the title of *Bible et Liturgie.*

First paperback edition, 1966

Reprinted in 2000, 2005, 2008, 2009, 2011, 2013, 2014

Library of Congress Catalog Card No. 55-9516

Copyright © 1956 by University of Notre Dame
Notre Dame, Indiana 46556
undpress.nd.edu
All Rights Reserved

Published in the United States of America

∞ *This book was printed on acid-free paper.*

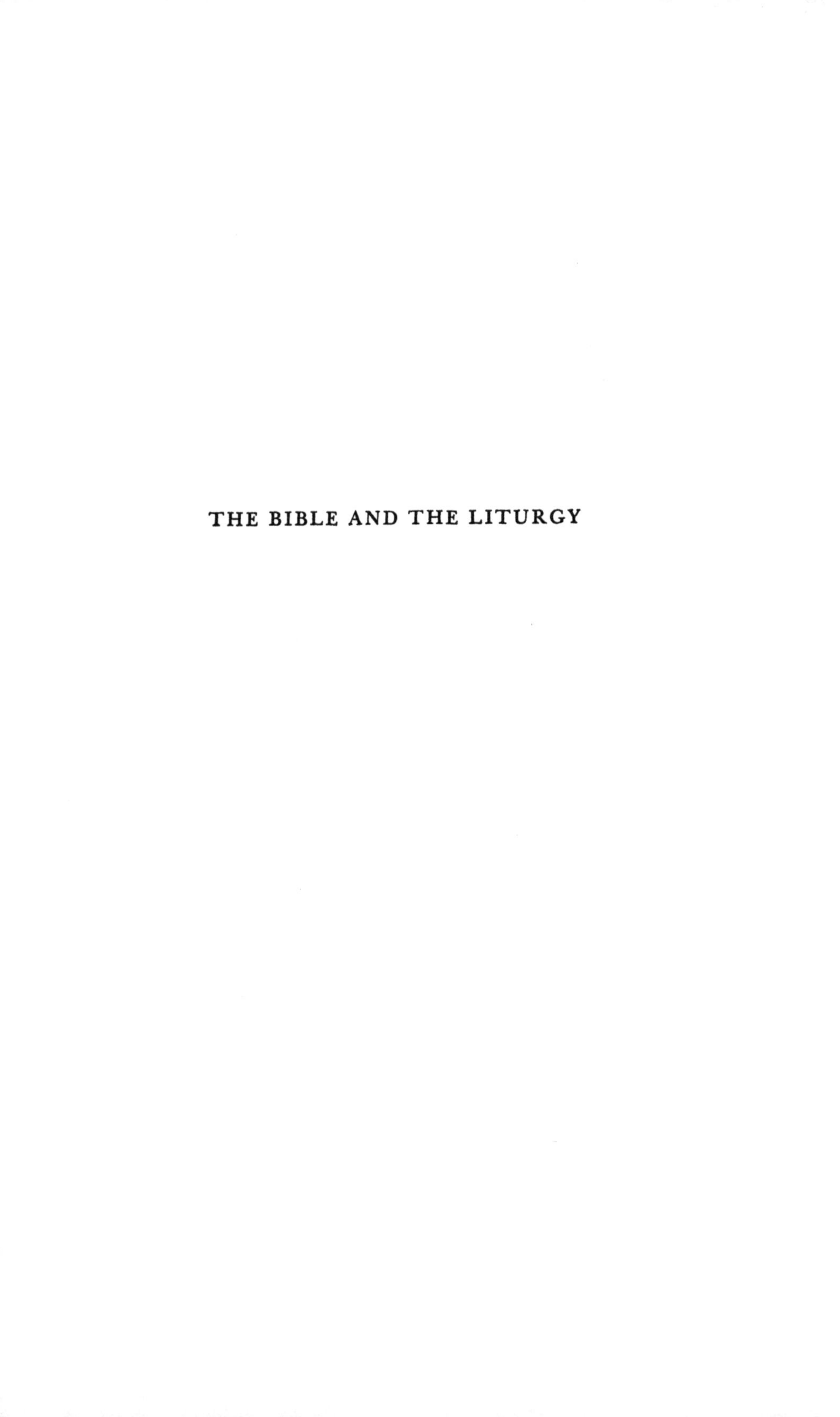

THE BIBLE AND THE LITURGY

Editor's Note

The rites of the Church and the greater feasts of Her liturgical year were intended to be an unfailing means, not only for transmitting the grace of the Sacraments, but also for instructing the faithful in their meaning and in the meaning of the whole Christian life.

During the last centuries, however, the faithful have too seldom taken proper advantage of this primal source of Christian initiation and growth. The reason is that they have lost familiarity both with the scriptural types and figures required for doing so and with the significance given to these types and figures by Christ Himself, by the Apostles, and by the Fathers. Too often, in fact, rites and feasts have come to be treated like sacred but mysterious heirlooms having no vital meaning for ordinary Christians today, since they do their work anyway, whether they are fully understood or not. It is to remedy, if only in part, this most unfortunate, not to say deplorable, situation that Father Danielou has written the present work. Taking advantage of the findings of modern scholarship, he here examines the sign-language of the Sacraments and of the Feasts—more particularly, that of Baptism, Confirmation, and the Holy Eucharist, as well as of the Sabbath—as this language is explained by the Fathers, who, in turn, based their interpretation on those given in the New Testament and in Tradition.

The present study is published in the hope, therefore, that it will prove of great value to all who are interested in learning, and instructing others in, the meaning of Christianity as this is expressed in its primary and basic idiom.

MICHAEL A. MATHIS, C.S.C.

Editor, *Liturgical Studies*

University of Notre Dame

June 6, 1956

Contents

THE BIBLE AND THE LITURGY

Introduction

THEOLOGY defines the sacraments as "efficacious signs,"—this being the sense of the scholastic saying (*significando causant*). But, as things are today, our modern textbooks insist almost exclusively on the first term of this definition. We study the efficacious causality of the sacraments, but we pay very little attention to their nature as *signs*. It is, therefore, to this aspect of the sacraments in particular that the chapters of this book will be devoted. We shall study the significance of the sacramental rites, and, more generally, that of Christian worship. But the purpose of this study is not simply to satisfy our curiosity. This question of the sacraments as signs is of fundamental importance for pastoral liturgy. Because they are not understood, the rites of the sacraments often seem to the faithful to be artificial and sometimes even shocking. It is only by discovering their meaning that the value of these rites will once more be appreciated.

There was no such problem in the early Church, for the explanation of the sacramental rites held an important place in the very formation of the faithful. During Easter week, for example, explanations of the sacraments were given to the newly-baptized who had received their first Communion after their baptism during the Easter vigil. Etheria, who, at the end of the fourth century, attended the Easter celebrations at Jersusalem, describes the bishop as saying in his last Lenten sermon to the catechumens: "So that you may not think that anything that is done is without meaning, after you have been baptized in the name of God, during the eight days of Easter week you will be given instruction in the church after Mass." [1] And also, in the sermons given on each feast of the liturgical year, the meaning of the feast was explained.

Our study will be based essentially on this teaching of the first Christian centuries, and will consist, therefore, of an interpretation of the symbolism of Christian worship according to the Fathers of the Church. We shall examine successively the symbolism of the three principal sacraments,—Baptism, Confirmation and the Holy Eucharist; and then that of the Christian week and of the liturgical year.

But before we study these patristic interpretations, we must first define the principles which inspired them. For this symbolism is not subject to the whims of each interpreter. It constitutes a common tradition going back to the apostolic age. And what is striking about this tradition is its biblical character. Whether we read the instructions concerning the sacraments, or look at the paintings in the catacombs, we are struck at once by figures taken from Holy Scriptures,—Adam in Paradise, Noe in the ark, Moses crossing the Red Sea,—these are the images used for the sacraments. It is, then, the meaning and origin of this biblical symbolism that we must first make clear.

That the realities of the Old Testament are figures of those of the New is one of the principles of biblical theology. This science of the similitudes between the two Testaments is called *typology*.[2] And here we would do well to remind ourselves of its foundation, for this is to be found in the Old Testament itself. At the time of the Captivity, the prophets announced to the people of Israel that in the future God would perform for their benefit deeds analogous to, and even greater than those He had performed in the past. So there would be a new Deluge, in which the sinful world would be annihilated, and a few men, a "remnant," would be preserved to inaugurate a new humanity; there would be a new Exodus in which, by His power, God would set mankind free from its bondage to idols; there would be a new Paradise into

[1] XLVI, 5; Pétré, (Sources chrétiennes), p. 231.

[2] This is the term adopted nowadays by most exegetes. See J. Coppens, *Les Harmonies des deux Testaments*, p. 98.

which God would introduce the people He had redeemed.[3] These prophecies constitute a primary typology that might be called eschatological, for the prophets saw these future events as happening at the end of time.[4]

The New Testament, therefore, did not invent typology, but simply showed that it was fulfilled in the person of Jesus of Nazareth.[5] With Jesus, in fact, these events of the end, of the fullness of time, are now accomplished. He is the New Adam with whom the time of the Paradise of the future has begun. In Him is already realized that destruction of the sinful world of which the Flood was the figure. In Him is accomplished the true Exodus which delivers the people of God from the tyranny of the demon.[6] Typology was used in the preaching of the apostles as an argument to establish the truth of their message,[7] by showing that Christ continues and goes beyond the Old Testament: "Now all these things happened to them as a type and, they were written for our correction" (I Cor. 10, 11). This is what St. Paul calls the *consolatio Scripturarum* (Rom. 15, 4).

But these eschatological times are not only those of the life of Jesus, but of the Church as well. Consequently, the eschatological typology of the Old Testament is accomplished not only in the person of Christ, but also in the Church. Besides Christological typology, therefore, there exists a sacramental typology, and we find it in the New Testament. The Gospel of St. John shows us that the manna was a figure of the Eucharist; the first Epistle of St. Paul to the Corinthians that the crossing of the Red Sea was a figure of Baptism; the first Epistle of St. Peter that the Flood was also a figure of Baptism. This means, furthermore, that the sacraments carry on in our midst the *mirabilia,* the great works of God in the Old Testament and the New: [8] for example, the Flood, the Passion and Baptism show us the same divine activity as carried out in three different eras of sacred history, and these three phases of God's action are all ordered to the Judgment at the end of time.

[3] See Jean Daniélou, *Sacramentum futuri,* Paris, 1950, p. 98.
[4] See A. Feuillet, *Le messianisme du Livre d'Isaïe,* Rech. Sc. Rel., 1949, p. 183.
[5] 'The only thing specifically Christian in the patristic exegesis of the Old Testament is the application to Christ' (Harald Riesenfeld, *The Resurrection in Ezechiel XXXVII and in the Dûra-Europos paintings,* p. 22).
[6] Harald Sahlin, *Zur typologie des Johannes evangeliums,* 1950, p. 8 et seq.
[7] Rendel Harris, *Testimonies,* 1, p. 21.
[8] Oscar Cullmann, *Urchristentum und Gottesdienst,* 2nd. ed., p. 114.

In general, then, sacramental typology is only one form of typology of the theological analogy between the great moments of Sacred History. But there is a special question in relation to the sacraments. For the sacraments present two aspects. First, there is the reality already accomplished, and this reality is in continuity with the works of God in the two Testaments. But there is also the visible sign,—water, bread, oil, baptizing, feasting, anointing,—by means of which the action of God operates. Here, properly speaking, is the sign, the sacramental symbol. But how are we to interpret this sign? Does it possess only the natural significance of the element or of the gesture that it is using: water washes, bread nourishes, oil heals. Or does it possess a special significance?

Here the recent studies on the history of liturgical origins are of service to us, for they have established the fact that we must not look to Hellenistic culture for the origin of the Christian sacraments as people have been so willing to do for the last fifty years, but rather to the liturgy of Judaism,[9] to which they are directly related. We must, therefore, ask ourselves the question: what significance did the signs used in the Jewish liturgy hold for the Jews of the time of Christ and for Christ Himself? It is also quite evident that the mentality of the Jews and of Christ was formed by the Old Testament. Consequently, it is in studying the significance for the Old Testament of the different elements used in the sacraments that we have the best method of discovering their significance for Christ and for the Apostles. We shall possess a typology that will bear not only on the content of the sacraments, but also on their form; and this typology will show us that we are quite justified in seeing the sacraments as prefigured in the Old Testament, since it is for this reason that these particular signs were chosen by Christ.

Let us consider some examples. We usually interpret the rite of Baptism by seeing in it a reference to water as cleansing and purifying. But now this does not seem actually to be the most important meaning of the rite. Two references in the Bible set us on the track of other interpretations. On the one hand, the water of Baptism is the water that destroys, the water of judgment; or "the waters" in Jewish symbolism are actually a symbol of the power

[9] See especially W. O. E. Oesterley, *The Jewish Background of the Christian Liturgy*, Oxford, 1925; Gregory Dix, *The Shape of the Liturgy*, Westminster, 1946.

of death. But the water of Baptism is also the water that brings forth a new creature, and this sends us back to the Jewish symbol of the waters as not only destructive but also creative. And, finally, Jewish baptism may also have referred to the crossing of the Red Sea. Or, again, in regard to the Eucharist: the choice of bread and wine may well have contained a reference to the sacrifice of Melchisedech; and the framework of a meal a reference to the sacred meals of Judaism, figures of the messianic feast; the season of the Pasch, a reference to the paschal meal, the symbol of the alliance between the People and God.[10] We can thus see how the deeds of Christ are charged with biblical memories which tell us the true significance of these deeds.

This biblical symbolism, therefore, constitutes the primitive foundation which gives us the true significance of the sacraments in their original institution. Later on, in the midst of a Hellenistic culture, other kinds of symbolism were grafted on to this primitive stock—symbols borrowed from the customs of the Greek world. In this way, for example, the imposition of the sign of the cross, the *sphragis,* was first interpreted in relation to the Jewish rite of circumcision, but later was compared to the brand or sign with which sheep, soldiers and priests were marked. Or again, the dove, originally referring to the Spirit of God hovering over the waters, was later considered to be a symbol of peace. But these later interpretations have never entirely covered over the original biblical foundation which the Fathers have preserved for us. And so their sacramental theology must be considered as essentially biblical.

This reference to the Bible has a double value.[11] First of all, it constitutes an authority justifying the existence and the form of the sacraments by showing that they are the expression of constant modes of the divine action, so that they do not appear as accidents, but rather as the expression of the very design of God. Moreover, these references to the Bible give us the symbolism in which the sacraments were first conceived, and they point out to us their various meanings, for the New Testament first defined them by means of categories borrowed from the Old. And so sacramental typology introduces us to a biblical theology of the sac-

[10] These statements will be vindicated later on.
[11] See Augustine, *De cat. rud.,* III, 6; P.L., XL, 313.

raments corresponding to their original significance, a significance which later theology was to continue to elaborate. The sphragis, for example, is, therefore, to be interpreted in line with the theology of the Covenant; Baptism in line with that of the judgment and of the Deliverance (redemption), the Eucharist in line with that of a meal and a sacrifice.

We can, therefore, now see the true value of our undertaking. We are not concerned with the personal theology of the Fathers; but what constitutes for us the supreme value of their work is that in them we meet apostolic tradition of which they are the witnesses and the depositaries. Their sacramental theology is a biblical theology, and it is this biblical theology which we are to try to recover. We are to look for it in the Fathers of the Church inasmuch as they are the witnesses of the faith of primitive Christianity. In them, we see this biblical theology as refracted through a Greek mentality, but this mentality affects only the method of presentation. The fact that the Good Shepherd appears dressed as Orpheus does not alter the fact that it is He Whom Ezechiel announced, and Whom St. John showed us as actually having come in the person of Christ.

A few words must now be said concerning the principal sources in which we discover this sacramental theology. The period of the first three centuries gives us only fragmentary witnesses, although these are particularly valuable by reason of their antiquity. If we must go back to the most ancient origin of treatises on the symbolism of worship, we should, perhaps, begin with the Gospel of St. John, if it is, as Cullmann believes, a kind of paschal catechesis commenting on the mysteries of Christ in relation to their biblical prefigurings [12] and also to their prolongation in the sacraments. But we are not going to speak only of the Fathers of the Church. We observe, first of all, that the ancient rituals often contain theological indications. Thus, one of the most ancient, the *Traditio Apostolica* of Hippolytus of Rome, mentions the explanations of the Eucharist given by the bishop to the newly baptized before giving them their first Communion during the Easter Vigil.[13]

[12] Cullmann, *Urchristentum und Gottesdienst,* 2nd. ed., 1950, p. 38-115.
[13] *Trad. Apost.,* 23; Botte (Sources chrétiennes), p. 54.

But such indications are only occasional. More important are those which we find in works explicitly concerned with the rites of worship. We have a small treatise of Tertullian's, *De Baptismo*.[14] This is the earliest document to put in systematic order the different aspects of the theology of Baptism. In it we find an interpretation of the figures of Baptism in the Old Testament: the different rites are enumerated with their significance. This treatise, known to Didymus the Blind, was to serve as a model for later works. It might seem astonishing that there is nothing like it to be found in relation to the Eucharist, but the reason is that the discipline of the *arcana,* of secrecy, forbade the revelation of the Mysteries. The only teaching given on this subject, therefore, could not be preserved for us in writing.

The subject most fully documented at this ancient time is, perhaps, that of the liturgical year, that is, essentially, of the paschal season, which was its principal feast. For the date of Easter caused several controversies and so gave occasion to various writers to treat of the subject. Two works on Easter by Origen have recently been found in Egypt, though unfortunately they have not yet been published. And, again, the feast of Easter, which was also that of Baptism, served as the occasion for sermons, some of which have been preserved for us. Thus, a *Homily on the Passion* by Melito of Sardis has been found and published by Campbell Bonner,[15] giving us a text of capital importance for paschal theology. Again, a homily that is substantially at least by Hippolytus of Rome, has been found by Fr. Charles Martin among the spuria of St. John Chrysostom.[16]

This material is sparse, but the fourth century gives us treatises on the whole subject. With the organization of the catechumenate, the custom spread of giving the new Christians an explanation of the sacraments which they had received. We have the good fortune to possess some of these sacramental catecheses given during Easter week, and they furnish us with the most important sources for our purpose. These documents, moreover, belong to

[14] P.L., 1, 1198-1224.

[15] *The Homily on the Passion,* by Melito, Bishop of Sardis, edited by Campbell Bonner, Studies and Documents, 1940.

[16] Established text, translated and annotated by Pierre Nautin, *Sources chrétiennes,* 1951. See Ch. Martin, *Un* περὶ τοῦ Πάσχα *de Saint Hippolyte retrouvé,* Rech. Sc. Rel., 1926, p. 148-167.

different times and places, the principal ones being the *Mystagogic Cathecheses* of St. Cyril of Jerusalem, the *De mysteriis* and *De sacramentis* of St. Ambrose of Milan, the Catechetical Homilies of Theodore of Mopsuestia, and, finally, the *Ecclesiastical Hierarchy* of Pseudo-Dionysius the Areopagite. We shall examine each of these in turn.

Under the name of Cyril, Bishop of Jerusalem, we possess a collection of twenty-four sermons addressed to the catechumens of Jerusalem.[17] That which is of special interest to us is the introductory sermon, or procatechesis, which must have been given on the First Sunday of Lent. To begin with, Cyril reminds the catechumens that Baptism demands a conversion, and that it must be received with a sound intention. Then he gives the significance of the exorcisms; he reminds his hearers that they must not reveal the content of their instructions to non-Christians; he insists on the importance of regularly attending the catecheses. Next, he gives some practical directions as to how they should conduct themselves during the periods of waiting: they should read or pray, but in a low voice so as not to annoy the others. And, finally, he shows what a great thing Baptism is and how important it is to prepare oneself properly for it.

The two first catecheses treat of penance and the mercy of God. The third, important for our purposes, gives a general teaching of Baptism. Cyril explains that it includes two elements, the water and the Spirit. He explains the meaning of the baptism of John the Baptist, and the reasons why Jesus was baptized by him. The catecheses that follow are commentaries on the Symbol of faith and contain few elements of sacramental theology.

Finally come the five mystagogic catecheses.[18] Their attribution to Cyril has been questioned, because certain reasons based on external criticism lead us to believe that they are by John of Jerusalem, Cyril's successor. But this does not matter to us, for in any case they are a document of the fourth century.[19] Cyril is now speaking to the newly baptized. He tells them why he has waited until this moment to give them the explanation of the significance

[17] P.G., XXXIII, 331-1128.

[18] An edition of the text with a translation by the Abbé Chirat will shortly be appearing in the collection entitled *Sources chrétiennes*.

[19] See W. J. Swaans, *A propos des Catéchèses mystagogiques attribués à saint Cyrille de Jérusalem*, Muséon, 1942, p. 1-43.

of the sacramental rites,—they had to remain surrounded with mystery. Then Cyril takes the rites one after the other. The first two catecheses are devoted to Baptism, the third to Confirmation, the two last to the Eucharist. We shall see how, in the case of each Sacrament, Cyril begins with its figures in the Old Testament, then the symbolism of the rites and, finally, the dogmatic explanations. These three aspects are also found in a general way in the other catecheses, and so also is the method which consists in following the development of the rites.

The Catecheses of Cyril of Jerusalem were given in Palestine in the middle of the fourth century. With the *De mysteriis* and the *De sacramentis* of St. Ambrose, we are in Milan, and in the last part of the century.[20] The two works are both mystagogic catecheses, analogous to those of St. Cyril, and they also deal with the three sacraments of Christian initiation. These catecheses were held during Easter week, as is shown by the beginning of the *De mysteriis*.

"The season now invites us to speak of the sacraments. If we thought it well to give some suggestions to the uninitiated before they received Baptism, this was done more by way of introduction than explanation. For we think that the light of the sacraments is better communicated if it is not expected than if some speaking has preceded it." (1, 2; Botte, 108.) We find the same idea with Cyril: the sacraments should preserve to the end their character of mysteries.

The relation of the two works has posed a difficult problem. Everyone agrees in seeing in the *De mysteriis* a work of St. Ambrose; but is this also true of the *De sacramentis?* Many arguments have been brought against its authenticity: the absence of any attribution to St. Ambrose by the manuscripts, a style very inferior to his, differences in certain rites: the *sputatio* and the prayer *ad orientem* are found in the *De mysteriis* and not in the *De sacramentis;* and, finally, the *De mysteriis,* in conformity with the law of the *arcana,* does not reveal the words of Baptism, of the Consecration, or of the Pater, while all these are found in the *De sacramentis.* Nevertheless, the resemblances are so considerable

[20] Established text, translated and annotated by Bernard Botte, O.S.B., *Sources chrétiennes,* 1950.

that criticism is now unanimous in seeing in both writings the work of St. Ambrose.[21]

But we still need to account for the differences between these two works, and Dom Morin has given an explanation which seems conclusive. This is that the *De mysteriis* was a literary work intended for publication, while the *De sacramentis* gives us the notes taken down by one of the audience during the catecheses. This would explain the absence of attribution; for this would be a document preserved for ordinary use in the Church of Milan. The style is negligent, because these are notes having the special quality of spoken instruction. And, finally, the disappearance of the two rites of the *sputatio* and the prayer to the east are explained by the fact that these two rites, having fallen into disuse, were taken out of a collection which was thought of as concerned with the ordinary ritual. We may, then, consider the *De mysteriis* to be an abridged version of the *De sacramentis* made for public use.

The first chapters deal with Baptism. Here Ambrose speaks at the same time—as St. Cyril does not—of the general doctrine and the symbolic meaning of the rites. He emphasizes especially the figures from the Old Testament. We find many usages peculiar to Milan, in particular that of washing the feet after Baptism, which Ambrose defends against the Roman custom (De Sacr. III, 4-7; Botte, 73-74). The treatment of Confirmation is quite brief, and the last chapters are concerned with the Eucharist. Here again St. Ambrose dwells at length on the figures,—those of Melchisedech and of the manna in particular. Like Cyril, he gives a commentary on the Pater. Like Cyril also, he explains clearly the reality of transsubstantiation. At once dogmatic and mystical, these two works are of the greatest possible interest for the theology of Christian worship.

The *Catechetical Homilies* of Theodore of Mopsuestia lead us to Antioch, a little after the time of St. Augustine. Msgr. Devreesse believes that they might have been given in 392. We have them only in a Syrian translation, recently discovered, of which, in

[21] See G. Morin, *Pour l'authenticité du De sacramentis et de l'explanatio fidei de saint Ambr.*, Jahr. Lit. Wiss, VIII, 1928, p. 86-106; O. Faller, *Ambrosius, der Verfasser von de Sacramentis,* Z.K.T., 1940, 1-14; 81-101; R. B. Connolly, *The De sacramentis Work of S. Ambrosius,* Oxford, 1942.

1933, Alfred Mingana made an English translation.[22] The Syrian text, accompanied by a French translation by Rev. P. Tonneau, O.P., and an introduction by Msgr. Devreesse, has just been published.[23]

The work begins with ten homilies making up a commentary on the Credo, parallel to the homilies of Cyril of Jerusalem, and as Msgr. Devreesse has shown, forming a valuable document for our knowledge of Theodore. The eleventh homily, on the Our Father, precedes the sacramental homilies, while in St. Ambrose's works, these are followed by the commentary on the Pater. Then come three homilies on Baptism and two on the Mass, which constitute the mystagogic catecheses properly so-called. As against the custom in the churches of Jerusalem and Milan, the explanation of the sacraments seems to have been given *before* their reception.

The sacramental symbolism of Theodore presents several characteristic aspects. In his Introduction, Msgr. Devreesse mentions "typology" several times; but what actually strikes us, when we compare Theodore to St. Cyril of Jerusalem, and, even more, to St. Ambrose, is the almost complete absence of any typology borrowed from the Old Testament. There is only one exception. Although Theodore ignores the baptismal figures of the Deluge or of the Crossing of the Red Sea, the theme of Adam appears several times, in particular in connection with the preparatory rites,—the examination, the exorcisms, etc.,—and the parallel between the situation of Adam in the garden and that of the catechumen in the baptistry dominates Theodore's presentation. But this is an exception, for his whole sacramental symbolism is founded on the parallel between the visible and the invisible liturgies. We are here in line with the symbolism of the *Epistle to the Hebrews.* We can certainly speak of typology, but we must make it clear that Theodore's is concerned more with the relation of things visible to the invisible than with the relation of things past to things to come, which is the true bearing of the word. Moreover, Theodore refers to the *Epistle to the Hebrews* in his first catecheses: "Every sacrament is the indication in signs and

[22] *Commentary of T. of M. on the Sacraments of Baptism and the Eucharist,* Woodbrooke Studies VI, Cambridge, 1933.
[23] *Les Homélies catéchétiques de T. de M.,* Cité du Vatican, 1949.

symbols of things invisible and beyond speech" (12:2), and he quotes Hebr. VIII, 5, and X, 1. He develops this line of thought especially in reference to the Eucharistic sacrifice, which he sees as the sacramental participation in the heavenly sacrifice.[24] And this leads us to remark that the sacramental platonism of Theodore is itself the consequence of the literal quality of his exegesis. Rejecting typology because he refused to see a relationship between historic realities, he was led to interpret sacramental symbolism in a vertical sense, as the relationship of visible things to invisible.

Nevertheless, this is not the only aspect under which he sees them: symbols of heavenly realities, the sacraments are for Theodore also a ritual imitation of the historic actions of Christ. We find here another basic aspect of sacramental theology, but it has a special character in the works of Theodore. Instead of relating only wholes to one another, he forces himself to try to establish relationships between the details of the rites and those of the Gospel narratives: the offertory procession is a figure of Christ led to His Passion, the offerings placed on the altar are figures of Christ placed in His tomb (XV, 25), the altar-cloths are the burial-cloths, the deacons who surround the altar are figures of the angels who guarded the tomb (XV, 27). We are at the beginning of a line of interpretation which was to have a great development in the East (we find it in Nicholas Cabasilas) and in the West with Amalarius). Seemingly a kind of typology along the lines of St. Matthew, it corresponded perfectly with one of the aspects of the temperament of Theodore, his care to hold himself to concrete realities. But it is obviously artificial. Theodore himself runs into complete absurdities, for example, when he tries to establish a comparison between the deacons who accompany the offertory procession and the Roman soldiers who accompanied Jesus to Golgotha (XV, 25).

With the Ecclesiastical Hierarchy of the Pseudo-Dionysius, we are still in Syria, but some two centuries later.[25] One of the results of the discovery of the *Homilies* of Theodore of Mopsuestia

[24] Francis J. Reine, *The Eucharistic Doctrine and Liturgy of the Mystical Catecheses of T. of M.*, Washington, 1942; J. Lecuyer, *Le sacerdoce chrétien et le sacrifice eucharistique selon T. de M.*, Rech. Sc. Rel., 1949, p. 481-517.

[25] P.G. I, 585A—1120A. French translation and Introduction of Maurice de Gandillac, Paris, 1943.

is that it allows us to determine more precisely the kind of culture with which the Areopagite writings were connected. We know the discussions which have arisen in the course of the search for the origin of these works: if Monsignor Daboy connects them with a convert of St. Paul's, Fr. Pira believes that they can be related to the writings of the Cappadocian Fathers.[26] But Fr. Stiglmayr, even though he was mistaken in attributing them to Severus of Antioch, already had seen that their place of origin was Syria.[27] And the striking resemblances, both in the order of the rites and in that of their symbolism, that exist between the *Homilies* and the *Hierarchy*, now render this origin certain.

But this work presents certain special characteristics. In the first place, it does not deal with an elementary catechesis, addressed to catechumens, like those of which we have so far been speaking. In one passage, having reminded his readers of the rites of Communion, the author writes: "And now, dear child, after giving these images ordered with piety toward the divine truth of their model, I will now speak for the spiritual instruction of the newly-initiated" (428 A). Following a number of explanations, the author continues: "But let us leave to the imperfect these signs which, as we have said, are magnificently painted on the walls of sanctuaries: they are enough to nourish their contemplation. For us, in Holy Communion, let us mount from effects to causes" (428 C). It certainly seems that the Pseudo-Dionysius distinguishes an elementary catechesis in which he meets the needs of the newly-baptized,—and this he only sketches out in passing,—from a deeper theology meant for advanced souls, which is the proper object of his work.

Another characteristic of the *Hierarchy* is that its symbolism is concerned with a more developed state of the liturgy itself. In connection with the rites of the Eucharist, we find here allusions to the incensing of the altar and the procession around the assembly: we are here concerned with the Byzantine liturgy. Dionysius treats at length of Confirmation and of the holy oils, which take up little space in the works of Ambrose or Theodore. Furthermore, after the three sacraments of initiation, he speaks of the

[26] *Denys le Mystique et la Theomachia,* R.S.P.T., 1936, p. 5-75.
[27] *Der sogennante D. Areopagiticus und Severus von Antiochen,* Scholastik, 1928, p. 1-27; 161-189.

Ordination of priests, of the Consecration of virgins, of the rites of betrothal; and there is nothing about these topics in the preceding writers. Here we are no longer dealing with the initiation of the newly baptized for whom these allusions would have no meanings; and we find also that the liturgy is much further developed.

The symbolic orientation which had already appeared in Theodore has now become very marked. Not only does Dionysius make no references to the figures of the Old Testament, but we find very few even to the New. The typology according to which the sacraments appear as events in sacred history, prefigured by the Old Testament and themselves the figure of the Kingdom to come, has given way to a mystical symbolism in which sensible realities are the images of intelligible. The waiting for the end of time characteristic of the first centuries has given way to the contemplation of the heavenly world. And so we can understand why the author very naturally went to the neo-platonist, Proclus, to find the forms of expression in which to express his vision of the world.[28]

The mystagogic catecheses are the most important documents for the theology of worship, but they are not the only ones. For we find in various other works passages related to the symbolism of the sacraments. So, to give only two examples: the *De Trinitate* of Didymus the Blind contains a passage on the figures of Baptism [29] and the *Treatise on the Holy Spirit* of St. Basil, has a symbolic commentary on a whole collection of rites, the prayer to the east, standing upright for prayer, etc.[30] And, in any case, the mystagogic catecheses are only concerned with the sacraments, whereas Christian worship contains other rites also charged with meaning, particularly, for example, the liturgical cycle of feasts. And here also we have valuable documents in the form of homilies pronounced on the occasion of the chief feasts of the year. It is impossible to give a complete list of these homilies, and we shall only point out certain texts.

In the eastern world, one group in particular deserves our attention, that of the Cappadocians. We possess liturgical homilies by St. Gregory of Nazianzen and St. Gregory of Nyssa containing

[28] Hugo Koch, *Pseudo-Dionysios in seinen Beziehungen zum Neuplatonismus und Mysterien weisen*, Mainz, 1900.

[29] II, 12-14; P.G., XXXIX, 668-717.

[30] XIV: Pruche (Sources chrétiennes), 162-167; XXVII: Pruche, 232-240.

elements of great value. Of those of the former, we should mention above all the homilies on the *Nativity,* on *Epiphany,* on *Pentecost,* on *Easter.*[31] Those of Gregory of Nyssa, though less celebrated, are also worthy of note. Besides three homilies on *Easter* and one on *Pentecost,* we have a brief homily on the *Ascension,* which now appears as a distinct feast, one on the *Baptism of Christ,* and, finally, one on *Christmas.*[32] All these texts are filled with symbolic interpretations.

The West is no less rich in works of this kind. We have a series of short *tractatus* on Easter, containing typological references, by Zeno, Bishop of Verona in the middle of the fourth century.[33] Gaudentius, Bishop of Brescia in the fifth century, has also left a series of *Sermons on the Easter season.*[34] The work of St. Augustine contains many sermons concerned with liturgical feasts, in particular Easter and Pentecost. And finally, to quote only the most important, we have a collection of homilies by St. Leo the Great commenting on the whole liturgical year.[35]

Besides these homilies, and in connection with the Easter season alone, we also need to consult the *Letters of the Feasts* which the Bishops of Alexandria customarily sent to their flock at the beginning of Lent, and which are the primitive form of the episcopal charge. The oldest are those of St. Athanasius,[36] and there also exists a collection of St. Cyril of Alexandria.[37]

This brief summary gives us an idea of the principal sources of liturgical symbolism in the first Christian centuries. It is also a witness to the important place held by this "mystagogic" teaching, in catechesis as well as in preaching. For the fact is that the life of ancient Christianity was centered around worship. And worship was not considered to be a collection of rites meant to sanctify secular life. The sacraments were thought of as the essential events of Christian existence, and of existence itself, as being the prolongation of the great works of God in the Old Testament and the New. In them was inaugurated a new creation which introduced the Christian even now into the Kingdom of God.

[31] P.G., XXXVI, 312-452; 608-664.
[32] P.G., XLVI, 578-702; 1128-1149. See Jean Daniélou, *Le mystère du culte dans les Homélies liturgiques de saint Grégoire de Nyssa,* Festgabe Casel, 1951.
[33] P.L., XI, 500-508.
[34] P.L., XX, 843-920.
[35] Text and translation by Dom Dolle, *Sources chrétiennes,* 1949.
[36] P.G., XXVI, 1360-1444.
[37] P.G., LXXVII, 402-981.

CHAPTER ONE

The Preparation

IN OUR study of the great liturgical unities, we shall begin with Baptism, since it is this sacrament which inaugurates the Christian life. During the fourth century, as we know, Baptism was usually given during the night before Easter Sunday, but the baptismal ceremonies actually began at the opening of Lent. The candidates were enrolled at that time and began their immediate preparation for the sacrament, whereas, up until taking this step, they had been simple catechumens. This remote period of preparation, as we know, could last for a long time; and the Fathers often protested against those who thus put off their entrance into the Church. But from the time of their enrollment at the beginning of Lent, the candidates constituted a new group, the *photizomenoi,* "those who are coming into the light." The ceremonies of these forty days form a whole, of which our Ritual today makes a single ceremony.

This preparation for Baptism was introduced by the rite of enrollment, which we find described in this way by Etheria in her account of her pilgrimage: "Whoever wishes to give in his name does so on the eve of Lent; and a priest notes down all the names. The next day, the opening of Lent, the day on which the eight weeks begin, in the middle of the principal church, that is, the church of the *Martyrium,* a seat is placed for the bishop, and one by one the candidates are led up to him. If they are men, they come with their godfathers; if women, with their godmothers. Then the bishop questions the neighbors of each person who comes in, saying: 'Does he lead a good life? Does he respect his parents: Is he given to drunkenness or to lying?' If the candidate is pronounced beyond reproach by all those who are thus questioned in the presence of witnesses, with his own hand the bishop notes down the man's name. But if the candidate is accused of failing in any point, the bishop tells him to go out, saying: 'Let him amend his life and when he has amended it, let him come to Baptism' " (*Per. Eth.* 45; Petre, p. 255-257).

Thus we see what this ceremony consisted of: the candidate gave in his name to the deacon in the evening; the next day, accompanied by his sponsor, he presented himself and underwent a kind of examination in order to ensure the purity of his motives; [1] then the bishop officially inscribed his name in the registers. The rite described by Etheria is that of Jerusalem, and is analogous to that of Antioch, thus described by Theodore of Mopsuestia: "Whoever desires to come to Holy Baptism, let him present himself to the Church of God. He will be received by the man who is delegated for this duty, according to the established custom that those who are to be baptized should be enrolled. This man will inform himself concerning the candidate's habits and way of life. This office is filled, for those who are baptized, by those who are called guarantors. The man who is delegated for this duty writes down your name in the Book of the Church, and also that of the witness. As in a trial, the person who is accused must stand up, so you are to hold out your arms in the attitude of one who prays, and to keep your eyes cast down. For the same reason, you are to take off your outer garment and to be barefoot, standing on haircloth" (*Hom. Cat.* XII, 1; Tonneau, 323).[2]

The literal meaning of these rites is obvious,—what interests us is the interpretation given to them by the Fathers. The examination which precedes the inscription in which the claims of the candidate are discussed, signifies for Theodore of Mopsuestia that at this moment Satan "tries to argue against us, under the pretext that we have no right to escape from his domination. He says that we belong to him because we are descended from the head

[1] This examination is mentioned as early as the *Apostolic Tradition* of Hippolytus of Rome (20; Botte, p. 47-48). St. Augustine gives an excellent explanation of the manner in which it was to be carried out. (*De catech. rud.* 9; P.L., XL. 316-317).

[2] See a similar description in the Pseudo-Denis, *Hier. Eccl.*, 393 D-396 A.

of our race," (XII, 18). Against him, "we must hasten to go before the judge to establish our claims and to show that by rights we did not belong to Satan from the beginning, but to God Who made us to His Own image" (XII, 19).[3] And Theodore compares this "temptation" to the scene in which Satan "tries to lead Christ astray by his wiles and temptations" (XII, 22). Even the attitude of the candidate is symbolic: he is clad only in his tunic and is barefoot, "to show the slavery in which the devil holds him captive and to arouse the pity of the judge" (XII, 24).

This interpretation brings out at the very beginning one of the themes of baptismal theology—the conflict with Satan. The baptismal rites constitute a drama in which the candidate, who up to this time has belonged to the demon, strives to escape his power. This drama begins with the enrollment and is not concluded, as we shall see, until the actual Baptism. Moreover, we notice that Theodore relates the trial which the candidate undergoes, on the one hand to the temptation of Adam, on the other hand to that of Christ. We are now in the center of biblical typology. A relationship between the temptation of Christ and that of Adam is perhaps to be found in the Gospel of St. Mark, where Christ is presented as the New Adam, ruling the wild beasts and served by angels (Mark I, 13).[4] The temptation of the candidate at Baptism is, in turn, a participation in the temptation of Christ. And so he also is contrasted with the first Adam. This parallelism of the scene in Paradise and that of Baptism, with that from the life of Christ in between, will appear all through the course of the baptismal catechesis. We notice that the Gospel of the Temptation is still today to be found in the Roman liturgy on the first Sunday of Lent, and this should be interpreted in the light of the fact that this was the Sunday of enrollment.

One detail given by Theodore of Mopsuestia deserves special attention. In Syria, the candidate stood on a haircloth during the examination. This appears again at the moment of the renuncia-

[3] "The justification of this idea may be found in St. Paul, when he says that at Baptism Christ destroys for us the *chirographum mortis,* the right which Satan claims over us (Col., II, 14), for that does seem to be the first introduction of juridical ideas into the theology of Baptism." (J. H. Crehan, *Early Christian Baptism and the Creed,* London, 1948, p. 104.

[4] See U. Holzmeister, *Jesus lebte mit den wilden Tieren,* Vom Wort des Lebens, Festschrift Meinertz, 1951, p. 84-92.

tion of Satan, and we find it also in the African liturgy.[5] This custom has been studied by Johannes Quasten.[6] It seems that the original significance was that of penitence; in fact, we find analogous practices in the Eleusinian mysteries. Theodore also points out this symbolism. But elsewhere the rite took on another meaning related to the interpretation of the Baptismal rites according to the symbolism of Adam. The haircloth appears as a figure of the "garments of skin" (Gen. III:21) with which Adam was clothed after the fall, the garments which signified his degradation. Henceforth the candidate will tread under foot these garments of skin. It is to this that Theodore is alluding when he speaks of the old sins, of which the haircloths are a figure.

After the examination, came the enrollment itself. This also is given a symbolic commentary. In this *Sermon against those who put off their Baptism,* intended precisely to invite the catechumens to have themselves enrolled, Gregory of Nyssa writes: "Give me your names so that I may write them down in ink. But the Lord Himself will engrave them on incorruptible tablets, writing them with His own finger, as He once wrote the Law of the Hebrews" (P. G. XLVI, 417 B). The visible writing in the register of the Church is the figure of the writing of the names of the elect on the tablets of heaven.[7] Theodore of Mopsuestia devotes a whole homily to a commentary on the *inscriptio.* For Gregory of Nyssa, the inscription on the church registers is a figure of inscription in the Church of heaven: "O you who present yourselves for Baptism,—he who is delegated for this office is actually inscribing you in the Book of the Church in such a way that you may know that from now on you are inscribed in heaven, where your guarantor will take great care to teach you, stranger as you are in this city and only recently come in, everything concerning life in this city, so that you may accustom yourself to it" (XII, 16; Tonneau, 348-349).

[5] Quodvultdeus, *De Symbolo ad Catech.*, I, 1; P.L., XL, 637.

[6] Johannes Quasten, *Theodore of Mopsuestia on the Exorcism of Cilicium,* Harv. Theol. Rev., 1942, p. 209-219.

[7] The idea of heavenly tablets on which are inscribed the names of the elect comes from Exodus XXXII, 32. The idea was common in Jewish Apocalyptic writings. It is found in the New Testament (Luke, X, 20; Apoc., III, 5) and in Christian Apocalyptic writings (*Apoc. Petri;* R.O.C., 1910, p. 117). On the origin of this idea, see Geo. Widengren. *The Ascension of the Apostle and the Heavenly Book,* Upsala, 1950.

Thus, on the first Sunday of Lent, the candidates were examined and enrolled. The forty days that followed were a time of retreat; "From this day on," writes St. Cyril of Jerusalem, "turn away from every wicked occupation; speak no unbefitting words" (P. G. XXXIII, 348 A). But "raise the eyes of your soul and contemplate the angelic choirs and the Lord of the universe seated on His throne, with His Son at His right hand and the Spirit beside Him" (XXXIII, 357 A). This whole period should be devoted to preparing for Baptism: "If your wedding-day were approaching, would you not leave everything else and devote yourself entirely to preparing for the feast? You are about to consecrate your soul to her heavenly Bridegroom. Should you not leave these material things in order to gain spiritual? (XXXIII, 345 A). This preparation consists on the one hand in strengthening faith against the attacks of error: this is the purpose of the catecheses. And, on the other, it is a time of purification in which "the rust of the soul should be removed so that only true metal will remain" (357 A).

During this time, the catechumens are to come to church every day, at the hour of Prime. This daily ceremony included, first of all, an exorcism. Etheria tells us: "The custom here is that those who are going to be baptized come every day during Lent, and first they are exorcised by the clerics" (46; Petre, p. 257). Cyril of Jerusalem gives some suggestions as to how the candidates should conduct themselves while the exorcisms were going on: "During the exorcism, while the others are coming up to be exorcised, the men should stay with the men and the women with the women. The men should be seated, having in their hands some useful book: and while one reads, the others should listen. On their side, the young women should gather to chant the Psalms or to read, but they should do so in a low voice, so that the lips may be speaking but the sound not reach the ears of the others" (XXXIII, 356 A-B).

Cyril treats at length of the meaning of the exorcisms. For one thing, they are the expression of the conflict which is being waged between Christ and Satan [8] around the faithful soul. The devil makes a supreme effort to keep the soul in his power. The trial,

[8] See A. Dondeyne, *La discipline des scrutins dans l'Église latine avant Charlemagne,* Rev. Hist. Eccl., 1932, p. 14-18.

which Theodore shows us as beginning at the time of the enrollment, continues during the preparation. "The serpent is beside the road, watching those who pass by," writes Cyril of Jerusalem. "Take care that he does not bite you by means of unfaithfulness. He follows with his eyes those who are on the way to salvation, and he seeks whom he may devour. You are going to the Father of spirits, but you must pass by the serpent. How can you avoid him? Have your feet shod with the Gospel of peace, so that, if he bites you, it will do you no evil. If you see any evil thought coming to your spirit, know that it is the serpent of the sea who is setting snares for you. Guard your soul, so that he cannot seize it" (XXXIII, 361 A-B).

Here is another witness to the importance of the struggle with Satan in the baptismal rites. But we must add that this theme of Satan barring the way which leads to God, and needing to be conquered if we are to come to God, is found in other places besides the baptismal rites. It appears particularly in connection with martyrdom. Thus during an ecstasy, Perpetua saw "on a ladder that mounted to heaven, a dragon lying, of an extraordinary size, who sets ambushes for those who climb the ladder." [9] In connection with this rite, Carl-Martin Edsman has remarked on the parallelism between the rites of Baptism and the theology of martyrdom,[10] and we shall have to mention it more than once. In a more general way, the demon is presented as trying to bar the way to heaven to the souls of the dead. St. Anthony sees in a vision "an enormous being, reaching to heaven, who, stretching out his hands, prevents the souls from rising up. He understood that this was the Enemy." [11] J. Quasten has shown the place of this idea in the ancient funeral liturgy.[12]

The rite of exorcism itself has for its precise purpose to free the soul little by little from the power that the demon has exercised over it. Cyril writes: "Receive the exorcisms eagerly, whether they be insufflations or imprecations, for this is salutary for you. Consider that you are gold that has been adulterated and

[9] *The Passion of Ss. Perpetua and Felicity MM.* (Tr. W. H. Shewring. Sheed & Ward, 1931) IV, 3. See F. J. Doelger, *Das Martyrium als Kampf gegen die Daemonen,* Ant. und Christ., III, 3, p. 177 et seq.

[10] C. M. Edsman, *Le baptême de feu,* p. 42-47.

[11] St. Athanasius, *Life of St. Antony,* 66.

[12] J. Quasten, *Der Gute Hirte in frühchristlicher Totenliturgie,* Miscell. Mercati, I, p. 385-396.

falsified. We are looking for pure gold. But as gold cannot be purified of its alloys without fire, so the soul cannot be purified without exorcisms, which are divine words, chosen from the Holy Scriptures. As goldsmiths, blowing on the fire, cause the gold to separate from the ore, so the exorcisms put fear to flight by the Spirit of God, and cause the soul to rise up in the body as if in its ore, putting to flight the enemy, the demon, and leaving only hope of life everlasting" (XXXIII, 349 A-B).[13]

After the exorcism every morning came the catechesis: "Then," writes Etheria, "they place a chair in the Martyrium [14] for the Bishop, and all those who are to be baptized sit in a circle around him, both men and women, and their godfathers and godmothers, and also all those who wish to hear, provided they are Christians. During these forty days, the Bishop goes through all the Scriptures, beginning with Genesis, explaining first the literal and then the spiritual sense: this is what is called catechesis. At the end of five weeks of instruction, they receive the Symbol, and its teaching is explained to them phrase by phrase, as was that of all the Scriptures, first the literal sense and then the spiritual" (46; Pétré, 257, 259). We are so fortunate as to have a series of these Catecheses, those of Cyril of Jerusalem.[15]

These catecheses end, on the Sunday before Easter, with the *redditio symboli* (the recitation of the Creed).[16]

The meaning of the catechesis is made clear by St. Cyril in these words: "Do not think that it consists of ordinary sermons. These are good, but if we neglect them today, we can still listen to them tomorrow. But the teaching that is to follow on the Baptism of rebirth,—if you neglect it now, when can you find it again? This is the time for planting the trees. If you neglect to spade and dig the earth, when can you plant properly a tree that has been badly planted? The catechesis is a building. If we neglect to dig its foundations, if we leave holes and the building is shaky,

13 See F. J. Doelger, *Der Exorcismus im altchristlichen Taufritual,* Paderborn, 1909.

14 The Martyrium was the main church at Jerusalem, built on top of the cistern where the instruments of the Passion had been found. See Vincent-Abel, *Jérusalem, Recherches de topographie, d'archéologie et d'histoire,* II, p. 183-194.

15 See also the *Catechetic Homilies of Theodore of Mopsuestia* and the *De catechizandis rudibus* of St. Augustine.

16 When the custom of having a *traditio* and a *redditio* of the Lord's Prayer became established, those of the Symbol were put forward one Sunday. See Dondeyne, *La discipline des scrutins,* Rev. Hist. Eccl., 1932, pp. 14-15.

of what use will be any further work?" (XXXIII, 352, A-B). The time of catechesis is, then, that in which the foundation of the faith is laid, while the purification of the soul is also being accomplished.

As for the *redditio symboli,* Theodore of Mopsuestia sees it as being the counterpart of the exorcisms. These have freed the soul from slavery to Satan. "By the recitation of the Creed, you bind yourself to God, by the mediation of the Bishop, and you make a pact to persevere in charity toward the divine nature" (XIII, 1; Tonneau, p. 369). We shall notice that the double aspect of struggle with Satan and of conversion to Christ will be found in the whole baptismal liturgy. All of it is a mystery of death and resurrection, and these preparatory rites are already marked with this character.

The last rite in preparation for Baptism took place during the Easter Vigil. This was the renunciation of Satan and adherence to Christ. This rite forms part of the preparatory ceremonies, although it is placed in the liturgy of the Easter Vigil. It also has been commented on by Cyril of Jerusalem in the first of the *Mystagogic Catecheses,* and we find it in all the writers and in all the Churches, in Jerusalem, in Antioch and in Rome. Its origin is ancient, being mentioned by so early an author as Tertullian.[17] It seems to be directly connected with the renunciation of idolatry. In this sense, it must have appeared, not in Jewish Christianity, where it would have had no meaning, but in the Christianity of the missions. And this explains why all the images it contains are connected more with the pagan world than with that of Judaism.

The renunciation of Satan is described by Cyril of Jerusalem: "You first entered into the vestibule of the baptistry, and, while you stood and faced the West, you were told to stretch out your hand. Then you renounced Satan as if he were present, saying: I renounce you, Satan, and all your pomp and all your worship" (XXXIII, 1068-1069). The formula of Theodore of Mopsuestia is analogous, "Once more you are standing on haircloth, with bare feet, you have taken off your outer garment, and your hands are stretched out to God in the attitude of prayer. Then you

[17] *De Corona,* 13; *De Spect.,* 4; *De Anima,* 35. For this last passage see the edition of J. H. Waszink, 1947, p. 414.

kneel but you hold your body upright. And you say: I renounce Satan, and all his angels, and all his works, and all his worship, and all his vanity, and all wordly error; and I bind myself by vow to be baptized in the name of the Father, of the Son, and of the Holy Spirit." (XIII, Introduction; Tonneau, 367).

Cyril explains to us why the renunciation of Satan takes place while the candidate faces the West: "I will explain to you why you stand facing the West. As the West is the region of visible darkness, and since Satan, who has darkness for his portion, has his empire in the darkness, so, when you turn symbolically toward the West, you renounce this dark and obscure tyrant" (XXXIII, 1069 A).[18] This symbolism goes back to the pre-Christian world. The ancient Greeks placed the gates of Hades in the West, where the sun goes down.[19] We meet it frequently in the Fathers of the Church: Gregory of Nyssa sees the West as "the place where dwells the power of darkness" (XLIV, 984 A).[20] St. Hilary comments on the verse of Psalm 47: *Ascendit super occasum* as being the victory of Christ over the power of darkness (P. L., IX, 446 B).[21]

Of greater importance is the formula of renunciation itself. It appears as the "breaking of the ancient pact with Hades" XLIII, 1073 B). Afterwards the soul will no longer fear "the cruel tyrant" who has held it in his power. "Christ has destroyed his power, abolished death by His death, in such a way that I am finally and decisively withdrawn from his empire" (XXXIII, 1069 A). We are now on the threshhold of the decisive act by which the liberation of the soul will be accomplished. Theodore of Mopsuestia, here again, insists on this aspect: "Since the devil, whom you, beginning with the heads of your race, once obeyed, has been the cause of many evils for you, you must promise to turn away from him. Yesterday, even if you had willed it, you could not have done so: but since, thanks to the exorcisms, the divine sentence has promised you freedom, you can now say: I

18 Likewise the Pseudo-Dionysius, Hier. Eccles., 401 A.

19 Cumont, *Recherches sur le symbolisme funéraire chez les Anciens*, 1942, p. 39 et seq.

20 See also Eusebius, P.G., XXIII, 726 A; Gregory of Nyssa, P.G., XLIV, 798 C; Athanasius, P.G., XVII, 294 B.

21 See F. J. Doelger, *Die Sonne der Gerechtigkeit und die Schwarze*, Munster, 1919, pp. 33-49; A. Rusch, *Death and Burial in Christian Antiquity*, Washington, 1941, pp. 8-10.

renounce Satan, indicating at the same time the association you once had with him, and the fact that you are turning away from it" (XIII, 5; Tonneau, p. 375). The gesture of stretching out the hand (Cyril), or the hands (Theodore) underlines the character of renunciation. For this was the gesture which in ancient times accompanied a solemn pledge made with an oath, or the denial of an oath. It expresses the candidate's denial of the compact that joined him with Satan in virtue of the sin of Adam.[22]

Certain liturgies add to the name of Satan, "and his angels." So in St. Basil (*Treatise on the Holy Spirit,*) 27; Pruche, p. 234). So also in Theodore of Mopsuestia, who adds this commentary: "These angels are not demons, but men who submit to Satan whom he makes his instruments, and of whom he makes use to make others fall" (XIII, 7). Theodore makes a list of these "angels": there are "those who apply themselves to profane learning and who cause the error of paganism to penetrate further into the world"; and "the poets who increase idolatry by their fables"; there are also "the leaders of heresies, Mani, Marcion, Valentin, Paul of Samosate, Arius, Apollinarius, who, under the name of Christ, have introduced their own vices" (XIII, 8).

Now come "the pomps, the service and the works of Satan." The first expression is the most difficult, and it has been the subject of much discussion. The expression *pompa diaboli* properly signifies the worship of idols, as Tertullian shows (*De Corona,* 13). But under what aspect is this worship considered? Rev. Hugo Rahner sees in the *pompa* the procession of the demons; the word would thus designate persons. The addition of *angeli* in the Syrian liturgy fits into this sense.[23]

But J. H. Waszink, following Dr. de Labriolle, maintains that the primitive meaning was that of the manifestations of the pagan worship, in particular the processions and the games, and that *pompa* stood for these.[24] This seems to be the original significance, and the personal one is an explanation of it related to the biblical and patristic idea of the worship of idols as being actually the worship of Satan.

This is the interpretation that we find in Cyril of Jerusalem:

[22] F. J. Doelger, *Die Sonne der Gerechtligkeit und die Schwarze,* pp. 118-119; J. H. Crehan, *Early Christian Baptism and the Creed,* pp. 96-110.

[23] *"Pompa diaboli,"* Zeitschr. Kath. Theol., 1931, p. 239 et seqq.

[24] *"Pompa diaboli,"* Vigiliae christianae, 1947, 1, p. 13 et seqq.

"The pomp of Satan is the passion for the theatre, for horse-races in the hippodrome, for games in the circus and all the vanities of this kind. And also it is the things which are laid out in the feasts of idols,—food, bread and other things that have been soiled by the invocation of impure demons. These foods, which are part of the pomp of Satan, are pure in themselves, but soiled by the invocation of demons" (XXXIII, 1072 A). This sentence reminds us of the old question of *idolothytes*—foods offered to idols—already under discussion in the times of the Apostles.

We observe that the spectacles of the theatre, the hippodrome and the circus formed part of the *pompa diaboli* inasmuch as they included acts of worship that were manifestations of idolatry. This is what we find treated, for example, in the *De Spectaculis* of Tertullian. But as idolatry receded, we find the accent is placed on the immorality of these spectacles. This is also to be seen in Theodore of Mopsuestia: "What are called the wiles of Satan are the theatre, the circus, the stadium, the athletic contests, the songs, the organs played by water, the dances, that the devil has sown in the world under the guise of amusements, to incite souls to their ruin. He who shares in the sacrament of the New Testament must keep himself from all this" (XIII, 12). The aspect of immorality was, moreover, associated even in the most ancient Fathers with that of idolatry. So Cyril, speaking of the pomps of Satan, speaks "of the folly of the theatre, where one sees farces and mimes full of things that should not be seen, and the foolish dances of effeminate men" (XXXIII, 1069 C).

As for the "worship of Satan," this means, for both Cyril and Theodore, all kinds of idolatrous and superstitious practices. As for the first, "the worship of the devil is prayer in the sanctuaries, honors given to idols such as lighting lamps, burning perfumes by springs and rivers, as do certain people who, deceived by dreams or demons, plunge into their waters thinking to find in them healing for their diseases. The worship of the devil is also to be found in auguries, divinations, signs, amulets, engraved scales, magic practices" (XXXIII, 1073 A). Theodore gives a similar list, and adds astrology (XIII, 10). We know that, even after the establishment of Christianity, such prohibitions were not uncalled for. The *Code of Theodosius,* at the end of the fourth century, still forbids "the offering of perfumes to the Penates, the lighting of lamps, the hanging of garlands around their altars" (XVI, 10, 201).[25]

To the renunciation of Satan and of his pomps, the *apotaxis,* corresponds the adherence to Christ, the *syntaxis.* Let us again take up St. Cyril's text: "When you have renounced Satan and broken the old pact with Hades, then the Paradise of God opens before you, the Paradise that He planted in the East from which our first father was driven out because of his disobedience. The symbol of this is that you turn from the West to the East, which is the region of light. So you were told to say: I believe in the Father, in the Son and in the Holy Spirit, and in the one Baptism of penance" (XXXIII, 1073 B). Theodore of Mopsuestia tells of an analogous rite, without saying precisely that the catechumen turns to the East, but showing him "with one knee on the ground, looking up to heaven with arms outstretched" (XIII, 1).[26]

The profession of faith made while facing the East complemented the abjuration made while facing the West. The rite is found in the baptismal liturgy of Milan: "You were turned to the East. For he who renounces the demon turns himself to Christ. He sees Him face to face" (De Myst., 7; Botte, p. 109). We know that this "orientation" of prayer is found in other places as well as the Baptismal liturgy. It was a general custom to turn to the East to pray. St. Basil ranks it among the most ancient traditions of the Church (De Spir. Sanct., 27; Pruche, 233). In places of prayer and even in private houses the East was indicated by a cross painted on the wall.[27] The prayer to the East appears particularly at the moment of martyrdom: Perpetua saw four angels who were to carry her to the East after her death (Passio Perpet., XI, 2). We find this custom of turning to the East also at the moment of death: Macrina, sister of St. Basil, "at the moment of her death, was conversing with her heavenly Bridegroom, on Whom she did not cease to fix her eyes, for her bed was turned toward the East" (P. G., XLVI, 984 B). And John Moschos

[25] See A. J. Festugière, *Le monde gréco-romain au temps de Notre-Seigneur,* II, pp. 40-41.

[26] The Pseudo-Dionysius, however, mentions the East, which shows that the rite existed at Antioch (Hier. Eccl., 400 A).

[27] Erik Peterson, *"La croce et la preghiera verso l'Oriente,"* Ephem. liturg., LIX, 1945, p. 525 et seqq; Jean Daniélou, *Origene,* pp. 42-44.

tells the story of a poor man, seized by brigands, who asked to be hanged turned toward the East (*Pré Spirituel,* 72).

The symbolism of the rite has led to discussion. F. J. Dolger thought that he saw in it a usage inspired by the pagan custom of praying in the direction of the rising sun.[28] But Erik Peterson has apparently established the fact that the usage is connected with the controversies between Jews and Christians as to the place in which the Messias will appear at the end of time. Prayer to the East thus would designate Christianity, in contrast with prayer toward Jerusalem for the Jews, and, later on, toward Qibla, or toward Mecca for the Moslems. This indicates its importance for distinguishing the three great forms of monotheism in the ancient Orient.[29] And here also appears the eschatological significance of the rite; it corresponds with what we have said of its being performed by those about to die:—they are waiting for Christ to come and take them.

Furthermore, a certain number of texts point out this eschatological meaning. It may have its origin in St. Matthew's Gospel: "As the lightning comes from the East, so shall the Son of Man appear" (XXIV, 27). The Didascalia of Addai explicitly connects it with this text: "It has been established that you should pray facing the East, because, as the lightning appears in the East and flashes to the West, so shall be the coming of the Son of Man" (II, 1; Nau, p. 225). This eschatological aspect appears clearly in this passage from Methodius of Olympia: "From the height of heaven, O virgins, the sound of a voice makes itself heard, awakening the dead: toward the Bridegroom, it says, let us all go in haste, clad in our white garments, our lamps in our hands, to the East" (Symp., II; Bonwetsch, p. 132).

But this primitive meaning, related to the waiting for the end of time, was soon attenuated; and often the East simply meant Christ Himself. This symbolism is connected with Zach., VI, 12: "The Orient is His name." This is the explanation of the baptismal rite found in St. Ambrose: "You are facing the East. The man who renounces the demon turns to Christ and sees Him face to face." This is also the meaning given by the antiphon of the

28 Tertullian relates that certain people accused the Christians of adoring the sun, because of this practice (Apol., XVI, 9).

29 Erik Peterson, *"Die geschichtliche Bedeutung der jüdischen Gebetsrichtung," Theol. Zeitsch.,* 1947, p. 1 et seqq; F. L. Doelger, *Sol Salutis,* pp. 220-258.

Roman liturgy: *"O Oriens, splendor lucis aeternae et sol iustitiae, veni ad illuminandos sedentes in tenebris et umbra mortis."* Gregory of Nyssa explains it in this passage: "The great day (of everlasting life) will no longer be illuminated by the visible sun, but by the true light, the Sun of justice, which is called the Orient (the rising sun) by the prophets because it is no longer hidden by any setting" (P. G. XLIV, 505 A). And St. John said that in the new Jerusalem "they shall have no need of light of lamp or light of sun, for the Lord God will shed light upon them" (Apoc. XXII, 5). So Christ appears as the eternally rising Sun of the Second Creation.[30]

But in the fourth century, the symbolism most frequently used is a different one. Prayer facing the East is connected with ideas of Paradise. For does not Genesis say that "Paradise was planted toward the East" (Gen. II, 8), and so to turn to the East seemed to be an expression of longing for Paradise. This is the reason given by St. Basil: "It is by reason of an unwritten tradition that we turn to the East to pray. But little do we know that we are thus seeking the ancient homeland, the Paradise that God planted in Eden toward the East" (*De Spir. Sancto,* 27; Pruche, p. 236). So also the *Apostolic Constitutions* show us this custom in the eucharistic liturgy: "Everyone, rising and turning to the East, after the catechumens have been sent away, prays to God 'Who mounts on the heaven of heavens to the East,' remembering the ancient home of Paradise, planted to the East, from which the first man fell" (II., 57: Funk, p. 162). St. Gregory of Nyssa shows the deeper meaning of this symbolism: "As if Adam lived in us, each time that we turn to the East—not that we can only contemplate God there, but because our first homeland, the Paradise from which we fell, was in the East—it is with good reason that we say, like the prodigal son: Forgive us our offenses" (P. G. XLIV, 1184 B-D).

But we should notice that this is the symbolism that Cyril of Jerusalem also gives us concerning the baptismal rite: "When you renounce Satan, God's Paradise opens to you, the Paradise that He planted to the East and from which our first father was driven on account of his disobedience. And the symbol of this is

[30] See also Tertullian, Adv. Val., 3; "The Holy Ghost loves the East which is a symbol of Christ"; Gregory of Nyssa, P.G., XLIV, 984 A; XLIV, 798 C.

your turning from the East to the West." Let us note here again the importance in the rites of Baptism of the symbolism of Paradise. In the contrast to Adam fallen under the dominion of Satan and driven out of Paradise, the catechumen appears as freed by the New Adam from the dominion of Satan and reintroduced into Paradise. A whole theology of Baptism as deliverance from original sin is thus written into the rites.

Facing the East, then, the catechumen pronounces his allegiance to Christ.[31] The word "alliance" (*syntheke*) is often used here.[32] Like the renunciation, this action was accompanied by a gesture of stretching out one's hand or hands, as Theodore says (XIII, 1) and also Pseudo-Dionysius (401 A-B). Theodore always interprets this gesture in the sense of a prayer and not of the taking of a pledge. Cyril says that he has already talked at length to the catechumens about the formula of this engagement. Actually it is the whole content of the Christian faith which is summed up here and to which the new Christian adheres. We do not need to dwell on this.[33] As Theodore of Mopsuestia well notes, the adhering to Christ is, properly speaking, the act of faith required for Baptism: "The divine nature is invisible, and faith is required on the part of the man who presents himself to promise to live henceforth without wavering in familiarity with it. Invisible also are the good things which God has prepared for us in heaven, and for this reason we must believe" (XIII, 13-14).[34]

With the renunciation and profession, the preparation for Baptism was finished, on the threshold of the Easter night. All through these different stages, we find one movement inspiring them all, which is to culminate in the solemn rite we are now going to describe. Now the aspirant for Baptism, having officially professed his will to abandon idolatry and to consecrate himself

[31] See J. H. Crehan, *Early Christian Baptism and the Creed*, pp. 95-110.

[32] Origen, *Exh. Martyr.*, 17; Koetschau, 16; Greg. Naz., Or., XL, 8; P.G., XXXVI, 368 B.

[33] See De Ghellinck, *Recherches sur le symbole des Apôtres, Patristique et Moyen Age*, I, p. 25 et seq.; J. N. D. Kealy, *Early Christian Creeds*, p. 30 et seq. Oscar Cullmann, *Les premières confessions de foi chrétiennes.*

[34] This adherence to Christ, which was both a profession of faith and a commitment for life, appears to assume a high degree of importance in early Christian times. This is the rite mentioned by the expression ἐπερώτημα in the famous baptismal text of I Peter, III, 21. See on this text E. G. Selwyn, *The First Epistle of St. Peter*, pp. 205-206; Bo Reicke, *The Disobedient Spirits and Christian Baptism*, pp. 173-201; J. H. Crehan, loc. cit., pp. 10-12.

to Christ, is able to receive the sacrament. But this long preparation is a witness to the personal nature of the action that has been accomplished. Nothing is further from the spirit of primitive Christianity than any magical ideas of sacramental action. Sincere and whole-hearted conversion is the condition required in order to receive Baptism.

CHAPTER TWO

The Baptismal Rite

THE ceremonies that we have been studying form the remote preparation for Baptism. Cyril of Jerusalem devotes his first catechesis to them, Theodore of Mopsuestia his two first homilies. These ceremonies constitute a well-defined whole, characterized by the fact that they take place outside the baptistry; the candidate is treated as being still a stranger to the Church. The entrance into the baptistry marked the beginning of the immediate preparation for Baptism, and it included two preliminary rites: the laying aside of clothing and the anointing with oil. Then the actual Baptism took place, carried out by immersion in the baptismal pool. It was followed by clothing in the white robe, corresponding to the previous stripping. These are the rites whose symbolism we shall now study.

At the beginning of the *Procatechesis,* St. Cyril says to those who come to be enrolled: "Henceforth you are in the vestibule of the palace. May you soon be led into it by the king" (XXXIII, 333 A). This is an exact description of the candidates' state. They were in the vestibule, "breathing already the perfume of beatitude. They are gathering the flowers of which their crowns will be woven" (XXXIII, 332 B). Here we find once more the symbolism of paradise. But they are not yet inside the sanctuary itself. The leading into the baptistry signifies the entrance into the Church, that is to say, the return to Paradise, lost by the sin of the first man: "You are outside of Paradise, O catechumen," says Gregory to those who would put off their Baptism. "You share the exile of Adam, our first father. Now the door is opening. Return whence you came forth" (P. G. XLVI, 417 C. See also 420 C and 600 A). In the same way, Cyril of Jerusalem says to the candidate: "Soon Paradise will open for each one of you" (XXXIII, 357 A).

In the primitive Church, this symbolism was brought out by the decoration of the baptistries. Here we usually find Christ represented as the Good Shepherd surrounded by His sheep in a paradisal setting of trees, flowers and fountains. The baptistry of Dura, which dates from the third century, shows us opposite to the representation of Christ, that of the fall of our first parents. This corresponds exactly, as L. de Bruyne has noted, to the inscription copies by Fortunatus in the paleo-Christian baptistry of Mayence: "The hall of holy Baptism, so difficult to enter, now is shining. Here it is that Christ washes away in the river the sin of Adam." [1] Thus every decoration of baptistries is charged with theological implications. It is the Paradise from which Adam was driven out and to which Baptism restores us.[2]

One feature of these decorations deserves an explanation,—that of the deer drinking at the springs. This image is drawn from an allusion to Psalm XLI: "As the hind longs for the running waters." We can understand how this text seemed to symbolize the thirst of the catechumens to receive Baptism; but the symbolism is carried much further than one would think possible at the first glance. In some baptistries, it has been noted that the deer have serpents in their mouths, because it was a tradition of ancient science that deer could eat snakes, and that to do so made them thirsty. And this idea, as H. Ch. Puech has seen, gives a richer symbolism to these pictures in baptistries.[3] It is only after vanquishing the serpent that the catechumen may come to the water of Baptism. We have already seen that this theme appears in the catecheses of Cyril.[4] And so the representation of the deer which,

[1] L. de Bruyne, *"La décoration des baptistières paléochrétiens,"* Mélanges Mohlberg, I, p. 198 et seq.

[2] On the Church as Paradise, see Cyprian, *Epist.,* LXXIII, 10; C.S.E.L., 785; LXXXV, 15; C.S.E.L., 820.

[3] *La symbolique du cerf et du serpent,* Cahiers Archéologiques, IV, 1949, p. 18-60.

[4] See above, pp. 23 and 24.

having eaten the serpent, quenches its thirst at the river of paradise, summarized for catechumens all the stages of their baptismal initiation.

The role of the baptistries is also symbolic. As Franz-Joseph Bolger has noted, they are often octagonal.[5] The origin of this shape may come from the Roman baths, but we are certain that in Christianity it took on a symbolic significance, as is shown by the inscription on the baptistry of the church of St. Thecla in Milan, which was that of St. Ambrose: "It is fitting that the hall of Holy Baptism should be built according to this number, which is that in which the People obtained true salvation in the light of the risen Christ." The number 8 was, for ancient Christianity, the symbol of the Resurrection, for it was on the day after the Sabbath, and so the eighth day, that Christ rose from the tomb. Furthermore, the seven days of the week are the image of the time of this world, and the eighth day of life everlasting. Sunday is the liturgical commemoration of this eighth day, and so at the same time a memorial of the Resurrection and a prophecy of the world to come.[6] Into this eighth day, inaugurated by Christ, the Christian enters by his Baptism.[7] We are in the presence of a very ancient baptismal symbolism, to which it may well be that St. Peter alludes in his first Epistle (III:20), and which occurs frequently in ancient Christianity.[8]

When he has been led into the baptistry, the catechumen is stripped of his clothing: "As soon as you entered," writes Cyril of Jerusalem, "You took off your tunic (XXXIII, 1077 A). For the Lenten exorcisms, the candidate took off only his outer robe and his sandals, but now he is to be completely naked. Theodore of Mopsuestia says: "You are now going to Holy Baptism, and first you take off your clothing" (XIV, I; Tonneau, p. 405). This rite, in preparation for the baptismal bath, is interpreted by various authors in a symbolic sense. Taking off one's old garments seems to Cyril as "the image of taking off the old man and his works" (XXXIII, 1077 A). This is also the symbolism of the Pseudo-Dionysius, who writes: "This is the teaching which symbolic tra-

[5] *Antike und Christentum,* IV, 4. 288; v, 294.
[6] See below, Chapter 15.
[7] F. J. Doelger, *Zur Symbolik des altchristlichen Taufhauses,* Ant. und Christ., IV, 3, p. 153 et seq.
[8] Jean Daniélou, *Sacramentum futuri,* p. 77 et seq.

dition suggests in taking away from the neophyte, so to say, his previous life; in stripping him of all his last attachments to things here below, and making him stand with his body and feet bare" (401 A). Gregory of Nyssa, speaking to those who deferred their Baptism, takes up the same idea: "Take off the old man like a soiled garment. Receive the tunic of incorruptibility which Christ is offering you" (XLVI, 420 C). For Theodore of Mopsuestia, the old garment symbolizes corruptible humanity: "Your garment, sign of mortality, must be taken off, and by Baptism you must put on the robe of incorruptibility" (XIV, 8).[9]

This "old man," symbol both of sinfulness and of mortality, was first stripped off the human race by Christ upon the Cross. If Baptism means configuration to Christ dead and risen again, this taking off of one's garments is, for St. Cyril, a configuration to the nakedness of Christ on the Cross: "You are now stripped and naked, in this also imitating Christ despoiled of His garments on His Cross, He who by His nakedness despoiled the principalities and powers, and fearlessly triumphed over them on the Cross (Col. 2:15). Since the powers of evil once reigned over your members, you should now no longer wear that old garment. I am not speaking now of your sensible nature, but of the corrupt 'old man' with his deceitful desires" (XXXIII, 1077 B). The stripping of Christ on the Cross is a figure of the "stripping off" of the old man, symbolized by one's garments. By this stripping, Christ had "despoiled" the powers of evil of the dominion that they exercised over mankind by means of this "old man." By the baptismal stripping, which is a participation in the stripping of Christ, the candidate in turn thus stripped or despoiled the powers of evil of the dominion that they had exercised over him.

But this old garment of corruption and sin which the baptized are to strip off, following Christ, is the very garment with which Adam was clothed after his sin. So we see the relationship between the scene in Paradise in which Adam, vanquished by Satan, is clothed with corruptibility; that of Calvary in which Jesus, the new Adam, the conqueror of Satan, strips off his tunic of corruptibility; and, finally, Baptism, in which the person being baptized takes off,

[9] On clothing as a symbol of the passions and of mortality in the ancient world, both pagan and Jewish, see P. Oppenheim, *Symbolik und religioese Wertung des Monchkleides im christl. Altertum,* Münster, 1932, pp. 8-18.

with his old garments, the corruptibility in which he shared as long as he was under the dominion of Satan. Mortality, put on by Adam, is symbolized for the Fathers by the "tunics of skin" of Genesis 3:21.[10] The stripping of the "old man" by the baptized is, therefore, the stripping off of the tunics of skin in which Adam was clothed. Gregory of Nyssa explains this clearly: "The soul, in taking off the tunic of skin with which it was clothed after the fall, opens itself to the Word by taking away the veil from its heart, that is to say, the flesh. And by 'flesh' I mean the 'old man' who must be taken off by those who desire to wash themselves in the bath of the Word" (XLIV, 1003 D).[11]

This baptismal nakedness signified not only a stripping off of mortality, but also a return to primitive innocence. This is the aspect stressed by St. Cyril. "How wonderful! You were naked before the eyes of all without feeling any shame. This is because you truly carry within you the image of the first Adam, who was naked in Paradise without feeling any shame" (XXXIII, 1080 A). This is also the interpretation of Theodore of Mopsuestia: "Adam was naked at the beginning and he was not ashamed of it. This is why your clothing must be taken off, since it is the convincing proof of this sentence which lowers mankind to need clothing" (XIV, 8). Here the reference is no longer to the tunics of skin of Genesis III:21, but to the loin-cloths of fig leaves of Genesis III:7. This is the clothing which Adam and Eve put on after their sin witnessing to their loss of innocence and of trust: "Shame and fear followed the sin, so that Adam and Eve did not dare any more to stand before God, but covered themselves with leaves and hid themselves in the woods" (P. G., XLVI, 374 D [12]).

So we see the true symbolism of the stripping of garments. It means the disappearance of the shame proper to sinful man before God, and the recovery of the sentiment, opposed to that of shame, of filial trust, the *parrhesia,* which was one of the blessings

[10] See Erik Peterson, *Pour une théologie du vêtement,* Lyon, 1943, p. 17. In the background of this symbolism can be found the old idea that clothes are peculiarly liable to attract the influence of spirits. See below, p. 51.

[11] See Gregory of Nyssa: "When the first men allowed themselves to be dragged into evil and were despoiled of their original blessedness, the Lord gave them clothes of skin. In my opinion, what is referred to is not ordinary clothes but our mortal lot" (XLVI, 521 D).

[12] In a certain number of authors, starting with Irenaeus, the fig-leaves are symbolic of concupiscence. The stripping off of the garment thus stands for the stripping off of concupiscence. See J. H. Waszink, *Tertullian, De Anima,* 1949, pp. 436-437.

of man's state in Paradise.[13] Gregory of Nyssa describes this return to the liberty of the children of God accomplished by Baptism: "Thou hast driven us out of Paradise, and now Thou dost call us back; Thou hast stripped us of those fig-leaves, those mean garments, and Thou hast clothed us once more with a robe of honor . . . Henceforth, when Thou callest Adam, he will no longer be ashamed, nor, under the reproaches of his conscience, hide himself among the trees of Paradise. Having recovered his filial assurance (*parrhesia*), he will come out into the full light of day" (XLVI, 600 A).

The catechumen, stripped of his garments, was next anointed with oil. St. Cyril of Jerusalem also comments on this rite: "stripped of your garments, you were anointed with oil that had been exorcised, from the top of your head to your feet, and you were made partakers in the true olive tree which is Jesus Christ. Cut off from the wild olive and grafted on the cultivated tree, you have been given a share in the richness of the true oil. For the exorcised oil is a symbol of participation in the richness of Christ. It causes every trace of the enemy's power to vanish. By the invocation of God and by prayer, the oil has gained the power, not only to purify you from the vestiges of sin by consuming them, but also to put to flight all the invisible powers of the Evil One" (XXXIII, 1080 A).

The most important symbolic meanings of oil appear in this text. Its action is, first of all, a healing one, since oil is used as a remedy: thus, the blessed oil heals the soul of the traces of sin which still remain in it. We find this idea in the prayer for the consecration of the baptismal oil in the *Euchology of Serapion:* "We anoint with this oil those who are approaching the divine re-birth, praying the Lord Jesus Christ to impart to it a power to heal and to strengthen, and, by its means, to heal, in the body, the soul, the spirit of those who are to be baptized, freeing it of every trace of sin and iniquity, so that they may have the strength to triumph over the attacks of hostile powers." [14]

These last words guide us to another and more important aspect of the symbolism of the oil. Oil is used, especially by athletes, to strengthen their bodies. "The high priest," writes the Pseudo-

[13] Jean Daniélou, *Platonisme et Théologie mystique,* pp. 110-123.
[14] Brightman, Journ. Theol. Stud., 1900, p. 264.

Dionysius, "begins by anointing the body of the postulant with holy oils, thus in symbol calling the initiate to the holy contests which he will now have to undertake under the direction of Christ, for it is He who, God as He is, orders the combat. He Himself descended into the arena with the combatants, to defend their freedom and to assure their victory over the forces of death and damnation. So the initiate also will throw himself gladly into these struggles which he knows to be divine. He will march in the footsteps of Him Who, in His goodness, was the first of athletes. So it is that, having overcome all the stratagems and all the powers that oppose his deification, in dying to sin by baptism, we can say that he partakes of the very death of Christ" (Hier. Eccl. 401D – 404A).

So the anointing with oil is meant to strengthen the initiate for his struggles with the demon. But it is important to notice that this does not refer only to the future struggles of the new Christian, but to the act of Baptism itself, as the Pseudo-Dionysius so well shows. We should keep before our minds the dramatic meaning of the Easter night as a struggle with the demon. We have seen that this conflict has been in progress since the beginning of the preparation, since the moment of the enrollment. Now comes the supreme struggle; like a good athlete, the candidate needs to be anointed before engaging in it.

Cyril of Jerusalem shows us that the descent into the baptismal pool is as it were a descent into the waters of death which are the dwelling-place of the dragon of the sea, as Christ went down into the Jordan to crush the power of the dragon who was hidden there: "The dragon Behemoth, according to Job," writes Cyril, "was in the waters, and was taking the Jordan into his gullet. But, as the heads of the dragon had to be crushed, Jesus, having descended into the waters, chained fast the strong one, so that we might gain the power to tread on scorpions and serpents. Life came so that henceforth a curb might be put on death, and so that all who have received salvation might say: O Death, where is your victory? For it is by Baptism that the sting of death is drawn. You go down into the waters, bearing your sins; but the invocation of grace, having marked your soul with its seal, will prevent your being devoured by the terrible dragon. Having gone down into the waters dead in sin, you come out brought to life in justice" (XXXIII, 441 A)[15].

Placed in this perspective, the anointing with oil is easily understood, as Baumstark has clearly seen: "The present rubrics of baptism prescribe that the anointing should be carried out *in pectore et inter scapulas*. Ancient Christianity prescribed at this point an anointing of the whole body. But what was the meaning of this ceremony? We are given instruction on this point by the Greek prayer for blessing the baptismal water: 'Thou, Thou hast sanctified the waters of the Jordan by sending from on high Thy Holy Spirit, and Thou hast crushed the heads of the dragons hidden therein.' This text is a clear witness to the belief that the depths of the waters were the dwelling of diabolic powers and that Christ had conquered them by His Baptism. And it was for this victorious struggle against the powers of darkness that the candidates for Baptism were prepared by receiving a symbolic anointing." [16]

We now come to the actual Baptism. In Antioch, it was preceded by the consecration of the water, as we see in the Apostolic Constitutions (VII, 43) and in Theodore of Mopsuestia: "First of all the Bishop, according to the law of the pontifical service, should use the prescribed words and ask of God that the grace of the Holy Spirit should come on the water and make it capable of this awe-inspiring birth" (XIV, 9). The other catecheses also insist on the consecration of the water, but without saying exactly when it took place. So Cyril of Jerusalem writes that: "Ordinary water, by the invocation of the Holy Spirit, of the Son and of the Father, acquires a sanctifying power" (XXXIII, 429 A). And Ambrose says, even more concisely: "You have seen the water, but all water does not heal; that water heals which has the grace of Christ. The water is the instrument, but it is the Holy Spirit Who acts. The water does not heal, if the Spirit does not descend to consecrate it" (De Sacr., 1, 15; Botte 58-59).

The baptismal rite is essentially constituted by the immersion and emersion, accompanied by the invocation of the Three Per-

[15] See P. Lundberg, *La typologie baptismale dans l'ancienne église*, pp. 148-150. There is the same exegesis of Job, XL, 18-20, in Didymus, XXXIX, 684 B.
[16] A. Baumstark, *Liturgie comparée*, p. 149.

sons. From the New Testament, the meaning of the rite appears fixed in its essential features. The symbolic immersion symbolizes purification from sin. Baptism is a *catharsis*. This was the meaning of the Jewish rite of the baptism of proselytes. The New Testament describes it as a bath (*loutron*) (Eph. 5:26). The coming out, or emersion signifies the communication of the Holy Spirit which gives a man the sonship of adoption (*huiothesia*). It makes the baptized a new creature by means of a new birth (*palingenesia,* Tit. 3:5) [17].

Here again, the baptized appear in contrast to Adam. Baptism is a new creating of man to the image of God, following the destruction of the old Adam. This parallelism is already to be found in St. Paul. Rudolph Schnackenburg had good reason to write that "the parallel between Adam and Christ is of supreme importance in St. Paul's theology of Baptism" [18]. The comparison of Baptism with the creation of the first Adam is often to be found in the Fathers: "By Baptism," writes Tertullian, "man regains his likeness to God" (De bapt., 5; P. L., 1, 1206 A). And Theodore of Mopsuestia develops the idea: "Since we fell and were corrupted by sin, the sentence of death caused our complete dissolution; but, in consequence, our Creator and Master, according to his indescribable power, once more fashioned us anew" (XIV, 11).

But this destruction of the old and creation of the new man is not achieved first in the baptized, but rather in Christ dead and risen again: "Baptism," writes St. Cyril, "is not only purification from sins and the grace of adoption, but also the antitype of the Passion of Christ" [19]. We find here once more the three planes: Adam, Christ, the baptized, that we have so often met before. But here the configuration to Christ dead and risen again becomes of primary importance. First developed by St. Paul in many passages,[20] this idea is seen by the Fathers of the fourth century to be the reality signified by the baptismal immersion and emersion. So, St. Cyril writes: "Then you were led to the holy pool of divine baptism, as Christ taken down from the cross was laid in the tomb already prepared. Each one was questioned in the name of the

[17] See, on these two aspects in St. Paul, Rudolf Schnackenburg, *Das Heilsgeschehen bei der Taufe nach dem Apostel Paulus,* Munich, 1950, pp. 1-15.

[18] Loc. cit., p. 107.

[19] P.G., XXXIII, 1081 B.

[20] Schnackenburg, loc. cit., pp. 26-74.

Father, of the Son and of the Holy Spirit. You made the profession of salvation and three times were you plunged in the water and came forth, signifying Christ's burial for three days. By this action, you died and you were born, and for you the saving water was at once a grave and the womb of a mother" (XXXIII, 1080 C).

The symbolism of this rite is first of all that pointed out by St. Paul: the sacramental configuration to the death and resurrection of Christ. This is the theme which appears everywhere. We find it, for Syria, in the *Apostolic Constitutions:* "Sanctify this water so that those who are baptized may be crucified with Christ, die with Him, be buried with Him, and rise again with Him for adoption" (VII, 43). St. Gregory of Nazianzen writes: "We are buried with Christ by Baptism so that we may rise again with Him" (P. G., XXXVI, 369 B); and, in Milan, St. Ambrose expresses the same idea: "You were questioned: Do you believe in Jesus Christ and in His cross? You said: I believe; and you were plunged into the water. This is why you were buried with Christ. For the man who is buried with Christ, rises with Him" (De Sacr. II, 20; Botte 66).

But what concerns us is the development and enrichment given to this teaching. Here our great master is St. Cyril. When he has explained that the three immersions symbolize the three days of the Paschal triduum, he continues: "What a wonder and a paradox! We have not actually died, we have not really been buried, and we have not, in reality, after having been crucified, risen again. But the imitation is effected in an image (*en eikoni*), salvation in reality (*en aletheia*). Christ was really crucified, really placed in the tomb; He really rose again. And all these things were done through love for us, so that, sharing by imitation in His sufferings, we might truly obtain salvation. O overflowing love for men! Christ allowed His pure hands and feet to be pierced with nails, and He suffered; and by communion in His sufferings, He has given me the grace of salvation without my having suffered or struggled." "Let no one, then," he continues, "think that baptism consists only in the remission of sins or our adoption as sons, when we know with certainty that, while it is purification from our sins and the pledge of the gift of the Holy Spirit, it is also the antitype of the passion of Christ. This is why St. Paul said to us just now: 'Do you not know that all we who have been baptized into Christ Jesus have been baptized into His death. For we were buried with Him by means of Baptism into death, . . .' He said these words to men who thought that Baptism procured the remission of sins and also adoption, but not that it was also the participation (*koinonia*) in a similitude (*mimesis*) in the true sufferings of Christ.

"But so that we may learn that what Christ suffered He endured for us and our salvation in reality, and not in appearance, and that we are partakers in His sufferings, Paul insists: 'If we have been planted together with Him in the likeness of His death, we shall be so in the likeness of His resurrection also.' And he is right in saying this; for now that the true Vine has been planted, we also at Baptism have been grafted into His death by participation. Consider this idea most attentively, following the words of the Apostle. He did not say: 'If we have been grafted into His death,' but 'into the likeness of His death.' For Christ actually died, His soul was really separated from His body. But for us, on the one hand, there is the imitation (*homoioma*) of His death and His sufferings, and on the other, not imitation, but the reality of salvation" (XXXIII, 1082 B-1084 B).

This text is admirable in every way. Baptism is an "antitype" of the Passion and the Resurrection, that is to say, it is at the same time like and unlike the original. And the text explains in what the likeness consists and in what the unlikeness. In the death and Passion of Christ, there are two aspects which must be distinguished: the historical fact, and the content of saving grace. The historical fact is only imitated: the sacramental rite symbolizes it, represents it. But the content of saving grace allows us a true participation (*koinonia*): The two aspects of the sacrament are thus defined perfectly: it is an efficacious symbol of the Passion and the Resurrection, representing them corporeally and actualizing them spiritually.

If we now consider the mystagogic teaching of the West, we find the same doctrine in St. Ambrose, and even in the same terms (so much so that a question of influence can be raised): "The Apostle cries (*boa*), as you have heard in the preceding reading: Whoever is baptized, is baptized in the death of Christ. What does this mean: 'in the death'? That, as Christ died, you also must taste death: as Christ died to sin and lives for God, so you also must die to the past pleasures of sin by the sacrament of Baptism, and rise again by the grace of Christ. This, then, is a death, but not in the reality (*veritas*) of physical death, but in a likeness (*similitudo*). When you plunge into the water, you receive the likeness of death and burial. You receive the sacrament of His cross, because Christ was hanged on the cross, and His body was fixed there by nails. And you, when you are crucified, you are joined to Christ, you are joined to the gift of Our Lord Jesus Christ" (De Sacr., II, 23; Botte p. 69).

Baptism thus effects a configuration to the one death of Christ, as St. Basil tells us in *De Spiritu Sancto:* "It was to lead us back to friendship with God that there took place the coming of Christ in the flesh, the examples of His public life recorded in the Gospels, His sufferings, His cross, His burial, His resurrection, so that man, saved by the imitation (*mimesis*) of Christ, might regain his original sonship. For a perfect life, then, the imitation of Christ is necessary, imitation not only of the examples of kindness, humility and forbearance that He gave us during His life, but also imitation of His death, as Paul, the imitator of Christ, says: Be conformed to His death, so as to come to the resurrection from the dead. How, then, do we enter into the likeness of His death? By being buried with Him by Baptism. There is only one death for the world, and one resurrection of the dead, of which Baptism is the figure (*typos*). This is why the Lord who orders our life has established the covenant (*diatheke*) of Baptism, containing the figure of death and of life, the water effecting the image (*eikon*) of death, the Spirit communicating the pledges of life. It is by three immersions and as many invocations that the great sacrament (*mysterion*) of Baptism is carried out, so that the image of death may be reproduced and so that, by the communication (*paradosis*) of the knowledge of God, the soul of the baptized may be illuminated" (*De Spiritu Sancto,* 15; Pruche 168-171).

The relation of Baptism to the death of Christ is especially emphasized by the triple immersion, an allusion to the paschal triduum, as Pseudo-Dionysius explains: "Consider with me how fitting are the symbols expressed in the sacred mysteries. Since to our eyes, death is the separation of parts that have been united, leading the soul into a world invisible to us, while the body, as it were hidden under the earth, loses all human form, it is fitting that the initiate should be entirely immersed in the water as a figure of death and burial in which all form is lost. By this lesson given in symbols, he who receives the sacrament of Baptism and is plunged three times into the water, learns to imitate mysteriously this triarchic death that was the burial of Jesus for three days and three nights, in the measure, at least, that it is permitted to man to imitate God without sacrilege" (404 B).

The opposition between the burial of Christ in the earth and the immersion of the baptized in the water marks clearly the difference between the reality and the sacrament. This is what Gregory of Nyssa points out: "Let us ask why the purification is effected by means of water, and what is the purpose of the triple immersion? Here is what the Fathers have taught on this subject and what we have received from them. Our Lord, in carrying out the economy of our salvation, came down on earth in order to raise up its life. We, when we receive Baptism, do so indeed in the image of Our Lord and Master, but we are not buried in the earth, for this will be the dwelling of our body when it is dead. But we are buried in the water, the element which is akin to the earth. And, in doing so three times, we imitate the grace of the resurrection. We do not do this by receiving the sacrament in silence, but the names of the three holy Hypostases are invoked upon us" (XLVI, 586 A-C. See also Disc. Catch. XXXV, 5-12). We should remark, however, that the sense of the analogy between the waters of death and the waters of baptism has been lost, and that Gregory is here making use of the hellenistic theory of the four elements and their relations.

But if the waters of Baptism are the tomb in which man the sinner is buried, they are also the vivifying element in which the new creature is generated. They are at once "tomb and mother," says Cyril of Jerusalem. This theme is directly connected with the idea of the maternity of the Church, which seems to have been developed especially in Africa. Tertullian writes at the end of *De Baptismo:* "You are blessed when you come out of the most holy bath of the new birth, and when you pray for the first time beside your Mother and with your brothers" (De. bapt. 20). We see here the connection between the motherhood of the Church and Baptism. It is made still clearer by St. Cyprian: "Since the birth of the Christian is accomplished in Baptism, and since the baptismal rebirth only takes place with the one Bride of Christ, who is able spiritually to bring to birth the sons of God, where could he be born who is not a son of the Church" (Epist. LXXXIV, 6; C. S. E. L., 804)[21].

We see how this theme grows more precise: the Church is the mother of the sons of God; it is in baptism that she brings them forth. So the symbolic meaning of the rite is ready at hand: the baptismal bath is the maternal womb in which the children of God are begotten and brought forth. This is clearly explained by Didymus the Blind, whose dependence on the Africans for his baptismal theology is well known: "The baptismal pool is the organ of the Trinity for the salvation of all men. She becomes the mother of all by the Holy Spirit while remaining a Virgin. This is the meaning of the Psalm: My father and my mother have abandoned me (Adam and Eve were unable to remain immortal) but the Lord has taken me up. And He has given me as a mother the baptismal pool; for Father, the Most High; for Brother, the Lord baptized for our sake" (P. G., XXXIX, 692 B).

In the fourth century, this theme assumes considerable importance in the catecheses preparatory to Baptism by Zeno, Bishop of Verona, written between 362 and 373: "Exult with joy, my brothers, in Christ, and all, inflamed with ardent longing, hasten to receive the heavenly gifts. The font, where we are born to eternal life, invites you by its healthful warmth. Our mother is eager to bring you into the world, but she is not in the least subject to the law which ruled over the child-bearing of your mothers. They groaned in the pains of birth, but this heavenly mother joyfully brings you forth, all joyful; free, she brings you into the world, freed from the bonds of sin" (Tract, 30; P. L. XI, 476 B)[22]. This is the text of the first *Invitation* to Baptism. The exhortations that follow it take up and develop the same theme, with the realism peculiar to Latins. What interests us is how the symbolism is made precise, thus giving the rite its meaning.

The same symbolism is developed with loving care in another part of the world, that of Antioch, by Theodore of Mopsuestia. He spends little time on the symbolism of the configuration to

[21] Joseph C. Plumpe, *Mater Ecclesia*, p. 100 et seqq.

[22] I follow the translation by M. Chirat, Vie Spirit., April 1943, p. 327.

death, but he is expansive on the symbolism of rebirth: "The Bishop must ask God that the grace of the Holy Spirit come down on the water to make it the womb of a sacramental birth, for Christ said to Nicodemus: unless a man be born again of water and the Spirit, he cannot enter into the Kingdom of God. As, in the birth of the flesh, the womb of the mother receives the seed but the divine hand forms it, so in Baptism, the water becomes a womb for him who is born, but it is the grace of the Spirit that forms therein him who is baptized for a second birth" (XIV, 9). Here we have a development parallel to that of the West.

After the rite of Baptism itself, there is still one final ceremony: the clothing with the white garment.[23] "After Baptism," says St. Ambrose, "you have received white garments, that they may be the sign that you have taken off the clothing of sin and that you have been clad in the pure garments of innocence" (De Myst. 34; Botte, 118). These white robes are given to replace the old garments taken off before Baptism which were figures of the "old man." These are the symbol of the new. One of the essential aspects of Baptism is thus here symbolized. The terms "clothing of incorruptibility" (*endyma aphtharsis*) (XXXIII, 1033 A; XXXVI, 361 C; XLVI, 420 C) or of "shining garment" XXXIII, 360 A; XXXVI, 361 C; XLIV, 1005 B) are the technical expressions for Baptism in the lists.[24] The origin of this symbolism is to be found in St. Paul: "You who have been baptized in Christ, have put on Christ" (Gal, III, 27). The rite of the white garment thus signifies one of the aspects of baptismal grace.

These white garments signify at once purity of soul and incorruptibility of body.[25] St. Ambrose brings out the first aspect, and we find it again in St. Cyril: "Now that you have taken off your old garments and been clad in white garments, you must also in spirit remain clothed in white. I do not mean to say that you must always wear white garments, but that you must always be covered with those that are truly white and shining, so that you may say with the prophet Isaias: He has clothed me with the garment of salvation and He has covered me with the vestment of joy"

[23] At this point the liturgy of Milan had a rite of washing of feet (Ambrose, *De Sacr.*, III, 4; Botte, 72-73).

[24] See J. H. Waszink, *Tertullian De Anima,* p. 420-421.

[25] On the symbolism of the white garments, see P. Oppenheim, loc. cit., pp. 33-43.

(XXXIII, 1104 B) Theodore of Mopsuestia emphasizes rather the incorruptibility regained by Baptism: "Since you came up from Baptism, you are clad in a vestment that is all radiant. This is the sign of that shining world, of that kind of life to which you have already come by means of symbols. When indeed you receive the resurrection in full reality and are clothed with immortality and incorruptibility, you will have no further need of such garments" (XIV, 26).

This glory is a participation in the glory of Our Lord at His Transfiguration when "His garments became white as snow" (Matthew XVII, 2).[26] "He who is baptized is pure, according to the Gospel, because the garments of Christ were white as snow when, in the Gospel, He showed forth the glory of His resurrection. For he whose sins are forgiven becomes white as snow" (Ambrose, De Myst., 34; Botte 118). And St. Gregory of Nyssa shows the baptized as wearing "the tunic of the Lord, shining like the sun, which clothed Him with purity and incorruptibility when He went up on the Mount of the Transfiguration" (XLIV, 1005 C. See also XLIV, 764 D).

Another series of texts find in the white robes the restoration of the original integrity in which the first Adam was created.

Here the symbolism of the clothing with white garments is again related to the symbolism of paradise which we have met already in connection with the taking off of the old garments, symbol of the garments of skin in which man was clothed after the Fall, the white robes being the symbol of the recovery of the vestment of light which was man's before the Fall. The relation of the baptismal robes to man's state in paradise appears in a passage such as this, in which Gregory of Nyssa speaks of Baptism: "Thou hast driven us out of Paradise and called us back; Thou hast taken away the fig-leaves, that garment of our misery, and clad us once more with a robe of glory" (XLVI, 600 A). More precisely still, Gregory shows us the father of the prodigal son clothing him with a robe, "not with some other garment, but with the first, that of which he was stripped by his disobedience" (XLIV, 1143 B. See also XLIV, 1005 D).

The underlying idea in all these passages is that Adam, before

[26] That is the text of the *Codex Bezae* and the main body of tradition in the West. All the Greek MSS, however, give 'white as light.'

he was clad in the garment of skin, had been stripped of another garment, since he discovered that he was naked. This idea has been finely stated by Erik Petersen: "Adam and Eve were stripped by the Fall, in such a way that they saw that they were naked. This means that formerly they were clothed. And this means that, according to Christian tradition, supernatural grace covered man like a garment." [27] So the garment of paradise was a figure of the spiritual state in which man was created and which he lost by sin. The baptismal robes symbolized the return to this state. Gregory of Nyssa often returns to this idea of the robe of glory lost by Adam's sin: "As if Adam were still living in each of us, we see our nature covered with garments of skin and the fallen leaves of this earthly life, garments which we made for ourselves when we had been stripped of our robes of light, and we put on the vanities, the honors, the passing satisfactions of the flesh instead of our divine robes" (XLIV, 1184 B-C).

Underlying this symbolism is a whole doctrine of religious significance of clothing. We have already remarked on the origins of these archaic beliefs: "It was a common idea among primitive peoples" explains A. Lods, "that clothing is especially likely to become impregnated with the spiritual forces that have surrounded its wearer. There is danger, then, that clothing would bring hostile emanations into sacred places, or, again, carry particles of the divine fluid out into the profane world.[28] Adam's loss of the robe of glory is thus seen to have been a kind of de-sanctification, a reduction to a state lacking in holiness. It corresponds to our expulsion from Paradise, which is the holy wood, the dwelling of God, and our entrance into the profane world, full of misery. Gregory uses precisely the expression 'stripping off the sacred robes.' " "The jealousy of the demon drove us away from the tree of life and stripped us of our sacred robes, to clothe us in ignominious fig-leaves" (XLIV, 409 B). The clothing with the baptismal robe, then, signifies the return to Paradise as the world of the holy.

We may note precisely that white is, in Holy Scripture, the color of sacred vestments.[29] In the Old Testament, priests wore

[27] *Religion et vêtement, Rhythmes du monde,* 1946, 4, p. 4. See *Pour une théologie du vêtement, by the same author,* Lyons, 1943, p. 6-13.
[28] *Israel des origines aux Prophètes,* p. 313.
[29] Dom Damasus Winzen, *Pathways in Holy Scripture,* The Book of Exodus, p. 10.

garments of white linen (Ex. XXXIX, 25). Again, the Apocalypse of St. John shows us the four and twenty ancients who celebrate the heavenly liturgy and represent the angels, as clothed in white garments (Apoc. 4:1). The white robes of Christ at the Transfiguration are, according to Harald Riesenfeld, an allusion to the white robe of the High-priest on the day of the Feast of Expiation.[30] The symbolism of the white robes of the baptized may include an allusion to this theme, but it does not seem, however, that it includes an allusion to the "priesthood" of the Christian.[31]

And, finally, the white garments have an eschatological meaning. In particular, they signify the glory in which the martyrs are clothed after their death. The Apocalypse says that those who have triumphed over the devil by martyrdom are clothed in white (Apoc. 3:5 and 18). And in Perpetua's vision, the martyrs who have gone before her into Paradise are clothed in white (*Passio Perpetuae, 4*). It seems difficult not to see here a connection with the baptismal garments. And this is not the first time that we notice the resemblance between sacramental and eschatological representations. Carl-Martin Edsman has pointed it out particularly in the case of the *Passion of St. Perpetua.*[32] And, in the Apocalypse, the heavenly liturgy of the martyrs is described in terms borrowed from the visible liturgy. This fact explains why it is often difficult to know whether the themes used in the decoration of ancient monuments are eschatological or sacramental.

More precisely still, the white baptismal garments, as Tertullian tells us, are the symbol of the resurrection of the body. In *De Resurrectione Carnis,* he comments on the text from Apoc. XIV, 4, which he weaves in with VII, 13: "We find in Scripture an allusion to garments as being the symbol of the hope of the flesh: these are those who have not soiled their garment with women, meaning by this, those who are virgins. This is why they will be in white garments, that is to say, in the glory of the virgin flesh. So this symbolism also furnishes us with an argument for bodily resurrection." (27; P. L., II; 834, A-B). This agrees with the belief, often to be found in the second century, that martyrs and virgins rose again with their glorified bodies immediately

[30] *Jésus transfiguré,* p. 115 et seq.
[31] Oppenheim, loc. cit., p. 37.
[32] *Le baptême de feu,* p. 42-47. See also C. A. Pusch, *Death and Burial in Christian Antiquity,* p. 217.

after their death, without having to wait for the general resurrection. The Church was later to define that this is only certain in the case of the Mother of God: this is the dogma of the Assumption.

We can now see that these different aspects of the symbolism of the white garments are not incoherent, but are ordered in an organic whole. They refer, first of all, to Adam, signifying his state in Paradise before the Fall. Then they are related to Christ, who came to restore the grace lost by Adam. In Baptism, they express configuration to the grace of Christ. And, finally, they are a prefiguring of future glory, anticipated in this present life. A whole theology is thus expressed in this symbolism, the theology of the New Adam. And this is also true of several of the other rites which we have been studying. A primary aspect of the biblical theology of the sacraments thus appears, one that we might call the theology of Adam, and others also will appear in the course of our study.

CHAPTER THREE

The Sphragis

THE ceremonies of Baptism include a rite that we have not taken up until now, because its particular importance merits a special study: this is the rite of the *sphragis*, that is to say, the imposition of the sign of the Cross on the forehead of the candidate at Baptism.[1] This rite is a very ancient tradition; St. Basil cites it with the prayer *ad orientem* as being among the unwritten traditions that go back to the Apostles: "Who taught us to mark with the sign of the Cross those who put their hope in the name of the Lord" (*De Spiritu Sancto.*, 27, Pruche, 233). The position of this rite has varied: sometimes we find it united with that of the enrollment at the beginning of the catechumenate, as is the case in the work of the Pseudo-Dionysius (396 A-400 D). Theodore of Mopsuestia places it between the renunciation of Satan, and Baptism (XIII, 17-18). More commonly, it seems to have been given after Baptism, and this is what we find in Cyril of Jerusalem and Ambrose. For them, it is associated with the anointing with chrism, and it is in connection with this rite that it is mentioned. Moreover, it may have been repeated in the course of the process of initiation, as it is in the present Rite for the Baptism of Adults.

The importance of the rite appears from the fact that it often serves to denote Baptism as a whole, this often being called the

[1] See F. J. Doelger, *Sphragis*, Paderborn, 1911; J. Coppens, *L'imposition des mains et les rites connexes*, Louvain, 1923.

sphragis.[2] We find this in various lists of the names for Baptism given by the Fathers; for example, Cyril of Jerusalem says: "How great is Baptism: it is the redemption of prisoners, the remission of sins, the death of guilt, the rebirth of the soul, the garment of light, the holy and ineradicable seal (*sphragis*), the vehicle to carry us to heaven, the delights of Paradise, the pledge of the kingdom, the grace of adoption" (XXXIII, 360 A). Gregory of Nazianzen gives us a similar list: "Baptism is the participation in the Logos, the destruction of sin, the vehicle to carry us to God, the key of the kingdom of heaven, the robe of incorruptibility, the bath of rebirth, the seal (*sphragis*)" (XXXVI, 361 C). We should notice the many similarities between the two lists.

The word *sphragis* in ancient times designated the object with which a mark was stamped, or else the mark made by this object. So *sphragis* was the word for the seal used to impress a mark on wax. These seals often have precious stones placed in the bezel or setting that holds them. So Clement of Alexandria recommends that Christians should have for seals (*sphragides*) a dove or a fish or a ship with sails unfurled, but not mythological figures or swords (Ped. III, 11; Staehlin, 270). These seals were used especially to seal official documents and wills. So St. Paul uses the symbol when he tells the Corinthians that they "are the seal of his apostolate in the Lord" (I Cor. 9:2), that is to say, that they are the authentic sign of it.[3] But more particularly—and here we come to the baptismal symbolism—the word *sphragis* was used for the mark with which an owner marked his possessions. Used in this sense, the word *sphragis* had various applications which are of particular interest to us here: the *sphragis* was the mark with which shepherds branded the beasts of their flock in order to distinguish them; again, it was the custom in the Roman army to mark recruits as a sign of their enlistment; this mark was called the *signaculum* and consisted of a tattooing made on the hand or the forearm which represented an abbreviation of the name of the general.[4] These various meanings came to be used by the

[2] Perhaps as early as St. Paul: II Cor., I, 22; Eph., I, 13—and in any case in the earliest Fathers: Clement of Rome, *Epist.*, VII, 6; Herm., *Sim.*, IX, 6, 3; 16, 4; Tertullian, *De pudic.*, IX, 9.

[3] F. J. Doelger, *Sphragis*, p. 15.

[4] Doelger, loc. cit., p. 32-33.

Fathers of the Church to give different emphasis to the baptismal *sphragis.* The sign of the Cross with which the candidate for Baptism is marked on his forehead shows that henceforth he belongs to Christ. And this can signify that he belongs either to the flock of Christ or to the army of Christ. These different interpretations are connected with the different themes of Baptism. The theme of the flock is in harmony with the idea, of supreme importance in Baptism, of the Good Shepherd who knows his sheep and defends them from wicked shepherds. By receiving the *sphragis,* the catechumen is seen to be incorporated into the flock of the Good Shepherd: "Come near," says Cyril of Jerusalem to the candidates, "and receive the sacramental seal (*mystike sphragis*) so that you may be recognized by the Master. Be numbered among the holy and recognized flock of Christ, so that you may be placed at His right hand" (XXXIII, 372 B).[5] Here we see one aspect of the *sphragis:* it allows the Lord to recognize His Own as the shepherd his sheep. In the same way, Theodore of Mopsuestia says: "This sign with which you are now marked, is the sign that you are from now on marked as a sheep of Christ. For a sheep, as soon as it is bought, receives the mark by which its owner may be known; and also it feeds in the same pasture and is in the same sheepfold as the other sheep who bear the same mark, showing that they all belong to the same master" (XIII, 17). Theodore emphasizes here our incorporation into the one Church, and the *consignatio* is seen as the sign of being made a member of the Christian community. Let us note that this is the aspect that the Pseudo-Dionysius at Antioch also emphasizes: "By the sign . . . the catechumen is received into the communion of those who have merited deification and who constitute the assembly of the saints" (400 D).

But the *sphragis* is not only a sign of ownership, it is also a protection. Gregory of Nazianzen unites the two ideas. The *sphragis* is "a guarantee of preservation and a sign of ownership" (XXXVI, 364 A). He develops this idea at greater length: "If you fortify yourself with the *sphragis,* marking your souls and your body with the oil (*chrism*) and with the Spirit, what can happen to you? This is, even in this life, the greatest security you can have. The sheep

[5] 'Make haste, O sheep, towards the sign of the Cross and the sphragis which will save you from your misery' (Greg. Nyssa, *H. Bapt.;* P.G., XLVI, 417 B).

that has been branded (*ephragismenon*) is not easily taken by a trick, but the sheep that bears no mark is the prey of thieves. And after this life, you can die in peace, without fear of being deprived by God of the helps that He has given you for your salvation" (XXXVI, 377 A). The *sphragis,* the mark that enables the Master to recognize His Own, is also a pledge of salvation.

Didymus the Blind uses the same language: "In many things, but above all in what concerns Holy Baptism, Scripture seems to mention, because of His identity of essence and of action with the Father and the Son, only the Holy Spirit and His saving mark with which we have been sealed, being restored to our first likeness. For the sheep that is not marked (*asphragiston*) is an easy prey for wolves, not having the help of the *sphragis* and not being recognized like the others by the Good Shepherd, since it does not know the Shepherd of the Universe" (XXXIX, 717 B). Here again, the *sphragis* is a guarantee of the protection of the Shepherd, at the same time as it is the mark of His ownership. And we see also here a new idea, the connection with the *eikon.* The *sphragis* imprints in the soul the image, the likeness of God, according to which man was created from the beginning.[6]

And Gregory of Nyssa, in his *De baptismo,* in which he urges the *procrastinantes* to have themselves baptized, says: "The soul which has not been enlightened and adorned with the grace of re-birth,—I do not know whether the angels receive it after its separation from the body. And, indeed, how could they do so, since it has no mark (*asphragiston*) and does not carry any sign of ownership? Truly it is carried about in the air, wandering and restless, without anyone to look for it, since it has no owner. It seeks rest and does not find it, crying vainly, and fruitlessly repentant" (XLVI, 424 C). This passage gives witness to the survival among Christian writers of ancient ideas of the hereafter, for the idea that the air is the abode of souls that are not able to raise themselves to the heavenly spheres, comes from pagan sources. We find it again in Origen: "The souls that are vile and dragged down to the earth by their faults, without being able even to take breath are carried away and rolled around here below, some of them near to tombs where the phantoms of souls appear

[6] See F. J. Doelger, *Sphragis,* p. 111-119. This entirely different idea is connected with Philo of Alexandria.

like shadows, others simply on the surface of the earth" (Contr. Cels., VII, 5).[7]

The *sphragis* is not only a mark of belonging to the flock of Christ, it is also the sign of our enlistment in His army. Here we pass to a different theme. Christ is not only the Shepherd, He is also the King who calls men to join His forces. In giving their names, at the beginning of the ceremonies of Baptism, the candidates have answered this call and have enlisted: "The inscription of your name," writes Cyril of Jerusalem, "has taken place, and the call to enter the campaign" (XXXIII, 333 A). The *consignatio,* then, shows our incorporation in the service of the king. Theodore of Mopsuestia connects this symbolism with that of the flock: "This signing, with which you are now marked, is the sign that you are now marked as a sheep of Christ's, as a soldier of the King of heaven . . . The soldier chosen for service, found worthy, because of his physique and health, first receives on his hand a mark showing what king he is henceforth to serve; so now you, you have been chosen for the kingdom of heaven, and you can be recognized, when anyone examines you, as a soldier of the king of heaven" (XIII, 17).

Cyril of Jerusalem defines the meaning of this engagement: "As those who are about to go out on a campaign examine the age and the health of their recruits, so the Lord, as He enlists souls, examines their wills. If anyone retains some hidden hypocrisy, He rejects him as unfit for the spiritual combat; if He finds him worthy, at once He entrusts to him His grace. He does not give holy things to dogs, but as soon as He sees a right conscience, He imprints his wonderful and saving *sphragis* which is feared by the demons and recognized by the angels, so much so that the former flee and the latter accompany it as a friend. Those, then, that receive this saving *sphragis* should have a will that corresponds to it" (XXXIII, 373 A).

The military character of the *sphragis* is still more apparent in another catechesis: "Each of us comes to present himself before God in the presence of the innumerable armies of the angels. The Holy Spirit marks your souls. You go to enlist (*stratologeisthai*)

[7] See also Basil, Hom. Bapt., XIII, 4; P.G., XXXI, 432 B. On this idea see Franz Cumont, *Recherches sur le symbolisme funéraire chez les romains,* p. 104 et seqq.

in the army of the great king" (XXXIII, 428 A). So also we read in St. John Chrysostom: "As the *sphragis* is imprinted on soldiers, so is the Holy Spirit upon those who believe" (LXI, 418). We find this symbolism again in another passage from Cyril of Jerusalem, but applied this time not to the sacramental character, but to the sign of the Cross made on the forehead: "After my battle upon the cross, I give to each of my soldiers the right to wear on their foreheads the royal *sphragis*" (XXXIII, 736 A).

We should note in passing that this idea of Baptism as enlistment in the service of Christ, sanctioned by the *sphragis* which is the seal of Christ's acceptance, is a theme familiar to Christian antiquity. It has been treated by Harnack in *Militia Christi,* by Doelger in *Sacramentum militiae* (Ant. und Ch. II, 4). The enlistment included the imposition of the *sphragis,* enrollment in the register, and the oath; thus it was easy to comment on the ceremonies of Baptism with the help of these images. We know particularly that in the Latin authors, and especially Tertullian, the word *sacramentum* is used in direct connection with the military oath, to bring out the aspect of Baptism as a military enlistment in the service of Christ.[8] Moreover this military vocabulary goes back to St. Paul, who speaks of the armor of the Christian and of his battles. The comparison of the new Christian to a young recruit is especially common; thus St. Gregory of Nazianzen writes: "He who only recently received the bath of regeneration is like a young soldier who has just been given a place among the athletes, but has not yet proved his worth as a soldier" (XLVI, 429 C).

We have noted in the course of the preceding pages that one of the points most frequently brought out by the Fathers of the Church concerning the *sphragis* is that it makes the Christian fearful to the demons. We are brought back again and again to this central aspect of Baptism and of the Christian life in general among the first Christians. The imposition of the Cross in Baptism is a phase of the struggle against the demon which, as we have seen, Baptism was considered to be from the outset. In the same way, the use of the sign of the Cross in Christian life is an expression of the fact that it continues to be a struggle against the demon. By Baptism, he has been conquered; marked with the

[8] See F. J. Doelger, *Die Sonne der Gerechtigkeit und die Schwarze,* p. 110-119.

sign of the Cross, the newly baptized no longer belongs to him; henceforth the Christian need only make this sign in order to repel the attacks of the demon and to put him to flight.[9]

This brings us to a new aspect of the symbolism of the *sphragis.* We have mentioned that in ordinary speech the word was used for the mark given both to soldiers and to sheep; but we have not as yet mentioned a third use, that of the mark of slaves. We have evidence of such a use in the East, where slaves were marked with an indelible sign of ownership by a kind of tattooing. In the West it seems that only runaway slaves were so marked. So St. Ambrose writes: "Slaves are marked with the sign of their master" (XVI, 437); [10] we call this mark *sphragis* or *stigma,* and its imprinting *stigmatization.*

But we must also add, for this is what is of interest to us, that the *sphragis* did not only mark the ownership of a slave by an earthly master; it could also be used for the mark by which the faithful servant of a god showed that he belonged to that god. Prudentius reports that, for the consecration of a devotee in the cult of Dionysius, red-hot needles were used to make the *sphragis* (Perist., X, 1077). Herodotus speaks of a priest of Heracles who, having consecrated himself to his god, bore the *stigmata,* the holy marks, so that nobody was allowed to lay hands on him (II, 113).[11] This sheds light on the passage in Gal. VI, 17: "Let no man from henceforth be troublesome to me, for I carry on my body the marks (*stigmata*) of Jesus." [12]

But in order to interpret this aspect of the *sphragis,* we do not need to look for analogies in the Greek world. For the imposition by God of a mark making a being inviolable is to be found in the Bible. The first example is that of Cain, whom God marked with a sign so that no one would kill him (Gen. 4:15).[13] This sign is one of protection; it is the statement of God's protection of sinful man. In Ezechiel, we read that the members of the future Israel carry the sign of God on their foreheads (9:4). Here, then, is the primary typology of the *sphragis.* And it is noteworthy that

[9] Greg. Naz. *Ho. Bapt.;* XXXVI, 372 A.

[10] Doelger, loc. cit., p. 23-32.

[11] The custom of tattooing the body was in use among Christians: "Many," says Procopius of Gaza, "tattooed themselves on the hand or the arm with the name of Jesus or the cross." (P.G., LXXXVII, 2401.)

[12] See F. J. Doelger, loc. cit., p. 39-51.

[13] See W. Vischer, *Les Livres de Moïse,* French translation, p. 103.

this sign is a T, for the New Testament also, in the Apocalypse, shows the saints as marked with the sign of the Lamb (7:4),[14] and this sign is probably that of the Cross, that is, a T. So if we recall the fact that the Apocalypse is filled with allusions to Baptism, it certainly seems as if this sign of the Lamb refers to the *sphragis* of the liturgy of initiation.

Be this as it may, we see the meaning that was given to the baptismal *sphragis* along these lines: it marked the character of inviolability of the Christian.[15] And this is directly connected with the sign of the Cross itself. For it was by His Cross that Christ despoiled the principalities and the powers. Henceforth they were conquered. And by Baptism the Christian shares in this victory of Christ. Henceforth the forces of evil have no power over him. This is why he need only sign himself with the sign of the Cross in order to remind these forces of their defeat and to put them to flight. This is true above all of the baptismal rite itself, as Cyril of Jerusalem explains: "The invocation of grace, marking your soul with its seal (*sphragis*) does not allow you to be swallowed up by the demon" (XXXIII, 441 C). The catechumen can face the demon without fear in the supreme struggle of Baptism when he goes down into the waters of death, for he is marked with the *sphragis*. And, further: "The Lord does not give holy things to dogs, but when He sees a right conscience, He imprints on it His holy and wonderful *sphragis* that the demons fear" (XXXIII, 373 A). But in speaking of the *sphragis*, Cyril does not mean only the imposition of the sign of the Cross at Baptism, but also the Christian custom of signing ourselves with the Cross on our foreheads in every circumstance of life: "Let us not be ashamed of the Cross of Christ, but even if someone else conceals it, do you carry its mark publicly on your forehead (*sphragizou*), so that the demons, seeing the royal sign, trembling, may fly far away. Make this sign (*semeion*) when you eat and when you drink, when you sit down, when you go to bed, when you get up, when you speak,—in a word, on all occasions" (XXXIII, 472 B). Further on, he takes up the same idea again: "Let us not be ashamed to confess the Cru-

[14] These last two passages are expressly connected by St. Cyprian with the sign of the Cross traced on the forehead of Christians (*Test.*, II, 22; C.S.E.L. 90).

[15] "The priest has marked thee on thy forehead with the sphragis," writes Cyril of Jerusalem, "that thou mayest receive the imprint of the seal, that thou mayest be consecrated to God" (XXXIII, 1102 B).

cified. Let us make the sign of the Cross (*sphragis tou stauro*) with assurance on our foreheads with our fingers, and so do in all circumstances: when we eat and when we drink, when we come in and when we go out, before we sleep, when we lie down and when we arise. Here is a great protection [16] that is free for the poor and easy for the weak; since the grace comes from God. It is a sign for the faithful and a terror for the demons. On the Cross, He triumphed over them: and so, when they see it, they remember the Crucified; they fear Him Who crushed the heads of the demons" (XXXIII, 816 B).

We have two remarkable illustrations of this power of the *sphragis.* The first is found in the *Life of St. Antony,* precisely in connection with his temptation. Some women came to visit Antony, and since he would not let them come into his cell, they were forced to spend a day and a night outside. "But see! they heard within, as it were the shouting of crowds, cries, groans and screams: 'Go away from us! What are you doing in the desert? You will not stand our attacks!' At first the people outside thought that there must be men inside who were fighting with Antony, but having looked through the key-hole and seen nothing, they understood that the noise was made by demons, and smitten with terror, they called Antony. He, giving them more attention than he gave the demons, came to the door and made them promise to go away: 'Sign yourselves (*sphragizate heautous*),' he said, 'and go in safety.' And so they went away, fortified with the sign (*semeion*) of the Cross" (*Vit. Ant. 13*).[17]

The other incident is found in the *Life of St. Gregory Thaumaturgus* by Gregory of Nyssa. He relates that a deacon, arriving one night in a city, wished to go to take a bath. "Now there ruled in this place a man-killing demon, who haunted the baths. His evil power was exercised after nightfall against any who came near, and because of this the baths were not used after sunset. The deacon came and asked the guard at the gate to open the door for him. But the guard assured him that none of those who had dared approach the waters at this time of day had come back on his feet, but that all had fallen into the power of the demon,

[16] On this word see Doelger, *Sphragis,* p. 119 et seq. Cyril uses it especially for the post-baptismal anointing. (XXXIII, 1093 B).

[17] See St. Athanasius, *The Life of St. Antony,* translated and annotated by R. T. Meyer, Westminster, 1950, p. 110-111.

and that many of such imprudent people had already fallen prey to incurable diseases." [18] But the deacon insisted, and the guard gave him the key. Scarcely had he taken off his clothes and entered, than all kinds of terrors were evoked by the demon, phantoms of all sorts appeared in a mixture of flame and smoke, striking his gaze with the forms of men and animals, hissing in his ears, coming so near he could breathe on them, spreading themselves in a circle all round his body. But he, protecting himself with the *sphragis* and invoking the name of Christ, crossed the first room without hindrance. In the same way, with the second room: new phantoms, another sign of the cross. And finally the deacon took his bath, and came out quite calmly, to the astonishment of the guard (XLVI, 952 A-C).

The various meanings of the *sphragis* that we have been studying so far have been chiefly connected with the use of the word in the Greek world. But one last text of St. Cyril sets us on another line of discovery, pointing out a new symbolism, and unquestionably setting us on the track of the true meaning of this rite. "After faith," he writes, "we, like Abraham, receive the spiritual *sphragis*, being circumcized in Baptism by the Holy Spirit" (XXXIII, 513 A). This is an entirely different order of ideas: the baptismal *sphragis* is related to the Jewish circumcision. As this was the seal of the alliance with God and of incorporation into the old Israel, so Baptism is the seal of the new alliance, and of incorporation into the new Israel.[19] Here the *sphragis* introduces us into the theology of the covenant, and, as a result, Baptism is related to its figure in the Old Testament.

What gives this interpretation its importance is that by means of it a whole group of texts from the New Testament are brought into the discussion,[20] St. Paul often alludes to the *sphragis*. For example, in the Epistle to the Ephesians: "It is in Him that you have believed and have been marked with the seal of the Holy Spirit" (1, 13). Let us note the connection thus established be-

[18] On the connection of the water with demons, in pagan circles, see Tertullian, *De bapt.*, 5.

[19] The expression 'seal of the covenant' is used by the Apost. Const., VII, 22, 2, in connection with Baptism.

[20] On the parallel between Baptism and circumcision, in the New Testament, see Oscar Cullmann, *Die Tauflehre des neuen Testaments,* pp. 56-63.

tween faith and the *sphragis,* recalling the text of Cyril in which he mentions Abraham:—the process of baptism, in which the *sphragis* is given after the profession of faith to seal it, reproduces the process followed by Abraham. And elsewhere St. Paul uses the word *sphragis* to describe the circumcision of Abraham: "Abraham received the sign of circumcision as the seal (*sphragis*) of the justice which he had obtained by faith when he was uncircumcised." (Rom. IV.: 11). The parallelism is perfect between the two passages. And we are therefore quite right in thinking that, when St. Paul speaks of the *sphragis* of the Christians which follows on faith, he is establishing a parallel between Baptism and circumcision which was the *sphragis* of the Old Covenant.[21]

The use of the word *sphragis* to describe circumcision is often met with elsewhere. We do not find it in the Septuagint: St. Paul is the first to employ it. But after his example, the Fathers use it frequently. To quote only one example, Eusebius of Cesarea writes: "Abraham, when he was an old man, was the first to undergo circumcision in his body, as a kind of seal (*sphragis*), handing on this sign to those who should be born of him as a mark of their belonging to his race" (Dem. Ev. 1, 6; P. G. XXII, 49 C). Circumcision, then, is the mark of membership in the race of Abraham, in the Old Israel, and the pledge of the promises made to Abraham by the Covenant.

But the circumcision was only a figure: the true *sphragis* is that of the New Covenant. This is suggested by St. Paul in a passage which we have already mentioned, but which we should quote in its entirety: "But as for me, God forbid that I should glory save in the Cross of our Lord Jesus Christ, through whom the world is crucified to me, and I to the world. For in Christ Jesus neither circumcision nor uncircumcision but a new creation is of any account . . . Henceforth let no man give me trouble, for I bear the marks of the Lord Jesus in my body" (Gal. 6:14-15). Perhaps there is in these *stigmata* an allusion to the marks of the pagan priests. But the whole text leads us to another conclusion: what St. Paul considers to be the sign of his dignity, what makes him a consecrated person, is no longer circumcision, it is the

[21] Moreover, the succession comprising the *consignatio* and then Baptism seems to correspond ritually with the incorporation of proselytes in the Jewish community—circumcision and then baptism. See Gregory Dix, "*The Seal in the Second Century,*" THEOLOGY, Jan., 1948, p. 7.

Cross of Christ. And he carries in his body the marks of this Cross. He received these marks for the first time when he became a new creature, that is to say, at Baptism. In the background of his thought here is the baptismal *sphragis* in the form of a Cross, contrasted with circumcision in the Old Testament as a sign of the covenant.[22]

This same baptismal context seems to be behind a text of the Pseudo-Barnabas: "You might say, perhaps, that (the Jewish people) were circumcised in order to set a seal (*sphragis*) on the Covenant. But the priests of the idols are also circumcised. Do they belong to the Covenant? Learn that Abraham, who was the first to be circumcised, did so in spirit, having his eyes on Jesus: for he received the teaching contained in three letters. Scripture says that he circumcised the men of his house to the number of 318. But 18 is written with an iota which stands for 10 and an eta which stands for 8. And as the Cross in the form of a T should signify grace, 300 (= T) is also added. The union of these two letters stands for Jesus" (IX., 6-8). Whatever the value of this interpretation may be, we should note that Barnabas shows that in circumcision is to be found the symbol of the sign T which was marked on the forehead of the baptized, and of the anagram of the name of Jesus, I H. As we have seen, certain of the faithful tattooed this sign on their skin.

Throughout all these texts, we see the parallelism drawn between circumcision and the *sphragis*. This is explicitly formulated by Asterius of Amasea: "Why did circumcision take place on the eighth day? Because during the first seven, the child was wearing swaddling clothes, but on the eighth, freed from these bonds, he received circumcision, sign of the seal (*sphragis*) of the faith of Abraham. And this also typified the fact that, when we have carried the seven days of life, that is to say, the bonds of sin, we should, at the end of time, break these bonds and, circumcised by death and resurrection, as if on the eighth day embrace the life of the angels. And it was to teach Christians that, even before they wrap them in swaddling clothes, they should mark their children with the seal (*sphragis*) by Baptism in the circumcision of Christ, as St. Paul says: In Him you were circumcised with a

[22] See also Col. II, 11-12; "To whom also you are circumcised with circumcision not made by hand, buried with him in baptism, as if in the circumcision of Christ."

circumcision not made by the hand of man, buried with Him in baptism, as in the circumcision of Christ (Col. 2:11-12)" (*Ho. Ps.* VI. P. G., XL, 445 A).[23]

As we see here, the comparison between circumcision and the *sphragis* is an aspect of the more general theme of circumcision as a figure of Baptism. In particular, the parallel between circumcision on the eighth day and Baptism as a participation in the resurrection of Christ on the day after the sabbath, that is to say, the eighth day, is often made. This was one of the aspects under which the Fathers saw the eighth day as prefigured in the Old Testament. Justin writes: "The precept of circumcision, commanding that children should be circumcised on the eighth day, is the type of the true circumcision which circumcised you from error and from sin by Him Who rose from the dead on the first day of the week, Jesus Christ our Lord. For the first day of the week is also the eighth" (*Dial.* XLI, 4).[24]

Light is also thrown on another aspect of the *sphragis* which relates it to circumcision. We note that, for St. Paul, there is a relation between the *sphragis* and the Holy Spirit (Eph. 1:13), although the sacramental character of the *sphragis* is not yet made clear. This relation is found also in the Fathers, and this time in a context that is explicitly one of worship. So Cyril of Jerusalem reminds the baptized "how the seal (*sphragis*) of the communion of the Holy Spirit was given to them" (XXXIII, 1056 B). So the theme of the *sphragis* presents an ambiguity: as an impression of the sign of the Cross, it is related to Christ Crucified,[25] but it is also related to the Holy Spirit. St. Ambrose bears witness to this plurality of aspects: "The Father, the Son and the Spirit are everywhere, with one working, one sanctification. But certain things are seen as particular to each Person. How may this be? God has anointed you, the Lord has marked you with the seal,

[23] "Circumcision was given on the eighth day," writes Gregory of Nazianzen, "was a sort of symbol of the sphragis" (P.G., XXXVI, 400 A). He is speaking of the baptism of infants. Now it is worth noting that Oscar Cullmann bases his attitude precisely on the parallel between circumcision and baptism to prove, as against Karl Barth, the New Testament character of the Baptism of infants (*Die Tauflehre des Neuen Testaments,* p. 51).

[24] See also Ambrose, *Exp. Psalm,* CXVIII, *Prol.;* Chrysostom, P.G., L., 807; Eusebius, *Co. Ps.,* VI, P.G., XXIII, 120 A.

[25] "The catechumen believes in the Cross of the Lord Jesus by which he himself is marked." (St. Ambrose, *De Myst.,* 20; Botte, 113-114).

and He has put the Holy Spirit into your heart. You have, then, received the Holy Spirit in your heart. Receive something else as well: for, as the Holy Spirit is in your heart, so Christ is in your heart. You possess that Christ Who said in the Canticle: Put me as a seal (*signaculum*) on your heart. Christ has marked you with a seal. How? Because you were marked with the form of the cross of His passion, you have received the seal in His likeness" (De Sacr. VI. 5-7; Botte, 99).

That the *sphragis* has so many implications is certainly due to the fact that many traditions come together in this rite. The christological interpretation is connected with the sign of the Cross, which is itself related to the biblical theme of the mark imprinted on the forehead, making the bearer inviolable. The interpretation of St. Paul should certainly be related to the theme of circumcision, that is to say, to the sign of the new Covenant. And it is a common idea that the second covenant is not sealed with a seal in the flesh, but with a spiritual seal; it is no longer a mark in the flesh, but a transformation worked by the Holy Spirit. This explains why the reference to the rite itself is less clear when we are dealing with St. Paul's point of view. And this explains also why the rite of giving the *sphragis* could be used sometimes in the sense of a configuration to the death of Christ, and sometimes in the sense of an outpouring of the Spirit.

But what concerns us, since it is the fundamental aspect of this second symbolic meaning, is the relationship between circumcision and Baptism as the seals of the covenant.[26] This enables us to understand one of the essential aspects of the baptismal "character." Circumcision was the sign of the covenant. Now it is the essential nature of the covenant to be an act of God's love by which He binds Himself to dispose of His blessings in favor of the man with whom He makes a covenant. Circumcision was the seal of this contract. But what characterizes this contract is the fact that it is irrevocable, that is to say that, though the infidelities of man may cause him to withdraw himself from the benefits of the promise, they can never cause the promise itself to be revoked. It constitutes a stable, definitive order, to which man can always appeal.

[26] On the general parallel between circumcision and Baptism, see Origen, *Co. Rom.*, II, 12-13; P.G., XIV, 900.

And if we now take up once more the characteristics by which the Fathers defined the baptismal *sphragis,* we see that there is a very important one which we have not yet discussed: that is, its indelibility. We meet in the writings of Cyril of Jerusalem the expression "the holy and indelible *sphragis*" (XXXIII, 359 A). And elsewhere he writes: "May God give you the ineffaceable seal of the Holy Spirit for eternal life" (XXXIII, 365 A). This is often interpreted, according to Greek imagery, as an indelible seal imprinted on the soul. But this image is a very material one. In reality, the ineffaceable nature of the baptismal character comes from the fact that it is founded on the irrevocable promise of God. The *sphragis* of baptism, then, signifies a contract of God with the baptized person whereby God grants him irrevocably a right to the blessings of grace. The baptized may withdraw himself from taking advantage of this right, but he cannot cause the right itself to be revoked.

We can see that the whole theology of the sacramental character is to be found here in germ, as St. Augustine made it more precise against the Donatists in condemning the repetition of Baptism. This sacrament is given irrevocably. By sin, a man may withdraw himself from its benefits, but there still endures something that we call the character, whose basis is the irrevocable contract of God's love, officially sealed by the baptismal *sphragis.* This doctrine was proposed by St. Paul, even before St. Augustine: "Although the Holy Spirit does not mingle with those who are unworthy, nevertheless, in a certain way, He seems to remain present with those who have been once marked with the seal (*sphragis*), awaiting their salvation by conversion. It is only at death that He will be wholly taken away from the soul who has profaned grace" (XXXII, 141 D).

Now we can understand the richness of the doctrine of the *sphragis,* as at once a special rite, and as an aspect of Baptism. It is quite clear that it is Baptism itself that is the seal of the covenant. As St. Cyril says in a brief formula: "If a man does not receive the *sphragis* by Baptism, he will not enter into the kingdom of heaven" (XXXIII, 432 A). But the diversity of rites is meant to bring out in a visible manner the riches actually effected by Baptism itself: the white garments, the restoration of incorruptibility; the immersion, the destruction of man the sinner; *the sphragis,* the new covenant. This is why their significance is important. Now the *sphragis* shows us in a characteristic manner that this significance of the sacraments is to be sought in their figures in the Old Testament. Around this biblical typology are grafted harmonious themes from Greek customs and thought; these also are rich in meaning, but they must always be brought back to their roots in Holy Scripture.

CHAPTER FOUR

The Types of Baptism: Creation and the Deluge

WHEN we were explaining (Chapter II) the symbolism of the immersion and emersion rite of Baptism, we did not touch upon the symbols which held the greatest place in patristic catecheses, that is, the types of this rite to be found in the Old Testament. We find enumerations of these types very early, the most ancient appearing in the *De Baptismo* of Tertullian. His list is reproduced and developed by Didymus of Alexandria (XXXIX, 693). Cyril of Jerusalem gives a list, not in the *Mystagogic Catecheses,* but in the catechesis on Baptism (XXXIII, 433). Ambrose, on the other hand, devotes a part of his mystagogic catecheses to these types (De Sacr., I, 11-24; Botte 57-61; De Myst., 8-27; Botte 110-116). The only exceptions are the Syrian catecheses of Theodore of Mopsuestia and of the Pseudo-Dionysius: the school of Antioch was, as we have said, hostile to typology.

When we read these lists, we are struck with their great resemblance to one another, a resemblance which proves that they form a common teaching going back to the first origins of the Church. For, in fact, even though the lists are of later date, the types themselves are to be found in the New Testament and the first ecclesiastical writers. The Crossing of the Red Sea and the Deluge are mentioned, the first in the First Epistle to the Corinthians (10:1-5); the second in the First Epistle of St. Peter (III; 19-21 [1]); the rock of Horeb is a type of Baptism for St. John (VII; 38);

[1] See Bo Reicke, *The Disobedient Spirits and Christian Baptism,* Lund, 1948.

Barnabas, Justin and Irenaeus mention these themes and others as well: the water of Marra, the bath of Naaman. The readings or "Prophecies" in the liturgy of Holy Saturday, preparatory to Baptism, are the echo of this traditional instruction.[2]

In the thought of the Fathers, these types are not mere illustrations: the Old Testament figures were meant first to authorize Baptism by a showing that it has been announced by a whole tradition: they are *testimonia* (Ambrose, De Myst., 9-12; Botte 110-111). And, above all, their purpose is also to explain Baptism, a purpose which still holds good today. In fact, if we wish to understand the true meaning of Baptism, it is quite clear that we must turn to the Old Testament. For, as Oscar Cullmann has well observed, in its fundamental significance Baptism is in the line of the great works of creation and redemption accomplished by God in the Old Testament. And, furthermore, Baptism was born in the land of Israel; we must interpret the material elements which it uses as a symbol according to the significance of these elements for the Jews of old. It is in a Jewish order of symbolism that we shall find the explanation of Baptism.[3]

In studying these types, we could proceed by means of a consideration of the various kinds of symbolism that they represent. But actually all these symbolic meanings have the same double aspect, an aspect which is found in each of them: water is, on the one hand, the principle of destruction, the instrument of judgment destroying the sinful world; and, on the other hand, it is the principle of creation, the life-giving element in which a new creature is born. We shall, then, simply follow the historical order of the types, the order which is that of our catecheses.

The first type of Baptism to be found in the most ancient catecheses is that of the primitive waters of Genesis. At first glance, this comparison may seem startling and artificial, but we must always be careful to look behind the "illustrative" resemblances which are concerned with images[4] for the theological analogies

[2] On the question as a whole, read Fr. Lundberg, *La typologie baptismale dans l'Ancienne Eglise,* Lund, 1941.

[3] See especially W. F. Flemington, *The New Testament Doctrine of Baptism,* London, 1948.

[4] I borrow this word from A. G. Hebert, *The Authority of the Old Testament,* p. 210-211.

which constitute typology, properly speaking. Here the theological analogy is clear: the Prophets announced that God, at the end of time, would undertake a new creation. This ideal holds an important place in Isaias. And it has been noted that the word "create," *bara,* appears first in speaking of this future creation.[5] Here we have an eschatological typology in which the first creation is presented as the type of the new creation which is to be accomplished at the end of time.

But the New Testament shows us that this new creation is already accomplished in Christ. The Incarnation is the creation of the new universe; and it is this creation which is continued in present history and takes place in Baptism.[6] It is truly a new creation, "regeneration" according to the word used in the Gospel of St. John (III, 5). And St. Paul calls the newly baptized a "new creature" (II Cor. 5, 17), and this re-creation is accomplished in the baptismal waters (John III, 5). The analogy of the primordial waters with the waters of Baptism is, then, an aspect, which is fundamentally biblical, of the parallelism between the first and the second creation.

Tertullian wishing, in the *De Baptismo,* to justify the use of water in Baptism from the unbroken witness of the Bible, turned first to the story of Creation in Genesis. In this narrative, the waters have two characteristics which Baptism reproduces: it is the primordial element in which life appears, and it is sanctified by the Holy Spirit. Tertullian develops this first aspect: "First of all, O man, you should have reverence for the antiquity of the waters as a primordial element" (Bapt. 2). It was in the midst of the waters that the earth appeared: "Once the elements of the world were set in order, when it was to be given inhabitants, it was the primordial waters which were commanded to produce living creatures. The primordial water brought forth life, so that no one should be astonished that in Baptism the waters are able to give life" (Bapt. 2).

And to this characteristic, another is added: the fact that the "Spirit of God was carried over the waters, He Who was to recreate the baptized. The Holy One was carried over that which

[5] Paul Humbert, *"Emplois et portée du verbe bara dans l'Ancien Testament,"* Theol. Zeitschr., Nov., 1947, p. 401 et seqq.

[6] See N-A, Dahl, *"La terre où coulent le lait et le miel,"* Mélanges Goguel, 1950, pp. 62-70.

was holy, or, rather, over that which could receive holiness from Him Who was carried. It is thus that the nature of water, sanctified by the Spirit, received the capability of itself becoming sanctifying. This is why all waters, by reason of their ancient original prerogative, may obtain the sacrament of sanctification by the invocation of God" (Bapt. 2). What is taught here is the consecration of the baptismal water, to which ancient Christianity attached great importance: "You have seen water. But all water does not heal, if the Spirit has not descended and consecrated that water." (Ambrose, De Sacr. 1, 15; Botte; 58).

Didymus of Alexandria takes the very text of Tertullian and develops it: "The indivisible and ineffable Trinity, foreseeing from eternity the fall of human nature, at the same time as It brought from nothing the substance of water, prepared for men the healing which would be given in the waters. This is the reason why the Holy Spirit, in being carried upon the waters, is shown to us as making them holy from this moment and as communicating to them their fecundity. With this we must connect the fact, and it is an important one, that at the moment of the baptism of Jesus, the Holy Spirit came down upon the waves of the Jordan and rested on them" (XXXIX, 692 C). Here we see a connection whose importance Didymus had reason to point out: the connection of the descent of the Holy Spirit on the primitive waters with His descent on the Jordan.

This interpretation, in fact, is not without foundation, for it brings out clearly the meaning of the dove of baptism: which seems to be a reminder, in the literal meaning of the text, of the Spirit of God, being carried "over the primitive waters." [7] And now we can see the whole meaning of the figure: as the Holy Spirit, hovering over the primordial waters, brought forth from them the first creation, so the Holy Spirit, hovering over the waters of the Jordan, brought forth from them the second creation; and it is this second creation to which the baptized person is born in the waters consecrated by the epiclesis. Thus the cosmic significance of Baptism is made clear. It is truly a new creation, and a renewal of the first creation. Now the typology stands out in its full meaning: it really expresses the correspondence between the two creative actions of God. And the symbolism of the

[7] C. K. Barrett, *The Holy Spirit and the Gospel Tradition,* London, 1945, p. 39.

water in Baptism is a sensible sign of this correspondence,—the water of Baptism does indeed refer to the primordial waters.[8]

As we have already said, this theme is to be found frequently. Thus St. Cyril of Jerusalem writes: "If you wish to know why it is by means of water and not some other element that grace is given, you will find the reason in going through the Scriptures. Water is a wonderful thing:—and the most beautiful of the four sensible elements of the cosmos—The sky is the dwelling of the angels, but the skies are made of water; earth is the home of men, but the earth has come out of the waters; and before the creation of visible things in six days, the Spirit of God hovered over the waters. The water is the principle of the Cosmos, and the Jordan of the Gospel" (XXXIII, 433 A). We should note that Cyril, following biblical cosmology, puts the waters above the dwelling of the angels.

But the most remarkable development of this theme is that of St. Ambrose. In the *De Sacramentis,* he shows that Baptism is a rebirth, that is to say, a new creation. And he asks himself why this regeneration takes place in the water: "Why are you plunged into the water? We read: 'May the waters bring forth living creatures (Gen. 1:20). And the living creatures were born.' This happened at the beginning of creation. But for you it was reserved that water should bring you forth to grace, as that other water brought forth creatures to natural life. Imitate this fish, who has received less grace (III 3; Botte, 72).[9] To understand this passage, we must remember that this fish, *ichthys,* is the image of Christ and so of the Christian. But what is less well known—and has been shown by F. J. Doelger [10]—is the baptismal origin of this theme. It appears in the *De Baptismo* of Tertullian: "We are little fishes (pisciculi) according to *the ichthys,* Jesus Christ, in Whom we are born, and we only live by remaining in the water" (De Bapt. I). The baptismal water begets the *pisciculi,* as the primitive waters begot the fish.[11]

[8] See also Clement of Alexandria: 'The new creation (ἀναγέννησις) comes about by water and the Spirit, like the creation (γένεσις) of the universe: The Spirit of God was borne upon the waters' (*Eclog, proph.,* 7; Staehlin, 138).

[9] See also St. Jerome: "The Holy Ghost was borne upon the waters, as upon a chariot, and brought forth the nascent world as a type of baptism." (*Epist.,* 69; P.L., XXII, 659).

[10] F. J. Doelger, *Pisciculi,* p. 120 et seq.

[11] See, earlier than this, Theoph. Antioch., *Ad Autolycum,* II, 16.

We might, perhaps, remark that in this first cycle of types, the waters appear only as a creative, and not as a destructive element. But this is not entirely correct. We find traces of this second aspect in the Coptic and Ethiopean liturgies for the blessing of the water, in which God is shown as having at the beginning: "created heaven and earth and enclosed the sea." [12] Here we have a trace of the primitive myth of creation as being a victory of God over the dragon of the sea, Leviathan, a myth which the narrative of Genesis has eliminated, but of which the Bible shows other traces. Lundberg can write: "In the Coptic and Syrian liturgies, the power of God over the water is evoked as it was manifested at creation, a power which causes the water of death to be transformed in a mystical manner, in the course of the consecration, into water creative of life. The consecration of the water is at once a purification and a sanctification." (Op. cit., p. 12-13).

We shall see again that this double aspect appears in the baptism of Christ in the Jordan, the relation of which to the narrative of creation we have already seen. Christ is shown as triumphing over the dragon hidden in the waters, before giving them the power of sanctification. So, alongside the theme of the creative waters, the theme of the waters of death is to be found in baptismal typology. But still, in the cycle of creation symbolism, the element of giving life, of regeneration is the most important. This is not true of the theme of the Deluge which we are now to study.

The Deluge is one of the types of Baptism most frequently cited by the Fathers and, as we shall see, one of the most obvious. Nothing can better aid us to rediscover the true meaning of the symbolism of Baptism, which is not primarily that of water as washing, but of water as destroying, and this will allow us to grasp the direct relationship between the rite itself and the theology of Baptism as configuration to the death of Christ. It is important here to connect the sign of the water with the theological idea of the Deluge. This may be reduced to its essential lines: the world is filled with sin; the judgment of God destroys the sinful world; one just man is spared to be the principle of a new cre-

[12] Denzinger, *Ritus Orientalium,* 1863 I, p. 205.

ation.[13] It is this *theologoumenon* that the Deluge, the Descent into the world below, Baptism and the Judgment all realize at different stages of sacred history.

The parallelism between the Deluge and Baptism is already expressed in the New Testament: ". . . Christ also died once for sins, the Just for the unjust, that He might bring us to God. Put to death indeed in the flesh, He was brought to life in the spirit, in which also He went and preached to those spirits that were in prison. These in times past had been disobedient when the patience of God waited in the days of Noe while the ark was building. In that ark, a few, that is, eight souls were saved through water. Its counterpart, Baptism, now saves you also . . ." (I Peter III, 18-21).

On this text, one of the most obscure in Scripture as Bellarmine had already noted, light has just been cast by a work of Bo Reicke.[14] The chief difficulty has to do with the word *keruttein* translated by "preach," which seems to imply a conversion of the spirits in prison. But the passage is not concerned with this, but with the proclamation of His victory made by Christ in the course of His descent into the lower world. The spirits in prison are the angels who, before the Deluge, were attracted by the daughters of men and who, because of this, as the Book of Henoch tells us (X, 4-6), were imprisoned in the great abyss until the day of Judgment. It is to them that Christ announced their defeat. But the demons, sons of the fallen angels, continue to act in the world, and they have a special connection with paganism and with the Roman Empire: as Christ fearlessly faced the fallen angels whom He had conquered, so Christians also should face without fear the world of paganism and its demons. Such seems to be the general meaning of this passage.[15]

But the author most particularly brings out the parallel between Baptism and the Deluge; the word *antitypos,* antitype, stands for the reality in opposition to the figure or type, *typos.* The Deluge is, then, a "type" that Baptism fulfills. We might

[13] The following pages on the Flood reproduce in part the chapter in *Sacramentum futuri* devoted to the same subject.

[14] Bo Reicke, *The Disobedient Spirits and Christian Baptism,* Lund, 1946, p. 95 et seqq. See also Geschwind, *Die Niederfahrt Christi in der Unterwelt;* W. Bieder, *Die Vorstellung von der Höllenfahrt J.C.,* 1949, p. 96, 120.

[15] Bo Reicke, loc., cit., pp. 85 and 131.

think that it is a question only of an analogy of images, but it appears that there is more than this to be found in it, and that we have here a whole interpretation of the baptismal rite. As sinful humanity in the time of Noe was destroyed by a judgment of God in the midst of the water, and one just man was saved to be the first-born of a new human race, so in Baptism the old man is annihilated by means of the sacrament of water, and the man who comes out of the baptismal pool belongs to the new creation. Between the Deluge and Baptism, we must also place the Descent of Christ into the world below, for it is here that we have the substantial realization of the mystery of the Deluge. In the death of Christ, the sinful humanity that He had assumed is annihilated by the great waters of death, and He rises from them as the First-born of the new creation. But Baptism, as St. Paul tells us, is a sacramental imitation of the death and the resurrection of Christ.[16]

We should note that, in presenting Baptism as the antitype of the Deluge, the First Epistle of St. Peter only prolongs what has been already indicated in the Old Testament. Just as the prophets announced that at the end of time God would raise up "a new heaven and a new earth" and as Christian typology affirms only that this new creation has been inaugurated with the resurrection of Christ and with Baptism that is a participation in it, so also here. Isaias announced a new Deluge at the end of time (LI, 9).[17] This is taken up in the Second Epistle of St. Peter (3:3-10). But the teaching of our text consists in saying that this eschatological judgment is accomplished in Baptism. This is important for the very nature of typology. For it has for its foundation the eschatalogical typology of the Old Testament, and this typology is verified in Christ and in Baptism as being the appearance of these "last times."

The sacramental typology outlined in the First Epistle of St. Peter was further developed by patristic tradition. We find it in Justin, in a passage where we are given explicitly the typology of St. Peter: "In the Deluge was accomplished the mystery (*mysterion*) of the salvation of men. Noe the just, with the other men

[16] Thus for example Chrysostom: "The immersion and emersion are the image of the Descent into Hell and the Return thence. That is why Paul calls Baptism a burial." (*Ho.* I *Cor.*, 40; P.G. LXI 348).

[17] See Jean Daniélou, *Sacramentum futuri,* p. 55 et seq.

of the Deluge, that is, his wife, his three sons and the wives of his sons, formed the number 8, and so showed the symbol of the eighth day (*tes ogdoes hemeras*) on which our Christ appeared risen from the dead and which is always, as it were implicitly, the first day. For Christ, the first-born of all creation, became in a new sense the head (*arche*) [18] of another race, of that which was regenerated by Him, by the water and the wood which contained the mystery of the Cross, as Noe was saved by the wood of the ark when he was carried on the waters with his family. When, therefore, the prophet says: 'In the time of Noe I saved you,' as I have said already, he spoke also to the faithful people of God, to the people who possess these symbols. . . . As the whole earth, according to Scripture, was flooded, it obviously was not to the earth that God spoke, but to the people who obeyed Him when He had prepared a place of rest (*anapausis*) in Jerusalem, as He showed beforehand by all these symbols of the time of the Deluge; and I mean those who are prepared by the water, the faith, the wood, and who repented of their sins, they will escape the judgment of God which is to come!" (*Dialogue,* CXXXVIII, 2-3).

Justin here makes more explicit what is said in the New Testament and in particular in the First Epistle of St. Peter. The water of the Deluge is the figure of the water of Baptism. We have mentioned above the foundation of this analogy. There are in fact two planes of comparison. On the one hand there is a *theological* resemblance between the Deluge, the Descent into the lower world, and Baptism, for here we see at work the same divine ways. In all three cases, there exists a sinful world which is to be annihilated by the punishment, and in all three cases a just man is spared: this just man, in the Deluge, is Noe; in the Descent into hell, Jesus Christ; in Baptism, the Christian by conformation to Jesus Christ. Thus Baptism is a sacramental imitation of the Descent into hell, both being prefigured by the Deluge. But, furthermore, in both the Deluge and Baptism, there is the element of water which might be called illustrative typology. This is not sufficient by itself to serve as a foundation for typology,— and it became the error of certain exegetes to try to recognize a type of Baptism wherever water is mentioned in the Old Testament. But these illustrations have real meaning when they are the signs by

[18] See Col., I. 18.

which we can recognize theological analogies. Thus, to the extent to which it symbolizes a judgment, the water of Baptism is clearly an allusion to the water of the Deluge.

We can finally note the relationship established between Baptism and the Judgment: "Those who are prepared by water, faith and the wood, will escape the Judgment to come." The fact of a relationship of Baptism with eschatology is connected with the New Testament, and in particular seems implied by the Baptism of John, which with good reason is interpreted as signifying a man's joining the messianic community in view of the judgment to come.[19] And Van Imschoot has well shown that the primitive meaning of the phrase: "I baptize you with water; he will baptize you with fire and the Spirit" was eschatological, and that St. John (3:33) modifies this into a sacramental statement, in which the Baptism of the Holy Spirit does not mean the Judgment, but Christian Baptism as contrasted with the baptism of John.[20] But what is new in the text of St. Justin quoted above is that Christian Baptism is shown not only to be a preparation for the eschatological Judgment—a leading theme which we shall find again—but also as a certain prefiguration of it. Baptism, by the symbol of immersion, is, as it were, a sacramental anticipation, through imitation, of the final Judgment, which will be baptism of fire. And it is thanks to Baptism that the Christian will escape the Judgment because in that sense, he has already been judged.[21] This idea is stated explicitly by Origen: "In the Baptism of water, we are buried with Christ: in the baptism of fire, we shall be configured to the body of His glory." [22] So Baptism is an efficacious memorial of the death and resurrection of Christ (which were considered to be a baptism by Christ Himself) [23]; and it is also an efficacious prophecy of eschatological death and resurrection. And these three realities are all prefigured by the Deluge.

Besides the symbolism of the water, the texts that we have seen present certain other themes. The first is that of the symbolism of the number eight, the *ogdoad*. It appears in the First Epistle of St. Peter in connection with the eight people saved in the Ark.

[19] See for example C. K. Barrett, *The Holy Spirit in the Gospel Tradition*, p. 33.
[20] *Baptême de feu et baptême d'eau*, Eph., Lov., 1936, pp. 653 et seq.
[21] Edsman, *Le baptême de feu*, pp. 124 et seqq.
[22] Co. Matth., XV. 23.
[23] Luke XII. 50.

And also in the Second Epistle of St. Peter, we find, "For God did not spare the angels when they sinned, but dragged them down by infernal ropes to Tartarus, and delivered them to be tortured and kept in custody for judgment. Nor did He spare the ancient world, but preserved (with seven others) Noe, a herald of justice, when He brought a flood upon the world of the impious . . . for the Lord knows how to deliver the God-fearing from temptation." (II Peter, II, 4-9). We find the number eight again in connection with Noe: and this time it is no longer the number of people saved in the Ark, but the number of generations before the Flood. We know that there was a tradition of their being seven generations before Noe (*Reconn. clementines,* I, 29), which seems to be in accord with the apocalyptic traditions influenced by the Babylonian idea of the seven sages who lived before the Flood.[24] This is one more sign of the points of contact this Epistle has with apocalyptic literature, but it does not explain why the Epistle of Peter emphasizes this theme in connection with Baptism. The reason is that the number eight stands for the eighth day, which is that on which Christ rose, since it was the day after the sabbath, and the Christian Sunday is the perpetual sacrament of this eighth day. But the Christian enters into the Church by Baptism, which was given on Easter Sunday, the Eighth Day *par excellence.* And so we also find very early the symbolism of Baptism as connected with the number eight.[25]

We find the symbolism of eight also brought out in the text of Justin. He explicitly mentions the eighth day which follows the week and "which is implicitly the first." And this eighth day is a figure of the Resurrection of Christ, which took place on the day after the sabbath; it is a figure of Baptism which is the beginning of a new era and the first day of the new week; it is, finally, the figure of the eternal "eighth day" which is to follow the whole time of the world.[26] A passage of Asterius, directly in the line of the tradition of Justin, taken from a *Sermon on Psalm 6* (P. G.,

[24] W. Staerk, *Die Säulen der Welt und des Hauses der Weisheit,* Zeitsch fur Neut. Wiss., 1936, pp. 245 et seqq.

[25] See above, p. 37.

[26] It is interesting to note that Cyril of Jerusalem represents the baptism of John as the end (τέλος) of the old Testament and the beginning (αρχή) of the New (P. G., XXXIII, 433 C).

XL, 448, B-D),[27] shows us the development of the theme of the eighth day: "Why did the Lord rise again on the eighth day? Because the first eight men, in the time of Noe, after the destruction of the ancient world, raised up a new universe in our race." We find again this idea of the end of the old world and of a new creation. Asterius sees, in these eight people from whom arose all the men who came after him, the figure of Christ also raising up a new race. And he goes on: "Just as the first resurrection of the race after the deluge took place by means of eight persons, so the Lord also inaugurated the resurrection of the dead on the eighth day, when, having dwelt in His sepulchre as Noe in the Ark, He put an end (*epausen*) to the deluge of impurity and instituted the Baptism of regeneration, so that, having been buried with Him in Baptism, we may become the participants of His Resurrection." [28] Here we find some new features which bring out more precisely the typology of the Deluge, particularly the comparison of the Ark with the Sepulchre. And the theme of the cessation of evil is in harmony with the name of Noe, which signifies repose (*anapausis*).

These texts of Justin give us a baptismal typology of the Deluge which is the development of that found in the First Epistle of St. Peter. This group is characterized by the importance that is given to the theme of the number eight. But besides this tradition, we find another which puts the emphasis on other characteristics, especially on the theme of the dove. This tradition appears in the *De baptismo* of Tertullian,[29] which brings together all the traditional figures of Baptism, in such a way that we may well suppose that it reproduces the primitive catechesis. "As, after the waters of the Deluge, by which the iniquity of the ancient world was purified,—after the Baptism, as it were, of the world,—the dove, sent from the Ark and coming back with an olive branch—which is even now a sign of peace among the peoples—announced that peace had come to the earth, according to the same plan, on the spiritual plane, the dove of the Holy Spirit descends on the earth, that is to say, on our flesh, when it comes out

[27] M. Marcel Richard sees in the author of this homily Asterius the Sophist and not Asterius of Amasea (*Symb. Osl.*, XXV, pp. 66-67).

[28] See also Augustine, *Contra Faustum* XII, 15 and 19.

[29] It is found in the same school in the Pseudo-Cyprian, *ad Novatian.*, 2; C.S.E.L. 55, 22-27. See also Hippolytus, *Sermo in Theophania* (Achelis, p. 261).

of the baptismal pool after the cleansing of its old sins, to bring the peace of God sent down from the height of heaven where the Church is, prefigured by the ark" (*De baptismo* 8; P. L., I, 1209 B). The chief feature of this typology is the symbolism of the dove, and it is this which sets us on the track of its origin. In an earlier passage, Tertullian tells us of the baptism of Christ "when the Holy Spirit descended on the Lord in the form of a dove and rested on the waters of baptism where He recognized His abode of old (De Bapt., 8).[30]

This is, then, another vein of typology that we find here, one which also is based on the Old Testament. Certainly, if the dove which came down upon Christ at His Baptism is an allusion to the Spirit of God hovering over the primal waters, Gen. I. 2, it seems also to be an allusion to the dove of the Ark.[31] It is, then, with good reason that patristic tradition saw in the Deluge a figure of the Baptism of Christ, in which He appears as the new Noe on whom the Holy Spirit descends to show the reconciliation of man with God.[32] For example, we find in St. Cyril of Jerusalem: "Some say that, just as salvation came in the time of Noe by the wood and the water, and there was the beginning of a new creation, and as the dove came back to Noe in the evening with an olive branch, so, they say, the Holy Spirit came down on the true Noe, the Author of the new creation, when the spiritual dove came down upon Him at His baptism to show that He it is Who, by the wood of the cross, confers salvation on believers, and Who, toward the evening, by His death, gave the world the grace of salvation." (P. G., XXXIII, 982 A). This passage is, indeed, in the manner of Cyril of Jerusalem, who tried to find in the events of the Old Testament the figure of the events of the life of Christ. But what is important for our purpose is that he gives us the intermediate link between the Deluge and the Baptism: the Deluge is a figure of the Baptism of Christ, which is in its turn a figure of the Baptism of the Christian, so that the dove of the Deluge is seen to pre-figure the coming of the Holy Spirit at Baptism.[33]

[30] The symbolism of the dove is contrasted with that of the raven, a symbol of the devil (Gregory of Nyssa, P. G. XLVI, 421 B).

[31] Barrett, *The Holy Spirit in the Gospel Tradition,* p. 39.

[32] Lundberg, *Typologie baptismale,* p. 73.

[33] See also St. Jerome, *Epist.,* LXIX 6: "The dove of the Holy Ghost, once the black bird has been driven out, flies towards Noe, as towards Christ in the Jordan" (P. L. XXII, 660A).

The other characteristic of this typology of Tertullian is to show us the Ark as the figure of the Church. We find this figure as early as Irenaeus (1093 B), but it is not scriptural.[34] We do not find it again in Justin, where the wood of the Ark is rather a figure of the wood of the Cross.[35] But it forms a part of the oldest sacramental catechesis and may go back to the very origins of Christianity. We find it again and again in Tertullian: *Qui in arca non fuit, in Ecclesia non sit* (De idol. 24; P. L. 1, 696 B). St. Cyprian in particular gives it a considerable place in *De unitate Ecclesiae:* "If anyone could have been saved outside the ark of Noe, then he who is outside the Church is saved" (6; C. S. E. L., 214), and this is the first expression of the aphorism: "Outside the Church there is no salvation." The connection of this theme with that of Baptism appears frequently: "Peter, in showing that the Church is one, and that only those who are in the Church can be saved, said: In the ark of Noe, certain persons to the number of eight only, were saved by water, which Baptism effects in like manner for you. He proves and shows that the one Ark of Noe was the figure of the one Church. If, at the time of this baptism of the world in which it was purified and redeemed, anyone could have been saved without having been in the Ark of Noe, then he who is outside the Church could now also be vivified by Baptism" (Epist. LXVIII, 2; C. S. E. L. 751). It is the typology of the First Epistle to Peter which St. Cyprian here develops explicitly. The same theme reappears in *Letter LXXXIII* in which Cyprian adds that the Church "was founded in the unity of the Lord according to the image (*sacramentum*) of the one Ark" (809, 10-12). See also Epist. LXXV 15; C. S. E. L. 820, 13-24). St. Jerome is the echo of unanimous tradition when he writes: "The ark of Noe was the type of the Church" (P. L. XXIII, 185 A).[36] And the liturgy itself gives a place to this idea. (*Const. Ap.* II, 14, 9).[37]

In direct dependence on Tertullian, Didymus of Alexandria, in

[34] St. Jerome thought nevertheless that it was meant in I Peter, III, 20. He writes: "The ark is interpreted by the apostle Peter as a symbol of the Church" (*Epist.*, 133; P. L., XXII, 1014).

[35] See Augustine, *De catech. rud.*, 32 and 34; *Contra Faustum.*, XVII, 14. The general theme of wood and water, symbolic of the baptismal water transformed by the cross, is an ancient one (Barnabas, XI, 5). See Lundberg, op. laud., p. 98 et seq.

[36] See also Augustine, *Contra Faustum,* XII, 17.

[37] See Lundberg, *La typologie baptismale,* p. 76.

the *De Trinitate,* takes up again and develops the themes of the *De baptismo.* We find here in particular the story of the axe of Eliseus and of the Pool of Bethesda which are found in Tertullian, and the Deluge also had its place: "The Deluge which purified the world of its ancient iniquity was a hidden prophecy of the purification of sins by the holy pool. And the ark, which saved those who went into it, is an image (*eikon*) of the awe-inspiring Church and of the good hope that we have because of her. As to the dove who brought the olive-branch into the Ark and so showed that the earth was uncovered, it designated the coming of the Holy Spirit and the reconciliation to come from on high: for the olive is thc symbol of peace" (II, P. G. XXXIX, 697, A-B).

The symbolism now is fixed in a manner henceforth unchangeable. We may note that the ancient symbols corresponding to archaic ideas, the eight persons in the ark, for example, have disappeared. Only those have lasted that were in harmony with the thought of men of the time. The most characteristic is the branch of the olive tree, which had no meaning for the Jews, but was connected with Graeco-Roman life. We may note also that the Ark, which was a figure of the Cross for Justin, henceforth prefigured the Church. Thus we go from a Christological kind of symbolism to an ecclesiastical. It is the realities of present Christian life,—the baptismal pool, the Church, which the symbols now prefigure.[38]

With the liturgical treatises of St. Ambrose, we get a similar point of view. He devotes a whole work to Noe: *De Noe et arca,* but this forms part of his moral treatises, inspired by Philo. If we wish to find him giving witness to liturgical tradition, we must consult the *De Mysteriis* and the *De Sacramentis.* Here we find a succession of baptismal figures which from that time on remains fixed. As with Tertullian and Didymus, the first is that of the Spirit borne upon the waters, of Genesis; the third is that of the crossing of the Red Sea; the second is that of the Deluge. "Receive another witness. All flesh was corrupted by its iniquities 'My spirit will dwell no longer in men,' says God, 'because they are flesh.' By this God shows that, by impurity of body and the stain of grave sin, spiritual grace is taken away. And so also God,

[38] Origen also knows the baptismal symbolism of the Flood: see for example *Co. Rom.,* III, I: P.G., XIV, 926 A.

wishing to make up for that which was lacking, caused the Deluge, and ordered the just man Noe to go into the ark. And he, when the waters were going down, sent first a crow which did not return, and then sent out a dove of which the text tells us that it came back with an olive branch. You see the water, you see the wood, you see the dove and can you doubt the mystery!" (De Myst., 10; Botte 110-111). Here we find once more the great symbols given in Tertullian. And in all these signs that form one whole, St. Ambrose finds the evidence for the validity of the figure.[39]

This traditional typology appears again in St. John Chrysostom: "The narrative of the Deluge is a sacrament (*mysterion*) and its details are a figure (*typos*) of things to come. The ark is the Church; Noe, Christ; the dove, the Holy Spirit; the olive branch, the divine goodness. As in the midst of the sea, the ark protected those who were inside it , so the Church saves those who are spared. But the ark only protected, the Church does more. For example, the ark took in animals without reason and kept them safe, the Church takes in men without *logos* and does not merely protect them, she transforms them" (*Ho. Laz.* 6; P. G., XLVIII, 1037-1038). We have here the witness of an author little inclined to allegory, and it has the more importance for us since it shows us that we have here a common ecclesiastical tradition. Moreover, in conformity with typological teaching, the author shows how the reality surpasses the figure. We have already met this point in St. Irenaeus. All these witnesses, borrowed from the elementary teaching of the Church, shows us to what degree the biblical figures were an integral element of primitive Christian mentality. For the Christians of the time, the narrative of the Deluge was their own history prefigured ahead of time: "By the Deluge was accomplished the mystery of the salvation of men," so writes St. Justin.[40]

[39] See also *De Sacram.*, II, 1; Botte, 62.
[40] On the Flood as a type of baptism on the decorated monuments of the first centuries, see *Sacramentum futuri*, p. 84-85.

CHAPTER FIVE

Types of Baptism: The Crossing of the Red Sea

TOGETHER with the Deluge, the Crossing of the Red Sea is one of the types of Baptism that we meet most frequently. Moreover, the central theme is analogous to that of the Deluge, for it concerns the waters of destruction, which are the instrument of the punishment of God, from which the people of God are preserved. Now we find ourselves in another part of the Bible, that of the Exodus. The whole narrative of the deliverance from Egypt is a figure of the Redemption. The prophets already had announced a new Exodus to come at the end of time, in which God would accomplish works even greater than those which He did for His people in the desert. The New Testament—and in particular the Gospel of St. Matthew—shows us that these works of God are accomplished in Christ. It is by Him that the true "deliverance" is accomplished, and this "deliverance" is effectively applied to each man by Baptism.[1]

Both the Gospel and the Liturgy, we should realize here, show us how striking is this relationship with the Exodus. For, in fact, it was at the time of the Pasch, which was for the Jews the commemoration of their deliverance from Egypt, that Christ accomplished our redemption by His death. And further, it is during this same night of the Pasch, Easter night, that Baptism was ordinarily given. So the coincidence of dates brings out in a strik-

[1] Jean Daniélou, *Sacramentum futuri,* pp. 131-142.

ing way the continuity between these different acts of God.[2] In the Exodus, in the death and resurrection of Christ, and in Baptism, it is the same redeeming action which is accomplished on different levels of history,—that of the figure, of the reality, and of the sacrament.[3] So it was quite normal for Christians to use the texts of the liturgy of the synagogue concerning the Pasch and to apply them to the Resurrection of Christ and to Baptism.

We are concerned here with a reality so central that it becomes the focus of the whole Christian Mystery: for this is indeed the "Paschal Mystery." But in this whole, various aspects may be distinguished. For one thing, the narrative of the Exodus includes successive events. Let us leave aside for the moment the first of these events, that of the immolation of the lamb and of the sparing of the first-born, which properly constitutes the Pasch. We shall speak of it again in connection with the Eucharist, although it also contains baptismal elements. Now we shall consider only the crossing of the Red Sea and the circumstances immediately surrounding it, and we shall dwell above all on those aspects of the Old Testament that are in the most direct relation to the baptismal rites themselves, that is to say, those of the crossing of the water.

The typological significance of the crossing of the water of the Red Sea was brought out in the Old Testament itself, and always with an eschatological meaning. In Isaias, God announced that "He would make a way for His people in the desert, a path in the dry waters" (Is. 43:19).[4] The crossing of the Red Sea is also the figure of the victory of God over Rahab, the sea-monster which symbolizes Egypt (Is. 51:10). Thus we see the outlines of a whole theme in which the crossing of the Red Sea is seen as a new victory of God over the dragon of the Sea, which was specifically identified with Egyptian idolatry. Beyond its historic significance, the crossing of the Red Sea is seen to grow to the proportions of a symbol of the future victory of Yahweh over the powers of evil.[5]

We find the echo of this eschatological typology in the New

[2] See Tertullian, *De bapt.*, 19.

[3] See J. Guillet, *Thèmes bibliques*, 1951, pp. 22-25.

[4] St. Cyprian expressly links this prophecy with Baptism (*Tertiom*, I, 12; C.S.E.L., 47).

[5] A Jewish work contemporary with the New Testament, the *Liber antiquitatum biblicarum*, shews the dividing of the waters of the Red Sea as a renewal of the dividing of the waters at the time of the creation (XV, 6; Kish, p. 155).

Testament. The Apocalypse of St. John compares the victory of the elect over death to the crossing of the Red Sea, and puts on their lips the victorious canticle of the sister of Moses: "And I saw as it were a sea of glass mingled with fire, and those who had overcome the Beast and its image and the number of its name, standing on the sea of glass, having the harps of God and singing the song of Moses, the servant of God, and the song of the Lamb . . ." (Apoc. 15:3). In the Beast we recognize Pharaoh, figure of the demon, who is destroyed by the water of judgment, while the servants of God, victorious, find themselves on the other shore, having crossed without harm the sea of death.[6]

But we are still in the realm of eschatological typology. The New Testament will show us that this crossing of the Red Sea is already realized in the baptismal rite of the crossing of the baptismal pool.[7] We find this in a famous text from the First Epistle to the Corinthians, one of the most important for the Biblical foundations of typology: ". . . our fathers were all under the cloud, and all passed through the sea, and all were baptized in Moses, in the cloud and in the sea . . . *Haec autem in figura facta sunt nostri.*" (I Cor. X:2-6). It was ourselves who were prefigured in these things. The relationship between the crossing of the Red Sea and Baptism could not be emphasized more clearly. The Exodus from Egypt was already a Baptism: the two realities have the same significance: they mark the end of slavery to sin and the entrance into a new existence.

Furthermore, the relationship of the Crossing of the Red Sea and of Baptism as brought out by St. Paul seems to be according to a line of interpretation belonging to the Judaism of his time. For we know that at the beginning of the Christian era, the initiation of proselytes into the Jewish community included, besides circumcision, a baptism. This baptism, as G. Foote-Moore writes, was "a purification that was neither real nor symbolic, but essentially a rite of initiation." [8] And the purpose of this initiation was to cause the proselyte to go through the sacrament received by the people at the time of the crossing of the Red Sea. The baptism of

[6] See Harald Riesenfeld, *The Resurrection in Ezechiel,* XXXVII, p. 23.

[7] On this question see F. J. Doelger, *Der Durchzug durch das Rote Meer als Sinnbild des christlichen Taufe.* Ant. und Christ., 1930, pp. 63-69; P. Lundberg, *La typologie baptismale dans l'ancienne Église,* pp. 116-146.

[8] *Judaism,* I, p. 334.

the proselytes was, then, a kind of imitation of the Exodus. This is important in showing us that the link between Baptism and the crossing of the Red Sea existed already in Judaism and that therefore it gives us the true symbolism of Baptism, as being not primarily a purification, but a deliverance and a creation.

Starting from the scriptural bases given by St. Paul, Christian tradition makes more precise the comparison between the Jewish people at the time of the Exodus and the catechumen during the Paschal night. As the Jewish people were under the tyranny of the idolatrous Pharoah, and were set free by his destruction in the waters of the Red Sea, so the catechumen was under the tyranny of Satan and is set free by his destruction in the waters of Baptism. This is what we find everywhere. Tertullian writes: "When the people, willingly leaving Egypt, escaped from the power of the King of Egypt by passing across the water, the water destroyed the king and all his army. What could be a clearer figure of Baptism? The peoples are delivered from the world, and this is done by the water, and the devil, who has hitherto tyrannized over them, they leave behind, destroyed in the water" (*De Bapt.* 9).

Here we have the primitive view of Baptism and of redemption. Redemption is understood as being the victory of Christ over the demon, the victory by which humanity is set free. It is this liberation that Baptism applies to each Christian. Again in Baptism, the demon is conquered, again man is saved, and this is accomplished by the sign of water. We have brought out above the importance of the theme of Baptism as a struggle with the demon, and the Exodus from Egypt offers us the image for this theological theme: what God did then, by the sacrament of the water, to deliver a people in the physical order of being from a tyrant in the same order, and to cause them to go from Egypt to the desert, He accomplishes now by the sacrament of water, to deliver a spiritual people from a spiritual tyrant and to cause them to go from the world to the kingdom of God.

In the *De Trinitate,* Didymus the Blind is led to speak of Baptism in connection with the divinity of the Holy Spirit. He gives us the figures concerned with this: the sanctification of the waters by the Spirit, the Deluge, and, finally, the crossing of the Red Sea: "And also the Red Sea which received the Israelites who did not fear it and delivered them from the evils with which the Egyptians were pursuing them, and the whole history of the going out from Egypt, are the type (*typos*) of the salvation procured by Baptism. Egypt, in fact, is a figure of the world, in which we make our own unhappiness by living evilly; the people are those who are now enlightened (that is, baptized); the waters, which are the means of salvation for the people, stand for Baptism; Pharoah and his soldiers, for Satan and his satellites" (II, 14; P. G., XXXIX, 697 A). We find here again the same order as in Tertullian, and the same interpretations. But this is not surprising, since the whole section of the *De Trinitate* which is concerned with Baptism is influenced by Tertullian.

The great Greek Doctors of the end of the fourth century love to dwell on this theme. So St. Basil: "What concerns the Exodus of Israel is told us in order to signify those who are saved by Baptism. . . . The sea is the figure of Baptism, since it delivered the people from Pharoah, as Baptism (*Loutron*) from the tyranny of the devil. The sea killed the enemy; so in Baptism, our enmity to God is destroyed. The people came out of the sea whole and safe; we also come out of the water as living men from among the dead" (*De Spiritu Sancto,* 14; Pruche, 163-164). We should note the last phrase in which the comparison is made with the Resurrection of Christ. Elsewhere Basil writes: "If Israel had not crossed the sea, they would not have escaped from Pharoah; so you, if you do not go through the water, you will not escape from the cruel tyranny of the demon" (P. G., XXXI, 425 B-C).

We find the same idea in Gregory of Nyssa: "The crossing of the Red Sea was, according to St. Paul himself, a prophecy in action (*di' ergon*) of the sacrament of Baptism. And in fact, now once again, when the people approach the water of rebirth as they flee from Egypt, which is sin, they themselves are freed and saved, but the devil and his aids, the spirits of wickedness, are destroyed" (P. G., XLVI, 589 D). In the *Life of Moses,* the army of the Egyptians—in a more allegorical line of thought—are figures of the passions of the soul: "The passions throw themselves into the water following the Hebrews whom they pursue. But the water becomes a principle of life for those who seek refuge there, and a principle of death for their pursuers," (P. G. XLIV, 361 C. See Origen, *Ho. Ex.* V, 5).

Around this essential theme, other themes gather. The first is that of the pillar of cloud which accompanied the Jews during their Exodus. This column, was the visible sign of the presence of God in the midst of His people. The theme of the cloud as the sign of God's dwelling in the tabernacle, is found all through the Old Testament. In the New Testament, the presence of the cloud witnessed to the fact that the Dwelling of God (John I, 14) is henceforth connected with the Humanity of Jesus: this cloud is what rested on Mary at the moment of the Annunciation (Luke I:35). It appeared in the Transfiguration and at the Ascension, which are precisely manifestations of the divinity of Jesus. More particularly, St. Paul directly establishes the relationship between the pillar of cloud of the Exodus, and Christian Baptism, when he writes: ". . . our fathers were baptized *in the cloud* and in the sea." The cloud clearly designates the Holy Spirit, the acting power of God, in the scene of the Annunciation. The presence of the cloud, accompanying the crossing of the sea in the narrative of the Exodus, also prefigures the union of water and the Holy Spirit, as the elements of Baptism.

The interpretations of the Fathers, therefore, rest on a solic Biblical foundation. Origen is the first to make this interpretation precise. In commenting on the narrative of the Exodus, in his *Homilies on the Exodus,* he recalls the interpretation of St. Paul and adds: "See how the tradition of Paul differs from the historic reading. That which the Jews consider to be the crossing of the Sea, St. Paul calls Baptism. That which they believe to be a cloud, St. Paul proves to be the Holy Spirit. And he wishes this passage to be interpreted in the same sense as the precept of the Lord, saying: If any man is not reborn of water and the Holy Spirit, he cannot enter into the kingdom of heaven." (Ho. Ex. V, 1; 184, 2).[9] We see here how the union of the water and the Spirit, prefigured by the dove and by the water in the Deluge and the Creation, is here represented by the union of the Cloud and of the Sea.

It is St. Ambrose above all who develops this theme. In the *De Mysteriis,* having enumerated the other figures of Baptism: the Spirit carried over the waters, and the Deluge, he comes to the crossing of the Red Sea: "The third witness is given us by the

[9] See also Basil, *De Spir. sancto* 14; Pruche 163-164; Gregory of Nyssa, *Ho. Bapt.,* P. G., XLVI, 589 D.

Apostle: All our fathers were under the cloud . . . etc. Furthermore, Moses himself says in his Canticle: 'Thou hast sent out Thy spirit, and the sea swallowed them up.' So you see that, in the crossing of the Hebrew people, in which the Egyptians perished and the Hebrews escaped, the figure of Baptism was already preformed. What else should we learn from this sacrament except that sin is drowned and error is destroyed while piety and innocence are saved?" (*De Myst.* 12; Botte, III). As to the cloud, it is the presence of the Holy Spirit: "It is this which came down on the Virgin Mary, and the power of the Most High covered her with its shadow." (*De Myst.* 13; Botte, III).

In the *De Sacramentis,* St. Ambrose takes up the same theme with new details. He shows the superiority of the Christian sacraments to the Jewish *mysteria:* "What was of greater importance than the crossing of the sea by the Jewish people? Yet the Jews who crossed over are all dead in the desert. But, on the contrary, he who passes through this fountain, that is to say, from earthly things to heavenly,—which is indeed the *transitus,* that is to say, the Passover, the passing over from sin to life,—he who passes through this fountain will not die, but rise again." (1, 12; Botte, 57-58). Ambrose, whose connection with Alexandrian exegesis is well-known, interprets Easter here in the Philonian sense of "a passage from earthly things to heavenly." As to the pillar of cloud, he gives us the same meaning as in the preceding passage: "The pillar of cloud is the Holy Spirit. The people were in the sea, and the pillar of fire preceded them, then the pillar of cloud followed them, as the shadow of the Holy Spirit. You see how by the Holy Spirit and by the water, the figure of Baptism is clearly shown" (1, 22; Botte 61).

But the cloud appeared only by day. By night it had the appearance of a pillar of fire. This leads to another line of typology the origin of which is equally biblical and which interprets the pillar of fire as the Word. Already the Book of Wisdom sees in it an image of Wisdom (10:17). "She will lead them by a way sown with marvels. And will be for them like the light of stars in the night." Philo sees here the figure of the Logos. And it seems that St. John's Gospel also shows us Christ as being the pillar of fire: "He who follows Me does not walk in the darkness, I am the light of the world." (8:12). Clement of Alexandria more precisely applies the pillar of light of the Exodus to the Incarnate Word (*Strom.*, 1, 24).

Thus, it is not astonishing that we find this interpretation in the baptismal catecheses. If the Holy Spirit, prefigured by the cloud, shows the power of God at work in Baptism, the Word, prefigured by the pillar of fire, shows that Baptism is *illumination*. We know that this (*photismos*) is one of the words for Baptism. And St. Ambrose writes in the same passage of the *De Sacramentis* in which he was speaking of the cloud: "What is the pillar of light, but Christ the Lord, Who has scattered the darkness of paganism and has spread the light of truth and of spiritual grace in the heart of men" (1, 22; Botte, 61).

We see this theme appearing again in the chief catecheses of the fourth century. We have some little sermons of Zeno of Verona, about a dozen lines each, on the Exodus, which are brief commentaries on the readings from this Book, given during the Easter season. In the first, he briefly recalls the historical sense, in accordance with the usage to which the *Peregrinatio Etheriae* gives witness,[10] and then he goes on to the spiritual sense: *Quantum spiritaliter intellegi datur, Aegypti mundus est; Pharao, cum populo suo, diabolus et omnis spiritus iniquitatis; Israel, populus christianus, qui proficisci iubetur ut ad futura contendat; Moyses et Aaron per id quod erat sacerdotium, per suum numerum demonstrabant duorum testamentorum sacramentum; columna viam demonstrans Christus est Dominus* (P. L. XI, 510). The pillar of cloud prefigured Christ, according to johannine typology. And its double aspect, of a cloud and of light, corresponds, says Zeno, to the two judgments, that of water which has already taken place, and that of fire, which is to come. We have here a clear allusion to the parallelism of the Deluge and of the final judgment, a theme common in ancient Christianity.[11]

We see in this text of Zeno a new aspect of the typology we are considering, that of the person of Moses. Zeno shows us that he is, on the one hand, the figure of the priest, minister of Baptism; and on the other, of the Old Testament. But he does not represent the usual tradition, in which Moses is a figure of Christ. This typology is founded on the New Testament, for the Gospel shows

[10] 46; Pétré, p. 256.
[11] See above, p. 79.

us Christ as a new Moses who gives the New Law, not on Sinai, but on a mountain in Galilee; not to the twelve tribes, but to the twelve apostles, prefiguring the universal Church.[12] And, in the crossing of the Red Sea, Moses plays a most important part: it is he who strikes the waters with his staff to cause them to divide, who is the first to enter the sea without danger, going ahead of his people, and who afterwards, following God's command, caused Pharaoh and his army to be engulfed in the water. Here again, in a special way, the New Testament shows us Moses as a figure of Christ.[13] We find this parallel between Moses and Christ indicated by Gregory of Elvira, together with other aspects of the baptismal typology of the Exodus: "It is a long and well-nigh gigantic task to speak of the descent of the people into Egypt and of their enslavement. Everyone knows this history, and it is clear. But what we must endeavor, dearest Brethren, to explain is also the spiritual meaning (*rationem atque mysterium*) of this passage, according to the spiritual understanding. For it is indeed that which contains a figure of the future reality which deserves to be explained, since also there is nothing in the holy and divine Scriptures which does not have as its principal value a spiritual one, either in manifesting things past, or in suggesting things present, or in intimating things to come. This is why Egypt was the figure of the world, Pharaoh of the devil; the children of Israel were images of the first parent, from whom they also are descended; Moses, sent to deliver them, was the type of Christ" (VII; Batiffol, 76-77).

Aphraates gives us a deeper interpretation of the part of Moses, also connecting the theme of the Red Sea with that of the waters of death: "The Jews escaped at the Pasch from the slavery of Pharoah; on the day of the crucifixion, we were freed from the captivity of Satan. They immolated the lamb and were saved by its blood from the Destroyer; we, by the blood of the well beloved Son, are delivered from the works of corruption that we have done. They had Moses for a guide; we have Jesus for our Head and Savior. Moses divided the sea for them and had them cross it; our Lord opened hell and broke its gates, when He went down into its depths and opened them and marked out the path for

[12] *Sacramentum futuri*, p. 137-138.
[13] I. Cor., X, 1; Ap., XV, 3.

those who come to believe in Him" (Aphraates, *Dem.,* XII, 8; P. O., I, 521).

In this passage, we can note the connection between the Red Sea crossed by Moses and the Abyss into which Jesus descended. We know that, according to ancient theology, the Descent into hell is the central episode in the redemption, the victory won by Christ over death in its own domain, and the deliverance of humanity in slavery to the power of the devil. Here is the Paschal Mystery. On the other hand, the idea of the river or the sea as the dwelling of the dragon is a theme both of the Bible and of the Fathers.[14] We have seen that Christian baptism was thought of as a struggle with the demon hidden in the waters. Here the crossing of the Red Sea is seen as the figure of the Descent into hell; but the context also implies a reference to Baptism.

If Moses is a figure of Christ, the sister of Moses is also interpreted by some commentators as a symbol of the Church. This theme appears with a baptismal reference in Zeno: "We should see in the sea the holy fountain in which those who are not fleeing but bearing their sin, are purified by the same waters by which the servants of God were delivered. Mary, who struck her tambourine with the women, is the figure of the Church (*typus Ecclesiae*), who with all the Churches that she has brought forth, leads the Christian people not into the desert but into heaven, singing hymns and beating her breast" (P. L. XI, 509-510). These lines add new elements. The Red Sea is expressly identified with the baptismal pool whose water takes away sins. So the image is made more precise and joins the liturgy. The crossing of the baptismal pool is prefigured by the crossing of the Red Sea. In the two cases, this crossing brings about the destruction of enemies temporal or spiritual. Finally, the theme of the Church who brings forth new children by Baptism is an important theme in primitive Christianity; we find it in Cyril of Jerusalem and above all in Zeno.[15]

One last feature of interest in the text of Zeno is the parallel between the canticle of Miriam and the hymns of the Church. Isaias in describing the eschatological Exodus writes, "Thou it is

[14] Orig., *In Joh.,* B VI, 48; Preuschen, 157. On the idea of the crossing of the Red Sea as the triumph of Yahweh over the Sea-Dragon, see Gunkel, *Schoepfung und Chaos,* pp. 31-32.

[15] J. Morgenstein, *The Despoiling of the Egyptians,* Journ. Bibl. Litt., 1949, 25-26.

Who hast made a path through the deep waters for the people to pass through. They will go to Sion with singing" (51:10-11). The Apocalypse also shows us those who have gone through the sea, that is, who have triumphed over death, singing the Canticle of Moses and the song of the Lamb (15:2-4). Zeno sees this eschatological prophecy as already realized in Baptism. This is expressed liturgically by the singing of psalms after the baptismal rite accompanying the procession to the Church. As Dom Winzen says, the canticle of Miriam was "the hour in which the Divine Office was born." [16] The singing of hymns in the Christian community fulfills the figure of the canticle of the Exodus and prefigures the heavenly liturgy. We must add that this liturgical aspect appears in the Old Testament itself: The Canticle of Miriam seems, in fact, to be the trace of the liturgical celebration of the Exodus in Judaism, which was incorporated into the narrative.[17] Thus again, the Jewish liturgy appears as the background of the Christian.

In this way, the series of episodes in Christian initiation is related to the series of events in the crossing of the Red Sea. In the mystagogic catecheses of St. Cyril of Jerusalem, this parallelism begins with the comparison of the renunciation of Satan compared with the beginning of the Exodus: "You must know that the symbol of Baptism is found in ancient history. In fact, when Pharoah, the harsh and cruel tyrant, oppressed the free and noble Hebrew people, God sent Moses to deliver them from slavery to the Egyptians. The posts of the doors were anointed with the blood of the lamb, so that the Destroyer would pass over the houses which had the sign of the blood. Let us now go from the old to the new, from the type to the reality. There we have Moses sent by God into Egypt; here we have Christ sent by the Father into the world; there is need to free the oppressed people from Egypt, here to rescue men tyrannized over by sin in this world; there the blood of the lamb turns aside the Destroyer; here the Blood of the true Lamb, Jesus Christ, puts the demons to flight; there the tyrant pursues the people even into the sea; here the shameless and bold demon follows them even to the holy fountains; one tyrant is drowned in the sea, the other is destroyed in the water of salvation." (P. G., XXXIII, 1068 A).

[16] Plumpe, *Mater Ecclesia,* p. 116.
[17] Dom Winzen, *Pathways in Holy Scripture, The Book of Exodus,* p. 6.

The interest of this passage lies in the fact that the beginning of the baptismal rites is connected with the Exodus. In the first place, the sign marked with the blood of the lamb on the lintels of the doors, the sign which turns aside the Destroying Angel, is a figure of the sign of the Cross marked on the forehead of the candidates, the sign which turns away the demon.[18] We have spoken of this rite at length, but it is important to see it here as prefigured in the Exodus. We note that further on, Cyril alludes to the pursuit of which the Hebrews were the object when they fled toward the Red Sea. He sees here the figure of the demon pursuing the candidates for baptism "as far as the holy fountain." As we have seen, the idea of the preparation for Baptism as being a period of trial and of struggle with the demon is common among the Fathers. It is not until it has eaten up the serpents, that the deer comes to the refreshing waters.

We find as early as Origen this theme of the Egyptians pursuing the Jews as a figure of the demons seeking to turn away the soul from Baptism: "(Paul) says that this baptismal passage was accomplished in the water and in the Holy Spirit, you may know that the Egyptians pursue you and wish to bring you back to their service, I mean to say, 'the rulers of this world' and 'the wicked spirits' (Eph. 6:12) that you have been serving up till now. They strive to pursue you, but you go down into the water and become healed and saved and, purified from the stains of sin, you come out a new man, ready to sing the new song." (V. 5; Baerhens 190, 10-15).

The same theme is found again in St. Cyprian and this time with even greater precision: it is connected with the exorcisms preparatory to Baptism: "The obstinate wickedness of the devil can do something up to the saving waters, but in Baptism it loses all the harmfulness of its poison. This is what we see in the figure of Pharaoh, who being struck down for a long time, but remaining obstinate in his wickedness, was able to continue it until he came to the waters. But when he arrived there, he was conquered and destroyed. But St. Paul declares that this sea was the figure of the sacrament of Baptism. . . . This takes place today, when by the exorcists the demon is struck down and burned by means of a human voice and divine power, but, although he often says that

[18] We shall come back later to the theme of the anointing of the doors, pp. 162-168.

he is about to go, he does nothing. But when a man comes to the saving water and to the Baptism of sanctification, we should have confidence that the devil is destroyed and that man, consecrated to God, is freed by divine grace" (*Epist.*, LXVIII, 15; C.S.E.L., 764).

So the parallelism between the Exodus and Baptism, culminating in the destruction by the water of the world of sin, reaches also to the events before and after. And this is important to show us that the analogy does not rest on any one detail, but on the whole of the two realities. Both are concerned with a great work of liberation accomplished by God for His people, enslaved by the forces of evil. And here is what gives a sure foundation in the literal sense of Scripture for the baptismal typology of the Exodus.[19]

[19] See J. Steinmann, *L'Exode dans l'Ancien Testament,* Vie spirit., March 1951, p. 240.

CHAPTER SIX

Types of Baptism: Elias and the Jordan

In the Coptic and Ethiopian prayers for the consecration of the baptismal water, after the figures of Creation, of the Deluge, of the Crossing of the Red Sea, of Marra and of the Rock of Horeb, we come upon a group of other figures characterized by the important place given to both the Jordan and to the prophet Elias. For instance, in the Ethiopian prayer: "It is Thou, O Lord, Who in the days of Joshua, the son of Nave, caused the powerful waves (of the Jordan) to flow back; it is Thou,—who can withstand Thy sight!—Who didst mark Thine acceptance of the sacrifice of Elias in the water by sending down fire from heaven; it is Thou Who didst show by Eliseus the water of the generation of life, and Who didst cause that Naaman should be purified by the water of the Jordan; Thou canst do all things and nothing is impossible to Thee. Give to this water the great gift of the Jordan, and may the Holy Spirit come down upon it." [1]

Now it is remarkable that we find these three figures grouped together in exactly the same order in the *Sermon on Baptism* of Gregory of Nyssa, given on the day of Epiphany (XLVI, 592-593). Previously, we meet this same group in the *Commentary on St. John* of Origen (VI, 43-48). But, on the other hand, it does not appear at all in the ancient western catecheses. We do indeed find the theme of Naaman in St. Ambrose. But joined to it is a third theme of the cycle of Elias and Eliseus,—that of the axe of Eliseus

[1] Grébaut, *Sacramentaire éthiopien*, p. 181.

floating on the waters. This association also appears in Didymus. We have, then, a whole separate series, including the crossing of the Jordan by Joshua, the bath of Naaman in the Jordan, and finally a miracle of water from the cycle of Elias and Eliseus.

Various features characterize this group. For one thing, as we have said, the sermon of Gregory of Nyssa was a sermon for the feast of the Epiphany. And, further, the Coptic and Ethiopian prayers are for the consecration of the baptismal water which took place perhaps on the same day. Thus we are here in a different context from that of Easter; and we need to remember that, for the Alexandrians, the Epiphany is above all the feast of the Baptism of Christ, and that this feast focused attention especially on the water of Jordan. We can understand, therefore, why it is the figures which are connected with the Jordan that are here mentioned by preference.[2] And the place of Elias is explained in the same way, for we know what a close connection he was held to have with St. John the Baptist. We can, therefore, now understand more clearly the importance in this group of the figures of Elias and of the Jordan.

Furthermore, the essential rite of the day is not, as at Easter, Baptism itself, but rather the consecration of the water. As a result, its figures have a different character from those which we have been considering. The water here is not water considered as destroying and creating, but rather as purifying and sanctifying. We enter into another aspect of the symbolism of water, that of the water which washes and, consequently, on the religious plane, of the ritual bath. As Gregory of Nyssa remarks,[3] the figures here indicate two aspects of Baptism: its purifying effect and its institution at the Jordan by the Baptism of Christ. In ancient tradition, in fact, it was the Baptism of Christ which instituted the sacrament of Baptism as to its form, if not as to its being actually administered—for this would presume that the Passion of Christ has already been accomplished.[4] And one last feature, less important but nevertheless noteworthy, is the Alexandrian origin of this group. It is in the works of Origen that we find it first set out,

[2] See F. M. Braun, *Le baptême d'apres le IVe Évangile,* Rev. Thom., 1948, p. 364-365.

[3] P.G., XLVI, 592 D.

[4] Harald Riesenfeld, *La signification sacramentaire du baptême johannique,* Dieu vivant XIII, p. 31 et seq.

and the writers who present it afterwards seem to depend entirely on him. And we should here recall the fact that it was at Alexandria that the feast of January 6th, as a feast of the Baptism of Christ, first appeared among the basilian Gnostics, according to the testimony of Clement of Alexandria (Strom. I, 21; Staehlin, 90). Thus we can see in what sense this group of figures can be called Alexandrian,—not as being a tendency towards this kind of symbolism, but as being a liturgical tradition of the Church of Alexandria. The witness of Origen is of value, then, not as a reflection of his personal ideas, but as a document of the tradition of his Church.[5]

It was quite normal that the crossing of the Jordan by Joshua should have been given a baptismal symbolism, for Joshua is a figure of Christ.[6] We should note that we do not find this typology in the Old Testament, nor in Judaism; probably because of its implying a depreciation of Moses. But the theme is frequently found in Christianity. Joshua, entering into the Promised Land, here appears as a figure of Christ. So with St. Cyril of Jerusalem: "Jesus, the son of Nave, in many ways offers us a figure (*typos*) of Christ. It was from the time of the crossing of the Jordan that he began to exercise his command of the people: this is why Christ also, having first been baptized, began His public life. The son of Nave established twelve (men) to divide the inheritance: Jesus sent twelve apostles into the whole world as heralds of the truth. He who is the figure saved Rahab the courtesan because she believed; He who is the reality said: 'The publicans and courtesans will go before you into the kingdom of God.' The walls of Jericho fell at the mere sound of the trumpets at the time of the type; and because of the word of Jesus: 'there shall not remain a stone upon a stone,'—the temple of Jerusalem is fallen before our eyes" (X, 11; P.G., XXXIII, 676 D—677 A). Here we have the chief features of the cycle of Joshua to which tradition has given a typological meaning: the crossing of the Jordan, the history of Rahab, the fall of Jericho. And we must also add the name of Joshua-Jesus. Two of these figures, the name of Jesus

[5] The theme of the crossing of the Jordan by Josue is linked with the crossing of the Red Sea as a symbol of Baptism as early as Clement of Alexandria (*Eclog. proph.*, 5-6).

[6] Jean Daniélou, *Sacramentum futuri*, pp. 195-250.

and the history of Rahab, have their foundation in the New Testament.

Can the same be said of the crossing of the Jordan? It does not seem as if the New Testament related it to the Baptism of Jesus in the Jordan. But Harald Sahlin has recently suggested that a relation may be found between this crossing of the Jordan and another incident in the Gospel,[7] in the eleventh chapter of St. John in which he tells of the raising of Lazarus. We are told at the beginning of this incident that Jesus was then west of the Jordan, "there where John had baptized" (John X; 40). He was told that Lazarus was dead. He waited two days, then crossed the Jordan and raised Lazarus from the dead. So Sahlin thinks that in this incident John wishes to show us in Jesus a new Joshua by recalling Joshua I:11 "In three days you will pass over the Jordan" and the announcement that after this crossing God will accomplish wonders. (Jos., 3; 5).

Thus the crossing of the Jordan by Joshua is the figure of its crossing by Jesus. But the incident of the resurrection of Lazarus also certainly seems to have a baptismal significance. The crossing of the Jordan followed by the raising of Lazarus is, (still according to Sahlin), the figure of the immersion in the water of Baptism which configures us to the Resurrection of Christ. And the word of Thomas: "Let us also go and die with Him" (XI, 6) does seem to suggest the idea of a configuration to the death of Christ in the crossing of the Jordan, corresponding to the other aspect of Baptism, at once death and resurrection. And so the crossing of the Jordan by Joshua appears to be presented in the New Testament as a figure not only of the resurrection of Lazarus, but of Christian Baptism.

This interpretation is to be found in the Fathers. But we should note that for them the intermediate link is not the resurrection of Lazarus, but the baptism of John. Gregory of Nyssa writes in the *De baptismo:* "You have been for a long time wallowing in the mud: hasten to the Jordan, not at the call of John, but at the voice of Christ. In fact the river of grace runs everywhere. It does not rise in Palestine to disappear in the neighboring sea; but it envelops the entire world and plunges itself into Paradise, flowing against the course of the four rivers which come

[7] *Zur typologie des Johannesevangeliums,* Upsala, 1950, p. 39-41.

down from thence, and carrying back into Paradise things far more precious than those which came out. For those rivers brought sweet perfumes, and the cultivation and semination of the earth: but this river brings back men, born of the Holy Spirit. Imitate Jesus, the son of Nave. Carry the Gospel as he carried the Ark. Leave the desert, that is to say, sin. Cross the Jordan. Hasten toward Life according to Christ, toward the earth which bears the fruits of joy, where run, according to the promise, streams of milk and honey. Overthrow Jericho, the old dwelling-place, do not leave it fortified. All these things are a figure (*typos*) of ourselves. All are prefigurations of realities which now are made manifest" (P.G., XLVI, 420D – 421A). This text is decisive for our theme. It comes from a document dealing with Baptism, and in it the crossing of the Jordan by Joshua appears as the type: the Ark is the figure of the Gospel; the desert represents sin; the Jordan is a figure of Baptism; the fall of Jericho, finally, is the destruction of sinful man, according to an idea which is found in Origen.[8]

In the same way, in his sermon on *The Baptism of Christ,* having given the crossing of the Red Sea as a figure of Baptism, Gregory continues: "The Hebrew people did not receive the land of promise before they had crossed the Jordan under the leadership of Joshua. And also Joshua, in setting up the twelve stones in the stream, clearly prefigures the twelve apostles, the ministers of Baptism." (*In Bapt. Christi;* P.G., XLVI, 592 A). Here we find once more the typology of Cyril of Jerusalem. Gregory then returns to the theme of the Jordan: "When the Jordan alone among all rivers had received the first fruits of sanctification and blessing, spread the grace of Baptism throughout the whole world, as from a spring, which is the true figure (*typos*). And these things are signs, in actions that actually happened, of the rebirth of Baptism" (593 A). We have here a remarkable definition of a figure, which is an action that really happened, signifying (*menyma*) a future action. Gregory also alludes to the Jordan in its relationship to Paradise: "The Jordan is exalted, because it regenerates men and plants them in the Paradise of God" (593 D).

We may remark that, in these texts, Gregory sees in the visible Jordan that waters Palestine, the figure of the baptismal waters

[8] *Ho. Jos.,* VI, 4-6; P.G., XII, 855-856.

that irrigate Paradise.[9] And Origen finds even more. For him, the Jordan is the symbol and the sacrament of Christ Himself, "It is this river whose streams gladden the city of God, as we see in the Psalm, this city being not the visible Jerusalem, (which in fact has no river to water it), but the immaculate Church of God, built on the foundation of the apostles and prophets. We must then understand by the Jordan the Word of God made flesh Who dwelt among us, and by Jesus (Joshua) who distributed the shares, the humanity that He assumed; It is the corner-stone which, having itself been introduced into the divinity of the Son of God by the fact of His assuming it, is washed (louetai) and then receives the innocent and sinless dove of the Spirit, which, united to Him cannot henceforth fly away" (VI, 42). The Jordan is the Word Himself, Who comes down into this world.

Moreover, the crossing of the Jordan becomes for Origen the best figure of Baptism, rather than the crossing of the Red Sea. This is connected with a more general opposition, in this author's writing, between Moses as the figure of the Old Testament, and Joshua, the figure of the New: "There (at the Exodus from Egypt), it was after celebrating the Pasch in Egypt that they undertook the Exodus: with Jesus (Joshua) it was after the crossing of the Jordan that they encamped at Galgala, the tenth day of the first month (when it was necessary, after the Baptism of Jesus, that, to celebrate the feast, they should first be circumcised on the hill of Araloth).[10] It was with a sharpened stone that all the uncircumcised sons of Israel who had escaped from Israel, were circumcised by Jesus; and the Lord recognized that He had taken away the reproach of Egypt on the day of Baptism in Jesus" (*Co. Jo.* VI, 44; Preuschen 154).[11] The crossing of the Red Sea is a figure of the first covenant in Moses, in opposition to the second covenant, that of the Jordan, in Joshua-Jesus.

Origen takes up the same contrast in the *Homilies on Joshua:*

[9] On the parallel between Paradise and the Holy Land, see N.A. Dahl, *La Terre où coulent le lait et le miel,* Mélanges Goguel, 1950, p. 65-66.

[10] The text of the MSS, as regards the last words of this sentence, are incomprehensible. As Staehlin has noted, πρόβατσν should be corrected to ἀκρόβυστον. Completing his correction, I read ἔδει (ἐν βουνῷ τῶν ἀκροβυστιῶν περιτμηθῆναι) τούς, which corresponds to *Jos.*, V, 4, and gives a satisfactory reading.

[11] The circumcision by Josue-Jesus appears as a type of Baptism, at the same time as the crossing of the Jordan. See H. Sahlin, loc. cit., p. 41. The theme is an ancient one. See Justin, *Dial.,* CXIII, 6-7.

"Let us see what things are here prefigured. I go into the Jordan not in the silence of flight, but to the sound of trumpets, sounding a divine and mysterious note, so that I may go forward to the preaching of the heavenly trumpet" (*Ho. Jos.* I, 3; P.G., XII, 828). But a new element appears: the crossing of the Red Sea is no longer compared to the Old Testament, but to the entrance into the catechumenate. The whole history of the Exodus is then thought of as a figure of Christian initiation, from the going out of Egypt, figure of the break with idolatry, to the crossing of the Jordan, figure of Baptism: "You who, having just now abandoned the darkness of idolatry, desire to come near to hear the divine Law, you begin by abandoning Egypt. When you have been added to the number of the catechumens and have begun to obey the precepts of the Church, then you have crossed the Red Sea. If you now come to the sacramental spring and, in the presence of the order of priests and levites, are initiated into the awesome and majestic mysteries which are known only to those to whom it is permitted (*fas*) to know them, then, having crossed the Jordan with the ministry of the priests, you will enter into the land of promise" (IV, I; P.G., XII, 843 A). There is a fascinating symbolism in such a vision; but the tradition of the Church which sees in the crossing of the Red Sea the figure of Baptism is too strong to be overcome by the idea of its being a figure of the Old Testament or of the catechumenate. What tradition has kept of Origen's symbolism is, therefore, the theme of the crossing of the Jordan as the symbol of Baptism. This figure is not opposed to that of the crossing of the Red Sea, but coexists with it.

After the history of Joshua, the second place in the Old Testament in which the Jordan plays a special role is in the cycle of Elias. And the catecheses and baptismal prayers also present a certain number of episodes belonging to the lives of Elias and Eliseus, in which the Jordan generally has a part. And as in the typology of the crossing of the Jordan by Joshua we have only one aspect of the whole typology of Joshua, so here. The typology of Elias is one of the most important of all; in the Judaism of the time of Christ, it was found in the material form of waiting for the return of Elias as a sign of the end of time, of which we hear the echo in the Gospel.

The New Testament, here as everywhere else, did not create the typology of Elias, but only shows us how this typology is fulfilled in the events of the history of Christ. It has been noted that this typology appears above all in the Gospel of St. Luke, while Mosaic typology is more important in Matthew.[12] Elias is sometimes the figure of John the Baptist, but most commonly of Christ Himself. The history of the widow of Sarepta (III Kings, 17:9) and that of the Syrian Naaman (IV Kings, V, 9) are figures of the calling of pagan peoples (Luke IV, 25-28). The demand of the Apostles that Christ send fire from heaven recalls the episode of Elias and the priests of Baal (Luke IX, 54). The Ascension of Elias is a figure of the Ascension of Christ (Luke IX, 51).[13]

It is noteworthy that two of these figures, the fire from heaven and Naaman, have been applied to Baptism. After the crossing of the Jordan, the second figure presented in the Ethiopian and Coptic liturgies is that of the sacrifice of Elias (III Kings XVIII: 1-40), and we find it also in the *Sermon* of Gregory of Nyssa: "This marvellous sacrifice, which surpasses all understanding, of Elias the Thesbite, what is it except a prophecy in action of faith in the Father, in the Son, and in the Holy Spirit, and of the redemption" (XLVI, 592 A). Elias is persecuted by the priests of Baal. He demands a judgment of God between them and himself. The sacrifice of the priests of Baal is marked by no sign. Then Elias prepares his sacrifice. He takes twelve stones to build the altar; on these he places the pieces of the victim. He has three times four pitchers of water filled and poured over the victim. He prays, and then "the fire of God fell and consumed the holocaust and the water" (III Kings, XVIII, 38).[34]

Gregory comments on this event in this way: "By this Elias prophesied clearly in advance the sacrament of Baptism (*he tou baptismatos mystagogia*) which was to take place in the future. The fire came down on the water that had been poured three times, to show that where the sacramental water is, there is also the Spirit, vivifying, burning, inflaming, which consumes the impious and illu-

[12] P. Dabeck, *Siehe, es erscheinen Moses und Elias,* Biblica, 1942, p. 180 et seq,
[13] J. Daniélou, *Le mystère de l'Avent,* p. 183-186.
[14] The theme seems to go back to Origen, *Co. Joh.,* VI, 23; Preuschen, 133.

minates (*photizei*) the faithful" (XLVI, 592 D). As often happens, we find here a double typology, one bearing on the profound meaning of the scene and the other on the material elements used. Under the first aspect, what is marked (as Lundberg has well observed) is the "complete rupture with paganism," (*loc. cit.* p. 30), which is one of the essential aspects of Baptism. It is remarkable that the Greek prayer introducing the liturgy of Epiphany includes the text of St. Gregory: "O Thou Who hast manifested to us in Elias the Thesbite, by the triple pouring of water, the Trinity of Persons in the One Godhead." [15] We notice the allusion to the triple pouring of the waters, but the essential idea is that of the affirmation of the true faith against idolatry.[16]

But Gregory also connects the function of the water in the sacrifice of Elias with its use in Baptism. More exactly, what is emphasized is the fact of the fire coming down on the water. This may well be explained, with Gregory, simply as being a figure of the outpouring of the Holy Spirit on the baptized. But it is doubtless more exact to remind ourselves that certain ancient narratives of the Baptism of Christ present the theme of the manifestation of a visible fire. This very ancient tradition, which is found in the *Gospel of the Nazarenes* and in the *Diatessaron* of Tatian is mentioned by Justin: "As Jesus went down into the water, fire was kindled in the Jordan; and while He came out of the water, the Holy Spirit, like a dove, hovered over Him" (*Dial.*, LXXXVIII, 3). And so we are brought back to the cycle of the Jordan.

But the theme of the sacrifice of Elias rarely appears in the baptismal catechesis.[17] Ordinarily we find instead other episodes in the same cycle. The most important is the crossing of the Jordan by Elias before his ascension. This is what we find in Origen's *Commentary on St. John* between the crossing of the Jordan by Joshua and the bath of Naaman: "We must observe again that Elias, when he was about to be carried to heaven by a hurricane, having taken his sheepskin and spread it out, struck the water with

15 Conybeare, *Rituale Armentorum*, p. 415. See also p. 419.

16 It must be added that one of the reasons which may have drawn attention to this episode is the fact that it occurred in the prayers of the liturgy of the synagogue, as an example of the deliverances wrought by God. Lundberg has noted that the Christian liturgy of Baptism took its inspiration from these Jewish prayers, as is evident from another example, that of the three youths in the furnace (Lundberg, loc. cit., p. 34-35).

17 However, see Ambrose, *De Sacram*, II, 11; Botte, 65.

it, which opened on either side, and they went through one after the other; I mean himself and Eliseus. So he was made more fit to be taken up to heaven, after having been baptized in the Jordan. For has not Paul actually called Baptism the miraculous crossing of the water?" (*Co. Jo.* VI, 46; Preuschen, 155, 9-15).

After Origen, we find the same figure used by St. Cyril of Jerusalem, not in the *Mystagogic Catecheses*, but in the *Catechesis on Baptism*: "Elias is taken up, but not without water. He begins by crossing the Jordan, and it is after this that the chariot carries him to heaven" (XXXIII, 433 A). We can remind ourselves in connection with this passage that, among the names for Baptism that we have met, both in Gregory Nazianzen and Gregory of Nyssa, we find the expression "what carries us to heaven." [18] This expression, was then, traditional, but it is nevertheless difficult to see in what context it is to be located. It could be given explanation by neoplatonism, in which the idea of the body as the vehicle of the soul during its ascension to Heaven is frequently to be found.[19] But it would be very strange if a neo-platonic idea were to be found at the origin of a traditional name for Baptism. We should, then, look for its origin in the Bible. And it is the chariot of Elias that seems to be the most probable reference.

Thus, there is a double biblical foundation of the baptismal typology of this episode. First, from the point of view of the Old Testament, the crossing of the Jordan by Elias was seen to be a repetition of the crossing of the Red Sea. Here there is, as it were, a double typological level in the Old Testament itself. Elias is already presented as a new Moses.[20] But, secondly, the specific element in this episode is the introduction of the theme of the Ascension. The ascension of Elias after crossing the Jordan is a figure of the Ascension of Christ after death. And Baptism in turn is seen as the ascension of the baptised which follows Baptism, as a configuration to the Ascension of Christ.[21]

But the episode most frequently found as a figure of Baptism in the cycle that we are now studying is that of the axe of Elias floating on the water of the Jordan (IV Kings VI: 1-7). Here we find a

[18] See above, p. 54.
[19] For example Proclus, *Elements of Theology*, (ed. Dodds), p. 182.
[20] Similarly the forty days spent by Elias in the desert (II Kings, XIX, 8-12) are a reminder of the forty days spent by Moses upon the mountain (Ex., XXIV, 18).
[21] See Ambrose, *De Myst.*, 35-36; Botte, 119.

different symbolic tradition connected with the texts of the Old Testament in which water and wood are both found. These texts were grouped together very early to designate the mystery of Baptism, in which the water acts by the power of the Cross. We find a first group in the *Testimonia* of the Pseudo-Barnabas (XI, 5). The theme first appears in Justin, in a context of the same order: "Eliseus threw a piece of wood into the stream of the Jordan. By this means, he retrieved from the water the iron of the axe with which the sons of the prophets wished to cut the wood to build their house. So our Christ has ransomed us at Baptism from our heaviest sins by His crucifixion on the wood and Baptism in the water." (*Dial.* LXXXVI, 6)

This miracle of Eliseus does not present any very profound analogy with Baptism, except insofar as it is a work of the power of God accomplished in the Jordan by means of wood, and this belongs more to the order of illustrative typology. Nevertheless the antiquity of this figure gained for it a great success. It appears in Irenaus (*Adv. Haer.* V, 17, 4); and in Tertullian (*Adv. Jud.* 13), from whom Didymus borrowed it and gave it a lengthy development: "By Eliseus, the man of God, who asked: 'Where did the axe fall in?' is prefigured the God coming among men Who asked of Adam: 'Where are you?' By the iron fallen into the dark abyss is prefigured the power of human nature, deprived of light. By the wood taken and thrown into the place where lay the object of the search is symbolized the glorious Cross. The Jordan is immortal Baptism. Indeed, it is in the Jordan that He Who made the Jordan deigned to be baptized for us. Finally, the iron which floated on the waters and came back to him who had lost it, signifies that we mount by Baptism to a heavenly height and find again the grace of our old and true home country" (XXXIX, 700 A).

Here we are in the full stream of allegorical development. Doubtless Didymus himself realized this, for he continues: "If anyone argues that this passage is not a prophecy of Baptism, what purpose, then, did the sacred writer have in writing down this passage?" (XXXIX, 700 A). The weakness of the argument appears clearly, but what to Didymus justifies the interpretation is the idea of Origen that everything in Scripture should have a figurative sense. This view is certainly questionable. But the weakness of Didymus' argument, although it prevents us from attaching any importance to the details of his interpretation, does not alter the fact that the episode as such was considered by tradition to be in a certain way a figure of Baptism. The true meaning that we should give it is shown by St. Ambrose. He cites the axe of Eliseus as a figure of Baptism in both the *De Mysteriis* and the *De Sacramentis,* a fact which testifies to us that it belonged to the common catechesis. But he clearly shows its significance: on the one hand, it is a miracle witnessing the power of God over the elements and thus prefiguring the miracle of Baptism (*Myst.* 51; Botte, 124). And, again, the recourse to Eliseus is a witness to the powerlessness of man to save himself without the intervention of the power of God (*Sacr.* II, 11; Botte, 65). The presence of the Jordan and of the wood accounts for the fact that this miracle was used as a favorite figure of Baptism.[22]

The third miracle of the cycle of the Jordan is the healing of Naaman the Syrian, who was told by the prophet to plunge three times in the river (IV Kings, V, 9-20). We find it mentioned in the Ethiopian and Coptic prayers for the consecration of the water, "Thou it was Who hast pointed out in advance by the prophet Eliseus the life-giving water of regeneration, and Who hast purified Naaman the Syrian by the water of the Jordan." [23] In Origen and Gregory of Nyssa, the episode comes last, after the crossing of the Jordan and the miracle of Elias. Here we find once more a common and constant tradition, as we do for the crossing of the Jordan. As Lundberg has well observed, the aspect of Baptism which is brought out by the figure of the bath of Naaman is that of purification,—as ordinary water washes stains from the body, so the sacred bath purifies us by the power of God. This power, which was exercised on a physical malady with Naaman, acts on the soul in Baptism: "The healing and purifying power which, according to the Biblical narrative, the river Jordan had for Naaman, is the image of the purification produced by the water of Baptism." [24]

We find this theme first developed in Origen. But we must not forget that the story of Naaman is mentioned in the New Testament (Luke IV, 27). And if here no allusion to Baptism is made directly, the meaning given to the incident is no less worthy of

[22] To this cycle could be added the miracle of Eliseus changing the water at Jericho, which is found in the Coptic prayer, in Didymus (XXXIX, 700B), in Gregory of Elvira (15; Batiffol, 162-163).

[23] Denzinger, *Ritus orientalium,* p. 205.

[24] Loc. cit., p. 17.

remark: it signifies the entrance of the pagan peoples into the New Israel. This particular aspect of the episode is brought out by certain authors when they are treating it as a figure of Baptism. Having spoken of the mantle of Elias, Origen then writes: "To understand the significance of the Jordan, which quenches thirst and fills with graces, it is useful also to mention Naaman the Syrian healed of his leprosy." (*Co. Jo.* VI, 47.) He recalls the fact that Naaman was first made very angry by Eliseus' words. That was because "he did not understand the great mystery of the Jordan. In the same way, indeed, as no one is good, save only God the Father, so among rivers, none is good except the Jordan which can purify from leprosy him who, with faith, washes his soul in Jesus" (VI, 47).

These last lines are explained by the interpretation which Origen gives to the Jordan, of which we have spoken above. For him, the Jordan is a figure of the Word Himself. Thus, to plunge into the Jordan means to immerse oneself in Christ. The Word is the river "which rejoices the city of God." As God is present in this river, so is the Father in the Son: "This is why those who wash themselves in Him are delivered from the shame of Egypt and become capable of being raised to heaven, are purified from the most frightful leprosy and ready to receive the Holy Spirit" (VI, 48). We should notice that, in these last words, Origen sums up the three figures:—the crossing of the Jordon by Joshua, the crossing of the Jordan by Elias, and the bathing in the Jordan by Naaman.

Origen goes back to the baptismal interpretation of the episode of Naaman, and precisely in connection with the passage from St. Luke's Gospel which mentions the incident: "No one was purified except Naaman the Syrian, who was not of Israel. See that those who are washed by the spiritual Eliseus, Who is Our Lord and Savior, are purified in the sacrament of Baptism and cleansed of the stain of the letter (of the law). It is you to whom it is said: 'Arise, go to the Jordan and wash, and your flesh will be renewed.' Naaman arose, departed, and, when he had washed, carried out the figure (*mysterium*) of Baptism. And his flesh became like that of a child. Who is this child? He who is born in the bath of regeneration." (*Ho. Luc.* 33; Rauer 198.)

After Origen, we find again in various catecheses the baptismal interpretation of the incident of Naaman. Didymus brings out two new features: the fact that Naaman was a stranger, as marking the universality of Baptism; the seven baths, as being an allusion to the Holy Spirit. The first is connected with the New Testament, and belongs to the best typology of the episode: "The prophet Eliseus announced in advance the ineffable riches contained in the baptismal waters and indicated at the same time that these riches would be extended to all those who wished to be converted, for he sent Naaman the leper, who was a stranger, who asked to be healed, to plunge seven times in the Jordan. He prescribed that he should plunge seven times, either that the stranger might learn that it was on the seventh day that God rested from his works, or to designate symbolically the divine Spirit." (XXXIX, 700 D).

St. Gregory of Nyssa emphasizes the part of the Jordan: "When Eliseus sent Naaman the leper to wash himself in the Jordan, and when he cleansed him from his sickness, he suggested what was to come, both by the general use of the water and by the special baptism in the river. In fact, alone among rivers, the Jordan received the first-fruits of sanctification and blessing, and poured out, like a spring, the grace of Baptism on the whole world" (XLVI, 593 D). So the bath of Naaman is seen to be a figure of the consecration of the waters of the Jordan by Christ, whose grace will be shared later by all consecrated waters. This is why it prefigures at the same time, as St. Gregory says, both Baptism and its institution.

St. Ambrose, in his sacramental catecheses, refers to the story of Naaman on three occasions, which shows us that this figure formed part of the elementary catechesis. But it is in his *Homilies on St. Luke* that he gives the richest development to the theme: "The people, made up of strangers, are lepers before being baptized in the mystical river; these people after the sacrament of baptism are purified of their stains both of soul and body. In the figure of Naaman, indeed, their future salvation is announced to the nations. Why was he given the command to immerse himself according to a number so charged with mystery? Why was it the Jordan that was chosen? Recognize the grace of saving Baptism" (Exp. Luc. IV, 50-51). We find here again the interpretation of Didymus which prolongs St. Luke's Gospel. The clearest feature of this incident is, actually, the fact that it was a stranger to the people of Israel who was admitted to receive the miracle.

With the cycle of Elias and of the Jordan, we have now gone through all the great scriptural figures of Baptism in the Old Testament. This is not to say that other texts have not been applied to Baptism by the Fathers,—we should mention in particular the texts of the Prophets and the Psalms. The Pseudo-Barnabas gives us a dossier of texts from Isaias (XI, 2-5). Gregory of Nyssa also quotes passages from Isaias and Ezechiel: "I will pour out upon you pure water, and you shall be purified of your stains" (Ezech. XXXVI: 25) (XLVI, 593 A-C). In the same way, the Psalms are often quoted as witnesses: Pseudo Barnabas quotes Psalm I: "He who does these things will be like a tree planted by a river of water" (XI, 2) and L. de Bruyne has shown that this text might have influenced the decorations of the baptistries.[25] We have seen the importance of the Psalm LIV: "As the deer longs for the running waters,"—and we shall see later on the importance of Psalm XXII. But the fact remains that prophecies draw their value from typology to the extent to which they manifest clearly the truth that the realities of the past of Israel are the expression of eschatological events accomplished in Christ. This is why it is that we should study these figures.

[25] *La décoration des baptistères judeo-chrétiens,* Mel. Mohlberg, 1948, p. 188-198.

CHAPTER SEVEN

Confirmation

THE history of the origins of the sacrament of Confirmation is one of the most obscure chapters in the origins of Christian worship. There is, first of all, some hesitation about the meaning of the sacrament. It is clear that it is related to the Holy Spirit. But the Holy Spirit is already given in Baptism. To what does this new outpouring correspond? There is also hesitation about the rite: does it consist in the imposition of hands, as the New Testament teaches, or in the anointing with holy Chrism, as the usage has prevailed in the East? And, finally, there is hesitation about the relation of Confirmation to the anointing after Baptism, which is to be found in many liturgies. All the documentation for this question can be found in the books of J. Coppens: *L'imposition des mains et les rites connexes* (Louvain, 1939) and of B. Welte, *Die postbaptismale Salbung* (Freiburg, 1939). And, furthermore, the question is raised of the relation between Baptism and Confirmation. Without entering into these discussions, we shall begin with the certain fact of the existence of an anointing made with a perfumed oil, the *muron,* in the Sacrament of Confirmation, and we shall look for the symbolism of this anointing.

The first characteristic of the rite is that it is an anointing (*chrisma*). This fact introduces us at once into biblical symbolism. Anointing was, in the Old Testament, the rite by which priests and kings were consecrated. It constituted a sacrament by which the

Holy Spirit was communicated to them in view of the functions which they were to carry out. We find in the Prophets a primal typology that is, literally, messianic. For they announce that at the end of time, an Anointed One will come, a Messias, a *Christos,* of whom the King of David's line and the High Priest were only the figures. This messianic typology holds an important place in the Psalms, which were part of the liturgy of the Temple, their relation to the priesthood being obvious.

This eschatological typology is realized in Jesus of Nazareth. This is the affirmation of the New Testament. The very name of *Christos* given to Jesus is the expression of it. This title was explicitly accepted by Him before Pilate (Matthew XXVII:12), and, furthermore, Christ attributed to Himself the prophecy of Isaias (XI: 1) describing the pouring out of the Holy Spirit on the Messias to come (Luke IV: 18).[1] The *Acts* apply to Him the texts of Psalms (II:34; Ps. CIX:1; IV:25; Ps. II:1)[2] But following the line of thought that we have been using, what is said of Christ is also true of the Christian. We have, then, a double sacramental typology in which the anointing is shown as related both to the Old Testament and to the New.

The oldest witness is that of Tertullian: "Having come out of the baptismal pool, we are anointed with blessed oil according to the ancient discipline in which it was customary to be anointed with oil spread on the horn to receive the priesthood. It is with this oil that Aaron was anointed by Moses; whence comes his name of the Anointed (*christus*) which comes from *chrisma,* meaning anointing. It is this anointing (*chrisma*) which gave its name to the Lord, having become a spiritual anointing. For He was indeed anointed with the Spirit by the Father, as it is said in the Acts: "They assemble together in this city against Thy Son Whom Thou hast anointed (Act., IV, 27). Thus on us the anointing is spread so

[1] Such is perhaps the meaning of the anointing of Jesus at Bethany: "This anointing no doubt means that Jesus is now taking upon himself his role as Messias. Till now he has been a second Moses, then a second Josue." (H. Sahlin, *Zur typologie des Johannes Ev.,* p. 46.) It will be noticed that this anointing (John XII 1-3) precedes the Messianic entrance into Jerusalem (John, XII, 19).

[2] "The Psalter is throughout a book of prophecy fulfilled by the coming of Christ" (Balthasar Fischer, *Die Psalmen froemigkeit der Maertyrerkirche,* Frieburg, 1949, p. 4).

that we can feel it, but it operates spiritually" (*De Bapt.*, 7; P.L., 1, 1207 A).[3]

Here we have an important theological theme: the sacramental anointing is connected with the priestly anointing of the Old Testament, in particular that described in Leviticus XXI. And it is also related to the royal anointing, and most especially to the anointing of the messianic king of Psalm II, 2. It is in fact to this anointing that the text of Acts refers, showing it to be fulfilled in Christ: but the anointing with the oil of the Old Testament is only the figure of the spiriual anointing, by which the Son is anointed with the Holy Spirit. This anointing, finally is called *chrisma,* and he who receives it, *christos.* This constitutes a new aspect of Confirmation: the oil is the chrism by which the baptized becomes a new *christos,* a *christianos.*[4]

Cyril of Jerusalem develops this idea, presenting the same tradition as Tertullian: "Having become worthy of this holy chrism, you are called Christians, making the name truly yours by regeneration. Before you were worthy of this grace, you did not truly merit this name, but you were on the way, aiming to become Christians. It is necessary that you should know that the figure of this chrism is to be found in the Old Testament. When Moses imparted to his brother the divine commandment, in constituting him high priest, having washed him with water, he anointed him. And he was called Christ, because of the figurative chrism. In the same way also the High Priest, in establishing Solomon as king, anointed him after washing him in the Gihon. But these things were done to them in figure, but to you not in figure but in truth, since you have been really anointed with the Holy Spirit. For the principle of your salvation is the Anointed One (the Christ)" (XXXIII, 1093 A).

We find again precisely the same theme as in Tertullian, but a little more developed. The royal anointing is expressly related to the anointing of Solomon, while this was only suggested by Tertullian. The term *christianos* is related with the anointing of Aaron with oil. It is again to the anointing of Aaron that St. Ambrose returns in the *De Mysteriis*: "After Baptism, you went up to the priest. What happened then? Was it not as David said: As when

[3] This passage is connected by B. Welte with confirmation (loc. cit., p. 23) and by B. Botte with Baptism, but this does not alter the question of symbolism.

[4] On the historical origin of the word, see Erik Peterson, *Christianos,* Miscell. Mercati, I. p. 355 et seq.

the precious ointment upon the head runs down over the beard of Aaron? Understand why this was done. It is because 'the eyes of the wise man are in *his head*' (Eccl. II, 14). It spreads out on the beard, that is to say in the grace of youth; it spreads on the beard of Aaron, so that you may become a race that is chosen, priestly, of great price. For in fact all of us are anointed with the spiritual grace, in view of royalty and of the priesthood" (*De Myst.* 29-30: Botte, 117).

Prefigured by the priestly and royal anointing of the Old Testament, the Christian anointing is, moreover, a participation in the anointing of Christ. Having devoted his first two catecheses to Baptism, Cyril of Jerusalem studies Confirmation in the third: "Baptized in Christ, and having put on Christ, you have become conformed to the Son of God. God, indeed, having predestined you for the adoption of sons, has conformed you to the body of the glory of Christ. Become participants in Christ, you are rightly called Christ. But you were made Christs when you received the sacrament of the Holy Spirit. And all these things were done symbolically, because you are the images of Christ. And He, having bathed in the Jordan and the Holy Spirit descended personally upon Him, Like resting on Like. And you also, when you came out of the pool of the sacred water, you received the anointing, the sacrament of that with which Christ was anointed, I mean to say, the Holy Spirit, of Whom blessed Isaias said, in speaking of the name of the Lord: The Spirit of the Lord is upon me, this is why He has anointed me" (XXXIII, 1088 B-1089 A).

And before this, Cyril had spoken to us twice concerning this sacrament of the Spirit. First, in his catechesis on the Holy Spirit, he recalls that "under Moses, the Holy Spirit was given by the imposition of hands, and that Peter by the imposition of hands gave the Spirit" (XXXIII, 956 C). But, he continues "grace will come down upon you when you have been baptized. And later I will tell you how." Here we have evidence both of the distinction between Confirmation and Baptism and also of the fact that, in spite of the change in the rite, it is still the same sacrament that Peter gave by the imposing of hands. In the catechesis on the resurrection of the body, he announces Confirmation in these terms: "Later, you will learn how you have been purified of your sins by the Lord by means of the bath of water together with the word, and how you have been made in a priestly manner participants of the name of Christ, and how the seal of the communion of the Spirit has been given to you" (XXXIII, 1056 B).

Cyril develops his thought in this passage: "Christ was not anointed by an oil or by a physical perfume given by the hand of men. But the Father, Who established Him in advance as Savior of the whole universe, anointed Him with the Holy Spirit, as Peter says: Jesus of Nazareth, whom God has anointed with the Holy Spirit (Act., X, 38). And in the same way as Christ was truly crucified, truly buried, truly risen again, and as it has been granted to you in Baptism to be crucified with Him, buried with Him, risen again with Him in a certain imitation, so it is with the chrism. He was anointed with the spiritual oil of exultation, that is to say, with the Holy Spirit, called the Oil of Exultation because He is the source of spiritual joy; and you, you have been anointed with perfumed oil, and become participants in Christ" (XXXIII, 1089 A-B).

This page is one of the most remarkable in sacramental theology. First of all, it states clearly what a sacrament is: a real participation in the grace of Christ, by a sacramental imitation of His life. And, secondly, it shows how this structure applies as well to the sacrament of Confirmation as to that of Baptism. In the same way as Baptism configures us to Christ dead and risen again, so Confirmation configures us to Christ anointed by the Holy Spirit. The Baptism of Christ, followed by the descent of the Spirit, is thus seen to be a prefiguration of His death followed by His royal enthronement, of which the Christian in turn partakes by means of the two sacraments of water and of the anointing.

If we now take the catechetical homilies of Theodore of Mopsuestia, we find an analogous teaching: "When you have received grace by means of Baptism, and when you have been clothed with a shining white garment, the bishop comes to you, signs you on the forehead and says: 'N. is signed in the name of the Father and of the Son and of the Holy Spirit.' Because as Jesus came up from the water, He received the Holy Spirit Who in the form of a dove came to rest on Him; and further because it is also said of Him that He was anointed with the Spirit; since, also to those who are anointed by men with an anointing of oil, the oil adheres and is not taken away from them, therefore you also must receive the signing on your forehead, so that you may have this sign that the

Holy Spirit has also come down upon you and that you have been anointed with Him" (XIV, 27). The formula of Theodore of Mopsuestia reminds us of the text of Cyril of Jerusalem: Confirmation is a participation in the anointing of Christ by the Spirit after His Baptism. We should notice that with this anointing is associated the more special in-dwelling of the Holy Spirit, and also that Theodore emphasizes the ineffaceable character of the oil, leading us to the doctrine of the sacramental character, here applied to Confirmation.

The doctrine of Confirmation is the same in the West: Ambrose sees it, as does Cyril, as a communication of the Holy Spirit: "Baptism is followed by the spiritual seal (*signaculum*) because, after the beginning, perfection is still to be achieved. This takes place when, at the invocation of the priest, the Holy Spirit is poured out, the Spirit of Wisdom and of understanding, the Spirit of counsel and of fortitude, the Spirit of knowledge and of piety, the Spirit of holy fear: seven, because the powers of the Spirit are seven. And indeed all the virtues are related to the Spirit, but these are, as it were, principal ones. These are the seven virtues that you receive when you are marked with the seal" (*De Sacr.* III, 8; Botte, 74-75).

This text shows us a new element which clarifies a point in our study hitherto obscure. We have said that the object of Confirmation is the communication of the Holy Spirit. But the new Christian has already been baptized in the Holy Spirit. Now this text brings out precisely what is still lacking after Baptism, that is, "perfection," [5] and this perfection consists in the gifts of the Holy Spirit. We come to the very object of Confirmation. This is not to give the Spirit, Who has already been given at Baptism. In Confirmation there takes place a new outpouring of the Spirit having for its object to bring to perfection the spiritual energies called forth in the soul by Baptism. As Mme. Lot-Borodine writes, "It is the setting in motion of the supernatural powers, of all the energies contained in the sacred bath." [6]

[5] See St. Cyprian: "The newly baptised ought to appear before the heads of the Church, to receive the Holy Ghost by invocation and the imposition of hands and to be made perfect by the seal (signaculum) of the Lord": (*Epist.*, LXXIII, 9; C.S.E.L., 785).

[6] *La grâce déifiante des sacrements d'après Nicolas Cabasilas,* Rev. Sc., Phil., Théol. 1937, p. 698.

The idea is clearly expressed by the Pseudo-Dionysius: "The most divine consecration of the holy oil perfects in us the freely given and sanctifying gift of the holy birth from God. . . . So, as I understand it, having received from God Himself the understanding of the hierarchical symbols, the various authorities of the human hierarchy call this rite that is so perfectly holy, the sacrament (*telete*) of the holy oils by reason of its perfecting action." (*Hier. Eccles.*, IV; P.G., I, 484 B-485 A). We should note that here there is no mention of the Holy Spirit. Only two characteristics remain: the rite of the perfumed oil and the idea of a perfecting of what is begun at Baptism.[7] Oriental tradition retains this aspect in seeing in Confirmation the sacrament of spiritual progress, while Baptism is that of spiritual birth.

This perfecting of the spiritual life is expressed in two ways by the Fathers. St. Ambrose connects it with the gifts of the Holy Spirit. The idea appears in the *De Mysteriis*: "You have received the spiritual seal, the spirit of wisdom and understanding, the spirit of counsel and fortitude, the spirit of knowledge and of piety, the spirit of holy fear. Preserve what you have received. The Father has marked you with the seal, Christ the Lord has strengthened you, and He has put into your heart the pledge of the Spirit" (*De Myst.*, 42; Botte 121). Later theology was, in fact, to see in the gifts of the Holy Spirit the very mark of the perfect soul, which is no longer led by ordinary virtues, but directly by the Holy Spirit by means of the Gifts which render the soul docile to His action.

But we find in Cyril of Jerusalem another line of thought, in which the *chrisma* is related to the teaching concerning the spiritual senses. We know that this teaching, which began with Origen,[8] is very dear to Oriental mysticism. But at Jerusalem, Cyril tells us, the anointing with chrism was carried out not only on the head, but also on the senses, to mark the awakening of the spiritual senses: "First you were anointed on the forehead, to be freed from the shame which the first man, after his sin, carried with him every-

[7] In a text in the *Apostolic Constitutions* on the symbolic meaning of the sacraments, the Holy Ghost is linked with the oil (of catechumens) and confirmation (βεβαίωσις) characteristic of the μύρου; "The water symbolizes burial, the oil the Holy Ghost, the sphragis the cross, the μύρου confirmation" (*Const. Ap.*, III, 16, 3). See also Didymus the Blind: "The sphragis of Christ on the brow, the reception of baptism, the confirmation (βεβαίωσις) by chrism" (XXXIX, 712 A).

[8] See K. Rahner, *Esquisse d'une doctrine des sens spirituels chez Origène,* R.A.M., 1932, p. 113 et seq.

where,—to be freed so completely that you may be able to contemplate the glory of God with open face, as in a mirror; then on the ears, so that you may find again the ears with which to hear the divine mysteries; then the nostrils so that, perceiving the divine perfume, you may say: We are the pleasant perfume of Christ" (XXXIII, 1092 B).

Cyril adds that a final anointing was given on the breast: "You were finally anointed on the breast, so that, putting on the breastplate of justice, you might stand up well against the attacks of the demon. Indeed, as Christ, after His Baptism and the coming down upon Him of the Holy Spirit, went forth to triumph over the adversary, so you also, after holy Baptism and the sacramental anointing, having been clothed with all the armor of the Holy Spirit, you resist the hostile powers" (XXXIII, 1092 C). This aspect of the sacrament is the one that our terminology has retained and called it "confirmation": as we have seen, this was already one aspect of the conception of the baptismal *sphragis*. What remains peculiar to Confirmation alone is the idea of perfecting the powers given in Baptism.

The study that we have just been making has shown us that among the different sensible elements: gestures, matter, etc. . . . that constitute Confirmation, there is one which has a special importance, that is, the use of the *muron*, the perfumed oil. This is, therefore, the rite whose significance we must discover.

The Pseudo-Dionysius in particular testifies to the very special importance of the *muron*. As against the oil of catechumens, the *muron* is the object of a special consecration that he compares to the Eucharistic consecration: "There is another consecration which belongs to the same order: our masters have called it the sacrament of the anointing. The high priest takes the holy oil, he puts it on the altar of the divine sacrifices, and he consecrates it by a very holy invocation" (*Hier. Eccles*, IV; P.G., I, 472 D-473 A. See also Cyprian, *Epist.* LXX, 2; C.S.E.L., 768).

Even before the Pseudo-Dionysius, this comparison of the consecration of the bread and wine with that of the *muron* is found in Cyril of Jerusalem: "Take care not to imagine that this *muron* is anything ordinary. In the same way as the bread of the Eucharist, after the invocation of the Holy Spirit, is no more ordinary bread, but the Body of Christ, so the holy *muron* is no longer ordinary, or, if you prefer the word, common, after the epiclesis, but the charism of Christ, made efficacious of the Holy Spirit by the presence of His divinity" (XXXIII, 1092 A). Here we find the idea of a certain presence of the Holy Spirit in the chrism, comparable to, though not the same as, the Eucharistic transubstantiation, and resulting in both cases from the consecratory epiclesis. This doctrine has persisted in the Oriental Church, and it shows us, in any case, that the chrism represents an element of eminent holiness, whose significance we should certainly study.

We know that the *muron,* which we call "chrism," is composed of a mixture of oil and balm, to which the Orientals add other aromatic herbs. What distinguished it materially, then, from the oil of catechumens is the presence of the balm and aromatic herbs, that is, the fact that it is perfumed. It is, then, the perfume which constitutes the essence of the symbol.[9] This appears clearly in the prayer of the Syrian Liturgy which accompanies the anointing of Confirmation: "Having baptized (them) in the name of the Father, of the Son and of the Holy Spirit, let the Bishop carry out the anointing with the chrism while saying: O Lord God, Who has spread abroad the pleasant perfume of the Gospel into all nations, now grant that this perfumed oil may be efficacious in the baptized, so that by means of it the pleasant perfume of Christ may dwell in him strongly (*bebaia*) and continually." (*Const. Apost.* VII, 44, 2).

The essential theme is here indicated: the *muron* is a symbol of Christ as He is perceived by baptized souls. This is the doctrine that the Pseudo-Dionysius develops more profoundly: "The holy oils are made up of a mixture of sweet-smelling substances perfuming those who perceive them according to the amount of the perfume that has reached them. We learn from this that the super-essential Perfume of Jesus, the most Thearchic, sheds His spiritual gifts on our intellectual powers, filling them with a divine delight. If it is pleasant to perceive sensible perfumes, provided that the organ which is given to us for perceiving scents is healthy; in the same way, our intellectual powers, provided that they have retained their natural vigor, remain also apt to receive the perfumes of the divine Thearchy" (477 C-480 A).

We see that this teaching rests on two ideas. For one thing, we

[9] Eusebius of Cesarea, *Dem. Ev.*, IV, 15; P.G., XXII, 289 D.

meet again that of the divine perfume, considered as a shining out of the divinity. This symbolism appears in Holy Scripture itself. Wisdom is called "an emanation of the glory of the Most High" (Wis. VII, 25). And Gregory of Nyssa commenting on the words of the Canticle: "The scent of your perfumes (*muron*) is above all sweet-smelling things" (1:3) writes: "The scent of the divine perfumes is not a scent perceived by the nostrils, but that of a certain immaterial power, the emanation of Christ Who draws us by the attraction of the spirit" (XLIV, 780 D).[10] We find once more the doctrine of the perception of spiritual things presented by the analogy of the senses, and particularly by the sense of smell: "You were anointed on the nostrils," writes Cyril of Jerusalem, "so that, perceiving the perfume (*muron*) of Christ, you can say: "We are the sweet perfume of Christ" (XXXIII, 1092 B). We should note that in this passage there appears the twofold idea of the perception of the perfume of Christ, and of participation in this perfume: it is this last aspect that is emphasized by the *Apostolic Constitutions.* The Pseudo-Dionysius makes this idea more precise in the following passage: "So the symbolic composition of the holy oils, giving in a certain way the figure of that which is without form, shows us that Jesus is the figurative source of the divine perfumes, that it is He Himself Who, in the measure that befits the Thearchy, spreads on the intelligences which have attained to the greatest conformity with God, most divine emanations which pleasantly charm these intelligences and which dispose them to receive the sacred gifts and to nourish themselves with a spiritual food, each intellectual power then receiving the sweet-smelling emanations according to the part that it takes in the divine mysteries" (480 A).

These last words introduce us to an important aspect of our study. The perception of the pleasant perfume of God is proportionate to the capacity of those who breathe it. This implies first of all the existence of this capacity. Here the Pseudo-Dionysius makes an important remark: "It is the duty of the High Priest devoutly to hide from the multitude the consecration of holy oils, and to remove them from the sanctuary, according to the laws of the hierarchy. . . . (For) these secret divine beauties, whose perfume surpasses every operation of the understanding, in fact es-

[10] See E. Lohmeyer, *Von Gottlichen Wohlgeruch,* 1919; H. Vorwahl, Εὐωδία Χριστοῦ Archiv. f. Relig., Wiss., 1934; J. Ziegler, *Dulcedo Dei,* 1937, p. 60-67.

cape from all profanation; they do not reveal themselves except to the understanding of those who have the power to grasp them" (473 B-476 B). The anointing of the *muron* is, therefore, foreign to the profane and reserved for initiates. And the initiation is Baptism. The non-baptized is excluded from the *muron* as from the Eucharist. The *muron* is, then, essentially post-baptismal; only a baptized person can receive it. For it is Baptism which gives the capacity to perceive the divine perfume, while Confirmation "sets in motion the energies given in the sacred bath." Here, again, therefore, Confirmation is shown to be a perfecting. It is the putting to use of the new dispositions which result from the new being created by Baptism. It represents the development of faith into "gnosis." We find here again its relation to the gifts of the Holy Spirit, and to the spiritual senses which signify this development.

But in the baptized person himself, the perception of the divine perfume is proportioned to his spiritual development. The divine essence is, in fact, in itself incomprehensible. We know it by means of the communication which it makes of itself and which, precisely, is designated by the image of perfume. And this communication is proportionate to the capacity of the souls who receive it. "By these words: 'Thy name is as oil (*muron*) poured out,' Scripture appears to me to signify that the infinite nature cannot be encompassed by any definition. It is inaccessible, unattainable, incomprehensible. But our spirit can make guesses about It by Its traces and reflections, as it were, and represent to itself the incomprehensible by the analogy of things it can grasp. All the conceptions that we form to designate the *muron* of the divinity do not signify the *muron* itself by their formulation, but they are as it were a feeble residue of the divine perfume" (XLIV, 781 D).[11] And Gregory of Nyssa compares what we perceive to the scent which remains in a flask from which the perfume has been emptied: it is not the perfume itself, which is the inaccessible essence of God, but it is His perfume which manifests His presence and which allows us to know something about It.

But there are degrees in the perception of this perfume. Gregory of Nyssa points out several of these. First of all, there is

[11] It is important to note that Ambrose sees in the "ointment poured forth" of the Canticle a symbol of the sacramental μύρου (*De Myst.*, 29; Botte, 117).

the visible world itself which is a reflection of God: "All the marvels that we see in the world furnish material for the divine names by which we say that God is wise, powerful, good and holy. They betray a remote quality of the divine *muron*" (XLIV, 784 A). The Church is a nearer manifestation of what God is: it is in this sense that the Apostle is "the good odor of Christ" and that "the perfume fills the whole house," that is to say, that the Church, the sweet perfume of Christ, fills the whole world. This is the aspect emphasized by the Apostolic *Constitutions*.[12] And finally, the life of grace, the supernatural virtues, are the perfume spread abroad by the divine Presence in the soul. To perceive this perfume, to experience the life of grace, which constitutes the mystical experience, is, therefore, to experience the presence of the hidden God. This is the aspect on which Gregory of Nyssa especially dwells (XLIV, 821 A-828 B).

There is, then, a whole hierarchy of spirits ranged according to their degree of perception of the divine perfume. The Pseudo-Dionysius begins this hierarchy with the creation of the angels: "It is clear to my understanding that the essences which are above us, because they are more divine, receive, as it were, from nearer the source, the waves of these pleasant scents. For them, this outpouring is clearer and, in their great limpidity, they receive the communication more fully. To intelligences that are lower and less receptive, by reason of its transcendence, the source of the scents hides itself and denies itself to them, for it only dispenses its gifts by reason of the merits of those who partake of them" (480 B). The liturgical symbol of this is the fact that "sacred tradition, at the moment of the consecration of the holy oils, covers them with the seraphic symbol (484 A), that is to say, with twelve holy wings."

This hierarchy is found again in the Church: If the rays that emanate from the most holy mysteries illuminate men of God in all purity and, with no intermediary, freely pour out their perfume on their intelligences, nevertheless this scent does not pour itself out in the same way on those who are on a lower level. But, if they have well-disposed souls, they will raise themselves spiritually to the extent of their merits" (476 B-C). We find again the

[12] See also Gregory of Nyssa, XLIV, 825 C. The source of this is Clement of Alexandria, *Pedag.*, II, 8; Staehlin, 194.

same idea in Gregory of Nyssa, but instead of connecting it with a more intimate perception of the divine perfume, he expresses it by the succession of perfume and taste: "There are two pleasures that the vine gives us: the first comes from its flower, when our senses delight in its perfume; the second comes from its fruit, coming later to perfection, which we enjoy by taste. So the Infant Jesus, born in us, and growing in different measure in those who receive Him, is not the same in all, but according to the capacity of him in whom He dwells, He shows Himself as a child, as growing, as come to full stature, in the manner of the vine" (XLIV, 828 D).

So the character of the *muron* appears clearly: it is the sacrament of the perfecting of the soul, as Baptism is that of its generation. It has for object the development of the spiritual energies infused in the baptismal water. It corresponds to the progressive setting to work of these energies, by which the baptised person, a child in Christ, becomes an adult, until he becomes a perfect man. That is just what Pseudo-Dionysius says when he sees in it the sacrament of *teleiotes,* of perfection. We know that Nicolas Cabasilas understands it in much the same way when he sees it as the Sacrament of those who are making progress, in opposition to Baptism, which is the Sacrament of beginning.[13]

Here also appears the connection between Confirmation and the spiritual life, considered as the development of the grace given in seed-form in Baptism. This also is where the idea of confirmation is given its meaning: it is concerned with the strengthening of the spiritual life, which is still weak in the baptized, and which is carried out under the action of the Holy Spirit.

[13] Lot-Borodine, *La Grâce déifiante des sacraments d'après Nicolas Cabasilas.* Rev. Sc. Phil, Theol., 1937, p. 705 et seq.

CHAPTER EIGHT

The Eucharistic Rites

IN THE Christian initiation which took place during the Easter Vigil, Baptism, Confirmation and the Eucharist formed one whole, constituting the introduction of the new Christian into the Church. And, in the catecheses made to explain to the new Christians the sacraments which they had received, these sacraments are presented as immediately succeeding one another. The Eucharist begins with the procession which conducts the newly-baptized from the baptistry to the Church, where the preparation of the offerings then took place. The whole fore-Mass with the readings that make it up, thus disappeared. And since in this study we have been placing ourselves in the framework of Christian initiation, it is within this framework that we shall now place ourselves here. We shall, therefore, leave to one side the fore-Mass and the dismissal of the catechumens which followed it. A commentary on this subject may be found in the *Ecclesiastical Hierarchy* of the Pseudo-Dionysius, which is the only one of our catecheses to consider the Eucharist in the setting of ordinary Masses.

Even reduced in this way, the Eucharist still includes three principal parts. First, there is the preparation, which we call the Offertory. Then, there comes the Eucharistic sacrifice properly speaking, constituted by the great prayer of thanksgiving pronounced over the elements of bread and wine. And, finally, there is the distribution of the consecrated elements at the communion of the faithful. We shall proceed as in the study of the other sacraments, beginning with the description of the essential rites and indicating their symbolism, and then deepening the significance of these rites by connecting them with their figures in the Old Testament.

If we go through the principal eucharistic catecheses, we find that two chief themes constantly recur in explaining the primary significance of the sacrament: the Mass is a sacramental representation of the sacrifice of the Cross, the Mass is a sacramental participation in the heavenly liturgy. These two essential themes run through the whole Eucharistic liturgy. They are explained mainly in connection with the very heart of that liturgy, the prayer of consecration; but these same themes command the interpretation of the various rites of the liturgy from its beginning. By the theme of death and resurrection, the Eucharist is seen to be the prolongation of the other sacraments: one could say that the whole Christian initiation is a participation in Christ dead and risen again: by the theme of the heavenly liturgy, on the other hand, we see a different aspect, which was introduced by the anointing with chrism, the rite which immediately preceded the Eucharist. And, as we have noticed, the baptismal liturgy takes us in succession through the themes of Creation, of Paradise, of the Circumcision, of the Covenant, of the Exodus, of Kingship, that is to say, through the actual series of Old Testament themes, so the Eucharist is seen to coincide with one further aspect, that of the priestly worship.[1]

These two themes, of the sacrifice of the Cross and the heavenly sacrifice, appear from the very outset of the Eucharistic celebration. After Baptism, the new Christians, in white robes with candles in their hands, form themselves in procession to go, in the Paschal night, from the baptistry to the Church, where they are to participate for the first time, in the Mysteries. This solemn moment, when the newly-baptized finally come into the sanctuary, at the end of the long waiting of Lent, is frequently recalled by

[1] It is noteworthy that Harald Sahlin, when studying the typology of St. John's Gospel, reached the conclusion that it is built up on the model of the history of the Hebrew people from the departure from Egypt until the consecration of the Temple (*Zur typologie des Johannes Ev*). This corroborates the thesis of O. Cullmann on the connection between the Gospel of St. John and the sacraments (*Urchristentum und Gottesdienst*) and shows the Paschal background which is common to both.

St. Ambrose: "The people who have been purified and enriched with wonderful gifts (Baptism and Confirmation) begin to walk in procession toward the altar, saying: 'I will go in to the altar of God, to God who rejoices my youth.' Having stripped themselves of the last traces of the ancient error, renewed in the youth of the eagle, they hasten to go to the heavenly banquet. They enter, then, and, seeing the holy altar prepared, they cry out: 'You have prepared a table before me' " (*De Myst,* 43; Botte 121).

This first procession has two stages: the procession and the entrance. We should notice that the first is commented on by a quotation from Psalm XLII, and the second by one from Psalm XXII; it seems, indeed, that these two Psalms were actually sung at this moment. The first is the Psalm *Judica me,* which is still today the Psalm of the *Introit,* the entrance, in the Roman liturgy. As to the second, it holds a most important place in the liturgy of initiation, as we shall see. But what we should notice is that the Eucharist is shown from the beginning to be the *heavenly* banquet. It is the entrance into the heavenly sanctuary which is prefigured by the entrance into the earthly church: "You begin to go towards the altar; the angels are watching you; they have seen you begin to walk in; they have seen your appearance, which previously was wretched, suddenly become shining" (*De Sacr.,* IV, 5; Botte, 79).

St. Gregory of Nazianzen develops this symbolism of the procession as a figure of the entrance into the heavenly sanctuary, taking his inspiration from the eschatological parable of the wise virgins: "The station which you will make immediately after Baptism, before the great throne, is the prefiguration of the glory on high. The chant of the psalms, with which you will be received, is the prelude to the hymns of heaven. The candles which you hold in your hands are the sacrament (*mysterion*) of the escort of lights from on high, with which we shall go to meet the Bridegroom, our souls luminous and virgin, carrying the lighted candles of faith" (XXXVI, 425 A).[2] All the details of the rite, the psalms, the procession, the candles, are interpreted in connection with the heavenly liturgy. In Gregory's vision, the paschal night opens out into eternity. The baptized have already entered into

[2] On the symbolism of the candles, see XXXIII, 372 A. They are linked with the wedding procession in XXXIII, 333 A.

it. The boundaries between the earthly world and the heavenly have been done away with. The baptized already mingle with the angels. They are about to take part in the liturgy of heaven.

Having entered into the sanctuary, they contemplate for the first time the hidden mysteries: "You have come to the altar, you have seen that which you had not yet seen, you have begun to see the light of the sacraments" (*De Sacr.* III, 15; Botte, 77). Here begins a second part of the liturgy, the preparation by the deacons of the offerings on the altar. This is the sight which is offered to the eyes of the newly-baptized. We may distinguish here three elements: the altar, the deacons, the preparation, which are all figures of heavenly realities. The altar is briefly explained by St. Ambrose: "The altar is the figure of the body, and the body of Christ is upon the altar" (*De Sacr.* IV, 7; Botte 80). As St. Cyril of Alexandria said still more fully: "Christ is the altar, the offering and the priest." [3]

The symbolism of the altar is developed by the Pseudo-Dionysius in connection with the consecration of the altar by the holy oils: "The most holy prescriptions for the sacraments command, for the consecration of the altar of the divine sacrifices, due outpourings of holy oil. Since, in fact, it is upon Jesus Himself, as upon the perfectly divine altar of our sacrifices, that the hierarchic consecration of the divine intelligences is accomplished, let us look with a gaze that is not of this world at this altar of the divine sacrifices. It is, in fact, Jesus the Most Holy Who offers Himself for us and Who dispenses to us the fullness of His Own consecration" (488 A).[4]

The deacons who arrange the offerings on the altar are the figures of the angels. This parallelism of the visible and invisible ministers of the sacrament was previously indicated by Didymus in connection with Baptism: "On the visible plane, the baptismal pool begets our visible body by the ministry of the priests. On the invisible plane, the Spirit of God, invisible to every intelligence, plunges (*baptizei*) into Himself and regenerates at the same time both our body and our soul, with the assistance of the angels" (XXXIX, 672 C). Theodore of Mopsuestia shows us the deacons

[3] P.G., LXVIII, 596-604. The expression comes from Origen, *Ho. Jos.*, IX, 6; P.G., XII, 868 C.

[4] On the symbolism of the altar, see F. J. Doelger, *Die Heiligkeit des Altars und ihre Begründung*, Ant. Christ., II, 3, p. 162-183.

as figures of the angels at the Offertory: "By means of the deacons who do the serving for that which is performed, we can follow in our understanding the invisible powers in their service of officiating at this ineffable liturgy; these are they who bring and arrange on the awe-inspiring altar this sacrifice or the figures of the sacrifice" (XV, 24).

As the altar is the figure of Christ perpetually offering Himself to the Father in the heavenly sanctuary, so the deacons represent the angels who surround this heavenly liturgy. From this it is clear that the Eucharistic sacrifice is the sacrament of the heavenly sacrifice. As it is Christ Who offers Himself under the symbol of the altar, so the angels are really present in the background of the visible liturgy. This idea of the presence of the angels at the Eucharistic liturgy is often pointed out by the authors of the fourth century: "The angels surround the priest. The whole sanctuary and the space around the altar are filled with the heavenly powers to honor Him Who is present on the altar." [5] This brings out the idea that the Eucharistic sacrifice is a sacramental participation in the unique heavenly sacrifice. And, as Erik Peterson has rightly remarked, this brings out the official character of the worship rendered by the Eucharist.[6]

As to the actual rite of the preparation of the offerings, Ambrose only alludes to it: "You have come to the altar, you have seen the sacred symbols placed on the altar, and you were astonished at the sight of this created thing itself, which still is only a common and familiar creature" (*De Sacr.* IV, 8; Botte, 80). Only Theodore of Mopsuestia gives this a symbolic interpretation, showing in this preparation a figure of the preliminaries of the Passion and of the Resurrection, according to a line of interpretation worked out by oriental mystagogy, which Nicolas Cabasilas in particular was to develop.[7] Here it is the second great theme, that of the Eucharist as the memorial of the Passion of the Resurrection, that we are shown as appearing at this point: "By means of the figures," writes Theodore, "we must now see Christ being led on His way to His Passion, and stretched out on the altar to be immolated. When indeed in the sacred vessels, in the patens

[5] Chrysostom, *De Sacerdotio,* VI, 4.
[6] *Theologische Traktate,* p. 329.
[7] *Explication de la Sainte Liturgie,* 24; Salaville, p. 137.

and in the chalices, the oblation appears which is to be presented, then you must think that Our Lord Christ appears, led to His Passion" (XV, 25).

Nevertheless, there is a difference from the Passion. There it was the guilty Jews who led out Christ to His death. But "it is not permissible that, in the figures of our salvation, there should be similitudes of evil." Therefore the deacons who prepare the offerings are not figures of the Jews, but of the angels: "You must consider that it is the image of the invisible powers who are serving that is taken on by the deacons, now that they bring in from outside the portion for the oblation" (XV, 25). Furthermore, "the invisible powers were also present at the moment of the Passion, exercising their ministry, since an angel appeared to Him to strengthen Him." We should notice how the two themes of the memorial of the Passion and of the heavenly liturgy here mingle with one another in a common symbolism.

Theodore continued this symbolism: "And when they have brought it in, it is on the holy altar that the angels place the oblation for the perfect carrying out of the Passion. For this reason also we believe that it is in a sort of tomb that Christ is placed on the altar and that He has already undergone the Passion. That is why some of the deacons, who lay out the cloths on the altar, show by this action the likeness of the burial cloths, and those deacons who, when the offering has been laid on the cloths, take their places on each side and fan the air above the sacred body, are figures of the angels who, all the while that Christ was in the tomb, remained there in His honor, until they had seen the Resurrection" (XV, 27). So in this paschal night, the anniversary of the Resurrection, the glance of Theodore sees, behind the gestures of the deacons, the angels gathering around the body of Christ laid in the tomb.

The preparation of the offerings is followed by two rites that we find commented on by all the catecheses: the washing of the hands and the kiss of peace. They are given in this order by Cyril of Jerusalem, in the reverse order by Theodore of Mopsuestia and the Pseudo-Dionysius. Cyril thus comments on the first: "You have seen the deacon hold out to the ministers and to the priests surrounding the altar of God, the water for washing their hands. This is not given them because of physical stains, but this washing of the hands is a symbol that you should be pure of all sin and all unworthiness. As the hands are the symbol of action, in washing them we signify the purity and innocence of our works" (XXXIII, 1109 B). The Pseudo-Dionysius presents an analogous commentary: "Thanks to this purification of the hands, living in the pure perfection of his conformity with God, he can proceed with generosity to inferior tasks, all the while remaining invulnerable to the attacks of impurity" (440 D. See also Theodore of Mopsuestia, XV, 42).[8]

The kiss of peace is of greater importance: "Next," St. Cyril tell us, "let us embrace one another and give the kiss of peace. Do not think that this is the kiss which friends are accustomed to give one another when they meet in the *agora.* This is not such a kiss. This unites souls to one another and destroys all resentment. The kiss is a sign of the union of souls. This is why the Lord said: If you bring your offering to the altar and you remember that you have anything against your brother, go first and be reconciled with your brother" (XXXIII, 1112 A). St. Augustine, in one of his sermons on Easter, commenting on the sacramental rites to the newly baptized, says: "After this is said: Peace be with you: and Christians give one another the holy kiss. It is the sign of peace. That which the lips show outwardly, exists in our hearts." (P.L., XXXVIII, 1101 A).

Theodore of Mopsuestia deepens the meaning of the rite: "All give the peace to one another, and by this kiss they make a kind of profession of the unity and charity that they have among themselves. By Baptism, indeed, we have received a new birth by which we are reunited in a union of nature: and it is the same nourishment of which we all partake, when we partake of the same Body and the same Blood: All of us, many as we are, we form one body because we partake of the same Bread. We must, then, before approaching the sacred Mysteries, carry out the rule of giving the peace by which we signify our union and our charity toward one another. It is not fitting to those who form one body in the Church that anyone should hate any of his brothers in the Faith" (XV, 40). Here a new aspect of the sacrament appears: it is the sign of the unity of the members of the Body of Christ, and

[8] See J. A. Jungmann, *Missarum solemnia,* II, p. 21.

the kiss of peace is seen as the sign of this unity. We find a similar development in the Pseudo-Dionysius (437 A).

The three rites that we have been studying constitute the preparation for the sacrament. Now we come to the sacrament itself, which is constituted by the prayer of consecration properly so-called, the great *anaphora* spoken over the bread and wine. It is introduced by the ancient formulae that our liturgy still retains. Cyril comments on them as follows: "The priest then cries: *Sursum corda.* Yes, truly at this moment, filled with holy fear (*phrikodestaton*) we must hold our hearts raised on high to God and turned no longer toward the earth and earthly things. The priest invites us all implicitly to leave at this moment all the cares of life and our domestic preoccupations, and to have our hearts turned to heaven, to God the Friend of men. Then answer: *Habemus ad Dominum,* giving by your answer your assent to the priest's words. Let there be no one who says with his lips: *Habemus ad Dominum* and who keeps his spirit among the cares of this life. We ought always to be mindful of God. If this is impossible because of human weakness, at least at this moment we must try to be mindful of Him" (XXXIII, 1112 B).

Cyril rightly emphasizes the symbolism of the *Sursum corda.* It is the expression of the holy fear (*phrike*) with which the hearts of the faithful should be filled at the moment when "the awe-inspiring liturgy" [9] is to be accomplished. Holy fear is the feeling which takes possession of man's heart when the living God manifests His presence. It is also the disposition of the angels in the heavenly liturgy: "They adore, they glorify, with fear they sing continually mysterious hymns of praise." [10] And this atmosphere of mystery which is that of the heavenly liturgy also penetrates the earthly liturgy. No one has better felt this fear than St. John Chrysostom: The moment of the consecration is "most fearful" (*phrikodestaton*) (XLVIII, 733 C). "Man should stand in the presence of God with fear (*phrike*) and trembling (*phrikodestata*) (XLVIII, 734 C). It is "with veneration that we must approach these most fearful realities (XLVIII, 725 C).[11]

[9] Theodore of Mopsuestia, XVI, 3.

[10] John Chrysostom, *On the Incomprehensible,* P.G., XLVIII, 707 B.

[11] See Jean Daniélou, *L'Incomprehensibilité de Dieu d'après Saint Jean Chrysostome,* Rech. Sc. Relig., 1950, pp. 190-195.

We must connect the *Sursum corda* with the chant of the Trisagion which follows it. Together they constitute the solemn introduction to the Canon. Both express the idea that the Eucharist is a participation in the heavenly liturgy. The Trisagion, in fact, is the hymn of the Seraphim who eternally surround the Trinity: "Man is as it were transported into heaven itself," writes St. John Chrysostom. "He stands near the throne of glory. He flies with the Seraphim. He sings the most holy hymn" (XLVIII, 734 C). The same idea is found also in Cyril of Jerusalem: "We speak of the Seraphim that Isaias saw in the Holy Spirit surrounding the throne of God and saying: 'Holy, Holy, Holy is the Lord, the God of hosts.' This is why we recite this theology that is transmitted to us by Seraphim, so that we may take part in the hymn of praise with the hosts above the cosmos" (XXXIII, 1114 B).

The Trisagion is commented on in the same sense by Theodore of Mopsuestia: "The priest mentions among all the Seraphim who cause this praise to ascend to God which blessed Isaias learned by a divine revelation, and transmitted to us in the Scripture, that which we all gathered together sing in a loud voice so that we may be saying the same thing as the invisible natures are saying" (XVI, 6). And Theodore shows the relation of the Trisagion to the spirit of fear and awe: "We use the awe-inspiring words of the invisible powers to show the greatness of the mercy which is freely lavished on us. Fear fills our conscience throughout the whole course of the liturgy, both before we cry out 'Holy!' and afterwards: we look down at the ground, because of the greatness of what is being done, manifesting this same fear" (XVI, 9).

Thus, these two rites taken together express both the fact that the Eucharistic liturgy is a participation in the heavenly liturgy and the dispositions of holy fear which should be possessed by those who participate in this liturgy. This constitutes the immediate preamble of the sacrifice. We are no longer on earth, but in some way transferred to heaven. This is what is meant by *Sursum corda* (XVI, 3) according to Theodore. Restored by Baptism to the angelic creation from which he fell by sin, the newly-baptized once more can unite his voice with that of the angels. He is admitted to the official worship of creation, of which the angels are the representatives. And the center of this worship is the priestly action of Christ in His Passion and His Resurrection. It is this priestly action which, abstracted from time and place, constitutes the heart of the heavenly liturgy and which is rendered present sacramentally by the Eucharist.[12]

We have now come to this central rite, and the first aspect of it on which the catecheses insist is that by the consecration the bread and wine become the Body and Blood of Christ: "Do not consider the bread and wine as being ordinary things," writes St. Cyril of Jerusalem, "they are the Body and the Blood of Christ, according to His word" (XXXIII, 1108 A). And he comments on the rite itself as follows: "After we have sanctified ourselves by the Trisagion, we pray God to send His Holy Spirit down on the offerings, so that He may make the bread His Body and the wine His Blood. And that which the Holy Spirit has touched becomes entirely consecrated and transformed" (XXXIII, 1113 C–1116 A).

In the same way, Theodore of Mopsuestia writes: "When the pontiff says that the bread and wine are the Body and Blood of Christ, he shows clearly what they have become by the coming of the Holy Spirit" (XVI, 12).

We should notice that in these two texts the consecration is connected with the descent of the Holy Spirit, invoked by the epiclesis. St. Ambrose, on the other hand, connects the consecration with the action of Christ operating by the words of institution: "As soon as the consecration has taken place, the bread becomes the Body of Christ. How can this be done? By the consecration. The consecration takes place by means of what words? By those of the Lord Jesus. Indeed what was said up to now was said by the priest. But here he uses the words of Christ. What is the word of Christ? It is that by which all things were made" (XVI, 440 A. See 405). So, on the one hand, the consecration, a work common to the Three Persons, is appropriated to the Spirit, by Whom God carried out His great works in history; and, on the other hand, it is attributed to the creative Word, which is also the instrument of the power of God.

But what is rendered present on the altar is not only the Body and Blood of Christ, it is His sacrifice itself, that is to say, the mystery of His Passion, His Resurrection and His Ascension, of which the Eucharist is the *anamnesis,* the efficacious commemoration: "Each time that the sacrifice of Christ is offered, the Death

[12] See Jungmann, loc. cit., p. 164-165.

of the Lord, His Resurrection, His Ascension and the remission of sins are signified" (XVI, 452 B). To signify does not here mean only to recall. The word also intends to state that the sacrifice offered is not a new sacrifice, but the one sacrifice of Christ rendered present. This doctrine has been particularly brought out by the doctors of Antioch, from whom I shall quote two examples.

In a Eucharistic catechesis, inserted in his Commentary on the Epistle to the Hebrews, St. John Chrysostom, having recalled the fact that the pagan sacrifices were repeated because they were inefficacious, explains that the sacrifice of Christ is efficacious and unique: "But do we not daily offer the sacrifice? We offer it, but in making the anamnesis of His death. And this is unique, not multiple. It was offered once, as He entered once into the Holy of Holies. The anamnesis is the figure of His death. It is the same sacrifice that we offer, not one today and another tomorrow. One only Christ everywhere, entire everywhere, one only Body. As everywhere there is one Body, everywhere there is one sacrifice. This is the sacrifice that we now still offer. This is the meaning of the anamnesis: we carry out the anamnesis of the sacrifice" (LXIII, 130). We see clearly in this passage the power of the anamnesis, as making present not to memory, but in reality, under the sacramental signs, the unique sacrifice of Christ.

St. John Chrysostom insists above all on the anamnesis of the sacrifice of the Cross. Theodore of Mopsuestia sees rather in the Eucharist the heavenly sacrifice rendered visible in the sacrament. But we always come back to the parallelism of these two aspects: "Although in the food and the drink we make commemoration of the death of Our Lord, it is clear that in the liturgy it is as if we accomplished a sacrifice, without its being anything new, nor its being His own sacrifice that the Pontiff carries out, but it is a kind of image of the liturgy taking place in heaven. . . . Each time, then, that the liturgy of this dread sacrifice is carried out—which is obviously the likeness of earthly realities—we must consider that we are like one who is in heaven; by faith it is the vision of heavenly realities of which we see the outlines in our understanding, considering that Christ, Who is in heaven, Who for us died, rose again, ascended into heaven, it is He Himself Who even now is immolated by means of these figures" (XV, 14 and 20).

So we see more clearly the profound meaning of the double theme which, as we have noted, has characterized the Eucharistic liturgy from its outset. It signifies that the sacrifice of Christ subsists under three different modes. It is the same priestly action which took place in a precise moment of history; which is eternally present in heaven; and which subsists under the sacramental appearances. Indeed the priestly action of Christ in its substance is the very action by which creation achieves its end, since by it God is perfectly glorified. It is this action which, since that moment, by a unique privilege, is taken from time in order to subsist eternally, and which the sacrament renders present at all times and in all places.

The last part of the sacrament of the Eucharist, the Communion, is preceded by two rites: the ostension and the fraction.[18] Pseudo-Dionysius thus comments on them: "Such are the teachings that the high priest reveals in accomplishing the rites of the holy liturgy, when he publicly unveils the offerings that before were hidden; when he divides their original unity into many parts; when, by the perfect union of the sacrament that he distributes to the souls who receive it, he admits to its perfect communion those who receive it. This shows us, in a sensible manner and as it were in an image, how Christ Himself came forth from His mysterious divine sanctuary to take the figure of a man for the love of man; how He descended progressively but without any alteration of His natural unity to the level of our sensibility; how the benevolent workings of His love for us grants to the human race the power to enter into communion with God" (444 C).

On the preparatory rites, let us mention only one commentary, which is on the fraction. Theodore of Mopsuestia, as he has already done concerning the rites of oblation, connects the fraction with the historic events that accompanied the Resurrection of Christ: "Now that the liturgy is accomplished, the Pontiff breaks the bread, as Our Lord first shared Himself in His manifestations, appearing now to this man and now to that" (XVI, 18). As with Pseudo-Dionysius, it is the communication of Christ

[18] See Jungmann, loc. cit., II, 259-260, who observes that this showing is found only in the Eastern liturgy at an early date. It was to appear much later in the liturgy of the West and was to take its place immediately after the consecration.

to all the multitude of different souls without division of His unity that is symbolized by the sensible rite. The other catecheses give no explanation of the breaking of the bread.

The essential rite, the distribution of the Body of Christ, is the subject of commentaries as developed as those on the Consecration itself, for it is indeed an essential aspect of the Eucharist to be spiritual food under the species of bread and wine. The symbolism of the bread and wine as signifying spiritual food is brought out by Theodore of Mopsuestia: "In the same way as, to live on in this life, we take as nourishment bread which possesses nothing of such a quality by its nature but which is capable of maintaining life in us because God has given it this power, so we receive immortality in eating the sacramental bread, since even though the bread has no such nature, nevertheless when it has received the Holy Spirit, it is capable of bringing those who eat it to immortality" (XV, 12).

The Eucharist is already an anticipation of heavenly blessings. As Theodore of Mopsuestia says, "by It, we who are mortal by nature, expect to receive immortality; corruptible, we become incorruptible; from the earth and earthly evils, we pass to all the blessings and delights of heaven. By means of these kinds of figures, we have faith that we possess the realities themselves" (XVI, 30). The Eucharist is, then, "the bread of angels" already shared in through the veil of the rites. It appears to us as an anticipated participation in the heavenly banquet which it prefigures and already realizes. We shall come back to this aspect in connection with the eschatological banquet. Here we find once more one of our essential themes, that of participation in heavenly realities.

But this spiritual nourishment is not to be thought of apart from the sacrifice of Christ. It is only a participation in this sacrifice, that is, in the Death and the Resurrection of Christ. Indeed the mystery of the Passion and the Resurrection is rendered present only in order to apply its effects to us. And Communion is precisely the manner in which these effects are applied to the soul. By this, the theology of Communion is seen not to differ from that of the Consecration in being a participation in the mystery of Christ dead and risen again. It is important, in fact, to note that, for our catecheses, Communion is seen to be as much a participation in the Death of Christ as in His Resurrection.

This has already been well noted by St. Ambrose: "Every time that you receive (the Eucharist) what does the Apostle say to you? Every time that we receive It, we announce the Death of the Lord. If we announce His Death, we announce the remission of sins. If each time that the Blood is poured out, it is poured out for the remission of sins, I should always receive It, so that my sins may be remitted" (*De Sacr.,* IV, 28; Botte 86-87). So it appears clearly that Communion is only the appropriation to the soul of the effect of the sacrifice rendered present in the Consecration. This aspect is emphasized also by St. Gregory of Nazianzen: "The Eucharist is the unbloody sacrifice by which we communicate in the sufferings and in the divinity of Christ" (P.G., XXXV, 576).

This connection of Communion with the death of Christ is particularly brought out by Theodore of Mopsuestia: "As, then, by the Death of Christ our Lord, we receive the birth of Baptism, so with food, it is also in a figure that we receive It by the means of His Death. To participate in the mysteries is to commemorate the Death of the Lord, which procures for us the resurrection and the joy of immortality; because it is fitting that we who, by the Death of Our Lord, have received a sacramental birth, should receive by the same Death the food of the sacrament of immortality. In participating in the mystery, we commemorate in figure His Passion, by which we shall obtain the possession of the good things to come and the forgiveness of sins" (XV, 7).

We should notice the great unity which the whole process of initiation is now seen to possess: from Baptism to Communion, this is all a participation in Christ dead and risen again. There is no other mystery than the Paschal mystery, this is the mystery which is the unique object of the whole sacramental life, and which this renders present in all times and in all places to apply to souls its life-giving fruits. We shall see that this overflows beyond the sacramental structure strictly so-callèd and extends to the whole Christian cult—the Christian week, the liturgical year are simply representations of the Paschal Mystery, efficacious representations which effect what they signify.

This fact has been remarkably expressed by Methodius of Olympus: "The Church could not conceive and regenerate believers by the bath of rebirth, if Christ, after He had been brought to nothing for them, so as to be able to be received in this recapitulation of His Passion, did not die afresh in descending from heaven; and if in uniting Himself to the Church, His Spouse, He did not provide in this way that a certain power should be taken from His Side, in such a way that all those who are grounded on Him, Who are regenerated by Baptism, may grow by drawing sustenance from His flesh and from His bones, that is to say, from His power and His glory. So the Church grows from day to day in stature and in beauty by the cooperation and communication of the Logos, Who condescends to us still now and continues His going out of Himself in the anamnesis of His Passion" (*Banquet* III, 8).

Other aspects of the Eucharist will appear as we study the figures of the Old Testament which announce it; it is the anticipation of the eschatological banquet, the sacrament of union, the source of spiritual joy, the document of the covenant. But it is important, first of all, to mark its central significance. For, as we have seen, from the beginning of the Offertory to the Communion, two themes dominate the theology of the Eucharist: that of the efficacious memorial of the Passion, the Resurrection and the Ascension, and that of participation in the sacrifice and the banquet of heaven. It is, then, these two themes that constitute its essential significance, symbolized by the sacramental rites.

CHAPTER NINE

The Figures of the Eucharist

THE consecration is carried out in the Mass by the great prayer of consecration which begins with *Gratias agamus* and ends with the epiclesis. The structure of this prayer deserves our study. The prayer begins with the recalling of the great works accomplished by God in the past. We have a remarkable example of this in the eighth book of the *Apostolic Constitutions.* The Pontiff gives thanks to God for His creation of the world and for that of man, for man's being placed in Paradise, for the sacrifice of Abel, the translation of Henoch, the deliverance of Noe, the covenant with Abraham, the sacrifice of Melchisedech, the deliverance from Egypt (VIII, 12, 20-27). The prayer continued with a remembrance of the great works of God in the New Testament and the mysteries of Christ: this is the only part preserved in our Preface. And the prayer was concluded by the epiclesis, which is the prayer addressed to the Holy Spirit, Who has done these great works in the past, to continue them in the present.

This double aspect of the *narratio,* which corresponds to thanksgiving, and the *expectatio,* which corresponds to the prayer of petition, is constitutive of Christian thought.[1] It rests on the faith in what God has done in the past in order to find the foundations for hope in what He will do in the present and in the future. We thus see how, by this very fact, it shows the continuity between the Old Testament, the New Testament and the Sacraments. It

[1] See St. Augustine, *De catech, rud.,* 7: P.L., XL, 317 C.

thus invites us to look in the Old Testament for the prefiguration of the New Testament and of the Sacraments. In this sense, the typology of the Eucharist is only the explication of the content of the prayer of Consecration itself, which is essentially typological. The Canon of the Roman Mass, as we have it today, conserves this structure in showing us first that the Eucharist is the memorial of the sacrifice of Abel, Melchisedech, and Abraham, and then that it is the memorial of the Passion, the Resurrection and the Ascension. So the Mass is seen to be the continuation in the present time of the priestly actions of both Testaments.

Nevertheless, these prefigurations are of two kinds. Some—and these are the great majority—are figures of the sacrifice of Christ, and therefore of the Mass inasmuch as it is the representation of this sacrifice: so, for example, the sacrifice of Abel and of Isaac. They are related to the reality which the Mass represents, not to the rites by which it is rendered present. What we need to establish here is the significance of the rites themselves, which are the offering and the eating of the bread and wine. And these rites appear as being prefigured principally by four episodes in the Old Testament: the sacrifice of Melchisedech, the manna of Exodus, the meal of the Covenant, the Paschal meal.

The bread and wine offered by Melchisedech were considered from a very ancient date to be a figure of the Eucharist. Clement of Alexandria already speaks of "Melchisedech, who offered bread and wine, the consecrated food as a figure (*typos*) of the Eucharist" (*Strom.* IV, 25; Staehlin, 319, 25). This idea is developed by St. Cyprian. His Letter LXIII, addressed to Cecilius, is actually devoted to combating the heretics who rejected the use of wine in the Eucharist. Here, Cyprian enumerates the principal texts of the Old Testament in which wine is presented as a figure of the Eucharist. And among these passages, the most important is that concerning Melchisedech: "In Melchisedech the priest, we see the sacrament of the sacrifice of the Lord prefigured according to the witness of Scripture; Melchisedech, king of Salem, offered bread and wine" (*Ep.* LXIII, 4; C.S.E.L., 703).

Cyprian begins by showing that Melchisedech is the figure, *typos,* of Christ, founding his statement on Psalm CIX:4 "Thou art a priest forever according to the order of Melchisedech."

"Who is more a priest of God Most High than our Lord Jesus Christ, Who offered to the Father the same offering as Melchisedech, that is, bread and wine, which is to say, His Body and His Blood?" (704). Thus, as Melchisedech is a figure of Christ, so his offering is a figure of the oblation of Christ. And as Cyprian remarks, not only a figure of the sacrifice of Christ, but of the sacrament of the sacrifice. The sameness of the offering of bread and wine emphasizes this relationship: "Thus the figure of the sacrifice, consisting of bread and wine, has taken place in the past. And it is this figure that the Lord fulfilled and accomplished when He offered the bread and the chalice of wine mingled with water: He Who is the fulfillment accomplished the reality of the figurative image" (704).

This figure of Melchisedech is a part of the common catechesis; St. Ambrose returns to it many times. For him, it is, together with the manna, the essential figure of the Eucharist. "We remember that the figure of these sacraments came before the time of Abraham, when holy Melchisedech, who has neither beginning nor end of days, offered the sacrifice" (*De Sacr.*, V, 1; Botte 88). This served St. Ambrose in particular to establish the anteriority of the Christian sacrifice over the Mosaic: "Receive what I say, to know that the mysteries of the Christians are anterior to those of the Jews. If the Jews go back to Abraham, the figure of our sacraments came before, when the high priest Melchisedech came before Abraham the victor and offered for him bread and wine. Who had the bread and wine? It was not Abraham, but Melchisedech. He it is, then, who is the author of the sacraments" (*De Sacr.*, IV, 10; Botte, 80).

The text of St. Ambrose alludes to the mysterious passage in the Epistle to the Hebrews in which St. Paul shows us Melchisedech "without father or mother, without genealogy, without beginning nor end of life," the figure of the Son of God (VII, 3). We know the speculations to which this passage gave rise in the first centuries and from which St. Ambrose himself did not completely escape, speculations which show us Melchisedech as an apparition of the Word and of the Holy Spirit.[2] But, in any case, the effect of the Epistle to the Hebrews is to present Melchise-

[2] G. Bardy, *Melchisédech dans la tradition patristique,* Rev. bibl., 1926, p. 416 et seq; 1927, p. 24 et seq.

dech as the figure of Christ the eternal Priest.[3] But we must remember also that this passage makes no allusion to the offering of bread and wine as being a figure of the sacramental Eucharist. Does this figure, then, possess a foundation in the New Testament, or does it result only from the speculation of the Fathers of the Church?

One fact should attract our attention, and that is the choice made by Christ Himself of bread and wine as the visible matter of the Eucharist. In fact, if we remember the extent to which the deeds of Christ were charged with reminiscences of the Old Testament, it seems probable that the choice of bread and wine in itself contains an allusion to the gesture of Melchisedech who also offered bread and wine. This has been observed by Father Feret: "To him who tries to realize, by means of the texts, but beyond the texts, what the Supper of Holy Thursday actually was in its concrete unfolding and in its power of biblical evocation, the developments of the Epistle to the Hebrews concerning the priesthood of Jesus according to the order of Melchisedech do not appear to be gratuitous, but solidly founded on the facts of the Gospel, especially on the offering of bread and wine." [4]

Thus, the development of the Epistle to the Hebrews rests on the very intention of Christ Himself in the institution of the Eucharist. The visible matter of the Eucharist was an effective allusion to the sacrifice of Melchisedech, an allusion willed by Christ and not imagined later by the Fathers. But we still need to inquire what is its foundation and its significance. We have in fact remarked, in connection with Baptism, the illustrative analogies,—the mention of water for Baptism, of bread and wine for the Eucharist,—are of value only to the extent to which they express underlying theological analogies. It remains, then, to ask what is the privileged analogy causing the sacrifice of Melchisedech to appear as the principal figure of the sacrifice of Christ. The question arises in particular concerning the superiority of the sacrifice of Melchisedech over those of Judaism, since this is brought out by the Epistle to the Hebrews and again mentioned by St. Ambrose.

[3] The Epistle to the Hebrews merely applies to the historical person of Jesus the Messianic typology of Psalm CIX.

[4] *La Messe et sa catéchèse,* p. 229 et seq.

This question has been profoundly treated by an author of whom we have not so far spoken, Eusebius of Cesarea. He remarks that, if the sacrifices of Judaism constitute a new step in the preparation for and the prefiguration of the New Testament, they also mark, in certain ways, a regression. For one thing, the priesthood in Israel became the property of a particular tribe and the others were excluded from it, while the sacrifice of Melchisedech was a universal priesthood, not the privilege of a particular caste: "Melchisedech was not chosen from among men, not anointed with an oil made up by man" (*Dem. Ev.* V, 3; P.G., XXII, 365 B-C). In the second place, the worship of the Old Testament was localized in one place, the Temple of Jerusalem. This was an advance, to the extent to which it was a visible symbol of monotheism: the one sanctuary manifesting the one God. But it was also a limitation to one place; the prophet Malachy announced it as a characteristic of the kingdom to come "that sacrifice will be offered in all places" (I, 11). The Fathers of the Church see in this vision a figure of the Eucharist, "the sacrifice of the new Law, offered in all places" (*Dem. Ev.* I, 10; XXII, 92 C).[5] And the sacrifice of Melchisedech was not limited to one place; it could be offered everywhere (XXII, 365 B).

This is true also of the matter of the sacrifice: "As he who was the priest of the nations does not appear at all as having used a corporal sacrifice, but as having blessed Abraham in the bread and the wine, so in the same way, Our Lord first of all, and after Him those who hold from Him their priesthood in all the nations, accomplish the spiritual sacrifice according to the rules of the Church, signifying by bread and wine the mysteries of the saving Body and Blood, Melchisedech having contemplated these things in advance in the Holy Spirit, and having used the figures of the realities to come (XXII, 365 D). There is, then, a greater resemblance to the Eucharist in the sacrifice of Melchisedech than in the Jewish sacrifices. And Fr. Feret gives the profound reason for this: "The bread and wine presented by Melchisedech to Abraham are a more spiritual offering, nearer to natural sim-

[5] Justin, *Dialogue,* XXVIII, 5; XXXIX, 1; XLI, 2; CXVI, 3; Tertullian, *Adv. Jud.,* 5; Irenaeus, *Adv. Haer.,* IV, 17 and 18; P.G., 1025 A.

plicity than all the sacred butcheries prescribed by the Jewish law" (*Loc. cit.*, P. 229).[6]

So the Eucharistic significance of the bread and wine is shown to us. "As Christ in instituting the Eucharist during the paschal meal, wished to show the continuity with the Mosaic covenant of the sacrament that He was instituting, so in instituting it under the appearances of bread and wine, He wished to show its continuity with the covenant with Noe of which Melchisedech was the High priest. Thus, Christ is the fulfillment not only of the figures of the worship of the Old Testament, but of all the sacrifices which in all religions and all times men have offered to God, which He takes up and transubstantiates in His Own sacrifice. It is the universal character of the sacrifice of the Eucharist which is signified by the appearances of bread and wine, and it is this that the liturgy of the Mass is stating when it shows us that it was prefigured in "the holy sacrifice, the immaculate victim, offered by the high priest, Melchisedech." [7]

The symbolism of the sacrifice of Melchisedech is concerned with the elements of the bread and wine. With the miracles of the Exodus, the correspondence to the Eucharist consists in the marvelous conditions under which the people of God were nourished. We have already met with the cycle of Exodus in connection with Baptism, when the crossing of the Red Sea was given us as a figure of Baptism itself. The Eucharist also is prefigured in the Exodus, the two essential episodes being the manna in the desert and the rock of Horeb, (This event is interpreted in two ways—one as a figure of Baptism, and this is connected with St. John; and the other, of the Eucharist, and this is Paulinian.)[8] Thus, the whole process of Christian initiation as carried out during the paschal night, is prefigured by the sacraments of the Exodus.

This sequence is brought out by the Fathers, as for example, St. John Chrysostom, who writes: "You have seen in connection with Baptism what the figure is and what the reality. Look, I

[6] See Eusebius, *Dem. Ev.*, I, 10; P.G., XXII, 84 A. Eusebius is here echoing the controversy against blood-sacrifices which appears at the end of the Jewish Church. See J. H. Schoeps, *Theologie und Geschichte des Juden christentums*, p. 220-223.

[7] Jean Daniélou, *Le mystère de l'Avent*, p. 35 et seq. (Eng. trans. *Advent*, Sheed & Ward).

[8] On the baptismal interpretation, see *Sacramentum futuri*, 170-176.

will show you the table also and the communion of the sacraments outlined therein, if as before, you do not ask to find it whole and entire, but rather that you examine the events as it is natural they should happen in the figure. Indeed, after his passage on the cloud and the sea, St. Paul says: 'And they all drank of the same spiritual drink.' In the same way, he says that you come out of the pool of water and go in haste to the Table, as they came out of the sea and went toward a new and marvelous table, that is, the manna. And as you have a mysterious drink, the saving Blood, so they had a marvelous kind of drink, finding water in abundance flowing out of a dry rock there where there was no spring nor running water" (*P.G.*, LI, 247, A-C).

In this passage, the sequence of Baptism and the Eucharist is well marked. The initiation as a whole is seen to be a sacramental imitation of the Exodus from Egypt, and the manna and the water from the rock also come in as figures of the Eucharist. The same themes are found in Theodore: "The events of the old were the figures of the new: the Law of Moses is the shadow, grace the body. When the Egyptians pursued the Hebrews, they, having crossed the Red Sea, escaped from their tyranny. The sea is the figure of the baptismal pool; the cloud, of the spirit; Moses, of Christ the Savior; his staff, of the Cross; Pharaoh, of the devil; the Egyptians, of the demons; the manna, of the divine Food; the water from the rock, the blood of the Savior. Indeed, as those men, having first crossed the Red Sea, then tasted a divine nourishment and a miraculous spring, so we, after the Baptism of salvation, participate in the divine Mysteries" (*P.G.*, LXXX, 257 B-C).

The first of these two figures is the manna. Although the whole Alexandrine tradition from Clement to Origen, following Philo, understands the manna to be a figure of the word of God, following Matthew IV:4, the Eucharistic interpretation based on John VI:31-33 is common in the catecheses. We shall quote only St. Ambrose.[9] Having established, by the example of Melchisedech, that the Christian sacraments are more ancient than the Jewish, He shows, by the manna, that they are also more efficacious. "The manna was a great marvel, the manna that God rained down on the Fathers. The heavens nourished them with daily food, as it

[9] See also Cyprian, *Epist.*, LXVIII, 14; C.S.E.L. 763.

is written: 'Man ate the bread of angels' (Psalm. 75:25). And nevertheless, those who ate this bread died in the desert. But this nourishment that you receive, the Bread descended from heaven, communicates to you the substance of eternal life. It is the Body of Christ. As the light is greater than the shadow, the truth than the figure, so the Body of the Creator is greater than the manna from heaven" (*De Myst.* 46; Botte, 123).

Ambrose emphasizes at the same time the real analogies of the manna and the Eucharist, and the superiority of the reality over the figure. But this superiority should not cause us to misunderstand the fact that the manna of the Old Testament was already something other than an ordinary profane food, and constituted a true sacrament. This is brought out strongly by St. Augustine: "The manna signifies the (Eucharistic) Bread, the altar of God signifies the (Eucharistic) bread. But these already were sacraments. The appearances are different, but the reality is the same. The bodily nourishment is different, since they ate the manna and we something else. But the spiritual nourishment was the same for them as for us" (*Tract. Joh.*, XXVI, 6, 12; P.L., XXXV, 1612).

This has consequences for the figurative meaning of the manna. The correspondence is not to be found in the analogy of the material element, since this analogy is missing, but is more profound, being concerned with the conditions under which the food is given in both cases and the effects which it produces. In the manna as in the Eucharist, there is no question of an aid given by God alone that man could not procure by his own efforts. It is, then, a supernatural grace. This food also is given daily, which distinguishes the Eucharist, the sacrament of every day, from Baptism, the sacrament which is given only once. And it is a spiritual food, which should be received with the dispositions proper to faith (I Cor. 10:3).

Even more than in the case of the sacrifice of Melchisedech, the application of the manna to the Eucharist, is thus seen to be founded in the very reality of things. And, further, it rests upon Scripture itself. Judaism had already given to the manna an eschatological significance. As God had nourished His people with a miraculous food in the time of the Exodus of old, so would He do again in the time of the new eschatological Exodus.[10] This eschatological significance of the manna appears in the New Testament: "To him who conquers, I will give a hidden manna" (II:17). The manna is put on the same plane with the tree of life (Apoc. II, 7), as a figure of participation in the divine blessings in the world to come.

But the precise object of the New Testament is to show that this eschatological nourishment is already present in the Church by the Eucharist. This is the teaching both of St. Paul and St. John. In the First Epistle to the Corinthians, St. Paul, having said that the Jews of the Exodus ate of the same spiritual food, says: "These things are the figures of those that concern us" (I Cor. 10:6). And St. John tells us that Christ said, "Your fathers ate the manna and they are dead. If anyone eat of this bread, he will live forever" (VI:60-51). The manna as a figure of the Eucharist, then, is part not only of the common tradition of the Church, but of the very teaching of Christ.[11]

We have already seen that Theodore and St. John Chrysostom associated the Rock of Horeb with the manna as a figure of the Eucharist, the manna being the figure of the bread and the water from the rock of the wine. This represents a tradition that has its origin with St. Paul (I Cor. 10:4), and there is another that we have mentioned, connecting the Rock of Horeb with Baptism, which has its origin with St. John. Cyprian in particular refuses to see in the water from the rock a figure of the Eucharistic wine (Epist. LXIII, 8; C.S.E.L., 705-707). Here, in fact, are two forms of typology, one insisting more on the visible elements, the other on the hidden realities. But in any case, the Eucharistic tradition of the Rock of Horeb is well attested—we have seen that it was found in the Fathers of the Church of Antioch, and it appears also in western tradition with St. Ambrose and St. Augustine.

The former gives it a place in his two catecheses. In the *De Mysteriis,* he associates it with the miracle of the manna to show

[10] See Behm, *Artos,* Theol. Woert, I, 476; H. J. Schoeps, *Theologie und Geschichte des Judenchristentums,* p. 91-93; Foote-Moore, *Judaism,* II, p. 367-368.

[11] On the eucharistic meaning of the words of Christ, see E. C. Hoskyns, *The Fourth Gospel,* p. 297; Oscar Cullmann, *Urchristentum und Gottesdienst,* 2nd ed., pp. 89-99. It will be noticed that the multiplication of the loaves is a fulfillment of the prophecy of the eschatological manna, which is itself a symbol of the Eucharist: we have here the two planes of Christological typology and sacramental typology. We shall find the same thing in the case of the Rock of living water and of the sacred banquet.

the superiority of the Christian sacraments: "The water flowed from the Rock for the Jews, the Blood of Christ for you; the water slaked their thirst for an hour, the Blood quenches your thirst forever. The Jews drank and thirsted once more; when you have drunk, you need never thirst again. That was a figure, this is the truth. If the figure seems wonderful to you, how much more the reality the figure of which you admire" (*De Myst.* 48; Botte, 123). The comparison with the Eucharist is still more precise in the *De Sacramentis:* "What does it contain, the prefiguration given to us in the time of Moses? We see here that the Jewish people were thirsty and that they complained because they did not find any water. Then Moses touched the rock and it produced water in abundance, according to the word of the Apostle: 'They drank of the spiritual Rock that followed them. And this rock was Christ.' Drink, you also, so that Christ will accompany you. See the mystery. Moses is the prophet; the staff is the Word of God; the water flows; the people of God drink. The priest knocks; the water flows into the chalice for life everlasting" (*De Sacr.* V 4; Botte 89). St. Augustine, like St. Ambrose, associates the miracle of the Rock and that of the manna as figures of the Eucharist, following St. Paul: "All drank of the same spiritual drink. They drank one kind of drink, we another. But these differ only in visible appearance, for they signify the same thing by their hidden power. How did they drink the same drink: 'They drank of the Rock that followed them, and this rock was Christ.' The Rock is the figure of Christ, the true Christ is the Word united to the flesh. And how did they drink it? The rock was struck twice by the staff. This double blow is a figure of the two arms of the Cross" (*Tract. Joh.* XXVI, 6, 12; P.L., XXXV 1612).

We should notice the allusion to the Cross of Christ, and Ambrose's speaking of the flowing blood of Christ. In the background of these two phrases, we see the theme of the blood flowing from the side of Christ on the Cross. For we know that ancient tradition saw, in the water flowing from the rock in the desert, the figure of the blood flowing from the pierced side of Christ.[12] We have here a typology on three levels,—in the blood

[12] See Hugo Rahner, *Flumina de ventre Christi,* Biblica, 1941, pp. 269-302; 367-403; P. M. Braun, *L'eau et l'esprit,* Rev. Thomiste, 1949, pp. 1-30. The whole of this is based on Scripture itself. Isaias (XLVIII, 21) had foretold that a spring would gush forth at the end of time, like that of the Exodus, and Christ asserted that this

and the water flowing from the side of Christ, the Fathers saw a figure of Baptism and the Eucharist; so the water flowing from the rock can at the same time be a figure of both the one and the other. It has more generally signified Baptism, but it was normal to see in it also a figure of the Eucharist. And to the man who might be astonished at this, Augustine answers, in the passage that have just been quoted, that the difference of the visible element matters little here, this was true also of the manna; what is important is the invisible power communicated in both cases, whether under the species of the water from the rock, or that of the wine in the chalice.[13]

In the passage from his *Letter to Cecilius* in which he gives the figures of the Eucharistic elements in the Old Testament, St. Cyprian adds to the episode of Melchisedech that of the banquet of Wisdom (Prov. IX:5): "By Solomon also the Spirit shows us the figure of the sacrifice of the Lord in making mention of the immolated victim, of the bread, of the wine, and also of the altar: Wisdom, he says, has built a house and supported it with seven columns. She has slain her victims, she has mingled water and wine in the cup, she has set the table. Then she sends her servants in a loud voice inviting the guests to come and drink of her cup, saying: Come, eat my bread and drink the wine that I have mingled for you. Solomon speaks of the mingled wine, that is to say, he announces prophetically the chalice of the Lord mingled with water and wine" (*Epist.*, LXIII, 5. See also *Test.* II, 2; C.S.E.L., 64).

A new theme appears here, corresponding to another aspect of the Eucharist: that of the meal, as expressing union with the

prophecy was fulfilled in himself (John, IV, 13). These texts are expressly connected with the sacraments by Cyprian (*Test.*, I, 12; C.S.E.L., 47; *Epist.*, LXIII, 8; C.S.E.L., 706-707). Cyprian understands the prophecy as referring to Baptism, but this does not alter the general interpretation.

[13] Just as the manna, after the crossing of the Red Sea, symbolizes the Eucharist, so the Promised Land, after the crossing of the Jordan, symbolizes the body of Christ. This piece of symbolism is a very ancient one. See Barnabas, VI, 10-17; Tertullian, *De res. carn.*, 16. The First Epistle of St. Peter (II, 2) may possibly contain an allusion to it. The milk and honey, offered to the newly baptized, gives it a place in the rites themselves (Hipp., *Trad. Apos.*, 23). See N. A. Dahl, *La terre où coulent le lait et le miel,* Mél. Goguel, p. 69.

divinity.[14] Here we are no longer in the cycle of the Exodus, but in that of the Temple. The Jewish liturgy included a sacred meal taken in the Temple on the mountain of Jerusalem, which was the visible sign of membership in the people of God. So we read in Deuteronomy: "You are to resort to the place which the Lord, your God, chooses out of all your tribes and designates as His dwelling . . . There, too before the Lord your God, you and your families shall eat and make merry over all your undertakings, because the Lord, your God, has blessed you" (Deut., XII:4-7. See also 17-18).[15]

And we meet throughout the whole Jewish tradition a series of texts describing the messianic blessings reserved for the end of time as a sacred banquet, of which the ritual banquets of the law were the figure. This is the meaning of the passage from the Book of Proverbs quoted by St. Ambrose. M. André Robert has shown that St. Ambrose also depends on a passage from Isaias II in which the prophet presents the happiness of the messianic age as a banquet:

> "All you that thirst, come to the waters,
> You that have no money, make haste, buy and eat. . . .
> Hearken diligently to me, and eat that which is good,
> And your soul shall be delighted in fatness." (Is. LV, 1-3)

This theme is also found in Isaias (LXV:11-13). This conception of the messianic banquet is developed especially in apocalyptic literature, appearing in the *Apocalypse of Isaias:* "And the Lord of hosts shall make unto all people in this mountain, a feast of fat things, a feast of wine, of fat things full of marrow, of wine purified from the lees" (Is. XXV:6).

The non-canonical Apocalypses present the same vision. So the Fourth Book of Esdras, describing the future world, writes: "Build the city and prepare the banquet" (VIII, 52). The Book of Henoch is particularly important, since its influence on the Judaism of pre-Christian times and on the New Testament itself

[14] See Jean Daniélou, *Les repas de la Bible et leur signification,* La Maison-Dieu XVIII, p. 133.

[15] The first of these meals is the one which, after the concluding of the covenant upon Sinai, brings together on Mount Sinai Moses, Aaron and the seventy elders (Ex., XXIV, 11). The ritual meals are its memorial. From this viewpoint the Eucharist is seen as the meal of the New Covenant.

is well known. The theme of the eschatological banquet appears here also: "The Lord of Spirits will dwell with them and they will eat with this Son of man; they will take their places at his table for ever and ever" (LXII, 14). We should notice that this future Banquet also possesses this characteristic of being a banquet with the Son of Man. We find this in the New Testament: "And appoint to you a kingdom, even as My Father has appointed to Me, so that you may eat and drink at My table in My Kingdom" (Luke XXII:29).

Thus, on the one hand, the messianic banquet presents the same features as does the liturgical meal in the temple of Jerusalem: It takes place "in the house of wisdom" (Prov. IX, I.), that is, the temple, as A. Robert has shown (*loc. cit.*, p. 377). It takes place on the Mountain (Isaias XXV, 6). The Mountain is the Mount of Sion, where God dwells and where the messianic manifestation will take place. It takes place in the City (Esdras VIII:52), the earthly Jerusalem being the figure of the heavenly. But at the same time, the messianic banquet surpasses the liturgical banquet which is only its figure, having a quality and an abundance indicating that we are no longer on the level of the present creation, but in a world transformed (Is. XXV:6 and LV:1); and that the blessings are spiritual ones (Is. LV:3) of which the visible foods of the liturgical meal are the symbols. Finally—and this is a very important point—although the members of the people of Israel were admitted to the Jewish ritual meals, it is "all the peoples" who are to be admitted to the eschatological banquet (Is. XXV:6).

The typology of the holy banquet thus appears from the time of the Old Testament. The New Testament, as in the case of the Manna and the Rock, only gives witness to the fact that the messianic banquet, more precisely described and enriched in its content, is fulfilled by Christ, since with Him the messianic times have come. In this connection, we must give special importance to the meals taken by Christ which are reported to us in the Gospel, for these meals seem to be permeated with a religious meaning, as it were, already realizing the messianic banquet prefigured by the ritual meals of the Old Testament. This significant character of the meals of the Gospel has been remarked by several recent writers, in particular by Lohmeyer,[16] by Cullmann,[17] and by Rev. de Montcheuill.[18] "The daily meals of Christ," writes the latter "have something sacramental about them. . . . The fact that Christ does not only appear as the master who teaches, but that He wishes to have this fellowship with men of eating at table with them, does it not mark both the social intimacy that He wishes to establish with them, and also the will to reunite them around His person? . . . But it does not suffice to remain in generalities which appeal only to the significance of fellowship at table—a significance which is in some way universal. . . . We must try to see what this might have represented in the thought of Christ Himself and of the evangelists. . . . But the Gospel, in continuity with the Old Testament, makes a religious use of the metaphor of the meal."

A more precise study of the meals of Christ as described in the Gospel shows us that this significance is not only religious, but truly messianic, that is to say, that these meals are shown to be the reality of which the meals of the Old Testament of which we have spoken, were the figures. In the first place, the very fact that Christ took part in banquets is shown as having a messianic significance, and as expressing the joy announced by the prophets. We see this in the passage which follows the account of the meal offered by Matthew to Christ. The disciples of John were scandalized: "Why, when we and the pharisees observe the fast, do your disciples not observe it?" (Mark II:18). Christ answers: "Can the friends of the Bridegroom be sorrowful while the Bridegroom is with them?" (II:19). Thus, these banquets attended by Our Lord seem to be the expression of the character of messianic joy which indicates the presence of Christ.[19] The period represented by John the Baptist, the period of waiting, has been succeeded by that of Jesus, the period of presence. We find the same contrast drawn between John and Jesus in another passage: "John the Baptist came neither eating nor drinking wine, and you say, 'He

[16] *Vom urchristlichen Abendmahl,* Theologische Rundschau, 1937, pp. 276 et seq.
[17] *'La signification de la sainte Cène dans le christianisme primitif.'* Rev. Hist. Phil. Rel., 1936, pp. 1-22.
[18] *'La signification eschatologique du repas eucharistique,'* R.S.R., 1936, pp. 5 et seq.
[19] These words come immediately before the episode of the disciples gathering ears of corn on the sabbath day. Harald Riesenfeld (*Jésus transfiguré,* p. 326) writes that this episode (Mark, II, 23-27) "denotes the eschatological meal and represents the Eucharist." The same author shows the link in this passage between the eschatological meal and the eschatological sabbath (p. 322).

has a devil.' The Son of Man came eating and drinking, and you say, 'Behold a man who is a glutton, and a wine-drinker, a friend of publicans and sinners!' " (Luke VII:33-34).

This passage indicates a second characteristic of the meals of Jesus which struck those who witnessed them and aroused the rebukes of the pharisees; this was the fact that He was willing to eat "with publicans and sinners." It is remarkable that this expression is immediately followed, in Luke, by the story of the meal with Simon the Pharisee, in which Jesus allowed the sinner of Magdala to come in. In the same way, the banquet of Jesus with Matthew the publican, which precedes the passage on fasting mentioned above, also aroused the objections of the Pharisees: "Why does your master eat and drink with publicans and sinners?" (Mark, II:16). To which Jesus answered: "I have not come to call the just, but sinners." These last words clearly indicate the meaning of this meal. Fr. De Montcheuil brings this out: "In accepting this intimate community with sinners, Jesus showed that He had come to destroy the barrier between sinful men and God. . . . It is an act with a religious significance which sheds light on what is most essential in the mission of Christ" (loc. cit., pp. 32-33).[20]

Thus, the meals of Christ in the Gospel are seen to be the realization of the messianic banquet announced by the prophets and the apocalypses. But as the multiplication of the loaves is both a realization of the figure of the manna and a prophecy of the Eucharist, so these meals of Christ are the prefiguration of the admission of the nations to the messianic community which is realized in the Church. So, in a passage from St. Luke, Christ declares that it is not the fact of having eaten and drunk with Him during His earthly life that constitutes the accomplishment of the promises; in fact "there will be weeping and gnashing of teeth, when you see Abraham, Isaac and Jacob and all the prophets in the kingdom of God, but you yourselves cast forth outside. And they will come from the East and West, from the North and the South and will feast in the Kingdom of God" (Luke XIII:28-29). And M. André Feuillet has shown that this

[20] This had been seen by St. Ambrose, *Exp. Luc.*, II, 11; LV, 66; "Christ eats with publicans and sinners. This means that he does not refuse to share the meals of those to whom he is to give the sacrament."

statement is to be understood of the admission of the Gentiles into the Church.[21]

This fulfillment of the eschatological banquet by the conversion of the pagan nations is, moreover, formally stated in what follows that same passage, the parable of the guests invited to the banquet. At a meal taken by Jesus with one of the chiefs of the pharisees, one of His fellow-guests had said: "Blessed is he who shall feast in the Kingdom of heaven" Christ answered: "A certain man gave a great supper, and he invited many. And he sent his servant at supper time to tell those invited to come, for everything is now ready. And they all began to excuse themselves. . . . Then the master of the house was angry and said to his servant: 'Go out quickly into the streets and lanes of the city and bring in here the poor, and the crippled, and the blind and the lame' " (Luke XIV 16-21). We should note that this passage certainly seems to allude to the Old Testament theme with which we began above, that of the banquet of Wisdom, as Origen had already noticed (*Co. Cant.* III; P.G., XIII, 155). As, in the Proverbs, Wisdom sent her servants to invite all the passers-by to the banquet prepared in the Temple, so the Father of the family sent His servant to invite all whom he meets to the feast that has been prepared. So the Church is seen to be the House of Wisdom in which bread and wine are distributed, not only in figure, but in the sacrament of divine realities. And so the liturgy rightly applies this passage to the Eucharist.

But the application of the eschatologic feast to the Eucharist here still has only a general character. It is in Patristic tradition that we find the prophecies of Wisdom and of Isaias explicitly applied to the Eucharist. We have already quoted the passage in which St. Cyrian shows that the banquet of Wisdom is one of the most explicit figures of the Eucharist, together with the Manna in the desert. Origen also connects the Gospel parable of the banquet with the invitation to the banquet of Wisdom in a Eucharistic context: "The Church asks the servants of the word to lead her into the wine-cellar, that is to say, into the place where Wisdom has mingled her wine and invited, by means of her servants all those who are ignorant, saying: 'Come, eat my bread and drink

[21] *Les ouvriers de la vigne et la théologie de l'alliance,* Bech. Sc. rel., 1947, p. 320 et seqq.

the wine that I have mingled.' It is in this House of the banquet that all those who come from the East and the West will take their places together with Abraham, Isaac and Jacob in the Kingdom of heaven. It is into this House that the Church and every soul desire to enter, by becoming perfect, to enjoy the teachings of Wisdom and the mysteries of knowledge as the good foods of a banquent and the joy of wine" (Co. Cant. III; P.G., XIII, 155).

The same interpretations appear in St. Gregory of Nyssa and in St. Ambrose, without explicit reference to the Eucharist, but with definite allusion to the sacrament. Thus the first writes: "The vine in flower announces the wine which will one day fill the cup of wisdom and will be poured out for the guests so that they may drink at their will in divine Revelation the sober inebriation which raises man from earthly to invisible things" (XLIV, 873 A). And, in a parallel context, Gregory explains that "for those who understand the hidden sense of Scripture, there is no difference between what is said here and the institution of the sacrament at the Supper" (XLIV, 989 C). Furthermore, we recall that the perfume of the vine is connected with Confirmation, as the wine from the vine to the Eucharist. Thus, we have here an example of that mystico-sacramental parallelism so characteristic of the Greek Fathers.[22]

The sacramental interpretation is more explicit with St. Ambrose: "You wish to eat, you wish to drink. Come to the feast of Wisdom which invites all men by a great proclamation, saying: 'Come, eat my bread and drink my wine that I have mingled.' Do not fear that in the Feast of the Church you will lack either pleasant perfumes, or agreeable food, or varied drink, or fitting servants. There you will gather myrrh, that is to say, the burial of Christ, in such a way that, buried with Him by Baptism, you also will arise from the dead as He Himself is risen. There you will eat the bread that strengthens the heart of man, you will drink the wine so that you may grow to the full stature of Christ" (*Of Cain and Abel,* I, 5; C.S.E.L., XXXII, 1, 356). The parallelism with Baptism and the allusion to the meal of the Church leave no doubt as to the Eucharistic meaning of the text.[23]

[22] See H. Lewy, *Sobria ebrietas,* pp. 3-34.

[23] See J. Quasten, *Sobria ebrietas in Ambrosius De Sacramentis,* Mélange Mohlberg, I, p. 124-125.

We have seen that the passage from Wisdom is not the only prophecy of the eschatological banquet, for, as we have noticed, this theme appears also in the prophets and in the apocalypses. We already mentioned two passages, one being Isaias LV:1, and the other Isaias XXV:6. These two passages are also applied by the Fathers to the Eucharist banquet. The first is quoted in Didymus the Blind. "You who thirst, come to the waters, you who have no money, come and drink precious wine and eat good meats. By the water, he means the Holy Spirit and the spring of the baptismal pool. The wine and the meat stand for what was offered by the Jews in times past, and now for the immortal communion of the Body and the Blood of the Lord" (XXXIX, 716 B). The application of this prophecy to Baptism is very ancient and the liturgy of Holy Saturday still retains it. But the Eucharistic application is also important. And here, Didymus brings out the cultural significance of the food and drink in the prophecy. It is concerned with the sacred banquet of the Old Law. And it is this sacred banquet in which the prophet sees a figure of eschatological blessings and which Didymus shows as fulfilled in the Eucharist.

The passage from the Apocalypse of Isaias is quoted by Cyril of Jerusalem in a sacramental context, but applied to the baptismal anointing: "It is of this anointing that blessed Isaias spoke in ancient times, saying: 'And the Lord will prepare for all nations a banquet on this mountain'—it is the Church that he means by this—; they will drink wine, they will drink of joy, they will be anointed with perfumed oil." The allusion to the *muron* is due to a mistranslation in the Septuagint version. The Hebrew text does not speak of perfumed oil, but of fat meats. But the passage shows us nevertheless that the text was used as a figure of the Eucharist. Its application to the Eucharist is also made by Eusebius. Having quoted the text with the same mistranslation, and having applied the *muron* to the baptismal anointing, he concludes: "The prophet announces to the nations the joy of the wine, prophesying by this the sacrament of the New Covenant established by Christ, which today is visibly celebrated in all nations" (*Dem. Ev.*, I, 10; P.G., XXII, 92 C).

Eusebius, like St. Ambrose above, clearly points out the essential characteristic of the messianic banquet as distinguished from the meals of Jewish worship: that is, that it is open to all nations. This leads us, then, well beyond the analogy of bread and wine presented by some of these texts, to the fundamental theological idea: the Eucharist is the fulfillment of the meal of Jewish worship; It signifies, then, as did these meals, participation in the blessings of the Covenant. But, while the Jewish meal was reserved for those who had received circumcision and carried out the ritual ablutions, what characterizes the new age inaugurated by the Messias is that the ritual meal is open to all. This is true of the meals of Christ, and the Fathers show us that it is also true of the Eucharist of which the meals of Christ were figures.

We should make one further remark: that this aspect of being the ritual meal of the New Covenant appears not only in the significance but also in the very origin of the Eucharist. As we have noted, the allusion to Melchisedech might have determined the choice made by Christ of bread and wine; in the same way—and still more so—the character of a meal possessed by the Eucharist is seen to be a resumption of the ritual meal of the Old Testament. In fact, the meal in the course of which Christ instituted the Eucharist seems to have been a ritual meal, a *chaboura,* such as was customarily celebrated by the Jewish communities. The prayer of consecration in fact, takes up the prayer of blessing over the bread and wine which person presiding at the meal was accustomed to make during its course.[24] It was, then, in this framework of a sacred Jewish meal that Christ instituted the meal of the New Covenant, as it was in the framework of the Jewish commemoration of the Pasch that He died on the Cross. This fact brings out expressly the relationship at once of continuity and of difference between these sacred meals and the Eucharist.

We can now see the importance of these symbols for understanding the Eucharist. As the significance of the baptismal rites is clarified for us by reference to the Old Testament, so is that of the Eucharistic rites. If we wish to understand why it was in the form of a meal in which bread and wine are shared that Christ instituted the sacrament of His sacrifice, we must refer to the allusions to the Old Testament contained in these rites, allusions

[24] See Gregory Dix, *The Shape of the Liturgy,* pp. 59 to 120; Louis Bouyer, *La première eucharistie dans la dernière Cène,* La Maison-Dieu, XVIII, p. 34-37.

which were present to the mind of Christ, rather than to any symbolism that we might think up for ourselves. And so we shall have an opportunty to come to know the true meaning of these rites. And this search leads us to see in the bread and wine an allusion to the sacrifice of Melchisedech, to the manna in the desert, to the meal in the Temple; by this we understand that the Eucharist is a spiritual and universal sacrifice; that it is the nourishment of the people of God in their journey toward the land of promise; that it is, finally, the participation of all nations in the communion of divine blessings.

CHAPTER TEN

The Paschal Lamb

UP TILL now, we have been studying separately the biblical figures of Baptism, Confirmation and the Eucharist. But there are certain especially important biblical passages in which the whole process of Christian initiation is prefigured. These are Chapter XII of Exodus, Psalm XXII and the Canticle of Canticles. These passages play a special part in the Paschal liturgy, constituting the readings and the chant. It is easy to understand, therefore their relationship to the sacraments given during the Paschal night should have been examined with special care. We shall now study these passages in concluding our study of the sacraments, which each passage will cause us to consider again as a whole, in the light of a particular biblical viewpoint.

Christian initiation took place during the night before Easter Sunday. This very circumstance relates it directly to the Death and the Resurrection of Christ. But the Resurrection of Christ was already set in the framework of the Jewish feast of the Pasch. We can understand therefore why the liturgy of initiation is so filled with echoes of the Exodus. Now the celebration of the Jewish Pasch as a whole has two aspects capable of being considered as figures of Christian initiation. One of these is the series of events made up of the crossing of the Red Sea, followed by the eating of the manna and the drinking of the water flowing from the rock of Horeb. We have studied these different figures separately in connection with the sacraments of Baptism and the

Eucharist, as the New Testament itself invites us to see them symbolized in these events.

But there is a second series of events which has also been considered a figure of Christian initiation, the series made up of the anointing of the posts and lintels of the doors of the Hebrews with the blood of the Paschal lamb, to preserve the first-born from the destroying angel, an anointing which was accompanied by the eating of the lamb with unleavened bread and bitter herbs. These two aspects of the Pasch correspond to the two translations of the word *Pascha* given by the Fathers of the Church. The majority, following Philo, translate it by *diabasis,* "crossing," and understand it to mean the crossing of the Red Sea, but others, in particular Theodoret, express it by *hyperbasis* "to pass over," and understand it to mean, that the destroying angel passed over the houses marked with the blood of the lamb; [1] this is the meaning, moreover, which corresponds to the true significance of the word. It is under this second aspect, then, that we shall now consider the rites of the Pasch as a figure of Christian initiation.

It is perfectly obvious why the event of the destroying angel sparing the first-born of the houses marked with the blood of the lamb should be an outstanding symbol of redemption. We have here one of the essential *theologoumenon* of Scripture: the world is under the dominion of sin, judgment is to strike the guilty world, but God spares those who are marked with the Blood of Christ. But it is the sacramental aspect in which we now are especially interested. This event clearly has a relationship to Baptism. For one thing, it prefigures what Baptism accomplishes: man is a sinner: Baptism is a judgment which destroys man the sinner: but, because of the death of Christ, when sin has been destroyed, Baptism brings forth the new man. In this light, the event of the Pasch is analogous to that of the Deluge and that of Rahab as prefiguring one of the aspects of the Redemption and therefore of Baptism.

But the anointing with the blood of the Lamb is seen by the Fathers as prefiguring not only the content but also one of the rites of Baptism. As the figure of the Deluge connects the theme

[1] *Sacramentum futuri,* p. 182-183.

of death and resurrection with the water of Baptism, so that of the Lamb relates it to the *consignatio*. For as the anointing with the blood of the lamb on the doors of the houses put the destroying angel to flight, so the anointing made on the forehead of the candidates at Baptism puts the demon to flight. Thus the anointing with the blood prefigures the sacramental *sphragis*. What makes this figure especially striking is that the *sphragis* consists of the sign of the Cross marked on the forehead, and, as the Fathers have noted, the anointing of the lintels and doorposts formed a kind of cross. It was, then, the Cross of Christ which kept safe the first-born of the Jews as a figure of the Cross which saves Christians.

This comparison appears very early, our first witness being Justin: "Those who were saved in Egypt, were saved by the blood of the Pasch, with which they anointed doorposts and lintels. For the Pasch was Christ, Who was later immolated. And, as the blood of the Pasch saved those who were in Egypt, so the blood of Christ was to preserve from death those who have believed in Him. Does this mean that God would have made a mistake if this sign, *semeion,* was not found on the doors? No, but it announced in advance the salvation that was to come by the blood of Christ, by Whom are saved (the sinners) of all nations, when, having received pardon for their sins, they sin no more" (*Dial,* CXI, 4). The word "sign," means (for Justin) the sign of the Cross. It is this sign of the Cross made with blood that preserved the Jews; it is this sign which saves the sinners who are marked with it in Baptism.

This sacramental interpretation is still more precise in later writers. So we read in the *Paschal Homily* of Hippolytus of Rome: "The blood as a sign is the mystery (*mysterion*) in blood of the seal (*sphragis*) of Christ. The sign is not yet the reality, but a figure of the reality to come. All those who have this blood imprinted on their souls, as the Law commanded that it should be imprinted and put as an anointing on the houses of the Jews, all these will be passed over by the destroying plague. The blood is like a sign of those to be saved on houses as on souls,—which are, in fact, by faith and the Holy Spirit, a consecrated house. Such is the mystery of the cosmic and universal Pasch" (Nautin 143). Let us notice the precision of the paschal theology of this passage.

And also that *sphragis* here clearly means the baptismal *consignatio*. It is the sign of the Cross marked on the forehead which consecrates the soul; and by this paschal mystery, is extended to the whole cosmos of souls.[2]

The baptismal significance of this figure also appears in its use in the mystagogic catecheses. We find it in particular in Cyril of Jerusalem, applied to the renunciation of Satan accompanying the imposition of the sign of the Cross: "You must know that the symbol of the renunciation of Satan is found in ancient history. Indeed, when Pharoah, that harsh and cruel tyrant, oppressed the free and noble Hebrew people, God sent Moses to free them from the slavery of the Egyptians. The doorposts were anointed with the blood of the Lamb, so that the Destroyer might pass over the houses that had the sign (*semeion*) of the blood. Let us go now from these ancient things to new ones, from the figure (*tupos*) to the reality. There we have Moses sent by God into Egypt; here we have Christ sent by the Father into the world. There the task is to free the oppressed people from Egypt; here to rescue men tyrannized in the world by sin; there the blood of the lamb wards off the destroyer; here the Blood of the true Lamb, Jesus Christ, puts the demons to flight" (XXXIII, 1068 A).

This last point is of special interest. We have seen in fact, that it is one of the characteristics of the *sphragis* to make the demons flee; the allusion to the demons put to flight by the blood of Christ is, then, certainly related to the sacramental *sphragis*. Furthermore, the explicit relation of the blood of the Paschal lamb to the *sphragis* is found elsewhere. Gregory of Nyssa writes in his *Sermon on Baptism*, speaking of the Baptism of children: "It is better to be baptized without being aware of it than to die without having been marked with the seal (*sphragis*) and without being initiated. We have proof of this in circumcision, given on the eighth day, which is a kind of figurative *sphragis* and which was given to children lacking reason—and also in the anointing of the doors which preserved the first-born by means of realities of which they were not aware" (XXXVI, 400 A). The parallel made with circumcision, which is the essential figure of the baptismal *sphragis*, is characteristic. And also the idea that there is question of a material rite and not only of a spiritual act.

[2] See also Melito, *Homily on the Passion*, 67; Campbell-Bonner, p. 131.

The application of this figure to Baptism is most evident in Cyril of Alexandria. Commenting on the Jewish feast of the Pasch in *De Adoratione,* he writes: "That the sprinkling of the blood saves those who have received the anointing is established by the text where it says that the entrances of the houses should be anointed, that is to say, the posts and lintels of the doors: the sacrament of Christ indeed forbids the entrance to death and renders it inaccessible to him. This is why we also, anointed with the sacred blood, shall become stronger than death and despise corruption" (LXVIII, 1069 A). The anointing of the lintels is the figure of the sacrament which marks souls with the seal of Christ and thus preserves them from the coming of death. What the blood of the lamb once effected for the Jews, now Baptism does for Christians. For the effectiveness of the various sacraments cannot grow less" (LXVIII, 897 C).[3]

This teaching is present in a still more explicit fashion in the *Paschal Homilies* of Pseudo-Chrysostom, in which we recognize the tradition of Cyril of Alexandria. The second homily treats successively of the "sacrament of anointing" and of the "eating which makes present in us the divine body" (LIX, 727 B). The Pasch truly becomes a figure of the whole process of initiation. "The redemption accomplished by Christ becomes a saving sign (*semeion*) for those who share in it. And seeing this sign, God saves those who have been anointed by faith. For there is no other way to escape the destroying angel than by the blood of God, Who by love has poured out His blood for us. And by this blood, we receive the Holy Spirit. Indeed the Spirit and the blood are related in such a way that by the blood which is connatural to us, we receive the Spirit which is not connatural, and the gate to death is closed to our souls. Such is the *sphragis* of the blood" (LIX, 726 D-727 A).

Here we see a whole sacramental theology of the baptismal anointing prefigured by the anointing of the doors. The anointing of the forehead with the sign (*semeion*) of the Cross is the visible sign prefiguring the anointing with the Blood of the lamb. And this visible sign works an invisible effect. He who is marked with it is recognized by God and spared by the destroying angel. The Spirit is poured out on him, and this effusion of the Spirit is

[3] See also *Glaphyres;* P.G., LXIX, 428 A.

the reality of which the *sphragis* is the sign. He who has in himself the life of the Spirit is henceforth incorruptible and is no longer under the power of death. The connection with the *sphragis* and the Holy Spirit relates this figure even more closely with sacramental theology.[4] It is the double aspect of the *sphragis,* as the seal of the Cross and the seal of the Spirit which is here expressed.

Western theology is no less precise, giving us the most formal witness to the baptismal symbolism of the anointing of the doors. St. Augustine in *De catechizandis rudibus,* in proposing a model for the instruction to be given to candidates for Baptism, writes: "The Passion of Christ was prefigured by the Jewish people when they received the command to mark the doors of their houses with blood. It is by the sign of His Passion and Cross that you must be marked today on the forehead, as on a door, and that all Christians are marked" (P.L., XL, 335). The allusion is explicitly to the rite of the *sphragis* which took place during the preparation for Baptism, and in a general way to the sign of the Cross with which Christians were marked in the forehead.[5]

This study has caused us to discover a new aspect of the theology of the *sphragis.* It is a sign which turns aside the detroying angel, and thus it is an expression of the gratuitous love of God, sparing those who are marked with the blood of His Son. This is one of the chief aspects of the Redemption, and it is this aspect which is incorporated into the symbolism of the rite of the *sphragis* by means of the figure of the sign on the houses. We should also notice that this symbolism helps us to understand the external sign of the *sphragis,* which consists of the sign of the Cross on the forehead. This sign of the Cross is indirect relation with the blood of the Passion. It is this double aspect of the blood and of the Cross which constitutes the rite of the Jewish Pasch, and which is echoed by the Christian rite of the sign of the Cross, symbol of the blood of the Passion.[6]

[4] See above, pp. 63-64.

[5] See Lactantius, *Div. Inst.,* IV, 26; P.L., VI, 531: "The Lamb is Christ who saves those who bear on their forehead the sign of blood, that is to say of the Cross."

[6] We may note that the anointing with blood is sometimes interpreted of the Eucharist (Theodoret, *Quaest. Ex.,* XII, P.G., LXXX, 252 D; Cyril, *Glaphyres:* P.G., LXIX, 428 A).

We have just seen that Pseudo-Chrysostom takes the anointing of the doors and the eating of the lamb as being figures of Baptism and of the Eucharist. It is the second element that we are now to examine. But, in fact, the question is raised in an entirely different way. For as the anointing on the doors has been seen from the beginning to be a figure of Baptism, so the Eucharistic symbolism of the eating of the lamb has been seen as secondary. I say the *Eucharistic* symbolism. For the symbolic interpretation of the Paschal meal is one of the most ancient in Christianity, but the oldest tradition sees it more as a figure either of the circumstances of the Passion of Christ, or of the spiritual life of Christian. The sacramental interpretation came later.

Like the banquet of Wisdom and the meals in the Temple, the Paschal meal was considered in Judaism as a figure of the kingdom to come, considered as a messianic feast. "The thought of the Paschal meal," writes J. Leenhardt, "was dominated by the memory of the redemption that had already been accomplished and by the waiting for a new redemption which should fulfill definitely the virtualities of the first." [7] We find in the New Testament the echo of this eschatological interpretation: "I have greatly desired to eat this Pasch with you before I suffer. For, I say to you, I will eat it no more until it is fulfilled in the Kingdom of God" (Luke XXII:15). Thus the Pasch, eaten by Christ with His disciples before the Passion, is a figure of the messianic banquet to which Christ will invite His own in the Kingdom of the Father.

Nevertheless, it is quite clear that these words, spoken immediately before the institution of the Eucharist, are not related to it. Between the Jewish Paschal meal and the messianic banquet, the Eucharistic meal is an intermediate link. It is the anticipated realization of the messianic banquet prefigured by the Paschal meal. So the First Epistle of St. Peter, which may be an exhortation addressed to the newly baptized in the framework of the Pasch, describes the Christian life by drawing its inspiration from the ritual of the Jewish Pasch. "Having girded up the loins of your spirit, be sober, and set all your hope upon that grace which is brought to you in the revelation of Jesus Christ" (1 Peter I:13). But we see that here the circumstances of the Pasch are inter-

[7] F. J. Leenhardt, *Le sacrement de la Sainte Cène*, p. 21.

preted of the dispositions of the Christian soul and not of the Eucharist properly speaking. This interpretation is the one we meet in all ancient tradition.

The first text in which we find a precise allusion to the Eucharist in this connection is the *Paschal Homily* of Hippolytus: "You will eat in a house: there is one synagogue, there is one house, there is one Church in which the holy body of Christ is consumed" (41; N. 163). The interpretation of the house where the Pasch is to be eaten as being a figure of the unity of the Church is very old. We find it as early as Cyprian, together with the Ark of Noe and the house of Rahab (*De unit. Eccles.,* 8; C.S.E.L., 217). This allusion to the Church probably led Hippolytus to the symbolism of the Paschal meal as being a figure of the Eucharist. To take part in it, indeed, one must be "in the house," that is to say, in the Church. It is, then, the idea of the Eucharist as the sacrament of unity that is prefigured by the Paschal meal.

But it is with Cyril of Alexandria that the Eucharistic symbolism of the Paschal meal was fully developed. In the *Glaphyres,* he interprets the precept of eating the Pasch in the evening as meaning the fact that the sacramental Eucharist is reserved to this present life: the text prescribes that the meat should be eaten in the night, that is to say, in the present world. For this is what Paul called it, when he said: 'The night is passed, the day is coming.' By the day, he means the future age of which Christ is the light. The text, then, says that the meat should be eaten in this world. Indeed, as long as we are in this world, it is by the holy flesh and the precious blood that we communicate in Christ in a way that is still imperfect. But when we have come to the day of His power and have gone up into the splendor of the saints, we shall be sanctified in another way known to Him Who distributes future blessings" (LXIX, 428 B).

The Paschal meal, celebrated by the people while it was still night before the day of their liberation, is a figure also of the Eucharist, as being a form of communion with Christ in the present life and a figure of the feast of the world to come. St. Cyril also connects the character of the Eucharist with the relation of the paschal lamb to the death of Christ. "The communion in the holy body and the drinking of the saving blood contains the confession of the Passion and the death received for us by Christ, as

He said Himself in instituting for His own the laws of the sacrament: 'Whenever you eat this bread and drink of this chalice, you announce the death of the Lord.' In the present world, then, by communion in these realities, we announce His death; when we shall be in the glory of the Father, it will be time no longer to confess His Passion, but to contemplate Him purely, as God, face to face" (LXIX, 428 C).

So we see under what aspect the paschal meal causes us to consider the Eucharist. What characterizes this meal is the eating of the immolated lamb. And the slain lamb is the figure of Christ in His Passion, as St. John taught (19:36). In consequence, as being a paschal meal, the Eucharist is the sacrament of Christ as put to death. It is a memorial of the Passion. And this is precisely the sense of the passage from I Cor. XI, 26 that Cyril quotes. We can even ask ourselves whether this passage is not an allusion to Christ in the paschal framework of the institution of the Eucharist,—all the more because there are many of the paschal echoes in the First Epistle to the Corinthians.[8]

We see how the theological importance of the eucharistic theme of the paschal lamb begins to appear, little by little.

The *De Adoratione* takes up the themes of the *Glaphyres*. We find here again the contrast of the present life, which is the time of the sacraments, with the future life, the time of clear vision.[9] The relation of the Eucharist to the spiritual life is connected with an allegory of the lamb: "The fact that he who has taken part in Christ by the communion of His holy Body and Blood, should also have His spirit and live to enter into His interior dispositions in having the understanding of what is in Him, is suggested to us by the text when it says that the head of the lamb must be eaten together with the feet and the entrails. Indeed, is not the heart the figure of the spirit, the feet that of the good deeds to be done, and the *interiora* of the victims that of the interior hidden life" (LXVIII, 1072 A).

This allegory may seem strange to us, but ever since the third century we find that the different parts of the lamb are given a symbolic interpretation. Hippolytus understood the head and the heart to mean the divinity of Christ, the feet, His incarnation

[8] See T. S. Manson, ΙΛΑΣΤΗΡΙΟΝ J.T.S., 1945, p. 20 et seq.
[9] *De adoratione*, 17; P.G., LXVIII, 1073 A.

(29; Nautin, 155). Gregory of Nazianzen presents an analogous interpretation (P.G. XXXVI, 645 A). And we read also in Gaudence of Brescia: "See whether by the head you do not understand the divinity, by the feet, the Incarnation at the end of time, by the *interiora,* the hidden mysteries" (C.S.E.L., LXVIII, 27). The interpretation of Cyril is different, seeing in the head the thought of Christ, in the entrails the disposition of His heart, in the feet His works. So the Eucharist should consist in putting on the dispositions, the spirit, the ways of Christ. Here we have a first outline of a doctrine of the "interior life of Jesus Christ."

We have already noted several times the interrelationship between the *Paschal Homilies* of Pseudo-Chrysostom and the writings of St. Cyril. This interrelationship is again corroborated here. The second *Paschal Homily,* having compared Baptism to the anointing of the doors, shows that the paschal meal is a figure of the Eucharist. The prescriptions concerning the eating of the lamb are interpreted as the necessary dispositions for Communion. The Law forbids the eating of the meat raw. This would seem astonishing if we held only to the letter. Who would ever think of eating raw meat? But for us this has a great meaning; it signifies that we must not approach with negligence the Communion of the holy Body. It is not shared by those who use it without respect and do not respond by good works to union with Him. In the same way, those who transform the Eucharist into an abundant meal, making the sanctifying Communion a pretext for eating and drinking, are rejected by the Apostle, because they do not come in a holy way to that which is holy. So they are guilty of impiety, those who do not prepare their bodies for communion with the Body of Christ, which He has given to us so that, mingled together with Him, we may be made worthy to receive the Holy Spirit" (LIX, 727-728).

We should notice how the necessity is stressed of a right intention for the sacrament, which seems even to make it a condition of validity. And also we find the emphasis on the Spirit, which characterizes these Homilies. The author continues, commenting allegorically like Cyril on the parts of the lamb, but with a different symbolism: the head signifies the first coming of Christ, the feet, His final Parousia. The whole method of eating the paschal meal is all interpreted in connection with the Eucharistic communion. And furthermore this is explicitly affirmed: "The preparation of the holy food was thus prescribed by the Law in these symbols, and this prefiguration was prescribed in view of its use to us" (728 B). We recognize in this last word the phrase of St. Paul concerning the rock in the desert; our author extends the principle to the paschal meal.

We now see the characteristics of the Eucharistic typology of the paschal meal. For one thing, it is seen to be founded on the New Testament itself, by the fact that Christ instituted the Eucharist in the framework of a paschal meal. The figure is concerned not with the elements, which are different,—bread and wine, on the one hand, a lamb, on the other—but with the meal itself. This meal was, even in Judaism, "a sacrament of salvation." [10] But this sacrament was figurative. In the Eucharist, the reality which the lamb prefigured is henceforth present under the appearances of bread and wine. The Eucharist now is seen to be the eating of the true paschal lamb, and its relationship with the paschal meal permeates it with all the symbolic significance of the paschal lamb.

This is the second important characteristic of this typology. It brings out a most important aspect of the Eucharist, that is, its relation to the Passion of Christ. The paschal lamb is, in fact, the figure of the Passion, according to the New Testament; and inasmuch as it is prefigured by the paschal lamb and thought of in the paschal framework, the Eucharist is seen to be the sacrament of the Passion. This is what Cyril clearly saw. It is the memorial of the Passion, and, further, it is the participation in the mystery of the Death and Resurrection of Christ. The paschal lamb was the sacrament of the Old Covenant, recalling God's free choice of the people of Israel.[11] So the Eucharist is the "blood of the New Covenant, shed for the remission of sins," not only of the Jewish people, but 'of a great multitude'; it is the sacrament of the covenant concluded with mankind by Christ on the Cross.

Among the directions accompanying the paschal meal, we have not yet touched upon those dealing with the azymes (unleavened

[10] P. J. Leenhardt, *Le sacrement de la Sainte Cène,* p. 21.

[11] "The meaning of the Paschal feast was to make a living reality each year of the covenant established by the divine grace between Yahweh and Israel" (Leenhardt loc. cit., p. 19).

loaves) which were to be eaten with the lamb. These azymes appear in two places in the text of Exodus in connection with the Pasch: as part of the paschal meal, and as the food of the people during the seven following days. This last usage is the most ancient. The feast of the azymes is mentioned several times in the Pentateuch (*Ex.* XXIII:15; *Lev.* XXIX:6-8; *Num.* XXVIII:17; *Deut.* XVI:1-4). It was originally a feast distinct from the Pasch and also from the feast of the first-fruits. It began on the 15 nizan, the day after the Pasch, and lasted for seven days. From this feast, the use of the azymes was introduced into the ritual of the Pasch; the blending of the two is noted in Deuteronomy.

We shall leave aside the distinction between these two aspects of the azymes to study only the symbolism of the bread itself. It has a special importance in paschal symbolism, because it was interpreted figuratively in the New Testament. In the First Epistle to the Corinthians, in fact, whose numerous references to the Pasch we have already noticed, St. Paul writes: "Do you not know that a little leaven ferments the whole lump? Purge out the old leaven that you may be a new dough as you are really without leaven, for Christ, our passover, has been sacrificed. Therefore let us keep festival, not with the old leaven, nor with the leaven of malice and wickedness, but with the unleavened bread of sincerity and truth" (I Cor. V:7-8).

St. Paul derives his symbolism from the fact that the azymes were a bread with no leaven, and leaven was made with some of the old dough fermented. The azymes were the first bread made with the wheat from the new harvest, when there was no leaven as yet. Thus they were the symbol of newness of life. Eaten after the Pasch, the azymes signify that after the immolation of Christ, of which Christian have been made participants by Baptism, they are dead to the old life and live with a new. We should notice that these seven days correspond to the paschal week which followed Baptism, and that during this week the white robes of the newly baptized symbolized the newness of the life into which they had entered.

This symbolism of St. Paul was to direct all later developments. The azymes never appear as the figure of the Eucharist properly speaking, but they are connected with the symbolism of the initiation inasmuch as they represent the dispositions of the newly initiated. Thus, they are the figure of the time that follows the baptismal initiation, and, more generally, of Christian life. We should also note that the symbolism of the azymes as representing a pure life is anterior to Christianity. Already for Philo "the azymes are prescribed by the Law to revive the embers of the pure and austere life which was that of the first ages of mankind —the feast of the azymes, indeed, is the annual commemoration of the creation of the world—and to give admiration and honor to the simplicity and poverty of primitive existence" (*De Spec. leg.* II, 160). Christianity has attached this symbolism to the new creation achieved by Christ instead of seeing in it a commemoration of the first creation.

The oldest Christian writers understood the symbolism of the azymes in the Paulinian sense, without finding any direct bond with the sacraments; the azymes symbolize simply Christian life and its newness. So for Justin, "what the azymes signify is that you should no more do the old works of the evil leaven. But you have understood everything in a purely carnal sense—(he is speaking to the Jews)—that is why God commanded you to knead a new leaven, after the seven days of the unleavened bread, which signifies the practice of new works" (*Dial.* XIV, 3). The symbolism is concerned with the new leaven, which thus represents the new life brought by the Gospel. The symbolism of the new paste, now applied to Christ, is found in Hippolytus: "Let the Jews, then, eat the azymes for seven days, let them strive on during the seven ages of the world. But as for us, Christ our Pasch is sacrificed, and we have received a new paste from His holy mixing" (39; Nautin, 161).

Here again, it is with Cyril of Alexandria that the relationship of the symbolism of the azymes and of the Eucharist is most clearly expressed. Not that he sees the azymes as symbols of the Eucharist, but he shows that they symbolize the life of the man who participates in the Eucharist. So in the *Glaphyres:* "The text prescribed that the Jews eat unleavened bread, signifying figuratively that those who have partaken of Christ should nourish their souls with desires unleavened and pure, making themselves familiar with a way of life that is innocent and with no admixture of malice" (LXIX, 429 A). We are again in the line of St.

Paul's thought, only with a more explicit allusion to the Eucharist.

The *De Adoratione* further develops the same idea: "We all, who have been sanctified and who have partaken of eternal life in the sacramental mode, we should try unceasingly to keep the law established for the Pasch. Indeed, we should not cease to celebrate the feast in Christ, doing away with all leaven from our territories, that is, from every land where we have to dwell. Nay, those who have been called to faith and to justice, who are in Christ, spiritually celebrating the feast, should not do so in the leaven of malice and sin, but, on the contrary, purifying the old leaven, should transform themselves into something better, and come forth as a new paste, with all their family and all their household, which means the immense crowd of those who have received the faith" (LXVIII, 1076 C).

Here we are in the purest line of Pauline thought. It is the more curious, therefore, to see that Cyril later goes back to a theme of Philo: "The text says that the first day of the week is to be called holy, showing this, I think, that the era of the origins of human existence was holy, in Adam our first father, when he had not yet violated the commandments. But holy and far greater is the time of the end of the world, that of Christ, Who is the second Adam, restoring our race after the misfortunes which happened in the middle era, to newness of life" (LXVIII, 1076 D). This striking text synthesizes perfectly the Philonian idea of the azymes as a symbol of the primitive age, with the Paulinian idea of the azymes as a symbol of the times that follow Christ, and so sums up the symbolic meaning of the azymes.[12]

From what has been said, we can see how the mystery of the Pasch lent itself in a very special way to prefiguring the Christian initiation. The further coincidence of the date of the Jewish Pasch with that on which Baptism was usually given invited this connection. But this coincidence itself did not come about by chance; it expresses a relationship between the two realities. For it is, in fact, the same mystery which is accomplished in both, that of the destroying angel sparing those who are marked with

[12] In these passages, Cyril is speaking of the Feast of the Azymes. When he is commenting on the azymes of the paschal meal, he sees in them the dispositions necessary for communion rather than those which follow it (*Ho. Pasch.*, XIX; P.G. LXXVII,, 825 A).

the blood, and that of the meal commemorating the covenant thus made. Thus, patristic tradition did no more than make precise a doctrine which is written in the events themselves before being written down in the Scriptures which report these events, and this doctrine is the expression of the unity of the plan of God revealed by the correspondences between the two covenants.

CHAPTER ELEVEN

Psalm XXII

IN READING the ancient catecheses, we are struck by the number and the importance of the allusions to Psalm XXII. For example, in the Fourth *Mystagogic Catechesis,* St. Cyril of Jerusalem writes: "Blessed David makes us know the power of the sacrament (the Eucharist) when he says: 'You have prepared a table before my eyes in the face of those who persecute me.' What does he mean by this, but the sacramental (*mystike*) and spiritual table that God has prepared for us. 'You have anointed my head with oil.' He has anointed your head on the forehead, by the *sphragis* of God which you have received, so that you may be imprinted with the *sphragis,* consecration to God. And you see also that he mentions the chalice, over which Christ when He had given thanks: 'This is the chalice of my blood' " (XXXIII, 1101 D-1104 A).

We see also that for Cyril the Psalm is considered to be a prophecy of Christian initiation. In the anointing with oil, he finds the postbaptismal *sphragis* made with consecrated oil; in the table and the chalice—and the chalice that inebriates me, how wonderful it is,—he shows us the figure of the two species of the Sacrament. We shall return to these figures later, but what we wish now to point out here is that Cyril alludes to the texts as if it were well known to the newly baptized. He seems to suppose that the Psalm had made the candidate acquainted in advance with the sacraments given to him during the paschal night, so that Cyril now need only explain to him the prophetic meaning of the Psalm.

This is explicitly affirmed by St. Ambrose, who also comments on this Psalm in his two catecheses: "Hear what sacrament you have received, hear David who is speaking to you. He also foresaw in spirit these mysteries and exulted and declared that he wanted for nothing. (1st Verse) Why? Because he who has received the Body of Christ hungers no longer. How many times have you heard Psalm 22 without understanding it? See how it fits the heavenly sacraments" (*De Sacr.* V, 12-13; Botte 91). The teaching here is more precise. The newly baptized has often "heard the Psalm without understanding it." It had, then, a part in the liturgy of Baptism.

Other texts help us to find more exactly what this part was. Didymus of Alexandria writes in the *De Trinitate:* "To those to whom earthly blessings are not given by reason of their age, the divine wealth is given in all its fullness, so that they can sing with joy: 'The Lord leads me and nothing is lacking to me' (XXXIX, 708 C). So the Psalm must have been sung by the newly baptized. We can go even further and learn from a passage of St. Ambrose at what point it was sung: "Having put out the stains of the old error, his 'youth renewed like the eagle's,' he hastens toward the heavenly banquet. He arrives and, seeing the altar prepared, he cries out: 'You have prepared a table before me' " (*De Myst.* 43; Botte, 121). Psalm XXII must, then, have been sung during the procession that conducted the newly-baptized in the paschal night to the church where they were about to make their first Communion.

We can see how the Psalm must have seemed appropriate to be sung at this moment, for it is a kind of summing-up of the whole process of baptismal initiation. We have a brief commentary of Gregory of Nyssa which shows us clearly how it could have been so considered: "By this Psalm, Christ teaches the Church that first of all you must become a sheep of the Good Shepherd; the catechesis leads you toward the pastures and the springs of doctrine. Then you must be buried with Him in His death by Baptism. But this is not death itself, but the shadow and the image of death. After this, He prepares the sacramental table. Then He anoints you with the oil of the Spirit. And, finally, He brings the wine that rejoices man's heart and produces the sober intoxication" (XLVI, 692 A-B) [1]

Here we have the model of the explanation of Psalm XXII which must have been given in the baptismal catechesis. Actually the text of Gregory of Nyssa only gives us in more complete form what we already found in the *Mystagogic Catechesis* of Cyril of Jerusalem. We know, then, that the Psalm was sung during the paschal night—and certainly also under other circumstances during the course of initiation—and further, from very ancient times, it was explained during the week of Easter. The commentary on the Psalm is, in fact, related to two other commentaries given at this time: those on the Canticle of Canticles, and on the Our Father. These three texts represented three hidden teachings whose meaning could only be given to the baptized.[2]

But a final question may be raised. If the baptized were to sing the Psalm during the paschal night, they must have already learned it. This is what Eusebius suggests: "When we have learned to make the memorial of the sacrifice on the table with the sacramental signs of the Body and Blood, according to the prescriptions of the New Covenant, we have learned to say by the voice of the Prophet David: 'You have prepared a table before me in the sight of those who persecute me. You have anointed my head with oil.' In these verses, the Word clearly designates the sacramental anointing and the holy sacrifices of the table of Christ" (*Dem. Ev.* 1, 10). This text confirms the fact that the words of the Psalm were sung at the moment when the newly-baptized came to assist for the first time at the Eucharistic sacrifice. It makes us certain also that the words of the Psalm had already been learned by heart.

We have also been told, in the case of one liturgy at least, under what circumstances the Psalm was learned. In a sermon wrongly attributed to St. Augustine, we have an explanation of the Psalm which was intended to accompany its *traditio:* "We have given you this psalm, O well-beloved who are hastening toward the Baptism of Christ, so that you may learn it by heart. For this is necessary, because of its hidden meaning (*mysterium*)

[1] This parallelism between Psalm XXII and initiation appears for the first time in Origen, (Hans Lewy, *Sobria ebrietas,* p. 127).

[2] Later on, Psalm XXII, like the Pater, was to be explained before Baptism.

which we shall explain to you by the light of divine grace" (P. L., XXXIX, 1646). We know that in the course of the Lenten preparation there was a *traditio* of the *Credo* and often of the *Pater,* which was to be learned by heart and then recited (*redditio*). And this text shows us that the same was true of Psalm XXII

Furthermore, in a series of discourses on the Psalms, studied by Dom Morin,[3] we find an explanation of Psalm XXII with similar directions, which must have been given to the aspirants for Baptism on the occasion of the rite of the *traditio:* "Learn by heart the verses of this Psalm," says the author, "and recite them aloud." And further on: "Keep this Psalm that has been given (*traditum*) you, so that, in possessing it by mouth, you may realize it in your life, your words and your manners." And the text continues with a sacramental explanation of the Psalm: the "table prepared" is the Eucharistic altar on which the bread and the wine are shown every day *in similitudinem corporis at sanguinis Christi.* The perfume spread over the head is the oil of the chrism, from which Christians take their name. These two texts, then, witness to the existence of a *traditio* of Psalm XXII. And we know that, in the liturgy of Naples at least, there was a *traditio psalmorum,* which certainly took place on the fourth Sunday of Lent.[4]

We have said that Psalm XXII was considered by the Fathers to be a mysterious summing up of the successive sacraments of initiation. We shall now see how tradition conceived the typological interpretation of its various verses, and later on, we shall study the bases for this interpretation. Verse 2 speaks of the pastures to which the Shepherd leads His sheep. St. Gregory of Nyssa sees in these pastures the catechesis preparatory to Baptism, in which the soul is nourished with the word of God. This interpretation is earlier found in Origen, who sees in the act of being led to green pastures, the instruction given by the Shepherd.[5] St. Cyril of Alexandria is even more precise: "The place of green pastures should be understood of the words that are always fresh

[3] *Études sur une série de discours d'un evêque de Naples au VIe siecle,* Rev. Bened., 1894, p. 385 et seq.
[4] Dom Morin, loc. cit., p. 400; A. Dondeyne, *La discipline des scrutins,* Rev. Hist. Eccles., 1932, p. 20-21.
[5] Co. Cant., 2; P.G., XIII, 121 B.

and green, the words of inspired Holy Scripture, which nourishes the hearts of believers and gives them spiritual strength." [6] This interpretation certainly concerns the word of God, but without special reference to the catechesis. Finally, Theodoret writes that by pastures Scripture means, "the holy doctrine of the divine words, with which the soul is to be nourished before coming to the sacramental food." [7]

Verse 3 is, in general, to be understood of Baptism; "He leads me beside waters of peace." Thus, we read in St. Athanasius: "The water of repose without doubt signifies holy Baptism by which the weight of sin is removed" (XXVII, 140 B). Cyril of Alexandria connects the place of pasture with the water of repose: "The place of pasture is the Paradise from which we fell, to which Christ leads us and establishes us by the water of rest, that is to say, by Baptism" (loc. cit., 841 A). Theodoret gives the same interpretation: "The water of rest is the symbol of that in which he who seeks grace is baptized: he strips himself of the old age of sin and he recovers his youth" (loc., cit., 1025 D). What is interesting here is that these commentaries are not mystagogic, from which it appears that the Psalm was interpreted in a general way in the sacramental sense.

Besides the tradition that sees Baptism symbolized in verse 2, there is another which connects it with verse 3: "Though I walk through the valley of the shadow of death, I fear no evil." This is the meaning found in Gregory of Nyssa: "You must be buried in death with Him by Baptism. But it is not death itself, but a shadow and an image of death" (XLVI, 692 B). It is noteworthy that Cyril speaks in the same way: "Since we are baptized in the death of Christ, Baptism is called a shadow and an image of death, which is not to be feared" (loc. cit. 841 B). We recognize here the sacramental typology of Baptism, a ritual imitation of the Death of Christ, accomplished by the immersion in the water, which produces the real effect of that Death.

The following verse is understood to refer to the outpouring of the Holy Spirit: "Thy rod and thy staff are my guide." The word "guide" translates the Greek *paraklesis,* and this is why an al-

[6] P.G., LXIX, 841 A.

[7] P.G., LXXX, 1025 C. See also Ambrose, *Exp. Psalm.*, CXVIII, XIV, 2; C.S.E.L., LXII, 299.

lusion to the Paraclete was seen in the verse.[8] So St. Gregory of Nyssa writes: "Then He guides him by the staff of the Spirit: for indeed the Paraclete (he who guides) is the Spirit" (loc. cit. 692 B).[9] But, more generally, the pouring out of the Spirit is connected with verse 5; "Thou hast anointed my head with oil." So for St. Cyril of Jerusalem: "He has anointed your head with oil on the forehead, by the seal which you receive from God, so that you may take the imprint of the seal" (XXXIII, 1102 B). In the same way, St. Athanasius writes: "This verse indicates the sacramental chrism" (loc. cit. 140 C). Theodoret is still more explicit: "These things are clear for those who have been initiated and have no need for any explanation. They recognize the spiritual oil with which their heads were anointed" (loc. cit. 1028 C).

Thus, the Fathers were pleased to find the sacraments of Baptism and Confirmation prefigured in the first verses of Psalm XXII. And besides, the last verses showed them a figure of the Eucharistic banquet. First, the application of verse 5: "Thou hast prepared a table before me." The application to the Eucharist is found everywhere, so frequently that it is one of the most usual figures. We find it in the sacramental catecheses:—In St. Paul of Jerusalem: "If you wish to know the effect of the sacrament, ask blessed David, who says: 'Thou hast prepared a table before me, in the face of those who persecute me.' See what he wishes to say. Before Your coming, the demons prepared for men filthy tables, full of diabolic powers. But when You came, O Lord, You prepared a table before me, which is none other than the sacramental and spiritual table which God has prepared for us" (XXXIII, 1102 B).[10]

As we have seen, St. Ambrose puts this same verse on the lips of the newly baptized coming before the altar to assist at Mass for the first time: "He comes near, and, seeing the holy altar made

[8] The Greek word παρακαλεῖν in the Old Testament sometimes means 'to guide.' It is thus a fitting word to use here in connection with the shepherd's crook (see Ex., XV, 3; Is., XLIX, 10). It is also one of the aspects of the Paraclete in the N.T. (John, XVI, 13). See C. K. Barrett, *The Holy Spirit in the Fourth Gospel,* J.T.S., 1950, pp. 1-16.

[9] For Ambrose (De Sacramentis, V, 13; Botte 95) and Theodoret (LXXX, 1028 B) this means the seal of the Cross marked on the baptized, which puts the demons to flight.

[10] In the *First Catechesis,* addressed to the catechumens, Cyril understands this verse as meaning the catechesis (XXXIII, 377 B).

ready, he cries out: 'Thou hast prepared a table before me' " (*De Myst.*, 43; Botte, 121). In the same way, St. Gregory of Nyssa says: "He prepares the sacramental table" (loc. cit., 692 B). We find the same figure in Athanasius (loc. cit., 140 D). St. Cyril makes it more precise: "The sacramental table is the flesh of the Lord, which fortifies us against our passions and the demons. Indeed Satan fears those who take part with reverence in the mysteries" (loc. cit., 841 C). And for Theodore of Mopsuestia, "it is the sacramental nourishment that He offers to us, He who has been established as our Shepherd" (loc. cit., 1028 C).

If the table prepared by the Shepherd is considered a figure of the Eucharistic banquet, this is even more true of the "overflowing cup," or, as the Septuagint translates it, of the "inebriating chalice," which He offers to His own. The application of the second part of verse 5: "My cup brims over" to the Eucharist is of ancient date and most important, since we find it in St. Cyprian [11] among the chief figures of the Eucharist: "The same figure (of the Eucharist) is expressed in the Psalms by the Holy Spirit, when He mentions the chalice of the Lord: 'Your inebriating chalice, how wonderful it is.' But the inebriation that comes from the chalice of the Lord is not like that given by profane wine. The chalice of the Lord inebriates in such a way that it leaves us our reason" (*Epist.* LXIII, 11).

We will return shortly to the question of the inebriation produced by the Eucharistic wine. Let us only note here that the expression *"calix praeclarus"* became so embodied in the Eucharistic liturgy as to form part of the Canon of the Roman Mass: "Accipiens et hunc *praeclarum* calicem." The connection between the cup of the Psalm and the chalice of the Supper was explicitly made by St. Cyril of Jerusalem in his Eucharistic catechesis: " 'How admirable is Your chalice that inebriates.' You see that this refers to the chalice which Jesus took in His hands and over which He gave thanks, before saying: This is My blood which shall be shed for many unto the remission of sins' " (XXXIII, 1104 A). In the same way, St. Athanasius interprets this verse as meaning "sacramental joy" (loc. cit., 140 D).

We must return to an important point, that of the expression

[11] Before this it appears in Origen (*Co. Mth. Ser.*, 85, P.G., XIII, 1734; *Co. Cant.*, 3; Baehrens, 184).

"inebriating" connected with the chalice. This is, in fact, the source of numerous developments emphasizing one aspect of the Eucharist, the aspect signified by the wine. The Eucharist produces spiritual effects analogous to those of wine, that is to say, spiritual joy, forgetfulness of the things of earth, ecstasy. But it does not produce these spiritual effects as wine produces its results. The inebriation given by the Eucharistic wine is a "sober inebriation," and we know that this is a traditional expression for denoting mystical states, found for the first time in Philo.[12] The interesting point is that this expression is found in a sacramental context, and brings out one aspect of the sacramental theology of the Fathers, that is, its relation to the mystical life.

A moment ago, we put to one side the end of the quotation from St. Cyprian. Having shown that the verse of the Psalm is a figure of the Eucharist, he continues: "But the inebriation which comes from the chalice of the Lord is not like that produced by common wine. This is why the text adds: 'It is truly wonderful.' The chalice of the Lord, indeed, inebriates in such a way that it leaves us our reason; it leads souls to spiritual wisdom; by it each comes from a taste for profane things to the understanding of the things of God. Finally, as common wine releases the spirit, sets the soul free and banishes all sorrow, so the use of saving Blood and of the chalice of the Lord banishes the memory of the old man, bestows forgetfulness of profane living, sets the soul at ease, by placing the joy of the divine goodness in the sad and gloomy heart which before was weighed down by the load of sin" (*Epist.*, LXIII, 11).

St. Ambrose also in his sacramental catecheses develops the theme of the sober inebriation, without quoting this Psalm, although in other places he gives it a sacramental meaning. But in his explanation of Psalm CXVIII,[13] he takes up the same theme using the same expressions in connection with this verse, so that the sacramental sense of the passage is made certain: "The chalice of the Lord gives remission of sins, the chalice in which the Blood is shed which has redeemed the sins of the whole world. This chal-

[12] See Hans Lewy, *Sobria ebrietas*, p. 3-34.

[13] J. Quasten, *Sobria ebrietas in Ambrosius De Sacramentis*, mel. Mohlberg, I. p. 117-125.

ice has inebriated the nations, so that they no longer remember their own sadness and forget their ancient error. This is why this spiritual inebriation is good, not affecting our physical powers, but lifting up the soaring spirit; the inebriation of the chalice is good, for its does away with the sadness of a sinful conscience and pours out the joy of everlasting life. This is why Scripture says: 'And Thy inebriating chalice is wonderful' " (*Exp. Ps.* CXVIII, 21, 4; C.S.E.L., 62, 475).[14]

Johannes Quasten remarks very rightly that here we find the same characteristics as in the *De Sacramentis:* the relation to the Cup of the Supper, the remission of sins. We should notice that the emphasis is placed, not on the mystical aspect, but on the conversion properly so called effected by Christian initiation. The Eucharist brings about the forgetfulness of past errors; it transports us into a new world; and this world is one of spiritual joy. This theme is dear to St. Ambrose. We find it again associated with Psalm XXII in other passages of his work. So in the *Exposition of Psalm I:* "Those who drink in figure have their thirst abated, those who drink in fact are inebriated. How good is the inebriation that gives eternal life. Therefore drink of this cup of which the prophet says: 'And his inebriating chalice, how admirable it is' " (C.S.E.L., 64, 8). See also *De Helia et jejunio,* 10, 33; C.S.E.L., 32, 429).

St. Gregory of Nyssa also gives an important place to the theme of the "sober inebriation."[15] In his sacramental catechesis on Psalm 22, he says: "In giving it the wine that rejoices man's heart, Christ produces in the soul this sober inebriation which raises the dispositions of the heart from passing things to what is eternal; 'And my inebriating chalice, how wonderful it is.' He, indeed, who has tasted this inebriation, exchanges that which is ephemeral for that which has no end, and lives in the house of the Lord all the days of his life" (XLVI, 692 B). It is in this passage of St. Gregory that the relationship of the Eucharist to mystical inebriation is best described. As H. Lewy has well noted, the *sobria ebrietas* means to St. Gregory the mystical ex-

[14] Loc. cit., p. 123.

[15] Jean Daniélou, *Platonisme et théologie mystique,* pp. 290-294.

perience, but this mystical experience is rooted in the Eucharistic life.[16]

So far we have considered Psalm XXII as occupying a particularly important place in the liturgy of initiation. But we have not yet brought out exactly what gives a special character to the typology of Psalm XXII, and this is what we are now to study. For there is one feature which we have already encountered, but have not especially noted, that is, the pastoral setting of this Psalm. It is in green pastures, a figure of heavenly food, that the Messias, under the form of a Shepherd, leads the sheep who make up his flock. And here we find a theme which was particularly dear to primitive Christianity,—we have already seen how widespread was the idea of the baptized as being sheep branded with the mark of Christ.[17]

This idea is already well defined in Origen. The pagans are the prey of bad shepherds, who are the gods of the gentiles: these are "flocks set under pastors who are angels" (Co. Cant. 2; P. G., XIII, 120 A). This is an ancient idea appearing as early as the *Book of Henoch* in which the seventy shepherds are the divinities of the pagan nations. Christ is the Good Shepherd (John X:11) Who comes "to separate His sheep from their companions and to make them feed apart from the others in order to have them enjoy His ineffable sacraments" (119 D). The Psalm shows us the Shepherd who first instructs the sheep with His teaching, in leading them into His pastures, then "He leads them from the pastoral meadows to the water of peace, and afterwards to the spiritual food and to the mysterious sacraments" (121 A). We find here the style of Origen, emphasizing the spiritual aspect more than the rite itself, but allusion is clearly made to the Christian initiation of the ancient pagans.

The connection between the sacraments and the pastoral theme is found elsewhere. St. Gregory of Nyssa writes: "In the Psalm, David invites you to be a sheep whose Shepherd is Christ, and who lacks nothing good, you for whom the Good Shepherd be-

[16] H. Lewy, loc. cit., p. 136. We may also quote John Chrysostom: "The chalice of our inebriation is wonderful. What is it? It is the spiritual chalice, the chalice of salvation, the chalice of the blood of the Lord. This chalice does not induce drunkenness but sobriety" (*De Res.*, II; P.G., L, 455 A).

[17] See above, pp. 55-57.

comes at once pasturage, water of rest, food, dwelling, way and guide, distributing His grace according to your needs. By this He teaches the Church that you should first become a sheep of the Good Shepherd, Who will lead you by the catechesis of salvation to the meadows and to the springs of sacred teachings" (XLVI, 692 A). In the same way, Cyril of Alexandria sees in the Psalm, "the song of converted pagans become disciples of God, who, spiritually nourished and satisfied, express their gratitude to their Leader for this saving food, calling Him Shepherd and father. For they have for guide not merely a saint, as Israel had Moses, but the prince of Pastors and the Master of doctrine, in Whom are all the treasures of wisdom and knowledge" (LXIX, 840 C).

But we should take into account an element of which we have not so far spoken. The influence of Psalm XXII on primitive Christian worship is shown, not only in the liturgical texts, but also in pictorial representations. Various recent studies, in fact, have gone to show that the representation of the Good Shepherd is particularly frequent in the ancient baptistries. We might ask the reason for this, and the authors of these studies all agree in seeing it to be the result of the influence of Psalm XXII.[18] It is through the medium of this Psalm, whose importance in the baptismal liturgy we have already studied, that the sacramental and pastoral themes are united. It is because of this Psalm that Christ was by preference presented to the newly-baptized as their Shepherd. So they saw reproduced before their eyes the same mystery which they celebrated in the Psalm.

In the baptistry of Dura, "the back of the apse in which the baptismal font is found is decorated with the figure of the Good Shepherd leading His flock. At His feet, to the left, the fall of the first human couple is reproduced on a smaller scale."[19] The theme of the Shepherd seems certainly to have been taken from Psalm XXII, although, as Msgr. de Bruyne has well observed, the connection with Adam here suggests, first of all, the theme of Christ giving His life for His sheep, as St. John shows him to us.[20] But in other baptistries the allusion to Psalm XXII is made more

[18] J. Quasten, *Das Bild des Guten Hirten in den altchristlichen Baptistieren, Pisciculi,* 1939, pp. 220-244; L. de Bruyne, La décoration des baptistères paléochrétiens, Mélanges Mohlberg, 1948, p. 188-198.

[19] De Bruyne, loc. cit., p. 189.

[20] Id., p. 199.

precise. So in the Baptistry of Naples "we do not find the Shepherd pictured, as at Dura, carrying the sheep on His shoulders, but the Shepherd at rest in a paradisal setting, with His sheep and flowers and springs. Peace and refreshment make up the atmosphere which reigns near the Good Shepherd." [21]

Moreover—and I do not think that any one has so far remarked upon this fact—we know that it was at Naples that the *traditio* of Psalm XXII formed part of the initiation of Baptism. And also the setting of the fresco corresponds much more to Psalm XXII than to John X. It is, then, quite possible that in this case it was the Psalm that inspired the picture. The descriptions we possess both of the baptistry of the Lateran and of that of the Vatican show us that such representations were common in the West. But we have a witness that is still more precise and entirely conclusive. For even today above the baptistry of Neon at Ravenna one can read this inscription: [22]

In locum pascuae, ibi me collocavit
Per acquam refectionis educavit me.

These are verses 1 and 2 of Psalm XXII;—their relation with the pastoral decoration of the baptistry is therefore evident.

We can now reconstruct the origin and establish the foundation for the interpretation of Psalm XXII. The Old Testament had a doctrine of the Shepherd Who should come at the end of time to gather together the scattered sheep of the house of Israel. This Shepherd would lead His sheep into marvellous pastures where springs gushed and green things grew in abundance; and these are described in terms which recall both the trees of Paradise and the springs of Exodus.[23] The New Testament teaches us that this eschatological figure is fulfilled in Christ. He is the Good Shepherd Who gives His life for His sheep and leads them to pasture (John X:10-11). The Fathers of the Church expressly state that He is the Shepherd announced by the prophets, applying to Him those texts (Cyprian, Test., 1, 14; C.S.E.L., 14). Here we find once more the great principle of the typology of the New Testa-

[21] Id., p. 197-198.
[22] Id., p. 198.
[23] See in particular Isaias, XLIX, 10; Ezechiel, XXXIV, 1 et seq.; Zacharias, XI, 4 et seq.

ment, which properly consists in affirming that the eschatological realities are fulfilled in Christ.

Psalm XXII is a liturgical development which, as we may well think, is not unrelated to the theme of the Prophets.[24] Its purpose, then, is to announce the Shepherd of eschatology, and this theme links up with that of the eschatological repast which we studied in the preceding chapter. We have here, then, the theme of the messianic meal with a pastoral coloring. The Fathers of the Church show us this theme as realized in two different, but parallel ways. First, there is the theme of the Good Shepherd who fights against the powers of evil, triumphs over them and leads His sheep into the pastures of Paradise,—and this theme appears in the setting of death and of martyrdom. M. Quasten has pointed out, in fact, that the theme of the Good Shepherd, apart from its use in baptistries, appears most frequently on tombs.[25]

This is shown in the prayers of the liturgy of the dead. Christ is the shepherd who rescues the sheep from the devouring wolves, the demons, who were trying to forbid its entrance to heaven. The most remarkable text, in particular because of its archaic character, is that of the *Passion of Perpetua and Felicity*. In her first vision, Perpetua saw a ladder rising up to heaven, on which a dragon was lying. In spite of him, she succeeded in reaching the top: "And I saw an immense garden, and in the midst a man sitting, with white hair, in the dress of a shepherd, milking the sheep, and men clad in white by the thousands surrounding him. He called me and gave me a mouthful of cheese which he pressed. I took it with joined hands and ate it" (IV, 8-10). The heavenly Paradise is presented, in the setting of Psalm XXII, as a smiling garden in which the Shepherd is standing surrounded by sheep and by men clothed in the white tunic of the baptized, who receive the heavenly Eucharist.

If we wish to convince ourselves of the antiquity of this representation of the heavenly Shepherd welcoming the saints into the everlasting pastures, it is sufficient to refer to the first text devoted to martyrdom, the *Apocalypse* of St. John. Here we meet a vision strangely resembling that of Perpetua, and this fact may be a sign

[24] See A. Robert, *Les attaches littéraires de Prov.*, I-IX, Rev. Bib., 1934, p. 374 et seq.

[25] J. Quasten, *Der Gute Hirte in frühchristlicher Toten liturgie und Grabenkunst*, Misc. Mercati, I, p. 373 et seq.

of the influence that Psalm XXII already had exercised on eschatological representations. We read in Chapter VII: "Those who are clothed in white robes are those who have come out of great tribulation. These have washed their robes and made them white in the blood of the Lamb. And He Who is seated on the throne shall bring them into His tent; they will no more hunger or thirst. For the Lamb who is in the midst of them will be their Shepherd and will lead them to the springs of the water of life" (VII:13-17).

But the Christian message is not only that of heavenly salvation, but of salvation already gained by Baptism and the Eucharist. So we see that the eschatological typology of Psalm XXII has also a sacramental form,—and it is this which we have been studying. But it is important to retrace its origin: the heavenly feast to which the Shepherd invites the sheep in the eternal pastures is already fulfilled in an anticipated way in the sacraments. It is, then, perfectly legitimate for the Fathers of the Church to show us that the waters of rest in Psalm XXII are the figure of Baptism, the table prepared, that of the Eucharistic feast, the inebriating chalice, that of the Precious Blood.

One of the conclusions which we can draw from this study is the influence exercised by the Old Testament on the representative art of primitive Christianity. M. Cerfaux has shown how the *theologoumenon* of the Redemption, as the annihilation and exaltation of the Servant, comes from Isaias LIII. We shall see further that the theology of the Ascension and of the seating of Christ at the right hand of the Father comes from Psalm CIX. And we see here how Psalm XXII has influenced the eschatological and sacramental representations of ancient Christianity. It has been the model of the representations expressed in the frescoes in the catacombs and the visions of the martyrs. It has also furnished the themes in which the first Christians loved to represent their first initiation and of which the paintings in the catacombs bear witness. And it is this Psalm which the Roman Mass still echoes today when it exalts the wonderful chalice containing the Blood of Christ which gives 'the sober inebriation.' "

CHAPTER TWELVE

The Canticle of Canticles

THE prophets of the Old Testament represented the covenant between Yahweh and Israel in the desert of the Exodus as being a marriage covenant. But this union was only the figure of a more perfect union which was to take place at the end of time, in the New Exodus: "I will lead her into the desert and I will speak to her heart" (Osee II:11, 16). Now the Canticle of Canticles is for certain exegetes the prophecy of this future marriage,[1] the epithalamion of the eschatological wedding of the Lamb described in the Apocalypse "I saw the New Jerusalem coming down from heaven, prepared as a bride adorned for her husband" (21:2). The New Testament shows us this eschatological marriage as fulfilled by the Incarnation of the Word in which He contracted an indissoluble alliance with human nature (John III:29). This marriage will be finally realized when the Bridegroom returns at the end of time and the souls of the just form a wedding escort to go forth to meet Him (Mat. XXV: 1-3).

But between its inauguration and its completion at the Parousia, the marriage of Christ and the Church continues—and does so in her sacramental life. This is another aspect of the theology of initiation, the nuptial aspect, and it by no means is least important. It holds good both for Baptism and for the

[1] See A. Robert, *Le genre littéraire du Cantique des Cantiques,* Vivre et penser, (Rev. Bibl.), III, 1944, p. 192 et seq.

Eucharist,[2] and we have many witnesses to it in connection with both sacraments. Concerning Baptism, this theme is found for the first time in Tertullian: "When the soul comes to the faith, re-created of water and the Holy Spirit by its second birth, it is received by the Holy Spirit. The flesh accompanies the soul in this wedding with the Spirit. O blessed marriage, if it allows no adultery" (*De anima,* XLI, 4; Waszink 57-58. See also *De res. Carn.* 63). The same idea is found in Origen: "Christ is called the Bridegroom of the soul, Whom the soul espouses when she comes to the faith" (*Ho. Gen.* X, 4; Baehrens, 98). We should notice that for Tertullian the Bridegroom is the Holy Spirit, for Origen, Christ.[3] In the fourth century, Didymus the Blind writes: "In the baptismal pool, He Who made our soul takes it for His Bride" (*De Trin.* P. G. XXXIX, 692 A). And the Eucharist also is presented as a marriage union between Christ and the soul: "Christ has given to the children of the bridal chamber the enjoyment of His body and His blood," writes Cyril of Jerusalem (XXXIII, 1100 A). And Theodoret says "In eating the elements of the Bridegroom and drinking His Blood, we accomplish a marriage union" (P. G., LXXXI, 128 B).

There is, then, a certain foundation for the interpretation of the Canticle, which is a prophecy of the eschatological marriage, as being a figure of Christian initiation, the feast of the wedding of Christ and the soul. To this reason, another may be added, of the liturgical order. In the fourth century, Baptism was ordinarily given during the paschal night. Now we know that in the Jewish liturgy, the Canticle was read during the time of the Pasch, and we know also that the ancient Christian liturgy was strongly marked by the Jewish liturgy. It is, then, quite possible that here also the Christian liturgy took up the order of readings the synagogal liturgy, and then showed in Baptism and the Eucharist the very realization of the text read during this liturgical season.

In the sacramental interpretation of the Canticle, we should distinguish two aspects. First, the Canticle as a whole is considered by the Fathers to be a figure of the sacraments as being a marriage union between Christ and the Church. And this appears

[2] St. John Chrysostom calls the Christian initiation regarded as a whole "the spiritual wedding (*Ho. Res.;* P.G., L, 441 A).

[3] See Waszink, *Tertullien, De anima,* pp. 456-457, which gives several references.

to be a legitimate development of the literal sense of the text. But the Fathers also tried to connect different verses of the Canticle with different aspects of the liturgy of initiation. Here we find elements of unequal value: certain of them have a scriptural foundation: for example the invitation to the banquet of Cant. V:1. Others at least are based on an ancient and common tradition: for example, the stripping of the tunic in Cant. V:3. And, finally, we find mere allegorisms founded on external analogies, and to these we need attach little importance. A commentary following the text would lead us to many repetitions, and so we shall follow instead the order of the baptismal initiation. Like Psalm XXII, in fact, the Canticle was seen as a complete figure of the sacraments as a whole.

The *Procatechesis* of Cyril of Jerusalem begins: "Already the perfume of blessedness is wafted to you, O catechumens. Already you gather spiritual flowers to weave heavenly crowns. Already the sweet perfume of the Holy Spirit is poured out. You are in the vestibule of the royal dwelling. May you be led into it by the king. From henceforth, indeed, the flowers have appeared on the trees. Now the fruit must ripen" (XXXIII, 333 A). The allusions to the Canticle of Canticles are clear: "The flowers have appeared" (2:12); "The perfume is poured out" (1:2); "the king leads into His dwelling" (1:4). The catechumens are on the threshold of the royal garden of Paradise, where the marriage is to take place. Already breaths of the air of Paradise are wafted to them. St. Ambrose speaks still more precisely, applying to the situation of the catechumens another verse of the Canticle: "Draw us. We shall run after the scent of your perfumes" (1:3). This perfume of Paradise, this sweet scent of the Holy Spirit, is the prevenient grace of God by which He draws souls to His Paradise. "See what this passage means. You cannot follow Christ unless Christ Himself draws you" (*De Sacr.* V, 10; Botte 90). And the same text is commented on in the *De Mysteriis:* "Draw us so that we may breathe the perfume of the resurrection" (*De Myst.* 29, Botte 117).[4]

[4] If we notice that "the captive Bride, who is Israel, expresses the desire that her bridegroom, who is Yahweh, may make her return to Sion" (A. Robert, loc. cit., p. 204), the lawfulness of the application of the verse to baptism becomes fully evident: it is through baptism that God makes the captive human race, symbolized by Israel, return to the true Sion, which is the Church.

We should notice that in the text of Cyril of Jerusalem, the theme of springtime is joined to that of the perfume of Paradise. The beginnings of the catechesis are like spring flowers whose fruits will be gathered at Baptism. And we should not forget that Baptism was given in the springtime, as Cyril himself remarks (XXXIII, 837 B). The spring, the season in which God created the world, is an annual anniversary of creation; [5] that the resurrection of Christ took place in the springtime, indicates that it is also a new creation.[6] And Baptism is, in turn, a new creation also. Thus, it is not only the liturgical text that connects Baptism with the spring, the seasonal setting itself is also found to be charged with symbolic significance.

Until now, the candidate for Baptism, although he breathes the perfumes of Paradise, is still outside. The introduction into the marriage-chamber, then, is seen as a figure of the entrance into the baptistry which inaugurates the sacramental marriage of the soul to Christ, and the catecheses see this prefigured in the verse: "The king has brought me into his store-rooms." So Cyril of Jerusalem says: "Until now you have been standing outside the door. May it come about that you will be able to say: 'The king has brought me into his store-rooms' " (XXXIII, 428 A). As we have seen, the Procatechesis already has alluded to this text (333 A). St. Ambrose, in one passage, applies it to the entrance into the hall of the Eucharistic banquet (*De Sacra.* V, 11; Botte, 90), but, in another, he interprets the chamber of the Bridegroom to mean the place where the mysteries of Baptism are carried out (Exp. Psalm CXVIII, I, 17; C.S.E.L., p. 17).[7]

As we have seen, the first rite after the entrance into the baptistry is the stripping off of the old garments. This rite is connected with the verse of the Canticle most frequently quoted in the sacramental catecheses: "I have put off my garment; how shall I put it on again" (5:3). Cyril of Jerusalem quotes it three times. In one passage which is not in his mystagogic catecheses, he gives the symbolism of the verse without a direct allusion to the rite:

[5] Philo, *De spec. leg.*, 150; Eusebius, *De pascha;* P.G., XXIII, 697 A.

[6] Cyril of Jerusalem, XXXIII, 836 A.

[7] This double interpretation is explained by the fact that the Latin translation used by Ambrose gave the translation *cubiculum,* whereas the Greek text gave ταμιειον, store-room (*De Sacr.,* V, 11; Botte 90).

"Take off the old man with his works, and say the verse of the Canticle: 'I have put off my garment, how shall I put it on'" (XXXIII, 438 B). A second passage applies it to Baptism in general: "So you, when you have been purified, in the future guard your actions like pure linen, and your robe will remain immaculate, so that you can always say: "I have put off my garment, how shall I put it on" (XXXIII, 908 A). And finally a last passage comments on the very rite of the stripping off the garments: "As soon as you entered, you took off your garment, which was the image of the stripping off of the old man with his works. May the soul henceforth no more put on the garment which it has once stripped off, and may it say, according to the word which the Canticle attributes to the Bride of Christ: 'I have put off my garment. how shall I put it on'" (XXXIII, 1080 A).

This theme is not peculiar to Cyril. St. Ambrose seems to refer to it, and Gregory of Nyssa above all has developed it in his *Commentary on the Canticle,* which is so full of sacramental echoes: "I have put off my garment, how shall I put it on?" By this the Bride promises not to put on again the garment which has been taken off, but to content herself with only one garment, according to the precept given to the disciples. This garment is that with which she was clothed, in being renewed by Baptism" (XLVI, 1004 A). Here it is the oriental Church which sees a figure of Baptism in this verse of the Canticle. We have explained above, in connection with the symbolism of the stripping of the garments, what aspects of the sacramental this rite particularly expresses.

Now we come to the rite of Baptism properly so called. The Canticle contains several allusions to water which have been interpreted in a baptismal sense. The verse: 'His eyes are as doves upon brooks of water which are washed with milk' (5:12) is connected by Cyril of Jerusalem with the Baptism of Christ, in which the Spirit descended on the waters of the Jordan under the form of a dove: "By this verse he foretold in a symbolic fashion that it would be in this manner that Christ would be manifested visibly to the sight of men" (XXXIII, 981 A). St. Ambrose dwells rather on the allusion to the milk, which signifies simplicitly: "The Lord baptizes in milk, that is to say, in sincerity, and those who are baptized in milk are those whose faith is without guile" (*Exp. Psalm,* CXVIII, XVI, 21; C.S.E.L., 364).[8] Further, the "fountain sealed" of 4:12, signifies for Ambrose that the sacrament of Baptism should remain sealed "without being either violated by actions, nor divulged by words" (*De Myst.,* 55; Botte, 126).[9]

But the verse whose baptismal significance is the most widespread and uncontested is "Thy teeth are as flocks of sheep, that are shown, that come up from the washing" (IV: 2). It was particularly dear to St. Ambrose who quotes it in the *De Mysteriis:* "This praise is not faint. The Church is compared to this flock of sheep, containing in herself the many virtues of the souls who have by Baptism put off their sins and been joined to her" (*De Myst.* 38; Botte 119). And this theme appears again: "As sheep, satisfied with good pasture and warmed by the heat of the sun, bathed themselves in the river and come out happy and clean, so the souls of the just come up from the spiritual bath" (*Exp. Psalm,* CXVIII, XVI, 23; C.S.E.L., 365-366). This allusion to the teeth of the Bride is further interpreted by St. Ambrose as signifying that, in the sacraments of the New Testament, "the baptized, as well as having their bodies purified, need also afterwards to be purified by spiritual food and drink, as in the Old Testament, the manna came after the spring of Horeb" (Id., 29; C.S.E.L., 367). (He is speaking here of the Eucharist and of its power to forgive sins committed after Baptism.)

It is certainly from St. Ambrose that St. Augustine borrowed this symbolism. We know that in the *De doctrina christiana* he quotes it as an example showing how a doctrine commonplace in itself becomes fascinating when it is presented under the mysterious veils of allegory,—a dangerous principle which transforms biblical typology into literary symbolism—.[10] "Why is it, I ask you, that if someone speaks of the good and faithful servants of God who, having laid down the burdens of the world, come to the bath of holy Baptism, he charms his hearer less than if he ex-

[8] But he alludes to the dove of baptism in connection with verse iv, 1; 'Thy eyes are doves' eyes' (*De Myster.,* 37, Botte, 119).

[9] Likewise Theodoret, *Co. Cant.,* 3; P.G., LXXXI, 144 C. This corresponds with the meaning of the text, which expresses the inviolability of the covenant (A. Robert, loc. cit., p. 208).

[10] See on this text H. I. Marrou, *Saint Augustin et la fin de la culture antique,* p. 489.

pressed the same idea by making use of the passage from the Canticle of Canticles in which it is said of the Church: 'Thy teeth are a flock of sheep coming up from the washing.' The thought is the same, and yet, I know not why, I contemplate the saints with more pleasure when I see them as being the teeth of the Church to cut men off from their errors; and I find a strong pleasure in seeing them as sheep that have been shorn, that have laid aside the preoccupations of the world, coming up from the washing, that is to say, from Baptism" (*De doct. Christ.* II, 6; P; L. XXXIV, 38-39).

This questionable exegesis is, however, not merely a literary device derived from Ambrose and Augustine, as this last text might cause us to believe. In fact we find it in Theodoret, who usually is so little given to allegory. It is, then, a common tradition: "I think that, by the flocks of sheep, the Bridegroom means us to understand those who have been purified by Baptism, having cut off their sins, according to the teaching of Paul, who speaks 'of the bath of water with the word.' So, he says, you have teeth that are clean and purified from every fault of speech, so that you seem like those who have been judged worthy of the Baptism of salvation" (*Co. Cant.* 2; P. G. LXXXI, 129 B). We see in the background of these texts, a whole incorporation of the Canticle into the liturgy of initiation, which goes beyond particular interpretations.

We have further evidence of this in the *Catecheses* of St. Cyril of Jerusalem, and here we are entirely in the line of the common catechesis. Now, Cyril also interprets this text in a baptismal sense, though giving a different symbolism: "The soul which formerly was a slave, now receives the Lord Himself as Bridegroom; and He, receiving the sincere promise of the soul, exclaims: 'Thou art beautiful, my love, thou art beautiful. Thy teeth are as flocks of sheep, all with twins.' He speaks of teeth because of the profession of faith given by an upright heart,[11] and of twins because of the doube grace which is wrought by water and the Spirit" (XXXIII, 446 C). It certainly appears, that the text was applied to Baptism and that this application was interpreted in

[11] The connection between teeth and the profession of faith is also made by St. Ambrose (C.S.E.L., 367).

various ways. Baptism here is signified not by the washing, but by the twins to which the rest of the verse alludes.[12]

When he comes out of the pool, after Baptism, the newly baptized is clothed with a white robe and welcomed by the Christian community. This rite evoked one of the most remarkable interpretations of St. Ambrose. Quoting verses 1:4 and 8:5, he shows us the baptized, in the radiance of grace symbolized by his robe of shining white, coming out of the baptismal pool and greeted by the admiration of the angels: "The Church clad in these garments which she has received by the bath of regeneration, says in the Canticle: 'I am black, but beautiful, O daughters of Jerusalem' (1:4). Black, because of the weakness of man's condition, beautiful because of grace; black, because coming from the midst of sinners, beautiful by the sacrament of faith. And, seeing these garments, the daughters of Jerusalem are overcome with amazement and explain: 'Who is this that cometh up, clothed in white?' (VIII:5). She was black, how has she suddenly become white?" (*De Myst.* 35; Botte 118-119).[13]

Thus, the angels cannot bear the brilliance radiating from the newly baptized. And this recalls to St. Ambrose the scene of the Ascension: "The angels also hesitated when Christ arose, the powers of heaven hesitated, seeing Him Who, although He was flesh, was ascending to heaven. They said, therefore: 'Who is this king of glory?' And while others said: 'Open, O eternal doors, and the king of glory will come in,' still others said: "Who is this king of glory.' And in Isaias also you find the Powers of heaven hesitating and saying: 'Who is this who cometh up from Edom, who cometh up from Bosra with his garments dyed red, in the splendor of his white robe' " (*De Myst.* 36; Botte, 119). Here we have an allusion to the New Testament theme of the wonder of the angels at the Ascension of Christ, going up to His Father after the Resurrection in the shining glory of His transfigured body.[14] Thus, the sacrament of initiation is seen as a configuration to Christ risen and ascending to His Father. Ambrose elsewhere ex-

[12] The myrrh of V, I and VI, 1 is also a symbol of baptism as a conformation to the death of Christ, according to Gregory of Nyssa (XLIV, 1016 D) and Theodoret (LXXXI, 148 C).

[13] The word black denotes 'the sufferings of the exile' (Robert, loc. cit., p. 204). The application to man's state before baptism is a lawful one.

[14] P. Benoit, *L'Ascension,* Rev. Biblique, 1949, p. 161 et seqq. On the application of Psalm XXIII see infra, p. 304.

plicitly presents Christian initiation as a participation in the Ascension: "The soul baptized in milk ascends to heaven. The Powers admire it saying: 'Who is this that cometh up clothed in white?' And, leaning on the Word of God, it is admitted into the heights" (Ex. Psalm CXVIII, XVI, 21).

In the *De Sacramentis,* Ambrose returns to this beautiful theme of the admiration of the angels for the newly baptized. But in this passage, he relates it to the procession going from the baptistry to the church. "You have still to come to the altar. You begin to walk on your way. The Angels see you. They saw you on your arrival, and they saw human nature, which before was all stained with dark ugliness, suddenly shining with bright radiance. And then they cried out: 'Who is this that cometh up from the desert clothed in white.' Thus, the angels also are lost in admiration. You wish to know why they wonder? Hear the Apostle Peter saying that the things which are given to us are those which the angels desire to see; and, further, that eye has not seen and ear has not heard what God has prepared for those who love Him" (*De Sacr.* IV, 5; Botte 19). Here Baptism is seen in its full wonder: If, for the eyes of men, there is only a white garment and a procession by night, the angels who see the reality of things wonder at the extraordinary event that has taken place. Baptism is an event that echoes in the whole of spiritual creation, a most marvellous event upon which the angels dare not gaze. The text quoted by St. Ambrose is taken from the First Epistle of St. Peter (1:12), and the important feature is the relationship established between Baptism and the reality of which the Epistle says that it fills the angels with amazement.

So the sacraments were seen as great events in sacred history, the *mirabilia* which fill the space between the *gloriosa Ascensio* and the glorious Parousia, their course constituting that shining train of divine works whose splendor the very angels cannot endure, which fills them with wonder.

St. Ambrose in particular has developed this typology, but he is only the inheritor of the mystagogic tradition. The Catechesis of Cyril of Jerusalem, in part, offer us an analogous commentary on this passage. In his *Catechesis on Baptism,* in order to increase the desire of the catechumens, Cyril tells them beforehand about the initiation and says: "The angels will surround you with their choirs and say: 'Who is this who cometh up, clothed in white, leaning on her Beloved?' " (XXXIII, 448 B). Baptism is seen as a participation in the Ascension of Christ above the angelic choirs. By means of these symbols, a whole theology, the deepest theology of the Fathers, is revealed to us little by little.

But it is not only the angels who admire the baptized as they come out of the purifying waters, clothed in the shining radiance of grace. It is Christ Himself who welcomes them and praises their beauty. The development of St. Ambrose follows exactly that of St. Cyril, so that the dependence appears clearly. Indeed the latter, after the text that we have quoted, continues: "She who previously was a servant, now receives the Lord Himself for her beloved. And He, receiving the sincere promise of the soul, exclaims: 'Thou art beautiful, my love, thou art beautiful' " (XXXIII, 448 B). Baptism is seen in its fullness as a nuptial mystery. The soul, until now a simple creature, becomes the Bride of Christ. When she comes out of the baptismal water in which He has purified her in His Blood, He welcomes her in her white bridal robe and receives the promise which binds her to Him forever.

St. Ambrose continues in analogous terms, after the passage which we have quoted: "Christ, seeing His Church in white garments, this Church for whom He, Himself, as you see in the prophet Zachary, was clad in a robe of ignominy, seeing the soul purified and washed in the baptismal bath, says: 'Thou art beautiful, my love, thou art beautiful, thine eyes are like doves and there is no stain in thee,' because sin was destroyed in the water" (*De Myst.* 37; Botte 119). He keeps the comparison of the eyes like doves: "Thine eyes are beautiful as doves, because it was in the appearance of a dove that the Holy Spirit came down from heaven" (*De Myst.* 27; Botte 119). It is the Holy Spirit, poured out in the soul by Baptism, who gives it the beauty with which it is clothed.

And then begins the wonderful dialogue which connects Baptism with the other sacraments. The soul is satisfied and yet she still desires something more: "I will take hold of thee and bring thee into my mother's house; there thou shalt teach me (VIII:1-2). You see how, filled with the gifts of grace, she desires to penetrate still more deeply into the sacraments, and to consecrate all her senses to Christ. She still seeks, she still asks for love; and she questions the daughters of Jerusalem, that is, the souls of the faithful, to ask for it for her, desiring that, through their intervention, her Bridegroom may be led to a still more generous love for her" (*De Myst.* 40, Botte, 120). The true meaning of the sacramental mystery appears, beyond the veil of the rites. It is the mystery of the love of God for the soul, arousing the love of the soul for God. Through these symbols, which seem to take us further away from the literal meaning of the sacraments, their deepest truth is unveiled to our eyes.

To the aspiration of the soul, Christ answers: "Then the Lord Jesus Himself touched by the ardor of such a love, by the grace of such a beauty which in the baptized is no longer obscured by any stain, says to the Church: 'Place Me as a seal upon your heart, as a seal upon your arm.' This is to say: 'You are all beautiful, my love, you are all beautiful, and there is no stain in thee.' Place me as a seal upon your heart, which will make your faith shine in the fullness of the sacrament. May your works shine also, and show the imprint of God, to Whose image you were made. May your love be shaken by no persecution, may the great waters not avail to sweep it away. It is for this that you received the spiritual seal" (*De Myst.* 41; Botte 120-121).[15]

The allusion to confirmation is beyond doubt. The *signaculum spiritale* is the Latin expression corresponding to the Greek *sphragis*. This is the seal which is prefigured by the *signaculum* which the Beloved of the Canticle puts on her heart. And the characteristics pointed out by Ambrose correspond to those of Confirmation, which is a fulfilling (*plenum*) which increases the light of faith and strengthens the vigor of love. The same verse is interpreted in a parallel way in the *De Sacramentis*. Ambrose well explains that, although the sacrament is the work of the Three Persons indivisibly, yet each works according to His own mode: "How? God has anointed you, the Lord has marked you with the seal and has placed the Holy Spirit in your heart. You have, then, received the Holy Spirit in your heart. Receive also something else. For as the Spirit is in your heart, so Christ is in

[15] Here again the patristic interpretation clings rigorously to the literal sense. 'The seal signifies that Yahweh asks Israel to stay faithful to him' (A. Robert, loc. cit., p. 210). Now the seal of baptism is precisely the expression of the promise of mutual fidelity between God and the soul.

your heart. How? You have this in the Canticle of Canticles: 'Place me as a seal upon your heart.' You have, then, been marked with the imprint of His Cross, with the imprint of His Passion. You have received the seal of His image, so that you may rise again in His image, so that you may live according to His image" (*De Sacr.* VI, 6-7; Botte 99).

The *signaculum* only alludes to the Cross marked on the forehead. But Ambrose observes that it also concerns an anointing. This other aspect of the rite appears to him to be prefigured in verse 1:2: "Thy is as oil (*unguentum*) poured out" (*De Myst.* 29, Botte 117). The same verse is also interpreted by Theodoret in a sacramental sense. But here he is concerned with the *consignatio*, which, as we have seen, took place, at Antioch, before Baptism: "If you wish to interpret this verse in the most sacramental way, remember the holy initiation (*mystagogia*) in which the initiates, after renouncing the tyrant and confessing the true King, receive, as a kind of royal imprint (*sphragis*) the anointing with the spiritual perfumed oil, being strengthened with the oil, as with a sign, of the invisible grace of the Holy Spirit" (LXXXI, 60 C).

But let us return to Ambrose, for whom the *signaculum* imprinted on the heart and the nard which diffuses its perfume both designate confirmation. Even after this new grace, which marks an increase, the soul is not satisfied. It desires still more: "Keeping hidden the sublimity of the heavenly sacraments and turning away from the violent assaults of the wind, she desires the sweetness of the grace of springtime, and, knowing that her garden cannot displease Christ, she calls the Bridegroom Himself, saying: 'Let my Beloved come down into His garden and eat the fruit of His apple trees' (IV:16). Indeed she has beautiful trees full of fruit which bathe their roots in the waters of the sacred fountain" (*De Myst.* 56; Botte, 127).

The purified soul, having become a paradise, nevertheless desires still more. She now wishes to receive her Bridegroom, to consummate her union with Him. And elsewhere St. Ambrose understands this text to mean the Church who invites Christ to come into the souls of the baptized by the Eucharist: "You have come to the altar, you have received the grace of Christ, you have obtained the heavenly sacraments. The Church rejoices in the redemption of a great number, and she rejoices with a spiritual joy in seeing around her her family clothed in white. You have this in the Canticle of Canticles. In her gladness, she invokes Christ, for she has a hall prepared, worthy of a heavenly banquet. This is why she says: 'Let my Beloved come down into His garden and let Him cut the fruit from His trees.' Who are these trees? You had become dry wood in Adam. Now by the grace of Christ, you are trees laden with fruit" (*De Sacr.* V, 14; Botte 91).

Christ answers this appeal and comes to visit the garden of His Bride: "The Lord Jesus willingly accepts and answers His Church with heavenly condescension: 'I am come into my garden, my sister, my spouse, I have gathered my myrrh with my aromatical spices. I have eaten the honeycombs, I have drunk my wine with my milk' (5:1)" (*De Sacr.* V, 15. See *De Myst.* 57). For St. Ambrose, this is a description of the Eucharistic banquet: "Why He speaks of food and drink will be understood by him who is initiated" (*De Myst.* 57; Botte, 127). In the *De Sacramentis,* where he is not bound by the secret of the arcana, he is more explicit: "You see that in this bread there is no bitterness, only sweetness. You see the nature of this gladness which is unsullied by any sin" (V, 17; Botte, 92).

But in this verse, it is only the allusion to bread and wine that suggests to Ambrose a Eucharistic meaning. The following verse, on the other hand, is the invitation itself, addressed by the Spouse to souls, to take part in the wedding-feast of His marriage with the Church. This is explained by Gregory of Nyssa: "For those who know the hidden sense of Scripture, there is no difference between what is said in the Canticle: 'Eat, O friends, and drink, and be inebriated, my dearly beloved,'—and the sacramental initiation (*mystagogia*) of the Apostles. Indeed, in both places the text says: 'Eat and drink' (XLIV, 989 C). We might object, nevertheless, Gregory says "that in the Gospel text there is no question of inebriation. But this is because this inebriation is Christ Himself Who raises us up out of inferior realities to those on high" (XLIV, 989 D).

The call to inebriation made by the Bridegroom in the Canticle is interpreted in the same way in our catecheses: "The Church, seeing such a great grace—the celebration of the wedding-banquet of Christ—invites her sons, invites her neighbors to run to the sacraments: 'Eat, my friends, drink, inebriate yourselves, my beloved.' What we eat and what we drink has elsewhere been described for us by the Holy Spirit through the Prophet: 'Taste and see that the Lord is sweet.' Christ is in this Sacrament, because it is the Body of Christ, not as physical, but as spiritual nourishment" (*De Myst.* 58; Botte 127). And in the *De Sacramentis,* he celebrates the sober inebriation that is given by the Eucharistic wine: "Whenever you drink, you receive the remission of sins and you become inebriated in spirit. He who is drunk with wine wavers and staggers, but he who is inebriated in the spirit, is rooted in Christ. What wonderful drunkenness which effects sobriety of spirit! This was what we had to go through concerning the sacraments" (V, 17).[16]

With the sober inebriation aroused by the Eucharistic wine, the thirst of the soul is at last satisfied. At the end of the sacramental initiation, she has passed from earthly to heavenly things. And this is why the Eucharist is the end of the sacraments. But we should remark nevertheless that, in this celebration of the wedding-feast of Christ and the Church which is realized in the Eucharist, the nuptial aspect is not brought out, and the symbolism is no different from that of the banquet of Wisdom or the inebriating cup of Psalm XXII. The nuptial aspect of the Eucharist more properly speaking appears in the interpretation of other verses of the Canticle in which not only the wedding-feast, but the marriage union itself prefigures the union of Christ and the soul consummated in the Eucharist.

St. Ambrose brings us back to the first verse of the Canticle: "You have come to the altar, the Lord Jesus calls you, for the text speaks of you or of the Church, and he says to you: 'Let him kiss me with the kiss of his mouth.' This word can be applied equally to Christ or to you. Do you wish to apply it to Christ? You see that you are pure from all sin, since your faults have been blotted out. This is why He judges you to be worthy of the heavenly sacraments and invites you to the heavenly banquet: May He kiss me with the kiss of His mouth. You wish to apply the same to yourself? Seeing yourself pure from all sins and worthy to come to the altar of Christ—for what is the altar, indeed, but the figure of the body of Christ—you see the wonderful sacraments, and you say: May He kiss me with the kiss of His mouth,

[16] See also *De Cain et Abel,* I, 20-21; C.S.E.L., 356-357.

that is, may Christ give me a kiss" (*De Sacr.* V, 5-7; Botte, 89-90). Thus, the Eucharistic communion in which the Body of Christ is placed on the lips of the baptized who has been purified from his sins, is truly the kiss given by Christ to the soul, the expression of the union of love which He has contracted with her. Here it is the marriage union which directly typifies the Eucharist.

This is found again in Theodoret: "If anyone whose thoughts are bad is troubled by the term 'kiss,' let him consider that, at the time of the sacrament, receiving the members of the Spouse, we kiss them and embrace them, and we place Him with His eyes upon our heart, and we imagine a kind of nuptial embrace, and we consider that we are uniting ourselves to Him and embracing Him and kissing Him, love casting out fear, according to Holy Scripture" (LXXXI, 53 C). This text is even stronger than that of St. Ambrose, but it proceeds from the same inspiration. The Eucharistic communion is really considered as a marriage union. It is the consummation of *agape,* of charity, by union. The idea returns elsewhere. Commenting on the expression "day of the marriage," [17] Theodore applies it to the Eucharist and writes: "Eating the members of the Bridegroom and drinking His Blood, we realize a nuptial union (*koinonia*) with Him" (128 A).

Thus, we see the whole catechetical tradition shows us in the Canticle of Canticles a figure of Christian initiation. The foundation of this hypothesis is obvious. From the fact that the Canticle is the prophecy of the eschatological marriage of the Messias and the New Israel, we are right in seeing it realized in the Christian sacraments, in which the perpetual marriage of Christ and the Church is carried out. But we may wonder whether this sacramental interpretation of nuptial theology finds authorization in the New Testament. There is a text in the Epistle to the Ephesians in which the mystery of Baptism and of the Eucharist is presented as the fulfillment of the eschatological marriage: "Husbands, love your wives, as Christ loved the Church and delivered Himself up for it, that He might sanctify it, cleansing it by the laver of water in the word of life, that He might present it to Himself a glorious Church, not having spot or wrinkle . . . He

[17] This expression denotes in the text of the Canticle "the eschatological advent" (Robert, loc. cit., p. 207). This eschatological advent is brought about by Christian initiation.

that loves his wife, nourishes and cherishes her, as also Christ does the Church, because we are members of His body. For this cause 'man and wife shall become one flesh.' This is a great mystery, but I speak of Christ and of the Church" (V:25-32).

This text is of interest here first because it shows how the rite of Baptism itself can be connected with the nuptial theme. We find here the theme of the nuptial bath; as Dom Casel has shown, the text here alludes to a rite known to the ancient world of the inauguration of the marriage celebration by a ritual bath.[18] This was a sacred bath, marking for the bride in particular her consecration to the worship of the family into which she was about to enter. This is the bath in which St. Paul sees a figure of Baptism. But we should notice particularly that the bath constitutes the purification, and that it is the marriage union itself which constitutes the full sanctification. The allusion to the Eucharist is evident. It is by this sacrament that Christ and the soul become one flesh, like husband and wife.[19] And this is precisely what the Fathers show us in their explanation of the Canticle of Canticles.

This fact has been noted by Methodius of Olympus. The marriage of Christ and the Church, which took place on the Cross, is continued throughout the whole Church by Baptism and the Eucharist: "The Word of God came down to earth to unite Himself to His Bride, willingly dying for her, to make her glorious and immaculate in the bath of purification. For otherwise the Church could not conceive those who believe and bring them forth anew by the bath of regeneration, if Christ did not die anew, did not unite Himself to His Church and give her the power from His side, so that all those may grow up who are born in the baptismal bath" (*Banquet,* III, 8). Baptism perpetually regenerates Christians by plunging them into the death of Christ, and the Eucharist continually makes them grow by giving them the strength which comes from His side, that is, by communion in His risen Body. Thus, the whole process of sacramental initiation becomes the expression of the nuptial mystery. The text from St. Paul itself gives the explanation of the figures which we have been examining. It is because the mystery of the Passion is

18 *Le bain nuptial de l'Eglise,* Dieu vivant, IV, pp. 43-44.
19 This eucharistic interpretation of Eph. V. 31, is expressly given by St. John Chrysostom in his *Commentary on the Epistle to the Ephesians.*

the carrying-out of the eschatological marriage of the Word and the New Israel, and because Christian initiation is the continuation of the mystery of the Passion, that Baptism and the Eucharist are a nuptial mystery.

CHAPTER THIRTEEN

New Testament Types

ONE of the gains of contemporary exegesis is to have shown how the Gospels are filled with allusions to the sacraments. As we love to see the Gospels, not only as being historical documents on the life of Christ, but also as being the expression of the faith and life of the Christian community, they seem to be constructed on two planes. The realities of the life of Christ in His earthly existence become also figures of His glorious life in the Church, particularly as this is expressed in her sacramental life. So the allusions to the living water, or to washings, to the ears of wheat rubbed in the hand, or to the multiplications of the bread, take on baptismal and Eucharistic echoes. This thesis is especially developed by Oscar Cullmann in *Urchristentum und Gottesdienst* and by Harald Sahlin in *Zur Typology des Johannes-evangeliums.*[1] We cannot study here all the sacramental allusions in the Gospels. We have already pointed out several: the multiplication of the bread; the water and blood flowing from our Lord's pierced side; the ears of wheat which the disciples rubbed in their hands on the Sabbath, the washing of the feet. These figures appear as being direct prolongations of episodes in the Old Testament, of those of the manna and the rock of Horeb in particular. Thus, the Gospel of St. John gives us a symbolism on three levels: the life of Christ is projected against the background

[1] See also E. Hoskyns, *The Fourth Gospel,* London, 1948; A. Correll, *Consummatum est,* Upsala, 1950.

of Exodus, and becomes also the figure of the sacramental life of the Church. We shall deal only with two episodes of this Gospel which show us new aspects of sacramental symbolism: the first, that of the pool of Bethesda, connected with Baptism; the second, the wedding at Cana, connected with the Holy Eucharist.

The fifth chapter of St. John's Gospel tells the story of the healing of a paralytic man at the pool of Bethesda. Ancient Christian tradition saw in this episode a figure of Baptism: Tertullian, Didymus and Ambrose commented on it in their catecheses. The Ethiopian and Egyptian prayers for the consecration of the baptismal water also mention it.[2] And furthermore, it is one of the motifs found in the frescoes of the most ancient baptistries. The *Capella Greca,* at the end of the second century, shows us this episode as a parallel to that of the rock of Horeb, which is a baptismal figure. The chapel of the Sacraments presents it alongside a representation of the Baptism of Jesus, and one of a fisher drawing out a fish, both figures connected with Baptism. We have here, then, one of the most ancient and common figures of Baptism.

Christian tradition here is simply the expression of the New Testament itself, for in the Gospel of St. John, the episode has a baptismal significance. And we can, therefore, consider this baptismal significance as going back to the apostolic community. The pool of Bethesda was a place where miracles of healing took place; but these miracles took place for only one individual, at one definite instant, by the mediation of an angel. With Jesus these conditions were abolished. He is Himself the salvation which is accomplished at all times, without any intermediary, for every man. Thus, He is seen to be the reality of which the healing by the angels was the figure. And we notice further that the healing took place on the Sabbath, a fact which scandalized the Pharisees: by this Christ showed that He is the master and the realization of the Sabbath.[3]

But this action of Christ's presents particular characteristics. For one thing, it is not only a healing of the body; it is connected with the pardon of sins (14-16). Thus, as often in the Gospel of

[2] Pere Lundberg, *La typologie baptismale dans l'Église ancienne,* p. 25.

[3] Oscar Cullmann, loc. cit., p. 87. Harald Sahlin adds that the episode shows the superiority of Baptism to the Jewish purifications. (loc. cit., pp. 20-21 and 73).

John, the visible reality appears as the sign of an invisible reality. The loaves of the multiplication are figures of the word of God and of the Eucharist. Of what, then, is this miracle the figure? Of the remission of sins, which is the very purpose of Baptism. This fact already directs us toward the sacramental significance of this miracle. But, as always in St. John, the sacraments are indicated, not only in their content, but also in their figure. The loaves of the multiplication are the figure of the bread of the Eucharist. And here the miracle takes place by a pool. We recall the fact that primitive Christian Baptism took place in pools, and in pools of running water, suggesting the stirring of the water by the angel. The Gospel scene thus signifies the remission of sins in connection with a pool of living water; and so it is clearly seen to be a figure of Baptism.

The Fathers, then, were in the true line of interpretation of this text when they explained it in a baptismal sense. Tertullian is the first author whom we find treating it in this way: "By his intervention, an angel stirred the Pool of Bethesda. Those who complained of illness were on the watch for this stirring, for the first who went down into the pool ceased to have anything to complain about after the bath. This figure of corporal healing prophesies spiritual healing, according to the law that things of the flesh should always precede and prefigure spiritual things. So, as the grace of God toward the human being advanced further, it was given to the angel and the waters to be able to do more. Then they brought healing to bodily evils only, now they heal the soul; then they effected only temporal well-being, now they restore eternal life: then they delivered only one person once a year, now every day they preserve whole crowds, destroying death by the remission of sins" (*De bapt.*, 5: P. L. 1, 1206).

We could not find a more precise commentary on the story told by St. John. Tertullian brings out admirably the points on which the baptismal symbolism is founded. In both cases, the idea is that of a power communicated to the waters. But in the Jewish pool this power was only concerned with a physical healing and procured only a temporal salvation. Here in Baptism it effects spiritual salvation and the remission of sins. In both cases, it is the power of the water which is being considered, and so the pool of Bethesda is a figure of the baptismal pool. Again, healing was effected only once a year at the pool of Bethesda, while Baptism is given every day. And, finally, only one person was benefited at Bethesda, while here there are crowds. Tertullian thus brings out the same points as those we have noticed in St. John as constituting the comparison between the figure and the sacrament.

Up until now, I have not mentioned one detail, because the special theology of Tertullian appears in it: that is, the angel.[4] For him, the role of the angel persists in Baptism and has an even greater efficacy than at the pool of Bethesda: *Plus aquis et angelo accesit.* This same idea is, in fact, the starting-point of Tertullian's whole explanation. He wishes to show that in Christian Baptism an angel acts by means of the water, that it is an angel who communicates to the waters their purifying power: "The waters having received a healing power by the intervention of an angel, the spirit is plunged in the water by means of the body, and the body purified in the water by means of the spirit." [4] To justify this statement, Tertullian brings forward examples, showing that the pagans themselves recognized the fact that demons work by means of water. He mentions first the baptisms of initiation were given in the mysteries of Isis and Mithra. "But let us continue further. It is not in these false sacraments only that the impure spirits come to cover the waters to make them serve their wicked deeds."

Tertullian gives two examples: "Do we not find that this is also true in the obscure fountains, the wild brooks, the thermal baths, the canals and cisterns of houses, of which it is said that they can make a man lose his reason by the power of a wicked spirit?" Why recall these things? "To make it less difficult to believe that a holy angel of God should be present at the waters which are to be prepared for the salvation of men, if an evil angel has the habit of frequent use of this element to destroy men." And elsewhere Tertullian has a still better argument: "If this intervention of an angel appears astonishing to you, it has precedents." And here is where the text concerning the pool of Bethesda comes in.

The interesting aspect to us from the point of view of the theology of Baptism is the question of the part played by this

[4] The evidence of Tertullian is important, not only for the meaning of the passage, but also for its authenticity. As is well known, several important MSS of the New Testament omit the verse in which the angel is mentioned (See E. Hoskyns, *The Fourth Gospel,* p. 265).

angel. To what does it correspond? The idea of a particular presence of an angel at Baptism is not peculiar to Tertullian. We find it particularly in Origen. Before Baptism, the soul is in the power of the demon. By Baptism, it is entrusted to an angel.[5] And, furthermore, the angel is present at Baptism. "When the sacrament of the faith has been given to you, the heavenly powers, the ministries of the angels, the Church of the first-born are present" (*Ho. Jos.*, IX, 4). The angel, indeed, even seems to be the minister of the sacrament: "Come, O angel, receive by the word him who is converted from the ancient error, from the teaching of demons; take him to give him the Baptism of the second birth" (*Ho. Ez.* I, 7). Thus, there is in Baptism as it were a twofold minister, the visible priest, and the invisible angel: "On the visible plane, the pool brings forth our visible body by the ministry of priests; on the invisible plane, the Spirit of God has regenerated at once our body and our soul with the assistance of the angels.[6]

As Erik Peterson has well remarked,[7] this presence of the angels at liturgical actions, and particularly at Baptism, expresses the official character of the sacramental acts of Christian worship. It is possible also that there is a connection here with the part the angels play in the entrance of the soul into eternal life. We have, indeed, already noted the frequent parallelism between the representations of Baptism and those connected with funerals. They are so closely related that it is often difficult to ascertain whether the allusion is to one or the other. The part of the angels in the liturgy of death is well known: in the Offertory of the Roman Mass for the dead, allusion is still made to St. Michael. Moreover, in certain apocrypha, we see the angel purifying the soul by a kind of baptism in the river of fire before bringing it into the presence of God.[8] Sacramental Baptism is an anticipation of the eschatological baptism. That an angel should take part in it is therefore quite normal.

Thus, Tertullian's concept is related to a whole tradition. But with him it takes on a special meaning: the angel of Baptism is seen as the precursor of the Holy Spirit, the purifying rite of the

[5] A. Bettencourt, *Doctrina ascetica Origenis*, p. 232.
[6] Didymus the Blind, *De Trinitate;* P.G., XXXIX, 672 C.
[7] *Theologische Traktate*, p. 361 et seq.
[8] C. M. Edsman, *La baptême de feu*, p. 65-67; P. Lundeberg, *La typologie baptismale dans l'Église ancienne*, p. 44-45.

water being especially reserved to him, and the outpouring of the Spirit being connected with the anointing: "It is not in the water that we receive the Holy Spirit, but, having been purified in the water under an angel, we are prepared for the Holy Spirit. From this also has come the figure. Thus, John was the precursor of the Lord, preparing His ways: so the angel who presides at Baptism prepares the way for the Spirit Who is to come, by the purification of sins which is obtained by faith, being signed in the Name of the Father, of the Son and of the Holy Spirit" (*De baptismo*, 6).

In this curious text, it appears that it is the angel who sanctifies the baptismal waters and gives them their purifying power. This same idea is also found in the comparison quoted above of the part of the angel in Baptism with the action of the demons in springs and rivers, and with the action of the angel in the pool of Bethesda. As the angel of Bethesda gave the waters a power that healed bodies, so the angel of Baptism gives the waters a power that heals souls. It seems to be true also that Tertullian understood the Spirit who hovered over the primeval waters and gave them a sanctifying power, to be an angel.[9] Here we have, then, an idea peculiar to Tertullian which is directly connected with the pool of Bethesda. After Tertullian, this idea is found again elsewhere in the West. So Optatus of Mileva challenges the validity of the Donatists' baptism by saying: "From whence do you have an angel who can move the waters for you?" (*Contra Parmenianum*, II, 16). The allusion to Bethesda is clear.

After Tertullian, the baptismal interpretation of the pool of Bethesda reappears in patristic tradition. We meet it again in Didymus, who depends closely on Tertullian: "Besides what we have recalled, the whole world agrees in seeing a figure of Baptism also in the pool of Jerusalem whose name is Bethesda. It was only a figure, not the reality. Indeed, the image was for a time, the reality is eternal. This is why it was only once a year that the water stirred by the angel healed only one man, the first who went down into it, and healed him of his bodily illness, not his spiritual. But true Baptism, after the manifestation of the Son and the Spirit, takes place every day, or rather every hour, or even every instant, and frees forever from all sin all those who go

[9] E. Amann, *L'ange du baptême chez Tertullien,* Rev. Sc. Rel., 1921, p. 298 et seqq.

down into it" (P. G. XXXIX, 708 A-B). We find here again the precise comparison already made by Tertullian. We should notice that for Didymus this interpretation is universal and common to the whole Church.

We shall not be surprised, therefore, to find it again in the baptismal catecheses which present the common teaching of the Church. St. Ambrose devotes to it a whole chapter of the *De Sacramentis.* He begins with an interesting comparison: "What was read yesterday?" (*De Sac.* II, 3) Thus we see that the fifth chapter of St. John was one of the liturgical readings for the octave of Easter, and thus we are here in the very context of the liturgy itself, as in the case of Psalm XXII. Ambrose recalls the text and continues: "Why an Angel? Because Christ Himself is the Angel of the great council. 'At his hour'—because he was kept for the last hour, so that he might seize the day at its setting and stop its decline. Every time that the Angel came down, the water was stirred. You will perhaps say: 'Why does this happen now?' Hear why. Miraculous signs are for the unbelieving, faith for believers" (*De Sacr.* II, 4).

We see the line of St. Ambrose's interpretation. It develops in detail the allegorical meaning of the event: the angel is a figure of Christ; the time when he came down is the hour of Christ, that is to say, the last hour. The interpretation continues along these lines: he who goes down first is the Jewish people. "But then only one was healed. How much greater is the grace of the Church in which all who go down are saved." Most curious is the interpretation of the phrase "I have no man (to carry me)." Ambrose sees here faith in the Incarnation: "He could not go down, he could not be saved unless he believed that Our Lord Jesus took flesh of a Virgin. From whence comes Baptism, if not from the death of Christ? Here is the whole mystery. He attained health because he believed in Him who was to come. But He would have been more perfect if he had believed that He Whom he had hoped to see coming, had already come" (II, 7; Botte, 63-64).

Nothing of Tertullian's interpretation remains here. The Angel is the figure of Christ. In the *De Mysteriis* also, Ambrose deals with Bethesda and affirms its figurative meaning: "This pool was a figure so that you may believe that a divine virtue descended into the Baptismal font" (*De Myst.* 23; Botte, 115). The Angel is the figure of the Holy Spirit, Who vivifies the baptismal water. The man who carries the paralytic is also interpreted as the Incarnate Word, "by Whose coming it is no longer the shadow which heals some few, but the reality which heals everyone" (*De Myst.* 24). The concept enduring throughout all these interpretations is that of the universal character of the salvation brought by Christ, in contrast to the limited nature of the healing found in the pool. And certainly this seems to be one of the characteristic features of the New Testament figures of the sacraments.[10] It marks one of the essential aspects of the contrast between the Jewish economy and the messianic times inaugurated by Jesus.

The texts that we have been examining are taken from treatises concerning Baptism. But the baptismal interpretation of the pool of Bethesda is also found elsewhere. In his twelfth Sermon against the Antinomians, St. John Chrysostom comments on the fifth chapter of St. John, which was the Gospel for the day: "Let us be obedient to this miracle which was read to us today" (P. G., XLVIII, 803 C). And he develops the comparison between the pool of Bethesda and Baptism along the same lines as our other texts: there only one person was healed, here, "even if you were to put the whole universe into the pool, the force of grace would not be lessened, but would heal everyone: it is the difference between the authority of the servants and that of the master" (XLVIII, 804). There, the healing took place only once a year; here, every day; that healing reached the body only, this the soul.[11]

If the healing of the pool of Bethesda is a figure of Baptism, it certainly seems as if the miracle of the wedding-feast of Cana must be one of the Eucharist. We find here again, on the level of the New Testament, the theme of the eschatological wedding. We notice, first of all, that the Gospel of St. Matthew presents us with two parables describing the world to come in terms of imagery taken from weddings. These are the parables of the guests

[10] See the episode of Naaman, for baptism (p. 112) and the meal of wisdom for the Eucharist (p. 152).

[11] See also *De Resurrectione*, 3; P.G., L, 439 D: "The angel went down into the pool and one alone was saved; the Lord of the angels went down into the Jordan and healed the universe in it."

invited to the wedding-feast (Matt. XXII:3) and that of the Wise Virgins (Matt. XXV:1). The meaning of these parables is certainly eschatological. But, as we have seen, the sacraments are an anticipation of this eschatological marriage-feast. It was natural, then, that Christian tradition should have applied these two parables to the process of initiation. And this in fact is what ancient tradition teaches. These two parables play a considerable part in this process, and many details have been directly connected with certain rites of Baptism and of the Eucharist. Let us, then, first consider the sacramental significance of marriage in general.

At the beginning of his *Procatechesis,* Cyril of Jerusalem explains to the candidates the necessity of having a right intention and of undergoing a serious conversion in order to receive the sacraments. To explain this, he uses the parable of the guests invited to the wedding-feast. The banquet to which the king invites the guests is the sacramental initiation; the wedding-garment represents the dispositions with which the candidate should be clothed: "A certain man, as the Gospel tells us, wanted to take part in the wedding-feast out of curiosity. He came in unsuitably dressed, sat down and ate. The Bridegroom allowed him to do so. But, when this man saw all the other guests dressed in white, he should have procured the same kind of robe for himself . . . So we, who are the servants of Christ, have allowed you to enter. But it is possible that you have a soul stained by the mud of sin. Strip off, we pray you, this garment that you now wear, and put on the white tunic of purity. I warn you to do so before the Bridegroom, Jesus, comes in, and sees your robe" (XXXIII, 336 B-341 A).[12]

The wedding banquet is a figure of baptismal initiation, which is the wedding of Jesus and the soul. Cyril points out that this wedding banquet is open to everyone, but that at the same time, it demands an interior conversion. This theme reappears later: "Begin by washing your robes by penance, so that, when you are admitted to the chamber of the Bridegroom, you will be found pure. For the Bridegroom calls everyone without discrimination. His grace is generous. And the voice of His heralds, resounding

[12] The *Clementine Recognitions* see in the wedding-garment a symbol of Baptism itself (which allows one to approach the Eucharistic banquet): 'The wedding-garment is the grace of Baptism' (IV, 35. See Waszink, *Tertullian, De Anima,* p. 457).

powerfully, gathers together all men. But He Himself will come to look at those who have come in to the symbolic marriage. May it not happen that any of those who have been enrolled will hear Him say: 'Friend, why did you come in without having a wedding garment?' Up until now, you have been standing at the door. May it come about that you all can say: 'The king has brought me into His store-rooms' (Cant. 1:3). And then may all your souls be found without spot or wrinkle or any such thing (Eph. V:27)" (XXXIII, 428, A-B).[18]

We should notice here the bringing together of the parable of the wedding-guests with two other texts: that of the Epistle to the Ephesians concerning the nuptial mystery of Baptism, and the Canticle of Canticles. We have here a whole symbolism of marriage as applied to the sacraments. Origen had previously connected this parable with the same verse of the Canticle: " 'The king has brought me into His store-rooms.' By these words, the Bride asks the friends of the Bridegroom to bring her into the place of gladness where wine is to be drunk and the feast is prepared. It is in this store-room that Wisdom has mingled her wine and, by means of her servants, invited the ignorant to come in. It is this banquet-chamber in which all those who have come from the east and from the west will take their places with Abraham, Isaac and Jacob in the Kingdom of heaven (Matt. VIII:11). David also, in admiration of the chalice of this banquet, said: 'How wonderful is my cup' " (*Co. Cant.* 3; P. G., XIII, 155).

We see how this passage brings together Psalm XXII, the banquet of Wisdom, the parable of the wedding-guests and the Canticle of Canticles, that is to say, all the various aspects of the eschatological banquet, realized in the Eucharist. More precisely, it is interesting to notice how the parable of the wedding-guest and the Canticle are brought together, and we see that the tradition for doing so must be very ancient. Concerning the theme of the old robe which must be taken off in order to be clothed with the wedding-garment, when this image is applied to the dispositions of the candidate, it is clear that it is in relation to the symbolism of the taking-off of the old garment and putting on the white tunic which forms part of the liturgy of Baptism. And

[18] It will be noticed that the beginning of the parable is used as a verse in the Roman Eucharistic liturgy.

elsewhere Cyril applies to both the same verse from Isaias LXI:10: "He has clothed me with the garment of salvation, and thrown around me the robe of gladness" (XXXIII, 428 A, and 1104 B).[14]

The second wedding parable from the Gospel is that of the Wise Virgins. Here the emphasis is not put on the laying aside of bad dispositions, but rather on the positive preparation for coming to the marriage-feast. Applied to the sacraments, the parable points out the dispositions necessary to take part in the Eucharistic banquet; and, liturgically, the procession of virgins going to meet the Bridegroom with their lighted lamps reminds us of the procession during the paschal night in which the newly-baptized, carrying their lighted candles in their hands, were led from the baptistry to the church where they were to take part in the Eucharistic banquet. This double aspect is recalled by St. Cyril, when, at the beginning of the Procatechesis, he presents the process of initiation as a whole: "You carry in your hands the lamps of the wedding procession, these lamps which are the desire of heavenly blessings, the firm resolution and the hope which accompanies it" (XXXIII, 333). The eschatological waiting signified by the lamps of the wise virgins is applied to the waiting for baptismal initiation which is an anticipation of the Parousia and a meeting of the soul with Christ the Bridegroom.

This connection between the procession of the paschal night and of the wedding parable is made explicitly by Gregory Nazianzen: "The station that you will make, just after Baptism, before the great throne, is the prefiguring of future glory. The chant of the Psalms with which you will be received is the prelude to the Psalmody of heaven. The lamps that you will light are the sacrament (*mysterion*) of the resplendent procession of heaven with which we will go before the Bridegroom, souls virginal and resplendent, with the burning lamps of faith. Let us not allow ourselves by negligence to become drowsy, so as to let Him for Whom we are waiting go by us when He comes unexpectedly, and let us not remain without sustenance and without oil, for fear of being excluded from the bridal chamber. There is no room there for the man who is proud and negligent, nor for him

[14] The parable is also applied to the Eucharist (Cyr. Alex., *Ho. Pasch.*, 14; P.G. LXXVII, 712 B).

who is clad in a stained garment and not in the wedding-robe" (XXXVI, 426 B-C).

This passage shows us that the baptismal procession is a figure of the procession of the elect at the time of the Parousia. Or, better still, this procession is the sacrament, the visible sign of the heavenly liturgy. It expresses that perpetual sacramental Parousia which is Christian worship, and which St. John describes in the Apocalypse. This text of St. Gregory is valuable also for our understanding of the baptismal liturgy in Cappadocia during the fourth century, with the station before the *bema,* the throne of the presiding bishop placed at the back of the apse. Let us notice, finally, the last allusion to the parable of the wedding-guests. In this discourse addressed to the catechumens, the two parables are, then, brought together with a definitely sacramental meaning. And this is one more confirmation of the Eucharistic meaning which the parable of the wedding-guest possessed for the Fathers.

The two parables that we have been considering are Christ's repetition of the announcement of the eschatological marriage; and the Fathers have applied them to Christian initiation. But, as we have seen in connection with the typology of the eschatological banquet, the meals of Christ showed that He had already fulfilled these types by His coming to earth. Thus, the multiplication of the loaves is the fulfillment of the manna of the New Exodus, the meal with Simon the Pharisee, of the messianic banquet. And these meals of Christ are, in turn, figures of the sacraments. This is equally true of the figure of the wedding-feast, for there is an event in the life of Jesus which is the fulfillment of the eschatological wedding-feast and which also most probably possesses a sacramental significance, analogous to that of the multiplication of the loaves: this is the wedding of Cana.

The sacramental significance of this event has been brought out by Oscar Cullmann.[15] It is a general characteristic of St. John's Gospel that his expressions have a symbolic, and, more specifically, a sacramental meaning. This is true of the meeting with the Samaritan woman, the multiplication of the loaves, the pool of Bethesda. And it is true also of the wedding of Cana. The expression "My hour has not yet come," the "three days" which

[15] *Urchristentum und Gottesdienst,* 2nd Edition, p. 67-72.

introduce the text are both allusions to the Passion. And thus the water changed into wine is an allusion to the Passion of Christ by which the legal purifications were abolished and the Blood of Christ washes away sins. The scrupulous observances of the Jews is to be replaced by the festive joy of the messianic age, symbolized by the wedding-feast.[16] And the Eucharistic wine is to be the sacrament by which participation in this nuptial feast is signified and effected.

This Eucharistic interpretation is confirmed by patristic tradition. Thus, St. Cyprian cites the event to justify the use of wine for the Eucharist: "How perverse and contrary it is, when the Lord at the wedding-feast made wine from water, for us to make water from wine, when the figurative meaning (*sacramentum*) of this event should rather teach us to offer wine in the sacrifices of the Lord. Indeed, since spiritual grace was lacking to the Jews, their wine was failing. For the vine of the Lord of hosts is the house of Israel. But Christ, teaching that the people of the Gentiles were to succeed the Jews, changed water to wine, that is to say, He showed that, at the marriage of Christ and the Church it is the people of the Gentiles who will crowd in, while the Jews will fail to come" (*Epist.* LXIII, 22; C.S.E.L., 711). Thus the wedding of Cana prefigures the marriage of Christ and the Church to which the nations are invited, as is signified by the substitution of wine, symbol of messianic joy, for the water of Jewish purifications. And the Eucharistic banquet is the sacrament of the participation of the nations in this wedding feast.

Cyril of Jerusalem also, in the *Mystagogic Catecheses* develops the same theme: "Christ has changed water into wine, which is akin to blood, at Cana of Galilee. And should we not consider it as even more worthy of faith that He has changed the wine into His Blood! Invited to the visible wedding, He accomplished this first miracle. And should we not much more confess that He has given to the children of the bridal-chamber the joy of His Body and Blood" (XXXIII, 1107 C). Let us notice that here again the emphasis is put at once on the symbol of the wine and on that of the marriage. Both the one and the other are related to the Eucharist. The wine is the visible sign; the marriage shows that

[16] Alf. Correl, *Consummatum est,* p. 257.

in the Eucharist the nuptial union of Christ and the Church is consummated in the soul of the Christian.[17]

Alongside this tradition (which seems to be the better founded) of seeing in the miracle of Cana a figure of the Eucharist, we should also mention another which makes it a figure of Baptism. The emphasis is here on the symbolism of the water instead of that of the wine. We have already met such an ambivalence with regard to the miracle of Horeb. Thus, Tertullian lists Cana as among the figures of Baptism (*De bapt.* 9; P. L. 1, 1210 A). Again, the Syrian prayer for the blessing of the water on the Vigil of Epiphany mentions the miracle of Cana next to that of Marra as figures of the transformation of the water. We recognize this typological sequence; and the text of Tertullian shows that this interpretation is also an ancient one.[18]

Let us observe, in connection with this Syrian prayer, the relationship of the miracle of Cana with the feast of the Epiphany. We know that today the Roman liturgy still brings together in this feast the three manifestations of Christ: the adoration of the Magi, the Baptism in the Jordan, the wedding-feast of Cana. And, furthermore, in the East at any rate, Epiphany was the day on which Baptism was given as well as on Easter. We can see how a whole sacramental typology was thus built up around this feast. Just as the Paschal initiation is placed in the perspective of the Exodus, so that the crossing of the Red Sea is a figure of Baptism, and the manna, of the Eucharist, so the typology of the Epiphany is placed in the framework of the New Testament: the Baptism in the Jordan is a figure of Christian Baptism, and the wedding at Cana of the Eucharist. And the characteristic feature of this cycle is its nuptial character: Christian initiation is seen to be the celebration of the marriage of Christ with the Church. We have seen the echo of this symbolism in the Roman liturgy of the Feast of the Epiphany in the Antiphon for the Benedictus: "Today the Church is united to her heavenly Bridegroom, since, in the Jordan, Christ washes away her sins, the Wise Men run with gifts to the royal marriage, and the guests are delighted with water changed into wine, alleluia."

[17] See also Eusebius, *Dem. Ev.,* 9; P.G., XXII, 684 D; Gaudentius of Brescia, *Serm.* 2; P.L., XX, 855 B.

[18] Pere Lundberg, *La typologie baptismale dans l'Ancienne Eglise,* p. 22-23.

CHAPTER FOURTEEN

The Mystery of the Sabbath

THE study of the sacraments has shown us that they are, in the present era of sacred history, the continuation of the great works wrought by God in the Old Testament and the New, and the prefiguration of Eschatology. And from this is follows that we cannot understand certain aspects of the sacraments fully unless we see them in this biblical perspective. This is also true of certain other aspects of Christian worship, and, in particular, of the liturgy of the great feasts. Here we have a double cycle, a weekly one and a yearly. We shall study first the one and then the other, confining ourselves, naturally, to the aspects of these cycles that are contained in the prolongation of Holy Scripture, and especially of the Old Testament.

There is, first of all, the weekly feast, that is, Sunday. Sunday is a purely Christian creation, connected with the historical fact of the Resurrection of the Lord. But since it is a weekly feast, the question arises of its relationship to the Jewish Sabbath. Before studying the symbolism of the Sunday, then, we need first to place Sunday in its proper relationship to the Sabbath, our concern being here with typology; and second with the Sabbath rest, our concern being with an institution. We shall only study this latter question in a secondary way.

The types of the Old Testament are persons, such as Noe or Isaac; events, such as the crossing of the Red Sea or the entrance into the Promised Land; and also institutions, such as the Temple, or circumcision. The Sabbath falls into this third category, of which it is one of the outstanding examples. Its character as a type is brought out in the New Testament: "Let no one, then, call you to account for what you eat or drink, or in regard to a festival or a new moon or a *Sabbath*. These are a *shadow* of things to come, but the substance is of Christ" (Col. 2:16). Here is the statement which will be the guiding principle of our whole study: the substance, the reality of the Sabbath is Christ. We need, then, to discover the religious reality of the Sabbath, for when it is thus set alongside the other types, it will show one aspect of what Christ is. This is the reason why the study of the Sabbath contains teaching which is always of value to us, even though the institution of the Sabbath as such has been abolished since Christ Who is its fulfillment has appeared.

The content of the idea of the Sabbath is expressed in two verses of Exodus which point out its two essential aspects. On the one hand, the Sabbath is "a day of rest (*anapausis*) consecrated to Yaweh" (Ex. 16; 25); on the other hand, the Sabbath is "the seventh day" (*hebdome*). A day of rest, the seventh day,—these are the two essential themes contained in the idea of the Sabbath. The Old Testament presents them as a literal prescription; the New Testament shows that they are now fulfilled: how Christ is the true rest, how Christianity is the true seventh day. And this shows us at once what is peculiar to the typology of the Sabbath,—that it is a typology of time.

This typology of the Sabbath is mentioned in the Old Testament itself. We have often remarked how the Old Testament gives us a primary spiritual view of Mosaic institutions, a primary Biblical typology. This remark here finds an outstanding application, and from a double point of view, as we shall now show. First of all, we find an eschatological interpretation of the Sabbath, that it is the symbol of time as sacred. We might say that it bears the same relation to time and history—that of being its great biblical symbol—as the temple, the other essential institution of Judaism, bears to the universe and to space. The Sabbath expresses the consecration of time to God, as the temple expresses that of space. And just as the temple, by the consecration of a limited enclosure, was the sacrament and prefiguring of the consecration of the whole universe, to be fulfilled in the resurrection of Jesus and the creation of the cosmos of the Church, so the Sabbath, by the consecration of a particular day of the week, was the sacrament of the consecration to God of the whole of history, which was also to find its principle in the resurrection of the incarnate Word.[1]

The other element in the Sabbath is the idea of rest (*anapausis*). Here also we find a primary typology in the Old Testament, consisting in a spiritualization of this idea of rest. In the prophets, and especially in Isaias, we find the statement repeated by the Fathers of the Church, that the true Sabbath, the true *anapausis,* is not to cease from physical work, but to cease from sinning. "The new moons and the Sabbaths and other festivals I will not abide, your assemblies are wicked . . . cease to do perversely, learn to do well . . ." (Is. I:13-19).[2] And this passage is the more important because, as we shall see presently, the teaching of Christ is its direct extension. This spiritualization of the idea of the Sabbath rest, which does not, obviously, exclude the idea of the actual practice of the Sabbath, is found again in Philo, transformed by its platonic setting, when he sees in the Sabbath the symbol of the soul "that rests in God and gives itself no more to any mortal work" (*De migr. Abrah.* 91).

We find a double typology of the Sabbath already sketched in the Old Testament and in apocalyptic and alexandrian Judaism. But this typology still lacks precision as to its content, and, above all, it is still indeterminate with regard to its object. As St. Paul tells us, it is Christ Who is the reality of which the Sabbath is only the shadow. Thus the Fathers of the Church were not the first to state this fact, for the christological interpretation of the Sabbath is already marked in the New Testament. We shall now take up again the two aspects of the typology of the Sabbath, but in the reverse order. The New Testament first of all extends the spiritualization of the Sabbath along the lines already marked out by Isaias; but it points out at the same time that the Sabbath is now gone by, since Christ is the reality which it prefigured. This

[1] On the eschatological aspect, properly so called, which appears in that type of Judaism in which eternity is considered as a Sabbath rest, see H. Riesenfeld, *Jésus transfiguré,* pp. 215 et seqq; A. G. Hebert, *The Throne of David,* pp. 147-149.
[2] See also LVIII, 13: "If thou callest the Sabbath a delight and honourest it by not following after thy ways."

aspect appears chiefly in the passages of the Gospel in which we see Christ in conflict with the Pharisees on the subject of the Sabbath rest. The typology of the Sabbath appears not as formulated in a theory, as it will be by St. Paul, but as existing and operative in the actual opposition between the Pharisees who incarnate the figure and Christ Who represents the reality. The first text is found in St. Matthew (XII: 1-13). The disciples were picking ears of a corn in a field on the Sabbath; the Pharisees protested, and Christ came to the defense of His Own.[3]

He begins by showing that the Old Testament itself gives examples of legitimate violations of the Sabbath: "Have you not read what David did when he and those who were with him were hungry? How he entered the house of God, and ate the loaves of proposition which neither he nor those with him could lawfully eat, but only the priests? Or have you not read in the Law, that on the Sabbath days the priests in the temple break the Sabbath and are guiltless?" (XII: 3-5).

And now come the important words: "But I tell you that One greater than the temple is here. But if you knew what this means, 'I desire mercy and not sacrifice,' you would never have condemned the innocent; for the Son of Man is Lord even of the Sabbath" (5-8). We must add to this passage another that follows it immediately, where we see Jesus, on the Sabbath day, healing a man with a withered hand, Jesus answered those who attacked Him: "It is lawful to do good on the Sabbath" (XII: 12).[4] We have here a criticism of the abuse caused by the formulation of the Pharisees in their way of understanding the Sabbath rest: this is obvious. But there is much more as well. In the first place, Jesus shows the secondary character of the Sabbath: it is not an absolute law, but a provisional institution. And He gives an example of this, inaugurating a line of argument which the Fathers were to take up and develop. He allows it to be understood that He is

[3] This passage is interpreted in a sense analogous to our own by H. Riesenfeld. He sees in the scene the foreshadowing of the eschatological Sabbath and of the heavenly meal (*Jésus transfiguré*, p. 318). Now this Sabbath is fulfilled in Christ. Here, then, we may have an allusion to the Sunday Eucharist (Cullmann, *Urchristentum und Gottesdienst*, pp. 60 et seq.).

[4] St. Epiphanius, commenting on this passage, writes that 'the Son of Man, Lord of the Sabbath, freed himself from its bondage and gave us the great Sabbath, which is the Lord himself, our rest and our Sabbath-keeping' (*De haer*, LXVI, 84; P.G., XLI, 165).

free to dispose of this institution,—and, by the example of His disciples, He lets it appear that its time has in fact gone by. But there is still more: the analogy with the Temple shows us that the two institutions are parallel. Jesus shows that He is greater than the Temple, and He clearly is also greater than the Sabbath. The Sabbath and the Temple are gone by because Christ Himself, the Sabbath and the temple of the New Testament, is here.

And the context gives us two examples of this reality of the new Sabbath which appears with Christ. On the one hand, the passage which we have quoted is immediately preceded by these words of Jesus: "Come to Me, all you who labor and are burdened, and I will give you rest. Take my yoke upon you, and learn from Me for I am meek and humble of heart; and you will find rest (*anapausis*) for your souls" (XI:29-30).[5] Christ is shown, then, as the true rest, the *anapausis* of the true Sabbath. And, in the second place, this episode is followed by the healing on the Sabbath day of the man with the withered hand. This healing, like all the miracles of Jesus, is an anticipated manifestation of the coming of His kingdom, of the true rest. The coincidence of this action with the Sabbath day shows us the relationship between the two events, just as the driving out of the merchants from the Temple shows that Jesus is the master of the Temple and Himself the true Temple. Thus, in these passages, Christ appears concretely as inaugurating the true Sabbath which replaces the figurative Sabbath. The opposition of the Pharisees is inexplicable otherwise, unless they saw that He pretended to give a substitute for the mosaic institution. Later typology was only to develop the consequence of this concrete attitude of Christ's.

The Gospel of St. John gives us an analogous episode; the healing on the Sabbath of the paralyzed man at the pool of Bethesda. We have already spoken of this event in connection with Baptism. The Jews persecuted Jesus because He did these things on the Sabbath day. Jesus answered: "My Father works until now, and I work" (V:17). And still more the Jews now seek to kill Him "because He made Himself equal to God" (V:18). The relation-

[5] It seems that there is here an allusion to the commandment forbidding the Jews to carry a 'burden,' on the Sabbath day. Christ is the true Sabbath who delivers us from the real burden which is sin. By a subtle contrast, the Sabbath rest is represented as a burden and the yoke of Christ as a rest. The connection is made by St. Augustine, *Epist.* II, 5, 10, 8.

ship of this mysterious word of Our Lord's with the Sabbath rest is clear. But Christ is speaking from an even higher level. The Jews of the time of Christ, in their exaltation of the Sabbath, thought that God Himself was subject to it. We find such an idea expressed in the Book of Jubilees (II, 16).[6] The word of Christ formally condemns the application to God of the Sabbath rest understood as idleness. In God there is no idleness; but His activity which, as St. Clement of Alexandria says, is identical with His love, is exercised without ceasing. And this is of great importance: the idleness, *otium,* of the Sabbath appears henceforth as a literal and inferior notion, giving room for seeking its spiritual meaning. The Fathers of the Church used this text to condemn the Sabbath rest by showing that it is not the law of the universe and that Christianity is the reality of which this idleness is the figure. Origen, using the same text of St. John, writes: "He shows by this that God does not cease to order the world on any Sabbath of this world. The true Sabbath, in which God will rest from all His works, will, therefore, be the world to come," (*Ho. Num.* XXII, 4). The working of Christ is seen to be the reality which comes to replace the figurative idleness of the Sabbath.

Thus, we have seen in the Gospel itself, in a concrete manner, the opposition between Christ and the Sabbath. This opposition is still veiled. There was a time in which the figure and the reality existed side by side. This coexistence continued in the primitive Christian community. We see the Apostles at Jerusalem observing the Sabbath after the Resurrection of Christ (Acts XIII:14; XVI:3). But this is a survival of a world which has passed away, while the reality which replaces it is already present. It is the same way with the Temple: there the Apostles continued to go and pray, while the new Temple, which is the Christian community, was already in existence. We find here one of those turning-points of history, an essential articulation in which the new reality appears and disengages itself step by step from an ancient world which is dying.[7] The destruction of Jerusalem brought

[6] See A. Marmorstein, *Quelques problèmes d'ancienne apol. juive,* Rev. Et. Juive, 1914, p. 161. However, even so early a writer as Philo opposes this idea: 'God never ceases to act. But as it is the property of fire to warm, so it is of God to create' (*Leg. All.,* I, 5-6).

[7] This is what is expressed by the theme of Christ as *telos-arche,* which we have met in the cycle of Noe.

about the destruction of Temple: St. Paul proclaimed the end of the Sabbath (Rom. XIV:6). Only a few judaising communities continued to observe it (Eusebius, Hist. Eccles. III, 27). And it is also St. Paul who formulated the meaning of this historical evolution. If the Sabbath was to die little by little, this was because it was only a provisional institution and a figure of the world to come. Now this world has come: the figure need only disappear: "Let no one, then, call you to account for what you eat or drink, or in regard to a festival or a new moon or a Sabbath. These are a shadow of things to come, but the substance is of Christ" (Col. II:16). Thus, the Gospel shows us in Christ Himself the true rest prefigured by the Sabbath idleness, the prophetic significance of which Isaias had already begun to perceive. The New Testament also shows us that Christ is the "seventh day," that is to say, the sacred time which succeeds profane days, of which the story of creation gives us the first theological interpretation. Here again the special quality of New Testament interpretation is that it is christological: it shows us in Christ Himself this seventh day, of which the Old Testament perceived only the prophetic significance. The capital text here is the prologue of the Gospel of St. Matthew. The ancestors of Christ are arranged in six groups of seven persons each. In this way, Christ appears as inaugurating the seventh age of the world, as being in Himself alone this seventh age. And it is clear that this is actually the meaning of this arrangement. The Book of Chronicles, in giving the genealogies of Abraham and of Noe, groups their descendents under the symbolic number of seventy. These groupings by sevens are obviously intentional. That given by St. Matthew is an application to Christ of the chronological symbolism of the sacred week. The genealogy given by St. Luke is also founded on the number 7, but in a different way: he gives seventy-seven names from Adam to Jesus. Gregory of Nyssa had already remarked upon the characteristic of sevens. And thus the genealogy of St. Matthew makes of the seventh day a figure of Christ.

The Epistle to the Hebrews justifies this interpretation by showing that the seventh day truly had this prophetic meaning (III:7; IV:11). The author begins with the words of Psalm XCIV:

11).[8] "They shall not enter into My rest," (*anapausis*), and connects this rest explicitly with the seventh day (IV, 4). We are dealing, then, with the repose of the seventh day, that is to say, with rest in its eschatological form. And this rest, as the author shows, cannot be that of which it is said that God rested on the seventh day. For indeed, "the works of God have been finished since the beginning of the world" (IV:3) and here it is the future of the world which is in question. So the "archeological" interpretation, that of the Old Testament, is done away with. There can be no further question of the entrance into the Promised Land, although this is the meaning obviously suggested by the Psalm. But, as the author says: "If Josue had led them into rest, David, such a long time afterwards, would not have spoken of another day (IV:8). Neither can the fall of Jericho after seven days be that which is meant by the *anapausis* of the psalm. Therefore, besides the rest of God, in the order of creation, and the rest of Israel, in the order of the Old Testament, there is a third rest, which is that of which the psalm speaks: "There remains, therefore, a Sabbath rest for the people of God. For he who has entered into his rest, has himself also rested from his own works, even as God did from his. Let us therefore hasten to enter into that rest" (IV, 10-11).

This text is remarkable especially for the parallelism which is established between the three "sabbatisms" of which the liturgical Sabbath is the figure. This is shown to be in Judaism a commemoration of creation and of its consecration to God; and later also to be a commemoration of the entrance into the Promised Land and of the temporal realization of the promise. But these two meanings are in turn the prefiguration and the prophecy of another *sabbatismus,* of a seventh day, which had not yet come about and which is realized in Jesus Christ, since henceforth this seventh day exists, and we should hasten to enter into it. Thus, we find once more, but commented on and justified, the eschatological theme indicated in the genealogy of Matthew. The symbolism of the seventh day serves above all to emphasize the character of Christianity as an eschatological event. We are now placed in the perspective of history, and this is, indeed, the mean-

[8] See the exegesis of this text in Chrysostum, *In Ep. ad Hebr.* IV, 8; P.G. LXIII, 55-58. He distinguishes three kinds of rest: that of God, that of the Promised Land, and that of Christ.

ing of the whole Epistle. God Who gave to the Jews the first opportunity for salvation, which they refused, is now offering a new one. This salvation is Christ. He is the seventh day, the seventh age of the world. A new era of grace is opening with His coming. We must not let it go by, as the Jews did theirs. Let us further notice that the theme of rest and the theme of the seventh day, the spiritual aspect and the eschatological aspect are reunited—and reunited in the one person of Christ Who gives them their meaning. The message of the New Testament is, above all, in fact, to point out that Christ is He Who was announced by all the prefigurations of the Old Testament.[9]

The New Testament shows us the abolition of the Sabbath and its fulfillment in Christ as an accomplished fact. The writers of the Church later on were to explain the meaning of this fact. This abolition gave rise, indeed, like that of the other mosaic institutions, to a difficult problem. On the one hand, the literal practice of the Sabbath is the object of an express commandment of God in the Old Testament, which was considered by the Christians to be an inspired book. But also, this practice was abolished by Christ, and the Sabbath now possessed for the Christian only the value of a symbol. How could these two statements be reconciled? It is impossible to say that God could contradict Himself. Two extreme solutions now present themselves. On the one hand, the judaiser maintained the literal practice of the Sabbath. They were, then, in agreement with the Old Testament, but in conflict with the Church. On the other side, the gnostics rejected the Old Testament by considering it the work of another God. This did away with the contradiction, but led to a rejection of the Old Testament, a rejection which was equally unacceptable. The Christians saw clearly that they must affirm both the inspiration of the Old Testament and the outmoded character of the Sabbath. But it took some time to see how it was possible to reconcile the two affirmations.

A first solution consisted in denying purely and simply that the literal practice of the Sabbath had ever been the object of a com-

[9] Are we to see an eschatological reference to the 'rest of the seventh day' in St. Peter's words at the Transfiguration: 'It is good for us to be here'? This attractive hypothesis is put forward by H. Riesenfeld (*Jésus transfiguré*, p. 259): it is not, however, decisive.

mandment of God. This is the solution of Pseudo-Barnabas. For him, the institutions of the Old Testament were purely a symbolic language, which it is the purpose of *gnosis* to understand. But the Jews did not posssess this *gnosis:* they took its language literally, and all their practices never ceased to be condemned by God. That of the Sabbath in particular was always reproved (II.5). As M. Lestringant well says: "For him, Christian exegesis did not need to give Scripture a new meaning, for at no time had it had any other meaning. God had always revealed one truth. The sacrifices, the temple, circumcision, were only signs. Their practice would constitute a flagrant violation of the will of God. And furthermore God had formally warned the unfaithful nation that He wished neither sacrifice nor offering" (*Essai sur l'unite de la revelation biblique,* p. 168). This solution simplified the question. Christ did not need to give a figurative meaning to the Sabbath, for it had never had any other meaning, it had never been anything but a symbol. The figurative sense of Scripture is the literal, since Moses intended to speak in symbolic language. This radical solution, which later was to be that of Pascal,[10] while it assured the unity of Revelation, took away from the Old Testament its own proper substance.

The solution of Justin was less absolute. He shows first how, even in the Old Testament, the commandment of the Sabbath was not the object of an unconditional obligation since it admitted of exceptions: "Did God wish to make your priests commit sin when they offered sacrifices on the Sabbath day, and also those who received or gave circumcision on the day of the Sabbath, since He commanded that new-born children should be circumcised on the eighth day even if it was the Sabbath" (*Dial.* XXVII, 5). Justin reproduces Christ's own line of argument as given in St. Matthew (XII: 5), and adds a second example to that given by Christ. We are at the beginning of a line of reasoning which we shall find again and again throughout patristic literature and which was constantly enriched by new examples. Tertullian gives those of the fall of Jericho on the Sabbath day (Jos. VI:4) and of the Machabees fighting on the Sabbath (*Adv. Jud.,* 4; P. L., II, 606 B-C). We find all these texts again in Irenaeus (*Adv. haer.,*

[10] A. M. Dubarle, *Pascal et l'interprétation de l'Ecriture* R.S.P.T., 1941, pp. 346 et seq.

V. 8; P. G. VII, 994-995), in *Aphraates* (*Dem.* XIII; P. S. I, 568-569), and in the *Testimonia adversus Judaeos* handed on under the name of Gregory of Nyssa (P. G., XLVI, 222 B-C.) This is a primary form of argument which continues that of the Gospel.

The second line of argument also proceeds from the Gospel: this is the fact that God does not observe the Sabbath in the government of the world. We have already remarked in connection with St. John V:17, that this is an answer to the Jewish notion that God Himself is subject to the Sabbath. St. Justin returns twice to this argument: "Look at the stars, they do not rest, they observe no Sabbath" (XXIII,3). And further on: "God governs the world on that day in the same way as He governs it on all the others" (XXIX, 3). Inside Judaism, certain men like Philo also rejected as being too excessive the idea of God being subject to the Sabbath. The argument of Justin was taken up by Clement of Alexandria: "Being good, if (God) ceased to do good, He would cease to be God" (*Strom.* VI, 16; Staehlin, 504, 1-5). We find it again in Origen: "We always see that God is acting, and there is no Sabbath on which He does not act" (*Hom. Num.* XXIII, 4). It is in the *Didascalia of the Apostles:* "The economy of the universe always continues, the stars do not cease for even an instant in their regular movements produced by the ordinance of God. If He says: "You are to observe the rest, how is it that He Himself acts, creating, conserving, nourishing, governing us and His creatures. . . . But these things (the precept of the Sabbath rest) were established for a time, in figure" (*Const. Ap.* VI, 18, 17).[11]

These two first arguments against the absolute value of the Sabbath rest are, then, developed from the Gospel itself. Justin adds a third, which is the most important for an understanding of his position with regard to the Sabbath: "Those who were called just before Moses and Abraham and who were pleasing to God, were not circumcised nor did they observe the Sabbath. Why did God not teach them these practices?" (XXVII, 5. See also XLVI, 2-3). Not only is the world not subject to the Sabbath, but the patriarchs, whom the Jews venerated, were not made subject to it by God. Certain Jews, like the author of the Book of Jubilees, do indeed show us the Patriarchs as observing the Sabbath. But this is an obvious exaggeration. The Sabbath is, then, in no way neces-

[11] See also Aphraates, *Dem.*, XIII, 3; P.S., I, 547; XIII, 9; 563.

sary to salvation, since the Jews themselves recognized that Abraham was saved without having practiced it (XLVI, 3). This line of argument, which is not to be found in the New Testament in explicit terms, but of which we find the equivalent, also was taken up by the whole of tradition (Tertullian *Adv. Jud.* 4; P. L. II, 606; Aphraates, *Dem.* XIII, 8; P. S. I, 558). We find it also in the *Didascalia:* "If God had wanted us to observe the rest after six days, He would have begun by making the patriarchs observe it and all the just men who lived before Moses" (*Const. Ap.* VI, 18, 16).

But, then, why was the Sabbath instituted? Justin does not go so far as Barnabas; he holds that God did will the practice of the Sabbath in its literal meaning. It is not, then, a pure figure. But this divine institution is not an honor for Israel; it does not mark any progress in the plan of salvation. On the contrary, it is only because of the wickedness of Israel that God imposed the Sabbath on them: "It was only for you that circumcision was necessary, for Noe and Melchisedech did not observe the Sabbath and nevertheless they pleased God, and also those who followed them, up to Moses, under whom we see your wicked people making a golden calf in the desert. . . . See why God adapted Himself to your people. The Sabbath was prescribed for you in order to make you keep God in mind" (XIX, 6. See also XXVII, 2; XLV, 3; XLVI, 5; CXII, 4). It is, then, because the Jews are unfaithful to the natural law of divine worship that, to lead them to it, God gave them the Sabbath as means of education. The Sabbath, then, is seen as the very sign of the reprobation of the Jewish people: "It is indeed because of your own wickedness and that of your fathers that, to mark you with a sign, God prescribed that you should observe the Sabbath" (XXI, 1).

Thus, the existence of the Sabbath is justified, but still not as a stage in history. Let us notice in fact that, according to Justin, not only was the Sabbath an inferior institution in God's eyes, while He had a better order in view, but this better order was that which He had instituted in the beginning. The situation of the patriarchs is superior to that of the Jews, which marks a decadence. Christ, then, reestablished the primitive order. In other words, Justin still sees no other way of avoiding contradiction in God, than to admit that His will always was that there should be no Sabbath, and that it was only a previsory infraction of the unchangeable order He had established. This is what Justin explicitly states: "God does not accept sacrifice from you; and if He once commanded you to offer them, it was not that He had need of them but because of your sins. . . . If we did not admit this, we come to fall into absurd ideas such as that it was not the same God Who existed in the time of Henoch and of all those who did not observe the Sabbath, since it was Moses who ordered it to be done. . . . It was because men were sinners that He Who is always the same prescribed these ordinances and others like them" (XXIII, 1). The immutability of God cannot be saved, according to Justin, except by the immutability of the world established by Him. He has no idea of any progressive revelation. And we find once more in Eusebius of Cesarea this same conception which denies all history.

In any case, we can see from the foregoing that God could suppress the Sabbath without contradicting Himself in any way, since He was led to institute it only because He was forced to do so by the wickedness of the Jewish people, and in consequence He had the desire to make it disappear as soon as He had accomplished His purpose of education: "So, just as circumcision began with Abraham, so the Sabbath began with Moses (and he showed that these institutions were made because of the hardness of your people); so also, by the will of God, they had to disappear in Him Who was born of a Virgin of the race of Abraham, Christ, the Son of God" (XLIII, 1). The coming of Christ marks the end of this provisional economy. It was intended only to prepare for Him. Its literal practice was a sketch of what Christ was to realize in fullness: "I can, by taking them one by one, show that all the prescriptions of Moses were only types, announcements, symbols of that which was to come with Christ" (XLII, 4). The true Sabbath does not consist in consecrating one day only to God, but every day, and not in abstaining from corporal work, but from sin: "The new law wills that you should continually observe the Sabbath, yet you think that you are pious because you rest and do nothing on one day. You do not reflect on the reason for the precept. It is not in these things that the Lord our God is pleased. If there be among you a perjurer or a thief, let him cease (*pausastho*); if there be an adulterer, let him do penance, and he will have observed the Sabbaths of delights, the true Sabbaths of God" (XII, 3).

These last lines are important. They clearly contrast the exterior practice of rest on one day of the week, which is only a figure, with the interior practice of which this rest is the symbol. In reality, the Sabbath, that is to say, the whole Christian life should be consecrated to God—and this not by abstaining from work with our hands, but by ceasing to sin. The context shows that this ceasing from sin should be understood of Baptism. It is Christ, then, Who is the true Sabbath, of which the Jewish Sabbath was the figure. What is important here is that we find the spiritual interpretation of Isaias, which is in the background of this whole passage (Justin quotes it at length, XII, I; XIII, 2-9; XIV, 4; XV, 2-7), related to the economy of Christianity. The true Sabbath of which Isaias spoke, and which consists in "ceasing to do evil" (1:16), is in Christ Who is the cessation from sin, which He alone fulfills. Christ introduces us into the unique Sabbath, of which the Sabbaths of the Law were only a prophetic prefiguration which did not give what they signified. The spiritualizing process begun by Isaias is continued by Justin and thus carried out in the Christian dispensation. We are now, therefore, in the most authentic line of biblical typology.

But there remains the fact that in Justin it is above all the negative aspect of the typology of the Sabbath which appears, that is to say, the justification of the disappearance of the observance of the literal precept. This is easily explained when we realize that his attention was focussed on the conflict with the Jews. Irenaeus had a different problem, for he was faced with the reverse error, that of the Gnostics. His thought on this point is not always perfectly homogeneous. Sometimes he accepts the presuppositions of Justin and admits that the appearance of the legislation is connected with the decadence of Israel in Egypt (IV, 16, 3; P. G. VII, 1017 A-B). But elsewhere his most profound thought appears: God is forming humanity according to a progressive economy (IV:38, 1.). It is quite normal, then, that the Law should have corresponded to a humanity still in a state of infancy, as it is normal that it should give place to a more perfect economy when humanity has been brought by it to a higher perfection. Thus the true idea of the Sabbath now appears. It may today be abolished, and yet, yesterday, have been the expression of the divine will: it is not God Who has changed, but rather that man exists in time. Thus Irenaeus can show that the Sabbath is an excellent institution (IV, 8, 2; P. G. VII, 994) and at the same time state that it is now abolished. It is not because of the wickedness of men that the Law appeared, as if it were a regression in relation to the unchangeable order willed by God, but it is because the development of humanity has been progressive; it needed to begin with an education adapted to its beginnings. But now that humanity has emerged from this state of infancy, the shadow of the Law must give place to the reality of the Gospel: "The Law will no longer command that man pass to one day in rest and idleness who observes the Sabbath every day in the temple of God which is his own heart" (*Dem.* 96).

The Jewish institution of the Sabbath now appears as being the figure of the perpetual Sabbath which is Christianity. We should note the parallelism with the temple. Here we find again the typology of Justin which Irenaeus develops still further: "God gave (the Sabbaths) as a sign. But these signs are not lacking in symbolism, that is to say, are not without teaching; neither are they arbitrary, since they were instituted by a wise artisan, for the Sabbaths taught perseverance in the service of God enduring all through the day. 'We are thought of,' says St. Paul 'as sheep to be slaughtered all the day long,' that is to say, we are consecrated, following our faith at all times, persevering it and abstaining from all covetousness, neither buying nor possessing any treasures upon earth. And by that was signified also, in some way, the rest of God after creation, that is to say, the kingdom in which the man who has persevered in following God will take part in His feast" (IV, 16, 1; P. G. 1015-1016).

This text affirms first of all and with great precision, the significant character of the Sabbath: "The signs were not without symbolism." He then develops this symbolism in a double ecclesiastical and eschatological sense. Thus, we find once more the two directions taken by the typology of the Sabbath which we had perceived in the Old Testament and found again in the Gospel. Concerning the first of these directions, Irenaeus brings out the two aspects which we have already met with in Justin: on the one hand, perseverance in the service of God during the whole of life, of which the one day reserved to Him was only the figure; and on the other, the ceasing to do evil; we should remark, however, that, according to an idea peculiar to Irenaeus, the Jewish Sabbath meant abstention from servile work, that is to say, from gainful work (IV, 8, 2; 994 B) [12] and thus was less the figure of the absence of sin than of detachment from earthly things. With regard to the eschatological aspect, he remains in the order of the Old Testament: the seventh day is not the figure of Christianity as it first appears, as in the texts of the Gospel and of the Epistle to the Hebrews, but it is the figure of the world to come.[13] This aspect of the typology of the Sabbath is related to Irenaeus, as by the Epistle to the Hebrews, to the text of Genesis. Thus, we find that the eschatological typology of the Sabbath was developed along the lines of Genesis, as taken up by the Epistle to the Hebrews, while the spiritual typology was developed along the lines of Isaias, taken up by the Gospel of St. Matthew.

With Irenaeus, the typology of the Sabbath appears as fixed in its essential lines, both negatively, in the justification for the abolition of the Jewish Sabbath, and positively, in the content of the symbolism of the Sabbath. We shall find it developed in these two directions by Tertullian and Origen. Tertullian takes the first aspect. His *Adversus Judaeos,* which continues the *Dialogue with Typho,* is a part of the controversy with Judaism in which the question of the Sabbath was in the forefront. Tertullian distinguishes the Sabbaths: "The Scriptures speak of an eternal and a temporal Sabbath" (*Adv. Jud.* 4). The temporal Sabbath is human, the eternal Sabbath divine. And it existed before the temporal Sabbath: "Thus, before the temporal Sabbath, there was an eternal Sabbath shown and predicted in advance. Let the Jews learn that Adam kept the Sabbath, and that Abel when he offered God a holy victim, pleased Him by fulfilling the Sabbath, and that Noe, builder of the Ark because of the great Deluge, observed the Sabbath" (*id*). This Sabbath, indeed, is the worship of God.

[12] See Isaias LVIII, 13.

[13] The eschatological interpretation is peculiar to Irenaeus. It is a taking up of the Jewish typology. The first Christian writers had shown that this typology was fulfilled in Christ. Irenaeus shows that there is an eschatology in Christianity itself. We have already remarked upon this aspect of his thought in connection with the theme of Paradise and that of the Flood. On the Jewish origins of this eschatological typology, see H. Riesenfeld, *Jésus transfiguré,* pp. 215 et seq.

Prefigured by the patriarchs, "we see that it is fulfilled in the time of Christ, when all flesh, that is to say, every nation, has come to Jerusalem to adore God the Father through His Son Jesus Christ." It is this Sabbath that "God wishes us to keep from now on." This is why "we know that we should abstain from all servile work, and that not only on the seventh day, but all the time."

We find again the idea of the true Sabbath conceived as the worship of God and abstension from servile work, understood in the spiritual sense, and this perpetually. The interest of the passage lies in the fact that Tertullian shows that the practice of the Sabbath by the patriarchs was a figure of its realization in Christ. But what about the temporal Sabbath, that is, the Mosaic institution of ceasing from work on one day of the week? This was a temporary institution, and Tertullian sees the proof of it in the fact that, even in the Old Testament, it was often suspended. He uses the examples that we have already quoted. "It is, then, clear that observances of this kind had a temporary value and were rendered necessary by the circumstances of the time, and that God did not give this law in the past to be a perpetual observance." So the Sabbath, decreed for a time, was destined to disappear: "This is why, when it is clear that a temporal Sabbath was established and an eternal Sabbath predicted, it follows that, all the physical precepts having been given in the past to the people of Israel, a time would come when the precepts of the ancient law of the old ceremonies would cease, and when the promise of the new law would come, when the light would shine for those who were sitting in darkness." [14] So Tertullian completes what had remained implicit in the thought of Irenaeus by showing that the eternal Sabbath which already existed in the Old Testament alongside the temporal Sabbath, was itself a prefiguration of Christ, the only true Sabbath, and was by this very fact the announcement that the temporal Sabbath was only a provisional economy.

As Tertullian thus makes more precise the typology of the Sabbath as to its form, so Origen continues the thought of Irenaeus by developing its content, and this in its double ecclesial and

[14] There is the same reference to the Epistle to the Hebrews in the Contra Celsum: 'Long, mysterious (μυστικός), deep and difficult would be the explanation of the creation of the world and the day of rest (*sabbatismus*) remaining to the people of God' (V, 59; Koetschau 63, 2).

eschatological meaning. In the *XXIII Homily on the Book of Numbers,* he treats the typology of the various Jewish feasts, along the lines of Philo in the *De Decalogo,* but without borrowing anything from him. "The just must also celebrate the feast of the Sabbath. But what is this Sabbath feast except that of which the Apostle says: 'There remains, therefore, a day of rest (*sabbatismus*), that is to say, the observance of the Sabbath reserved to the people of God.' Leaving aside, then, the Jewish observances of the Sabbath, let us see what ought to be the observance of the Sabbath for a Christian. On the Sabbath day, none of the works of the world are to be done. If, then, you abstain from all works that are worldly, and do not busy yourself with any worldly affair but keep yourself free for spiritual things, go to the Church, listen to readings and divine homilies, meditate on heavenly things, concern yourself with the hope to come, consider not the things that are present and visible but those that are future and invisible,—this is the observance of the Christian Sabbath. He who abstains from the works of the world and frees himself for spiritual things, he it is who celebrates the feast of the Sabbath. He bears no burden on the journey. For the burden is any sin, as the Prophet says: They weigh on me like a heavy burden. On the Sabbath day, every one stays seated in his own place. What is the spiritual place of the soul? Justice is its place, and truth, wisdom, holiness, and everything that Christ is, this is the true place for the soul. And it is from this place that it should not go out if it is to keep true Sabbaths: 'He who dwells in me, I also will dwell in him.' " (John XV:5) (*Ho. Num.* XXIII, 4).[15]

Here, then, is the spiritual and ecclesial sense. The fulfillment of the figure of the Sabbath is the whole Christian life, which is wholly spiritual and consecrated to God. To this meaning, Origen adds the eschatological. "Since we have spoken of the true Sabbaths, if we seek, going still higher, to learn what the true Sabbaths are, it is beyond this world that we find the true observance of the Sabbath. This is, indeed, what is written in Genesis, that 'God rested on the seventh day from all His works.' We see that

[15] For Origen the rest symbolized by the Sabbath is the recollected mood of contemplation rather than abstention from sin. This comes from Philo, *De spec. leg.*, II, 64.

it was not fulfilled on the seventh day, and that it is not even fulfilled now, for we see that God is always acting and that there is no Sabbath day on which He does not act, on which He does not cause the sun to rise on the just and the unjust, to strike and to heal. This is why the Lord, in the Gospel, accused by the Jews of acting and of healing on the Sabbath, answered them: 'My Father works even until now, and I work,' showing by that that on no Sabbath of this world does God cease to administer the world and to provide for the needs of the human race. Indeed, He made, at the beginning of creation, substances to exist, as numerous as He, the Creator, thought necessary for the perfection of the world; but to the consummation of the ages He will not cease to administer them and to conserve them. The true Sabbath, after which God will rest from all His works, will therefore be the future world, when sorrow, sadness, and groanings will disappear and God will be all in all. May God grant that we may feast on this Sabbath with Him and celebrate it with His holy angels, offering the sacrifice of praise and giving thanks to the Most High. Then indeed the soul will be able ceaselessly to be present with God and to offer Him the sacrifice of praise by the High Priest, Who is a Priest for eternity according to the order of Melchisedech." (*Ho. Num.* XXIII, 4).[16]

We find here again the echo of the former tradition. With Justin, Origen recalls that God is not subject to the Sabbath, since He does not cease to govern creation. And we should notice that he connects the Sabbath with the text of John V:17. This idea was taken up again by Clement of Alexandria (*Strom.* VI, 16; Staehlin, p. 504, 2), but without being connected with the evangelical text. With Irenaeus, he shows that the rest of God which is signified in Genesis is not only the present time, but rather the world which will follow on after this creation. The Sabbath henceforth is a figure of the entrance of man into this future world where he will rest from his works, that is to say, where he will take part in the divine banquet, in the liturgy of the angels, where he will eternally offer with Christ the High Priest the sacrifice of praise. Here are the true Sabbaths of God, of which

[16] See also *Ho. Lev.*, XIII, 5: "The number six has a certain connection with this world"; *Ho. Jud.*, IV, 2: "The number six is symbolic of this world, which was completed in six days."

the Jewish Sabbath was the far-off prefiguration, of which continual prayer is the sacramental beginning in the Church, and of which the heavenly liturgy is the full accomplishment.

This figurative aspect of the Sabbath is that which appeared the most striking to the first Christian generation. Preoccupied first of all with marking the end of the Jewish order and its replacing by the Christian reality, it insisted above all on the fact that the *institution* of the Sabbath was fulfilled by the whole Christian mystery. But it appeared also that this Christian mystery included a sacramental structure, that is to say, that in the Church spiritual realities expressed themselves by means of visible signs. The loaves of proposition were abolished, but the Church possesses another Bread. The Temple of Jerusalem was destroyed and fulfilled in the whole Christ, the place of the divine Presence, but the Church also possesses churches of stone, connected with the Eucharistic presence. Christianity is not a purely spiritual reality. Its spiritual essence expresses itself by means of these visible realities, and this precisely is the Liturgy. And this is true of our topic also. The Sabbath was abolished and fulfilled in the risen Christ, but the Resurrection of Christ had a visible commemoration, that is, the Sunday.

CHAPTER FIFTEEN

The Lord's Day

THE celebration of the Lord's Day is one of the most ancient rites of Christianity. As early as the second century, Ignatius of Antioch defined the Christian by the celebration of the *Kyriake:* "Those who once lived according to the ancient order of things have come to the new hope, observing no longer the Sabbath, but the Lord's Day, the day on which our life was raised up by Christ and by His death" (*Magnes.*, VI, 1).[1] At about the same time, a pagan, in trying to describe what was characteristic of the conduct of a Christian, could find nothing better than to say: "They have the custom of gathering together on a fixed day (*stato die*) before dawn, and to say a prayer to the Christ as to God" (Letter of Pliny the Younger to Trajan, *Epist.* X, 96). This "fixed day"—which Pliny had no other way of defining since in the official calendar there was no weekly recurrence—is our Sunday. And this gathering which had for its object a prayer to Christ as God, or *Kyrios,* is the Eucharistic synaxis of the Lord's Day.

The Lord's Day is a purely Christian institution; its origin is to be found solely in the fact of the Resurrection of Christ on the day after the Sabbath. The custom of gathering together on this day appears in the very week following the Resurrection, when

[1] The word κυριακή appears for the first time in Apoc., I, 9. The Latin equivalent is *dominicus dies* (Tertullian, De or., 23), from which the French *dimanche* is derived.

we find the Apostles gathered in the Cenacle. Sunday is the continuation of this weekly reunion. It is the commemoration of the Resurrection of Christ, the sacrament of His presence in the midst of His Own, the prophecy of His second coming. In the beginning, this constituted its unique significance: as being the weekly Easter. But, at the same time, this day had various characteristics capable of being taken as symbols: it was the first day of the Jewish week; it fell on the day of the sun in the astrological calendar; and it was the eighth day.

We shall now examine these meanings. But, first, we must say something about the relationship between the Sunday and the Sabbath. Originally, what made the Sunday was the synaxis which took place only on the Lord's Day. But this presented the difficulty of separating the day of worship from the Sabbath day of rest. The day of rest had, even in paganism, a religious significance: "It is something common to both Greeks and barbarians," writes Strabo, "to associate sacrifices with the relaxation proper to feasts. Nature itself teaches this. For relaxation indeed, turns the spirit away from its preoccupations and turns it to God" (X; p. 467, 9). And this natural reality was taken up by Judaism into the idea of the Sabbath. Philo clearly shows us the transition from one to the other: "Since we are made up of a body and a soul, Moses gave to the body the activities proper to it, and to the soul those befitting it, and he took care to found the one upon the other, so that, when the body was working, the soul could rest, and when the body in turn rested, then the soul worked: Thus the best ways of life, the contemplative and the practical, follow each other alternately, the practical life having six days as its own for corporal needs, the contemplative life having the seventh day to be free for study and for the perfect life of the spirit" (*De spec. leg.*, 64).[2]

The day of Christian rest could have been inserted into, and

[2] See Pierre Boyancé, *Le culte des Muses*, 1939, p. 210 et seq. We may wonder how far Philo alters the meaning of the Aristotelian idea of contemplative rest when he embodies it in the Sabbath. The question is all the more important for us in that, through Eusebius, this Aristotelian idea was to pass from the Sabbath to Sunday. The (Aristotelian) idea of contemplation (θεωρία) was to take the place of the (biblical) idea of waiting. In proportion as the biblical aspect is done away with, we should speak of there being a deformation; insofar as the Aristotelian aspect merely colours the biblical aspect, without taking its place, we should speak of a contingent, but lawful, embodiment.

so made to transform, the day of cosmic rest already represented by the Jewish Sabbath. But this is not what we find in primitive Christianity: the day of rest is separated from the day of worship. Thus the Lord's Day was dissociated from the Sabbath. Here, in fact, Christianity met with a major difficulty in achieving its sacramental realization: as far as it was concerned, the day of worship was absolutely fixed as Sunday, and this in such a radical way that nothing could ever modify this institution of the Lord Himself. But the day of rest was a different one in the civilizations in which Christianity developed. The Romans had holidays which alternated with working days according to a variable rhythm which was not that of seven days; and the Jews had Saturday. We must add the fact that the custom of the Sabbath rest had spread into pagan milieux as Tertullian testifies: "Certain people among you devote the day of Saturn to idleness and good cheer, following in this the Jewish custom of which they are ignorant" (*Apol.* XVI, 11).

We understand now the situation in which the Christians found themselves, being unable to make the Lord's Day coincide with the weekly day of rest. This is one of the aspects of the drama of primitive Christianity, that it was lived out in the midst of a civilization that was strange and hostile to it. Tertullian admirably describes this situation, showing that Christians must at once be present and be instransigeant, refusing to leave the society of men, and yet never denying the demands of Christianity which are opposed to the customs of that society.[3] Thus, in the case we are considering, the Christians remained faithful to the Lord's Day, trying to include in it as much leisure as possible, (*differentes negotia*) as Tertullian says (*De Or.* 23), in order to be free for worship and for the assembly, and at the same time continuing the practice of rest on the days fixed by the society of their time, but doing away with their idolatrous aspect. Finally, the Lord's Day succeeded in taking over the observance of the day of the rest; and then the abnormal division which had existed in primitive Christianity was done away with.

For, in the fourth century, profiting by the fact that, as the day of the Sun, the first day of the week was venerated by pagans as well as by Christians, Constantine made it a holiday, consecrated

[3] Apol., XLII, 2-4.

to worship.[4] I do not need to examine here the sociological aspect of this question, but it is certain that this decree gave to the institution of the Lord's Day a quite new importance, and brought out still more its substitution for Saturday, which was formerly the holiday for certain pagans as well as for the Jews. This decree was thus a visible sign of the triumph of Christianity. We can understand, then, why the writers of the fourth century so often treated of the symbolism of the Sabbath and of the Lord's Day. This symbolism was supported by the liturgical fact of the Sunday, even when no direct allusion was made to it. And the expansion of the practice of the Lord's Day caused an equal flowering of the mysticism connected with that Day.

In an important text, Eusebius gives us the perfect expression of the transposition of the symbolism of the Sabbath to the *Kyriake*. "It is necessary to examine what the Sabbath signifies. Scripture characterizes it as the rest of God: it introduces it, indeed, after the creation of the sensible world. What, then, could be the rest of God, except His dwelling in the realities that are intelligible and above the world. Indeed, when He looks at the sensible world and gives Himself to the operations of the providence of the cosmos, He is said to act. And it is in this sense that we should understand the word of Our Lord: 'My Father works until now and I work' (John V:17). But when He turns to the realities that are intelligible and above the world, and when He is, so to say, in the observatory (*periope*) to be found there, then we may consider Him as resting during this time and so fulfilling His Sabbath. In the same way, when men of God turn themselves away from the works that weary the soul (such are all the works of the body and those dear to earthly flesh) and turn themselves wholly toward God, giving themselves up to the contemplation of things that are divine and intelligible, then they observe the Sabbaths that are dear to God and the rest of the Lord (*Kyrios*) God. And it is of these Sabbaths that it is said: 'Now there remains a Sabbath rest for the people of God' (Heb. 4:9). For, in-

[4] Eusebius, *Vit. Const.*, IV, 18 (P.G., XX, 1165, B-C): "(Constantine) ruled that the day which is truly the first (πρώτη) and the chief (κυρία), the Lord's day, the day of salvation, was to be considered as a day of prayer. . . . He ordered all those who lived beneath the Roman authority to make holiday on Sundays and likewise to honour the Fridays" (See Jean Gaudemet, *La législation religieuse de Constantin*, Rev. Hist. Egl. Fr., XXXIII, Jan. 1947, pp. 43 et seq.).

deed, the perfect Sabbath and perfect and blessed rest is found in the kingdom of God, above the work of the six days and outside everything sensible, in the realities that are intelligible and incorporeal, where, freed from the realities of the body and the slavery of the flesh, with God and beside Him, we shall celebrate the Sabbath and we shall rest" (*Co. Ps.* XCI; P.G., XXIII, 1168 D).

This is an interpretation of the rest of the seventh day which is the same as that of Philo. From him comes the idea that the rest of God is the creation of the intelligible world (*Leg. all.* I, 5-6), as well as the idea, which Eusebius combines with the foregoing, that rest is a kind of contemplation (*De Decalogo* 96). Eusebius connects this theme with the sentence from St. John concerning the continual activity of the Father. Like Philo again, Eusebius shows that it is acting in imitation of God when man turns himself from exterior actions to give himself to contemplation. A theme from Hellenism appears in the image of the *periope*.[5] And, finally, this contemplation practised during the present life is only an anticipation of the true Sabbath, which will be life beyond death, when the soul, freed from the works of the body prefigured by the six days of creation, will be wholly absorbed in things intelligible and divine. So much for the theology of the Sabbath rest. It remains to make its liturgical application. And here we see the appearance of the correlative realities of the Jewish Sabbath and the Christian Sunday. Eusebius gives us first his theory of the Jewish Sabbath: "It is the image (*eikon*) of that (heavenly) Sabbath and of that perfect and blessed rest shown us here on earth by the men of God; they abstain from things that lead one too much away from God, and they turn themselves wholly toward the contemplation of divine things, applying themselves day and night to meditation (*melete*) on the Holy Scriptures; then they pass over into rest and keep holy Sabbaths and a rest agreeable to God. This is why it was right that the law of Moses, which has transmitted to us the shadows and the figures of that of which we have been speaking, has appointed a particular day for the people, so that on this day at least they may leave their ordinary work and give themselves to meditation on the divine law" (XXIII, 1168 C-1169 A).

[5] See Maximus of Tyre, XVII, 6. The word occurs again in Gregory of Nyssa (P.G., XLIV, 1194 D).

In order fully to understand this passage, we must recall the position of Eusebius on the Old Testament. For him, perfect religion was already being practiced in the time of the patriarchs. They believed in the one God and in the Word (*Dem. Ev.,* I, 2; P.G. XXII, 24); they practiced the morality of the Gospel (I, 6; XXII, 65). The law came in only later because of men's sin (I, 6; XXII, 57); the Gospel is merely a return to the primitive state, not before original sin, but at the time of the patriarchs. Thus, the patriarchs appear as the models of "true philosophy." Eusebius conceives this, in the manner of Origen and of the monks of Egypt who were his contemporaries, as a continual meditation on Scripture. Their life is thus a perpetual feast-day. And this contemplative life, at once that of the patriarchs and that of Christians, is the image, the *eikon* of the "blessed rest," that of heaven, where, freed from all servitude to sense, one can contemplate intelligible realities. The Sabbath itself was introduced by the law of Moses because of the people (*plethos*), as an educational means to lead them to the more perfect practice of the perpetual and spiritual Sabbath. This is the very thesis of Origen on the origin of feast-days (*Contra Celsum,* VIII, 23; Koetschau, 240, 3-15), and Eusebius now brings it out explicitly: "The Sabbath was not prescribed for priests, but only for those who were not capable for the whole duration of their lives of giving themselves to divine worship and to works agreeable to God" (1169 C).

Now the Christian Sunday is the New Testament equivalent of the Jewish Sabbath. Here again the ideal is the perpetual feast-day which is the contemplative life. We recall the word of Origen: "The perfect man, who is always occupied with the words, the actions, the thoughts of the Word of God, is always living in His days, and all His days are Lord's Days" (*C. Cels.,* VIII, 22). But because of the people, there has to be a particular day to mark the duty of divine worship. But "the Jews having been unfaithful in the New Testament, the Word has transferred the feast of the Sabbath to the rising of the light (*anatole*) and has given us, as the image of true rest, the day of the Saviour, the Lord's Day (*kyriake*) and the first day of the light, on which the Saviour of the world, after all the works that He accomplished among mankind, conquered death and opened the gates of heaven, going beyond the creation of six days and receiving the blessed Sabbath and beatific rest when His Father said to Him: "Sit at My right hand" (1169 C). This passage is a summary of the theology of the Lord's Day. This day is the *kyriake,* the day of the Lord, because —and the whole primitive theology of the Redemption appears here—it is the day on which Christ conquered death and, going beyond the six days which are a figure of the world here below and its miseries, opened the gates of heaven and entered into the Sabbath, into the rest of the seventh day. We find here, once more, Philo's contrast between the six days which are a figure of the sensible world, and the seventh, the figure of the intelligible world, christianized by the entrance of the theme of the *anabasis,* the Ascension of Christ. We see here also the Sabbath mystery of the *kathisis,* the seating of the Lord at the right hand of the Father, of which the *anapausis* is the figure.

In what does the Sunday worship consist? It is Eusebius who further explains this, drawing his inspiration from Psalm XCI, that is to say, transposing the Jewish worship into the Christian. "On this day, which is that of the light, the first day, and that of the true sun, we also gather together after the interval of six days, and, celebrating holy and spiritual Sabbaths, we fulfill that which was prescribed for the priests, of observing the Sabbath according to the spiritual law. Indeed, we offer spiritual victims and offerings (*anaphoras*) and cause perfumed incense to go up, according to the word: *Let my prayer go up as incense in Thy sight.* And we also offer the loaves of proposition, renewing the saving memory (*mneme*) and the blood of aspersion, that of the Lamb of God Who takes away the sin of the world and purifies our souls; and we also light the lamps of *gnosis* [spiritual understanding] in the presence of God. . . . In a word, everything that was prescribed concerning the Sabbath, we transfer to the Lord's day (*kyriake*) as being more appropriate and more worthy than the Jewish Sabbath" (1172 A-B). And Eusebius goes on to show that the Christians have "the tradition of gathering together on this day" for confession (*exomologesis*) for the Eucharist, for the night vigil, and prayer in union with all the Churches.

We should notice that these last texts describe the Lord's Day particularly as the first day, the eighth day, and the day of the sun. This introduces us to the symbolism of the Sunday. If it inherits the prerogatives of the Sabbath, this is because it possesses a superior dignity. This dignity consists essentially in the fact that it is the day of the Resurrection. But even while it remains in the framework of the Jewish week, it appears as having a special value. To begin with, it is the first day of the week. In honoring it, the Christians are in opposition to the Jews: "You say that the Sabbath is superior to the Lord's Day because the Bible says that the Lord made everything in six days and on the seventh He rested from His works and made that day holy. But, we ask you, which is the first, the Aleph, or the Tau? The first is then the beginning of the world" (*Didasc.*, 113).

The *Didascalia* indicates a primary symbolism. The Lord's Day, as the first day, is the anniversary of the creation of the world. Eusebius of Alexandria, in the 5th century, shows the relationship between the first day of creation and the Resurrection which is the first day of the second creation: "The Holy Day of Sunday is the commemoration of the Lord. It is called the Lord's (*kyriake*) because He is the Lord (*Kyrios*) of all days. Indeed, before the Passion of the Lord, it was not called the Lord's Day, but the first day. It was on this day that the Lord began the first-fruits of the creation of the world; and, on the same day, He gave to the world the first-fruits of the Resurrection. This is why this day is the principle (*arche*) of all doing good; principle of the creation of the world, principle of the Resurrection, principle of the week" (P.G., LXXXVI, 416). St. Ambrose echoed this teaching when he wrote in the hymn from Lauds of Sunday:

Primo die quo Trinitas
Beata mundum condidit
Vel quo resurgens Redemptor
Nos morte victa liberat.

We can add to these texts a treatise *De sabbatis et circumcisione.* This is to be found among the works of St. Athanasius, though it is not proved certainly to be his, and it can be considered as a little Summa of the theology of the week.[6] We do not need to date it before the end of the IV century. The treatise is presented as a commentary on the precept of Exodus 31:16 concerning the observance of the Sabbath. It was, the sacred author tells us, the sign which recalled the creation of the world. It was therefore to have

[6] See also Eusebius of Emesa, *On the Sunday*, P.G., LXXXVI, 1413 et seq.

been observed so long as this first creation subsisted. "But when a new people was created, according to the word: *Populus qui creabitur laudabit Dominum* (Ps. CI:19), it was no longer necessary for this (new) people to observe the end of the first creation, but rather to seek the beginning of the second. And what is this, but the day on which the Lord rose again. It is from here that the new creation began, of which St. Paul says: 'If, then, anyone is in Christ a new creature.' God ceased His making of the first creation: this is why men of the former generation observed the Sabbath on the seventh day; but the second creation has no end: So God has not ceased from His work, but *usque modo operatur*. This is why we do not keep the Sabbath (we do not rest) on this day as if in memory of the first creation, but we await the Sabbaths of Sabbaths to come, which the new creation does not take as an ending, but shows forth and celebrates perpetually. This is why indeed this Sabbath was given to the former people, so that they would know the end and the beginning (*telos kai arche*) of creation. But the new creation was not commanded to observe the Sabbath, so that while it recognized its beginning on the Lord's Day, it would know also that the grace (of this creation) has no ending" (P.G. XXVIII, 133 B-C).

The author then develops the contrast between the Sabbath and the Lord's Day: "This is why (God) pointed out the beginning, that is to say, the Lord's Day, so that you may know that the former generation has ended. The first being finished, the beginning of the other succeeded. This is why it is after the Sabbath that the Lord rose again." Also the Lord's Day, the day after the Sabbath, is as it were the sign of the second creation. What then was the meaning of the Sabbath: "The Sabbath did not stand for idleness (*argia*), but in part for the knowledge of the Creator, and in part for the ending of the figure of this world" (106 C). The author quotes in this connection the texts concerning the sacrifices offered by the Levites on the Sabbath day, the fall of Jericho on the seventh day, and circumcision which also could fall on the Sabbath. We find here again the criticism of the Sabbath idleness. And, further, Scripture calls Sabbaths days which are not seventh days. "So the Sabbath is not the seventh day, but the remission of sins, when someone ceases to fall into sin. And the Sabbath is not idleness, but confession and humility of soul" (137 A). Here we recognize the primitive idea of the Sabbath as the ending of sin. The author concludes this section: "This is why the Sabbath is not primarily the law of idleness, but of *gnosis,* of propitiation and of abstaining from all evil" (137 C).

The second aspect was that the Sabbath was the figure of the end of this world: "God did not give the Sabbath for the sake of idleness, but so that they would know of the ending (*katapausis*) of creation. He willed that, knowing of the end of this creation, they would look for the beginning of the other. Indeed, the Sabbath was the end of the first creation, the Lord's Day (*kyriake*) was the beginning of the second in which He renewed and restored the old. In the same way as He prescribed that they should formerly observe the Sabbath as a memorial of the end of the first things, so we honor the Lord's Day as being the memorial of the beginning of the new creation. Indeed, He did not create another one, but He renewed the old one, and completed what He had begun to do." The most curious idea found here, and one that we have not encountered before, is that of the Sabbath as the memorial of the end of the first creation. This is a new application of the symbolism of the week and the octave. What makes it still more precise is the fitting together of the two orders of symbolism, those of the Sabbath and of the first day in connection with the succession of the two creations: On the sixth day, creation was finished; on the seventh, God rested from all His works. But in the Gospel, the Word says: 'I have come to finish the work.' He Who rests from all His works wishes to say by this that His works need the completion that He Himself has come to bring. Indeed, His Work would have been imperfect, if, Adam having sinned, man was dead. But it was perfected when he was brought to life. This is why, having renewed the creation made in six days, He assigned a day to the renewal, which was announced in advance by the Holy Spirit in the Psalm: *Haec dies quam fecit Dominus.*" The world of creation, symbolized by the seven days, thus appears as a preliminary stage of the plan of God.

This interpretation of the Lord's Day as the first day is not the only one. In a whole group of writers—Clement, Eusebius of Cesarea—we find another, in which the first day is interpreted as being the beginning, not of the creation of the world, but of the generation of the Word. It is this generation of the Word which these authors find expressed in the verse of the first chapter of Genesis: "Let there be Light . . . and it was the first day." This idea appears first in Clement of Alexandria: "The seventh day, by banishing evils, prepares the primordial day, our true rest. This is He Who is the light brought forth first of all, in which everything is seen together and separately.[7] From this Day, wisdom and knowledge shine out on us. It is, indeed, the light of the Truth which is the true Light without shadow, sharing indivisibly the Spirit of the Lord with those who are sanctified by Him" (*Strom.* VI, 16; Staehlin, 501-502).

So the Lord's Day, the first day of the week, before becoming the day of the Resurrection, that is to say, of the birth of the Word as the first-born from the dead, is the day, which existed before creation, of the generation of the Word. Clement returns several times to this idea: "The day on which God created heaven and earth, that is to say, in which and by which He made everything, shows his working through the Son. It is He of Whom David speaks: 'This day that the Lord has made, let us rejoice and be glad in it' (Psalm 117:24). What is called day, indeed, is the Word, illuminating hidden things, by Whom every creature has come to the light and to existence" (Strom. VI, 16; Staehlin, 506, 15-25).[8]

This idea of the First Day as meaning the Word Himself, in His generation before the creation of the world, brings with it a certain risk of subordinationism; it did so, certainly, with Clement, for whom the Word is begotten to be the light of the world. We find this again in Eusebius of Cesarea, who once more clarifies the relationship between the day of the generation of the Word and that of His Resurrection, of which the Lord's Day is the memorial: "On this day (Sunday) which is that of the light, the first, and also that of the true sun, we gather together after the interval of six days and, celebrating holy and spiritual Sabbaths, we carry out that which He prescribed for the priests to do on the Sabbath according to the spiritual Law. . . . It was on this day that at the time of creation, when God said: Let there

[7] The expression comes from Aristotle, according to Eusebius, *Prep. Ev.*, XIII, 12, 9-12. The latter, however, identified the first day with the Sabbath, not with the day after the Sabbath.

[8] It will be noticed that Justin gives Day among the names of the Son (*Dial.*, XXIV, 1; CXI, 13).

be light, there was light; and on this day also the sun of justice arose on our souls" (P.G. XXIII, 1172 B).

It is this same idea of the First Day as being both that of the generation of the Word and that of the Resurrection which Eusebius takes up again in commenting on the verse of the Psalm: "Thou hast delighted me with Thy works, O Lord, and I rejoice in the works of Thy hands." He writes: "The Work of God could indeed be the Day of which it is said: 'This is the day that the Lord has made, let us rejoice and be glad in it.' He means the Lord's Day of the Resurrection, as we have shown elsewhere in explaining what concerns the creation of the World. God said: 'Let there be light, and there was light.' You see that on this Day there was no other creation for which the word would be fitting: 'This is the Day that the Lord has made,' except that Day itself which was the first Lord's Day. It is of this day that it is said: 'Lord, Thou hast delighted me with Thy works.' As to the works of His hands, these are they that were created in the days that followed" (P.G., XXIII, 1173 B-1176 A).

We should notice that we find here again the same quotation from Psalm CXVII as in Clement of Alexandria. This Psalm is eminently that of the Lord's Day and it is still a Sunday Psalm today in the Roman Breviary. Even at that remote date, this Psalm was commented on in relation to Sunday. Here we find a whole tradition of the exegesis of the Psalms. We observe also the contrast between the work of God, which is the Word, and the work of His hands, which is creation. As early as Irenaeus, the hands of God mean the Son and the Spirit, instruments of the Father in the work of creation and redemption.

We can now bring together the idea of the Lord's Day as the first day, and as the Sun-day, the *dies solis.* These are two kindred aspects, in fact, the first day being that of the creation of light. But they actually come from entirely different origins. The day of the sun is connected with the planetary week, which came from the Orient, and began to spread in the West about the time of early Christianity under the influence of the Hellenized magi.[9] This day consecrated to the Sun was found to coincide with the

[9] See Cumont, *La fin du monde selon les mages occidentaux,* Rev. Hist. Rel., 1931, p. 55; Schuerer, *Die Siebentätige Woche in Gebrauche der christlichen Kirche der ersten Jahr.,* Zeit. Neu est. Wiss, 1905. p. 1 et seq.

first day of the Jewish week and so with the Christian Lord's Day. One result was that in the eyes of certain pagans, the Christians could pass for a sect of devotees of the sun. Tertullian defends them from this accusation: "If we give ourselves to rejoicing on the day of the sun, for a reason quite different from that of giving worship to the sun, we are following in the steps of those of you who devote the day of Saturn to good cheer and to leisure, and who introduced seven days into the calendar" (*Apol.* XVI, 11, See *AD Nat.* I, 13). This passage, addressed to pagans first under the influence of Judaism, seems to bear witness also to the fact that the custom had spread in the Roman world of devoting the Sabbath day to rest, the Sabbath day happening to fall on the day of Saturn.[10]

Tertullian bears witness also to the fact that the custom of calling this day *dies solis* had then spread in the Roman world. As we know, this expression is still that for the Lord's Day in many countries—Sunday, Sonntag—and, in the writings addressed to pagans, this is the expression used by the Fathers. Thus, Justin writes in his *Apologia* "On the day that is called the day of the sun, all of us, in the cities and in the country, come together in the same place. The Acts of the Apostles and the writings of the prophets are read. When the reader has finished, he who presides gives a discourse. Then we all rise and we pray together aloud. Then they bring bread, with wine and water. He who presides sends up to heaven prayers and thanksgivings, and all the people answer: Amen" (LXVII, 5). We have here one of the most ancient witnesses to the synaxis on the Lord's Day. But even if, in the second century, the custom of calling this day *dies solis* had spread, it had not yet been taken up in official life. This is why Pliny calls it simply *status dies*. Later on, things changed. With the development of the cult of the sun throughout the Empire, the day of the sun took on a greater importance. This was how Constantine was able, as we have seen, to make Sunday a holiday without thereby displeasing the pagans.

From this coincidence the Christians drew another line of symbolism. The Lord's Day was the day of the sun. But does not Scripture say that Christ is the "Sun of Justice"? The Lord's Day,

[10] Influence may also have been exerted by the Neo-Pythagoreans, for whom the day of Saturn was the anniversary of the creation, of the *Saturnia regna*.

on which Christ rose again, is seen as the day on which arose the sun of the second creation. Thus we meet again, but from a different starting-point, the Jewish symbolism of the first day. This symbolism appeared as early as in Justin: "We come together on the day of the sun, for this is the first day on which God, drawing matter from darkness, created the world" (*Ap.* LXVII, 7). We see the fusion of the two themes, which was developed particularly in the fourth century. St. Jerome writes, for example: "The day of the Lord, the day of the Resurrection, the day of the Christians is our day. And if it is called the day of the Sun by the pagans, we willingly accept this name. For on this day arose the light, on this day shone forth the sun of justice" (*Anecd. Mareds.*, 1897, III, 2, p. 418).[11]

Sunday was seen as a renewal of the first day of Creation and, beyond that, as an echo of the eternal generation of the Word, this aspect remaining secondary. But there is another of great importance, although its origins are still mysterious: this is the description of Sunday as the "eighth day." We have already met with this name in Barnabas: "We celebrate with joy the eighth day, on which Jesus arose again and on which He rose up to heaven" (XV, 8-9). Tertullian uses it as a current name: "For the pagans, there is only a yearly feast; for you every eighth day (*octavus dies*)" (*De idol.*, 14). And Justin shows us a hidden meaning in it: "We can show that the eighth day contains a mystery" (*Dial.* XXIV, 1). Here, then, is a name which was frequently used and rich in significance. But what was its origin? Reitzenstein thought that it was anterior to Christianity: "The value of the eighth day was taken up by the Christians and by them related to the Resurrection of the Saviour on the morning of Sunday, but that was not its birthplace." [12] He wanted to connect it with an idea of the octave as the "Rest of God" which is found in Philo and in mandeism, and which would be one of the elements of prechristian gnosis. But the example that he gives from Philo gives witness to a contrary meaning. For Philo takes up the astrological idea of the seven planetary spheres which are figures of the world

[11] See H. Rahner, *Griechische Mythen in christlicher Deutung*, pp. 141-149.
[12] *Die Vorgeschichte der christlichen Taufe*, p. 314. See also F. J. Doelger, *Die Achtzahl in der altchristlichen Symbolik*, Ant. und Christ., IV, 3, p. 181.

of change and are contrasted with the sphere of things that are fixed, but he does not precisely call this the eighth sphere (*De Dec.* 102-104). As for the mandean texts, their late date does not allow them to be used in this argument.

We must therefore look elsewhere. We have already met, several times in the course of these studies, with allusions to the octave as the eighth day. These allusions are also found in Jewish apocalyptic literature. The eighth day appears in the Second Book of Henoch as the figure of the future world which will follow the seventh millennium: "I blessed the seventh day, which is the Sabbath, and I added to it the eighth day, which is the day of the first creation. When the seven first days have gone around, under the form of a thousand years, the eighth millennium will begin, which will be an endless age in which there are no more years, or months, or days, or hours" (II Henoch, XXXIII, 7). We can see how Judaism was led to this idea by the separation of the two eschatologies: the earthly one, to which the seventh millennium is reserved, prefigured by the Sabbath; and the heavenly, which constitutes an extra day, the eighth.

But if the succession of the seventh millennium and of the world to come clearly seems to have been a doctrine of Judaism, it does not seem that this was true of the designation of this world to come as the eighth day—for this implies a depreciation of the seventh day not very compatible with the cult of the Sabbath. And we should note the fact that the text of the Second Book of Henoch dates from after the beginning of the Christian era [13] and that it is therefore quite likely that the mention of the eighth day is due to some Christian influence. There is no need, then, to seek any further in Jewish eschatology for the origin of this term.

We are thus led to the conclusion that the doctrine of the eighth day is of purely Christian origin.[14] The point of departure here was the fact that the Resurrection of Christ took place on the day after the Sabbath. This day thus gained a pre-eminent place in Christian liturgy and was substituted for the Sabbath: "Those who live in the old order of things have come to the new hope, observing no longer the Sabbath, but the Sunday." [15] But

[13] H. H. Rowley, *The Relevance of Apocalyptic,* p. 95.
[14] See Carl Schmidt, *Gespräche Jesu mit seinen Jüngern,* p. 279.
[15] Ignatius of Antioch, *Magne.,* IX, 1.

since the Sabbath was the seventh day of the Jewish week, the Lord's Day, as we have said, could be considered either as the first or as the eighth day. We find both these names used. St. Justin speaks "of the eighth day on which our Christ appeared risen again, the day which is found implicitly always to be the first. (*Dial.* CXXXVIII, I.) But it is its designation as the eighth day which has taken on the greatest importance. We meet it as early as Barnabas: "It is not your Sabbaths that I love, but the one I have made, wherein, putting an end to the universe, I shall inaugurate a new world. This is why we celebrate with joy the eighth day on which Jesus rose again" (XV, 8).

The substitution of the eighth day for the seventh appears, therefore, to be the expression, at once symbolic and concrete, of the substitution of Christianity for Judaism. This leads us to touch on a primary aspect of the symbolism of the eighth day. Like the symbolism of the first day, it was used by the Christians to exalt the superiority of the Sunday over the Sabbath, and thus it became an instrument of Christian polemics. The passage from the religion of the seventh day to that of the eighth was to become the symbol of passing from the Law to the Gospel: *Septenario numero expleto postea per ogdoaden ad Evangelium scandimus* (Jerome *In Eccles.* II, 2). This explains the fact that the typology of the eighth day appears especially in the writings of anti-Judaic polemics, such as the *Epistle* of Barnabas and the *Dialogue with Trypho*. It is under this aspect, in fact, that the *kyriake* appeared most clearly as being contrasted with the Sabbath. St. Hilary gives this contrast its classic expression when he writes: "Although the name and the observance of the Sabbath had been established for the seventh day, it is the eighth, which is also the first, that we ourselves celebrate, and that is the feast of the perfect Sabbath" (*Inst.* Ps. 12; C.S.E.L., XXII, 11). And he sees in the fifteen Gradual Psalms "the continuation of the seventh day of the Old Testament and the eighth day of the Gospel, by which we rise to things holy and spiritual" (16; XXII, 14).

This dignity with which the eighth day found itself thus liturgically invested at the expense of the seventh day could only rest on the typology of the week. We have seen that, in the perspective of the Bible, the seventh day was a figure of the repose of the future life. The appearance of the eighth day here gives rise to a problem, for we are now presented with two distinct lines of symbolism. On the one hand, we shall continue to find a symbolism which is purely Biblical, in which the sixth day is a figure of the present world and the seventh of the world to come. But alongside this symbolism, we shall find another being formed, in which it is the seven days that constitute the present world and the eighth the world of the future. We see this already appearing in the text of Barnabas: "It is not your Sabbaths that I love, but the one I have made, wherein, putting an end to the universe, I shall inaugurate a new world. This is why we celebrate the eighth day with joy." We see this symbolism, together with the preceding ones, explicitly stated by Origen: "The number eight, which contains the virtue of the Resurrection, is the figure of the future world" (*Sel. Psalm;* P.G., XII, 1624 B-C).[16] This eschatological symbolism of the eighth day is sometimes combined with that of the seventh: this is what we find especially in the millenarianism in which the seventh day is a figure of the earthly millennium which is to come before the eternal eighth day; but this combination is also found outside of the millenarian point of view.

Here, in fact, we have to recognize the introduction of a new element. While the typology of the eighth day was developing in orthodox gnosis, it was having a considerable success in the doctrine of the octave in heretical gnosis. The importance of this octave in gnosis does not seem to be pre-Christian, as Reitzenstein thought. It is in Christianity, and in particular in the Christian liturgy, that the theme of the eighth day first became important and that it appeared as a symbol of salvation as opposed to the Jewish Sabbath. The gnostics, who were decided enemies of Judaism, were carried away by this theme. But they completely transformed it by taking it over into their own way of thinking, substituting the vision of a hierarchy of spheres set one upon the other for the successive historical stages of the theology of the Church. They borrowed this vision from astrology, which had spread its notions throughout the Hellenistic world of the time and especially in neo-pythagoreanism. Basic to this idea was the contrast between the seven planetary spheres which are the domain of the *cosmocratores,* the archontes, who hold man under the tyranny of the *heimarmene,* and, beyond, the heaven above,

[16] See also *Co. Ro.,* II, 13; *Ho. Lev.,* VIII, 4; *Co. Jo.,* II, 33.

that of the fixed stars, which is the place of incorruptibility and repose (Cumont, *Les religions orientales dans le paganisme romain,* p. 162).[17] The salvation of the soul is effected by an ascension in the course of which it rises beyond the seven planetary spheres, stripping off the tunics of its corporeality, which become more and more ethereal, to arrive finally at the divine and eternal sphere of the stars. These notions come from a septenary symbolism distinct from that of the seven-day week with a Sabbath, with which is connected another septenary symbolism of the Old Testament, that of the candlestick with seven branches (Exodus XXV: 32), of the seven spirits (Isaias XI:2), of the seven chief angels (Tobias XII:15). This symbolism is often mingled with that of the sabbatical week, but it is better to make a careful distinction between the two.

In this astrological conception, we encounter again the theme of the octave, standing for the sphere of the fixed stars as contrasted with that of the planets. (Orig. *Contr. Cels.* VI, 22; Proclus *Co. Tim.* III; 355, 13).[18] The special quality of the syncretism of the gnostics was to bring together the supreme dignity of the eighth day in Christianity with the pythogorean view of the planetary spheres. Thus they were led to the conception of the octave as meaning, not the kingdom to come of Judaeo-Christian eschatology, but the world on high, of which all creation is only the degradation. Irenaeus, summing up the theories of the gnostic Valentinus, thus describes the octave in a text in which we can recognize the mixture, so characteristic of the gnostics, of a Christian vocabulary with strange ideas: "It is the dwelling of (Sophia) whom they call Mother, Ogdoad, Wisdom, Earth, Jerusalem, Holy Spirit, Lord. She dwells in the place above the heavens. The Demiurge dwells in the heavenly place, that is to say the hebdomad; the cosmocratores in our world" (*Adv. haer.* I, 5, 3).[19] Here we have, transposed into the perspective of superposed spheres, the succession of six days, of the hebdomade and the

[17] The sphere of the stars is sometimes considered to be the highest; sometimes a higher sphere beyond it is admitted. On this point see Boyancé, *Étude sur le songe de Scipion*, pp. 65-78. This latter point of view was to occur again in gnosis.

[18] See Doelger, *Die Achtzahl in der altchristlichen Symbolik,* Ant. und Christ., IV, 3, p. 181.

[19] See F. M. Sagnard, *La gnose valentinienne et le témoignage de saint Irénée,* pp. 174-175.

ogdoade. The vocabulary is still Christian; but the historical perspective of Christianity has been totally abolished.

That what occurred was a mythological transposition of the liturgical fact of the eighth day is shown in a text of another gnostic, Theodotus, whose ideas are reported to us not by Irenaeus, but by Clement of Alexandria: "The rest of spiritual men will take place on the Day of the Lord (*kyriake*) in the ogdoade which is called the Day of the Lord (*kyriake*). It is there that the souls that have been reclothed will be beside the Mother until the end; the other faithful souls are with Demiurge. At the consummation, they will also penetrate into the ogdoad. Then comes the wedding-feast, common to all the saved, until all are equal and know one another" (*Excerpt. Theod.* 63). Here it is not only the ogdoade, whose origin could be disputed, but the *kyriake* itself, the special creation of Christianity and its distinctive sign, which is associated with the ogdoad, to designate the super-celestial kingdom, that which is found immediately beneath the Pleroma, the divine world properly speaking, and above that of the hebdomad. The eschatological symbolism of the *ogdoas* is here transposed into cosmological symbolism. We should remark here also to the theme of the *anapausis* associated with the ogdoad by Justin in order to characterize the kingdom to come after the seventh millenium, and which designates the kingdom superior to that of the hebdomad. There is perfect parallelism between the two ideas.

This parallelism, moreover, we find explicitly affirmed in a passage of Clement of Alexandria in which Christian gnosis is influenced by heretical (*Strom.* VI, 16).[20] Elsewhere he puts the eschatological and the cosmological visions side by side. He is dealing with the passage from Ezechiel: "The priests are purified for seven days" and the sacrifice is offered on the eighth (XLIV: 27). Clement writes: "They are purified for seven days by which creation was brought to its completion. The seventh indeed is consecrated to rest (*anapausis*). On the eighth, he offers the sacrifice by which the promise obtains its fulfillment. Indeed, the true purification is faith in the Gospel, received from the prophets,

[20] See A. Delatte, *Études sur la littérature pythagoricienne,* pp. 232-245; A. Dupont-Sommer, *La doctrine gnostique de la lettre Waw,* pp. 35-80; F. M. Sagnard, *La gnose valentinienne,* p. 358-386.

and purity by obedience with detachment from the things of the world, until the restoration of the tabernacle of the body. Therefore whether we consider the times which, by the seven ages of the world, lead to the restoration (*apokatastasis*) of the supreme rest, or the seven heavens which some count in an ascending order and call the ogdoad, it means that the gnostic must come forth from the state of becoming and of sin. During seven days the victims are sacrificed for sin, there is fear of change" (*Strom.* IV, 25). Clement leaves the choice open between the two conceptions. The essential thing for him is the idea of the ogdoad as supreme rest.[21] But in any case, the cosmological interpretation appears as a deviation from the Christian symbolism of the eighth day, which is the figure of the world to come.

[21] See also *Strom,* VI, 14; Staehlin, 485-486; VII, 10; St., 20 et seqq.

CHAPTER SIXTEEN

The Eighth Day

THE position of the day of the Resurrection in relation to the Jewish week and to the planetary week could thus lend itself to different kinds of symbolism. But among these, this symbolism of the eighth day took a preeminent place and this is why we must dwell on it. The seven days, figure of time, followed by the eighth day, figure of eternity, appeared to the Fathers of the fourth century as being the symbol of the Christian vision of history. This symbolism, however, was developed along two different lines. The Alexandrians, more inclined to allegory, conceived the seven days as a pure symbol of the whole epoch of this world in contrast to the eighth day, the figure of life everlasting, and they did not concern themselves with trying to make each of these seven days coincide with a special period in history. But the westerners, continuing the speculations of the apocalypses, and thinking more realistically, tried, on the contrary, to make the seven days into precise historical epochs and to use these as the basis for calculations which enable them to foretell the date of the Parousia. These two currents of thought, freed from their immediate associations of Alexandrine allegorism or millenarianism, were expressed in the fourth century by the Cappadocians and by St. Augustine in two theologies of history.

In a text of capital importance, St. Basil the Great, the master of the Cappadocian School, outlines its design with the greatest clarity. Basil has just recalled that there are in the Church, besides the written teachings, other things coming from the tradition of the Apostles, which have been handed on to us *en mysterio*. He mentions some of these and then continues: "We make our prayers standing on the first day of the week, (*mia tou sabbatou*) but all do not know the reason for this. For it is not only because we are risen with Christ and that we should seek the things which are above, that on the day of the resurrection (*anastasimo*) we recall the grace that has been given us by standing to pray; but also, I think, because this day is in some way the image of the future age (*eikon tou prosdochomenou aionos*). This is why also, being the principle (*arche*) of days, it is not called the 'first' by Moses, but 'one.' 'There was,' he says, an evening and a morning, one (*mia*) day, as though it returned regularly upon itself. This is why it is at once one and the eighth (*ogdoe*) that which is really one and truly the eighth, of which the Psalmist speaks in the titles of certain Psalms, signifying by this the state that will follow the ages, the day without end, the other aeon which will have neither evening, nor succession, nor cessation, nor old age. It is, then, in virtue of an authoritative claim that the Church teaches her children to say their prayers standing on this day, so that, by the perpetual recalling of eternal life, we may not neglect the means which lead us to it" (*De Spir. Sancto*, 27; Pruche, 236-237).[1]

This text constitutes a valuable witness in the history of the liturgy because of the fact that it forbids prayers to be said kneeling on Sunday (see also Tertullian, *De Cor.* 3; *De oratione* 23). But, above all, it marks an important moment in the theology of the Lord's Day. Let us notice first of all that it deals with mystagogy properly so called, that is to say, with explaining the symbolism of the rites to the faithful. Basil first recalls the essential meaning of the Lord's Day, that it is the day of the Resurrection. And, referring to *Col.* III:1, he connects prayer said standing with the seeking of things on high proper to Christians who have risen with Christ. But this symbolism is not the only one. The Lord's Day is the memorial of the Resurrection, but it is also the

[1] The Psalms whose titles are alluded to in the text are Psalms VI and XI, 'for the ogdoad.' The Gnostics even in their time understood this to mean the ogdoad. See Irenaeus, *Adv. haer.*, I, 18, 3. We find this again in the Fathers. Thus Eusebius (P.G., XXIII, 120 A; Athanasius, P.G., XXVII, 7; Didymus, P.G., XXXIX, 1176 A; Asterius, P.G., XL., 444-449; Chrysostom, P.G., LV, 543 A).

figure (*eikon*) of the age to come. It has an eschatological meaning. Its pedagogical value is to preserve among Christians eschatological expectation, in frequently recalling to them the heavenly life to come, and to keep them from being absorbed in the things of earth. So the theology of the Lord's Day is seen to be formed in the image of that of the sacraments and of Christian worship in general, in which the double aspect of memorial and of prophecy is always clearly marked.

Elsewhere this symbolism of the Lord's Day is commented on by Basil with the help of certain features which are the development of previous speculations. The Lord's Day is the *arche,* the principle. Here we have a transference of the idea of the Sabbath as *archon,* in connection with the text of Genesis 1:1 in which it is said that in the beginning (*arche*) God created the light.[2] In the second place—and this idea is the most original—Basil explains that, according to Scripture this day is not called "first," but rather "one." He has expressed this idea at greater length in the *Third Homily on the Hexaemeron:* "Why did he (Moses) not call this day the first, but one (*mia*)?" Basil gives a first reason, that Moses was speaking of this day as made up of day and of night. Then he continues: "More important perhaps is the reason that is handed on to us in secret traditions (*en aporretois paradidomenos*), that is, that God, Who created time, gave it the periods of the days as measures and signs, and, measuring it by the week, He established that the week, returning always upon itself (*anakuklousthai*) should mark the measure of time. And the week itself constitutes one single day, returning seven times on itself. Here is the form of the cycle, which has its beginning and end in itself. Now the property of the aeon is to return on itself and never to end. This is why the principle of time is called not the first day, but one day, so as to indicate, by its name, its relationship with the aeon. Having the characteristics of oneness and of incommunicability, it is properly and fittingly called one" (*Ho. Hex.* II, 8; P.G., XXIX, 59 B-C).

[2] This occurs as far back as Philo (*De opif.*, 100; *De Dec.*, 106); it is the result of a blending of the Pythagorean theme of the number seven as ἄρχων (Philolalos, ap. Lydus, *De mensibus,* II, 12) and the biblical theme of the first day, ἀρχή. Clement of Alexandria was the first to transpose the title of ἄρχων to the eighth day. We must also recognize, with Reitzenstein (*Die Vorgeschichte der christl. Taufe,* p. 351.) that the idea of the eighth day, as being a renewal of the first day after the week, is far more usual than that of the seventh day as identical with the first.

The passage gives the detailed explanation of what Basil only indicated in passing in his *Treatise on the Holy Spirit.* If the day which begins the week is called "one" it is to indicate that the week, returning on itself, forms a unity.[3] Here we encounter two ideas. The first is that the world of time is ruled by the seven-day period: this is the Pythagorean theme, to be found as early as Philo.[4] The second is that this week represents a closed cycle, returning perpetually on itself, having therefore no beginning or end, and thus it is a figure of eternity. Here is the Hellenistic idea of time very clearly expressed. And here also appears again the idea of the connaturality between the monad and the hebdomade, the one and the seven, as Philo developed this also. Let us notice, however, that Philo tried to make this doctrine coincide with that of the Sabbath by showing that this was the "first day."[5] Basil rejects such an interpretation with a violence that makes us ask whether he is not taking a position against Philo. But another question also comes to mind: is this cyclic idea of time compatible with the Christian view of history? Basil attacks the problem: "But if Scripture shows us many ages (*aiones*) in speaking often of 'the age of ages' or 'the ages of ages,' let us notice that no age is called the first or the second or the third, in such a way as to show that these are less circumscriptions, limits, and successions of aeons than differences of state and diverse realities" (52 A). The aeons seem to be defined as universes differing in quality, not as ages successive in time. Each *aion* has its proper individuality, it is "incommunicable," and, in consequence, cannot be counted with the others; it is "one," but not first or second. And it is of this unity that cyclical time is the image. History could not be more completely emptied of all significance; we are here in the midst of Hellenistic thought.

We may seem to be wandering from our subject, but Basil now brings us back to the liturgy. And the interest of this text is pre-

[3] This comes directly from the school of Pythagoras. Thus, in the *De mensibus* of Lydus, we read: 'The first day, according to the Pythagoreans, ought to be called one (μία) of the monad, not the first (πρώτη) of the hebdomad, because it is unique and cannot be communicated to the others' (II, 4; Wuensch, p. 21). Here we have an interesting case of a connection between the biblical text (μία ἡμέρα, Gen., I, 5) and a Pythagorean interpretation. See Y. Courtonne, *Saint Basile et l'hellénisme*, p. 35-36.

[4] *De spec. leg.*, II, 56; *De opif.*, 111; *De Dec.*, 103.

[5] *De spec. leg.*, II, 59; *De opif.*, 103.

cisely in the connection which he establishes between speculations on the nature of time and the liturgical institution: "The Day of the Lord (*hemera Kyriou*) is great and celebrated (Joel II:11). Scripture knows this day without evening, without succession, without end; the Psalmist calls it also the eighth day because it is outside of this time of seven days. Whether you call it day or age, the sense is the same. If this state is called day, it is one (*mia*) and not multiple; if it is called aeon, it is alone (*monakos*) and not part of a whole (*pollostos*). To raise our spirit toward the future life (Moses) called 'one' the image of the aeon, the first-fruits of days, the contemporary of the light, the holy Lord's Day (*kyriake*) honored by the resurrection of the Lord" (*kyrios*) (52B).

St. Basil's thought now is clear. The Day of the Lord is the future age, the eighth day which is beyond the cosmic week. This day is without succession. We find here once more the expressions used in the *Treatise on the Holy Spirit,* and this seems to indicate a touch of anti-Origenism. When Scripture thus speaks of "ages" in the plural, it means the differences of condition in the one unique aeon: it is the celestial hierarchy, not a succession of cosmic ages, which is thus indicated. But the visible symbol, the sacrament, meant to guide our spirits towards this unique aeon, is the first day of the week, that on which light was created, on which the Saviour rose from the dead, of which the Sunday of each week is the liturgical commemoration; it is called one to signify that it is the figure of the oneness of the age to come. The whole theology of the Sunday is now seen clearly; it is the cosmic day of creation, the biblical day of circumcision, the evangelical day of the Resurrection, the Church's day of the Eucharistic celebration, and, finally, the eschatological day of the age to come.

We might have been afraid for a moment that St. Basil meant to do away with history and lead us back to Hellenism. But Hellenism only served him to do away with the aeonian history of Origen. St. Basil brings us back to a truly Christian vision, with the fundamental contrast of the seven days, figure of the present world, and the eighth day, figure of the world to come. The text of the *Homily on the Hexaemeron* has given us a commentary on the other characteristics attributed to the Lord's Day in the *De Spiritu Sancto*. We see why it is at once "one" and "the eighth":

—"one" inasmuch as the future life is "one" without any succession of time, without decline; and "eighth" inasmuch as the world to come is to follow this world, the figure of which is the seven days. The essential contribution of St. Basil is the connection he makes between the "monad" of Greek thought and the biblical *mia.* The theme of the monad, indeed, had not up to that time been conquered by Christian thought. Clement, in the line of Philo, contrasts the world above with this world of change, and thereby runs the risk of doing away with history. Origen did not take up this idea, but instead with him the unity of the spiritual world was threatened. Basil succeeded in overcoming this opposition and in introducing the theme of the monad into an eschatological perspective. By this means, the whole contribution of Greek thought was not rejected, nor was it introduced to the detriment of the true Christian conception of time; it was incorporated into a higher view. Here precisely is one of the points of interest of the work of the Cappadocians.

The same characteristic is found in the followers of Basil. St. Gregory Nazianzen develops the theology of the Lord's Day in a *Sermon on Pentecost:* "The Feasts of the Hebrews honor the hebdomad, as the Pythagoreans honor the tetractys, by which they take oaths, and the disciples of Simon (the Magician) and of Marcion honor the ogdoad and the three hundred, by which they designate I do not know what Aeons of the same number. I do not know in virtue of what symbolic reasons, nor according to what property of this number, but they do honor it" (*Or.* XLI in Pent; P.G. XXXVI, 429 C).[6] Let us notice the connection established by Gregory between the ogdoad and gnosis. This goes to confirm what we have said on this topic, and in no way excludes the Christian origin of the ogdoad in gnosis itself. Gregory thus comes to the biblical symbolism of the hebdomad: "What is clear is that God, having created and formed matter in six days, and having adorned it with various species and organisms, and having made this visible present world, rested from His Works on the seventh day, as is also clearly signified by the word 'Sabbath' which in Hebrew means rest. If there is herein a more sublime meaning, let others seek for it. This honor the Hebrews extend

[6] On the tetractys, see A. Delatte, *Études sur la littérature pythagoricienne,* p. 249-268.

not only to days, but also to years. The honor of days is the Sabbath, as is shown both by the perpetual honor with which it is surrounded and the time during which the leaven is forbidden.[7] And the honor of years is the sabbatical year of remission. This is found not only in weeks, but in weeks of years, that is, the Jubilee, which contains at the same time a respite for the earth, the liberation of slaves and the restitution of purchased property. . . . For the number seven, multiplied by itself, produces fifty minus one day, and we add this by taking it in the world to come: it is at once the first and the eighth, or rather one (mia) and indestructible. And indeed we must there cease the Sabbath-keeping of our souls, so that one part of seven may be given to some, of eight to others, as certain men who have come before us have explained on the subject of the word of Solomon" (432 A-B).

Gregory here brings together in the concise style which is his very own the essential ideas of the Old Testament on the number seven. He himself is "no philosopher," and he leaves to others "sublime" speculations on the subject. Of these speculations, he keeps only one, which is an application of the theology of the eighth day to the pentecostal week of weeks. After the forty-nine days of the week of weeks, there needs one more in order to make fifty. This day represents the future age. "It is at once first and eighth, or rather one and indissoluble." Such was already the idea of Basil concerning the eighth day, the figure of the future world; it has exactly the same characteristics. Gregory finds again the contrast between the hebdomad and ogdoad in the text of Eccl. XI:2: "Give a part of it to seven and even to eight" which certain of his predecessors interpreted in this sense.[8] The typological sense given to this text may seem to be labored, and we might prefer to see it as an invention of the Fathers of the Church. But here again they are only following a tradition, for actually the rabbis were the first to see in this text of Ecclesiastes the figure, not of the Sabbath and of the Sunday, but of the Sabbath and the circumcision.[9] St. Jerome knew of this interpretation (*Co. Eccles.*

[7] See Justin: "God ordered them to knead a new leaven, after the seven days of the unleavened bread, thus signifying the practice of new works."

[8] This interpretation is later found in Chrysostom, P.G., LV, 543 D; Augustine, P.L., XXXIII, 215.

[9] Foote-Moore, *Judaism*, II, 16; Bacher, *Agada der Tannaiten*, I, 156; Bonsirven, *Exégèse rabbinique et exégèse paulinienne*, p. 242.

XI, 2). Thus, what the Fathers did was merely to apply this idea to the Sunday. This is the Palestinian foundation upon which, ever since apostolic times, the Christian typology was built up which we find again through the Fathers.[10]

In connection with another feast of the liturgical year, the Sunday which is the Octave of Easter, Gregory returns to this symbolism of the eighth day. We have other witnesses to the celebration of this octave. It appears already in the *Apostolic Constitutions* (V, 20). "After eight days, may the octave-day be for you a great feast." This was the day on which the newly baptized returned to normal life and took off the white robe worn during the week *in albis*. Gregory also gives witness to the importance of this feast, and then he adds: "That Sunday (Easter) is that of salvation, this is the anniversary of salvation; that was the frontier between burial and resurrection; this is entirely of the second creation, so that, as the first creation began on a Sunday (this is perfectly clear: for the Sabbath falls seven days after it, being repose from works), so the second creation began on the same day, which is at once the first in relation to those that come after it, and the eighth in relation to those before it, more sublime than the sublime day and more wonderful than the wonderful day: for it is related to the life above. This is what, as it seems to me, the divine Solomon wishes to symbolize when he commands to give a part, seven to some, that is to say, this life; and to others, eight, that is to say the future life: he is speaking of doing good here and of the restoration (*apokatastasis*) of the life beyond. The great David seems to sing of this day in the psalms on the octave" (612 C-613 A).

We are always in the same context of ideas. Sunday is defined as both the memorial (*genethlion*) of the Resurrection, and the figure of the future life *(apokatastasis)*. The new element—which is really only a development of the same theme—is the parallelism between the two creations, which both began on the Lord's Day, this Day being at once that of creation and that of the Resurrection. The world of grace is thus as it were a *deutera ktisis,* a second creation, more admirable and more sublime than the first; here is a theme that we shall find again in Gregory of Nyssa. This

[10] Modern exegetes do not know the meaning of this verse. See H. Kruse, *Da partem septem necnon et octo,* Verbum Domini, 1949, pp. 164-169.

is a new stage in the formation of the Christian vision of history, which now appears as a sequence of two creations, of which the second is a more sublime re-expression of the first, without depreciating the first for all that: it is still *thaumaste,* wonderful. We have here a first expression of the formula from the Offertory of the Roman Mass: *Deus qui humanae substantiae dignitatem mirabiliter* (*thaumastos*) *condidisti et mirabilius* (*thaumastoteros*) *reformasti.* The Christian optimism of Irenaeus reappears, triumphant over the Greek depreciation of creation which would make of the hebdomad the symbol of change and of illusion.

Gregory Nazianzen is, therefore, a witness to the eschatological symbolism of the ogdoad. But he did not insist on it further. This "sublime philosophy" which he denies that he possesses, we find again—and it is perhaps to him that he alludes—in the brother of Basil, Gregory of Nyssa. He takes up this same theme and develops it philosophically and mystically: as a philosopher concerned with the mystery of time, and, as a mystic who desires the coming of the Eighth Day. He does this chiefly in connection with Psalms VI and XI, in which Basil and Gregory of Nazianzen have already shown it to be contained. We find a first allusion to this theme in his *Treatise on the title of the Psalms:* "The theme of the ogdoad is akin to those that we have explained. The whole business of the interior life is turned toward the future age whose principle is called ogdoad, because it follows the sensible world which is enclosed in the hebdomad. The titular introduction *On the eighth* urges us, therefore, not to consider the present time, but to have our eyes turned to the ogdoad. When this time that flows and passes has come to an end, the world of generation and corruption will exist no longer, and then the hebdomad which measures this time will also be completely ended, and the ogdoad will follow it, which is the future age and forms altogether one single day, according to the word of the Prophet which calls "a great day" the life which we are awaiting. And it is no longer the visible sun which lights up this day, but the true light, the sun of justice, which is called Orient by the Prophet because it is no longer hidden by any setting" (*Co. Ps.* II, 8; P.G., XLIV, 504 D-505 A).

This is exactly the same idea as that found in Basil and in Gregory Nazianzen, and henceforth we shall find it in this established form. Gregory depends particularly on his brother Basil. In both of them we find the same quotation from Joel II:11 on the "great day." The ogdoad in Scripture has for its purpose, according to Gregory, as does the Sunday for St. Basil, that of keeping our eyes fixed on the future life.[11] We recognize the special mark of Gregory of Nyssa in the philosophic ideas about the world of generation and corruption: we shall see them developed later on. We recognize also his poetic genius in the passage on this day "which is not enlightened by the visible sun, but by true light which is called the Orient." [12] The theology of the Lord's Day as the day of the sun is united with that of the eighth day. This text thus furnishes us with a particular application of a theme that we have seen making its appearance in Gregory Nazianzen, that of the second creation; the application is inspired by the passage from the Apocalypse on the future world in which there will be no need of any sun for "the Lord God will be its light." Gregory comes back to this a little further on (548 C). "The octave (ogdoad) is the end of the present age and the beginning of the future aeon. The special property of the ogdoad is to give no further place for the preparation (*paraskeue*) of good things or evils to those who are found in it, but that what each one has sown for himself, of that sowing will he reap the sheaves." We have found in Gregory of Nazianzen this contrast of the time of merit and that of reward. The word *paraskeue* seems to be an allusion to the command not to gather the manna on the Sabbath, which is commented on in this sense by the *Life of Moses* (P.G. XLIV, 369 B-C).[13] And that of *dragmata* (sheaves) could be an allusion to the ogdoad *par excellence,* that of Pentecost, which is the feast of the harvest *(dragmata).*[14]

But the most important work is the little treatise *On the Ogdoad* which Gregory devotes entirely to this subject. Gregory addresses himself to men "who are not ignorant of the mystery of the octave" (XLIV, 608 C). He recalls the circumcision on the eighth day and its symbolic meaning. Then he begins his exposi-

[11] P.G., XXIX, 52 B.
[12] See also P.G., XLVI, 1184 D.
[13] See also on this point Origen, *Ho. Ex.*, VII, 6, which sees in the six days that time of the world in which one gathers merit; Cyril of Alexandria, *Glaphyres;* P.L., LXIX, 460 C. sees in them the image of the law which we do not reject even when we have entered the spiritual Sabbath which is Christ.
[14] Philo, *De Spec. leg.*, II, 162.

tion, which constitutes a religious philosophy of time expressed by the symbol of the week and the octave: "The time of this life, in the first realization of creation, was accomplished in a week of days. The creation of beings (*onta*) began on the first day, the end of creation was accomplished with the seventh. There was, in fact, says Scripture, one day on which the first beings were created, then a second day on which the second, and so until the seventh, which is the end of creation and closed in itself the time coextensive with the creation of the world. As, therefore, no other heaven was made except this one and no parts of the world added to those which were made at the beginning, but creation was established in itself, abiding in its dimensions without augmentation or diminution, so no other time has existed except that which was determined with creation, and the reality of time is circumscribed in the week of days. This is why, when we measure time with days, beginning with one day and closing the number with seven, we go back again to one day, measuring the whole extent of time by the cycle of weeks until, the things that have motion have passed away and the flux of becoming being ended, there shall come, as the Apostle says, the things that are no longer tossed about, that suffer neither alteration nor change, and this creation shall remain always like itself in successive ages" (609 B-C).

We encounter in this passage one of the aspects of the philosophy of Gregory of Nyssa, that of the essentially finite nature of creation. It is enclosed in determined limits which it can not go beyond. Time, in particular, which was created with the world,[15] is a finite time, enclosed in the measure of the Week until the day when it will cease together with the world of becoming with which it is inseparably bound up.[16] Here the contrast between the week and the octave takes on a more metaphysical character. It is concerned less with the world of sin and that of grace than with the world of biological becoming and that of the spiritual creation. And to describe this contrast, Gregory also uses a philosophical vocabulary. The octave is defined in platonic terms as that which is not susceptible "of growth or diminution," which

[15] This also occurs in Philo, *De Op.*, 26, which depends on Plato.

[16] H. Urs von Balthasar, *Présence et pensée*, p. 6; E. von Ivanka, *Vom Platonismus zur Theorie der Mystik*, Scholastik, 1936, pp. 185 et seq; Jean Daniélou, *Platonisme et Théologie mystique;* p. 139.

is "inaccessible to alteration and change," which "remains unchanged in the same things." Furthermore, the definition of time as *diastema,* the interval of cosmic motion, is of stoic origin (Diogenes Laertes, VII, 141).[17] We find it again in Philo (De Op. 26). In this treatise, then, we have the first attempt by a Christian philosopher to elaborate a philosophy of duration.

In contrast to this world of time, Gregory then defines, but now in the theological terms, that of eternity: "In (this other world) we shall see the true circumcision of human nature in the taking off of biological life and true purification from true stain. For the stain of man is sin, brought forth with human nature, which He who has effected the purification of our sins will then purify completely. It is in this sense that we take the law of the octave, which purifies and circumcises, that is to say that, this septenary time having ceased, the eighth day will appear after the seventh. It is called the eighth because it comes after the seventh, but it does not allow any succession of numbers after it for it remains always unique, never being interrupted by the obscurity of night. It is another sun which makes this day, that sun which sends forth the true light, which, once it has shone on us, as the Apostle says, is no longer hidden by setting each night, but, embracing all things in its illuminating power, enlightens all those who are worthy of it, with the light that is everlasting and without alteration (609 D-612 A). We have already studied these biblical allusions to circumcision and to purification on the eighth day. We know also these characteristics of the eighth day which is a figure of the world to come. It comes after the cosmic week, but has nothing after itself. It is "one" as Basil said, and knows no interruption or succession. "The memory of the octave," Gregory finally adds, "introduces into the Psalm an exhortation to penitence, for the inheritance is prepared for the just in the octave, and there also is the judgment of God." We are thus led back in conclusion to the eschatological meaning of the mystery, the octave having for its purpose to renew in us the memory of the future life, to keep alive our zeal.[18]

But it is a more mystical aspect that is brought out by one last

[17] See *The Meaning of Time in the Ancient World,* New Scholasticism, Jan., 1947, pp. 1 et seq.

[18] See also in this sense *Ho. Cant.,* XV; P.G., XLIV, 1116 A-C.

text of Gregory's on the octave. In his *Commentary on the Beatitudes,* when he reaches the eighth, which promises the Kingdom of God to those who are persecuted for the sake of justice, Gregory writes: "I think that it is good first to consider what the mystery of the octave (*To tes ogdoes mysterion*) means to the Prophet, the octave which is a part of the title of two psalms; what also are the Purification and the Law of Circumcision, both being observed by the Law on the eighth day. This number has perhaps a certain relationship to the eighth beatitude, which, as being the summit of the beatitudes, is placed at the peak of the ascending virtues. Indeed, by the symbol of the octave, the Prophet describes the day of the Resurrection; the Purification expresses the return to purity of man's nature stained by sin, the Circumcision symbolizes the stripping off of the dead skins with which, when we were stripped of life after our disobedience, we clothed ourselves; in the same way, the eighth beatitude contains the restoration (*apokatastasis*) in the heavens of those who had fallen into slavery and who have been recalled from slavery to royalty" (*De beat.* 8; P.G. XLIV, 1292 A-B).[19] We see reappearing in this passage the biblical figures of the octave, and its connection with the day of the resurrection. The contrast between the restoration and the *douleia* seems clearly to be an allusion to the week of weeks. But we recognize Gregory's thought at once by the mystical significance which the octave has for him. It represents the summit of the spiritual life, for here eternal life has already begun. And the symbols by which he describes it are those by which he defines the spiritual life: it is the return of man to his true nature, the stripping off of the garments of skin, symbols of mortality and the carnal life, purification from the stains of sin, restoration to the royal dignity.

In the Cappadocian exegesis, and in particular that of the *Commentary on Psalm VI* of Gregory of Nyssa, we must add a Commentary of St. John Chrysostom on the title of this Psalm, which is found in the second *Treatise on Compunction* (*katanuxis*): "What is the eighth but the great and manifest day of the Lord which burns like straw, which makes the powers on high tremble? Scripture calls it the eighth, showing the change of state

[19] See *Platonisme et Théologie mystique,* p. 52-65 (tunics of skin); p. 164-165 (purity); p. 114-119 (royal dignity).

(*katastasis*), and the inauguration (*ananeosis*) of the future life. Indeed, the present life is nothing but one week (*hebdomas*) which begins on the first day and ends on the seventh and returns (*anakukloumenos*) to the same unit (*diastemata*) and goes back to the same beginning, to continue to the same end. This is why no one calls the Lord's Day the eighth day, but the first. Indeed, the septenary cycle does not extend to the number eight. But when all these things stop and dissolve, then the course of the octave will arise. Its course indeed does not go back to the beginning, but is made up of successive units. This is why the prophet, animated by profound compunction, having before him continually the memory of the judgment, wrote this Psalm" (*De compunctione* II, 4; P.G., XLVII, 415 D-416 A). All this reminds us of Gregory's commentary, without the philosophical developments. The vocabulary is the same, the thought also. And this text also marks the furthest point of the eschatological interpretation of the eighth day, since it formally denies this name to the Lord's Day and reserves it for the age to come.[20]

While the Oriental tradition interpreted the biblical week in a symbolic manner as a figure of the whole time of the world in contrast to the eighth day of eternity, Western tradition, more realistic and historical-minded, sought to find in the week a key to the succession of the ages. This interpretation of the week as a figure of the seven millenia which constitute the history of the world originated in the Pharisaic milieu of the apocalypses. It is because certain disciples of Christ, those whom Irenaeus calls the presbyters (in a non-ecclesiastical sense), had contacts with these apocalyptic milieux, that the millenarian way of thinking pervaded ancient Christian mentality. So we find it in a Papias.[21] As a result, it was particularly cherished by these Christians who were the most traditional-minded, since they saw in it an inheritance from primitive Christianity. We meet it in Irenaeus,[22] in Hippolytus,[23] in Tertullian.[24] It is remarkable that since the very

[20] This eastern tradition is found in St. Ambrose (*Exp. Luc.*, VIII, 23; C.S.E.L., XXXII, 401). See F. J. Doelger, *Die symbolik der Achtzahl in den schriften der Ambrosius*, Ant. Christ., IV, 3, p. 160-165.

[21] Eusebius, *Hist. Eccl.*, III, 39.

[22] *Adv. haer.*, V, 28, 3; 33, 2.

[23] *Co. Dan.*, IV, 23-24.

[24] Adv. Marc., IV, 39; De An., XXXVII, 4. See J. H. Waszink, *Tertulliani de Anima*,

beginning it was the old teachers in the West—Irenaeus at Lyons, Justin and Hippolytus at Rome—who represented this tradition. We might, then, consider that it constitutes the Western version of the symbolism of the Week as the religious interpretation of history, at least up to St. Augustine.[25]

It is interesting to see St. Augustine wrestling with the symbolism of the Week, that is to say, with the theology of history, for we know the importance of the work of St. Augustine from this point of view. *The City of God* represents the greatest effort of ancient Latin thought to give a Christian interpretation to history. Furthermore, the symbolism of the Sabbath was also related, for St. Augustine, with the theology of the person, as being *anapausis* rest. And, since we have here the two essential axes of the thought of St. Augustine,—the progress of history toward the future world of glory and the progress of the soul toward the interior world of peace—the result is that the theme of the Sabbath is at the center of Augustinian thought. Finally, it is interesting to see how St. Augustine, faced with the millenarist tradition, first accepted it and then, when he had given thought to it, went beyond it. This marks—and we have here a third aspect—a most important stage in Western thought, that in which it detaches itself from an archaism which was paralyzing it, and aims toward a construction of its own. Here the Middle Ages begin.

It is in connection with the Sunday within the octave of Easter that St. Augustine treats in his sermons of the problem of the octave. We have seen that this octave-day was solemnly celebrated in Cappadocia, where Gregory of Nazianzen devotes a whole sermon to it. It was especially celebrated in Africa (*Epist.* II, 55, 32; P.L. XXXIII, 220). This was in a way the "eighth day" *par excellence,* the most privileged octave-day. Thus, it was normal that on this occasion the theology of the octave should be expressed. This allows us once more to bring out the connection between the liturgy of the Lord's Day and the theology of history as this is found in the Fathers. For them, liturgical time was the sacrament of the time of sacred history. The Bible, the liturgy, theol-

pp. 428-429, and *Tertullians eschatologische Deutung der Siebenzahl,* Pisciculi, p. 276 et seq.

[25] See J. Danielou, *La Typologie milleniariste de la Semaine dans le christanism primitif,* Vigiliae christianae, 1948, I, p. 1-16.

ogy and mysticism converged in the same eschatological perspective, of which they represented different aspects which were interrelated. We are therefore in the very heart of a conception in which one and the same theme, that of the week and the eighth day, exists in different modes, prefigured in the Old Testament, accomplished in Christ, sacramentally present in the liturgy and to be fulfilled by eschatology. Each school of thought emphasized a different aspect, but all are connected with the same central idea.

A first passage is found in Sermon 259 (P.L., XXXVIII, 1197 sq.): The eighth day signifies the new life at the end of the ages, the seventh the future rest of the saints on this earth. For indeed, the Lord will reign on the earth with His saints, according to the teaching of the Scripture. This will be the seventh day. The first, indeed, in the whole of time, is that which lasted from Adam to Noe; the second from Noe to Abraham; the third, from Abraham to David; the fourth from David to the Captivity in Babylon; the fifth, from the Captivity to the coming of Our Lord Jesus Christ. With the coming of the Lord begins the sixth age in which we are living. And this is why, as man was made on the sixth day, according to Genesis, so it is in our age, which is as it were the sixth of all ages, that we are reborn in Baptism to receive the image of our Creator. When the sixth day has passed, then rest will come, after the winnowing of the threshing-floor, and the saints of God will keep the Sabbath. And after the seventh, when there is seen in the field the glory (*dignitas—time*) of the harvest, the splendor and the merit of the saints, then we shall go into that life and into the rest of which it is said that eye has not seen, and ear has not heard what God has stored up for those who love Him. Then we return, so to say, to the beginning. In the same way, indeed, when seven days have gone by, it is the eighth which is also the first, since after the seven ages of the world that passes have been ended and finished, we shall return to that immortality and beatitude from which the first man fell. And the octaves accomplish the mysteries (*sacramenta*) of the children of God" (1197-1198).

This text, showing a very definite millenarianism [26] is interest-

26 The essence of millennialism is the idea of a glorious reign of Christ and his saints upon earth, corresponding to the seventh millennium, before the eighth day, which is life everlasting.

ing from several points of view. First, we find here the perspective of the seven millenia combined with another perspective, that of the five ages of the world, as primitive exegesis derived them from the parable of the workers brought into the vineyard at different times. According to St. Augustine's way of counting, the two series fit nicely into one another, since the fifth age ends with Christ, Who inaugurates the sixth. St. Augustine remarks, however, that, to arrive at this result, he uses the divisions of the genealogy of St. Matthew. For there existed a more ancient division which seems to have been that of the primitive tradition of the parable. According to this older division, the first age lasted from Adam to Noe; the second, from Noe to Abraham. So far, it is the same. But from there on, as St. Augustine himself remarks, the differences begin. The next age goes from Abraham to Moses, then from Moses to Christ, so that Christ inaugurates the fifth age, and this does not harmonize with the septenary method of counting the ages.[27] Nor does the perspective or Augustine coincide with Hippolytus' method of counting.[28] He founds his method on the weeks of Daniel, and says that Christ appeared in the *middle* of the sixth millennium, so that the end of the world will be in the 500.[29] For St. Augustine, Christ *inaugurated* the sixth millennium, so that the end of the world was to come in the year 1000. This is the view retained by the middle ages. But we find again the authority of Lactantius [30] for the parallelism between man created on the sixth day and Christ incarnated in the sixth age of the world.

A few more remarks are here required. The eschatological theme of the harvest is found here. This is connected with Matthew XIII:39, but, on the other hand, Pentecost, feast both of the harvest and of the octave of weeks is connected with the eighth day. And this eighth day, as a return of the first, is interpreted as a return of man to his primitive beatitude. But the Greek Fathers, more profoundly and more Christianly, had already shown that it was the seven-day period which returned on itself, and that the eighth day, which is outside of the cycle, introduced

[27] See for example Origen, *Co. Matth.*, XV, 32, which represents this interpretation as coming from the 'presbyters.'

[28] Pseudo-Chrysostom, P.G., LIX, 724 B, follows Origen.

[29] *Co. Dan.*, IV, 24.

[30] *De div. Inst.*, VII, 14.

a *new* creation, or, inasmuch as it renews the first, a second creation superior to the first. Augustine seems to be more Platonic than the Greeks. He returns to the same themes in another sermon on the octave of Easter. This sermon was collected under the title of No. 94 in the first volume of the *Bibliotheca Nova* of May (pp. 182 sq.). Its millenarianism is less pronounced. "The solemnity of octaves (*octavarum*) which, over the whole surface of the earth, the nations have undertaken in the name of Christ, is celebrated with a special devotion by those who have been reborn by His Baptism." We are again in the line of the eighth day after Easter, especially dear to the newly-baptized, and it is the symbolic meaning of this octave which Augustine is going to explain, in bringing us back first of all to the theme of the Flood.

He continues: "What the meaning is of such a mystery we shall try to explain in a few words. Who does not know, indeed, that in other times the earth was purified from its stains by the Flood. And that the mystery of holy Baptism, by which all the sins of man were cleansed by the water, was preached already beforehand? For the Ark, made of incorruptible wood, which was a figure of the Church, contained only eight persons. Thus the truth which is attested by there being eight men saved from the waters of the Deluge by which sins were wiped out, this same truth is shown in there being eight days in the case of waters of Baptism by which sins are destroyed. Thus, just as one and the same thing can be said by many words, so one and the same thing is accustomed to be signified by many figurative events. Thus, the fact that in one case there are eight persons and in the other eight days does not mean that different things are signified but it is the same thing which is signified in different ways by the difference of signs, as it might be by a diversity of words" (183).

Augustine comes back to the ancient symbolism of the First Epistle of St. Peter, the most traditional of all the baptismal figures which use the number 8.[31] And we should notice how he observes that the eight persons could well have the same significance as the eight days. It does seem, indeed, as if this must be true of the literal meaning of the text itself. Then he goes on to the eschatological significance which we are now concerned with: "This is why the number 8 prefigures that which is related to the

[31] IV, 20-21. See above, p. 79.

future age, where there is neither growth or decline by the revolution of time but everything endures in secure blessedness. And as the times of this world (*saeculum*) are measured by the cyclical return of the week of days, that this day is rightly called, in some way, the eighth, when, after the works of time, the saints having come hither, no longer distinguish activity from rest by the alternation of day and night, but possess a rest which is always awake, and an activity which is not lazily, but unwearyingly, rested." We see appearing here the eschatological conception, in terms which recall St. Basil. St. Augustine then mentioned Psalm VI and the connection between the octave and meditation on the judgment. We should notice the depth of St. Augustine's thought in the analysis of this blessed activity which is beyond both action and repose. Here it rejoins the page of the *Life of Moses* in which Gregory of Nyssa shows that it is the property of the spiritual activity to be rested by exercise itself.[32]

St. Augustine then comes to millenarianism. Psalm VI ends with the verse: *Custodies nos a generatione hac in aeternum,* "as beginning on the seventh and leading to the eighth, from glory to glory as under the Spirit of the Lord. What further is meant by this peace more than the peace that the Prophet promises? What, then, except that the Sabbath, which is signified by the seventh day even though it is contained in the same temporal cycle of days, has also a rest of its own, that which was promised on this earth to the saints, in which no distress of this world will trouble them further? It was to signify this a long while ahead that God Himself, having made all things very good, Himself rested on the seventh day. And if this day has no evening, it is because, with no history intervening, it leads the saints to the eighth day, that is to say to eternal blessedness. For it is one thing to rest in the Lord while yet being in the midst of time—and this is signified by the seventh day, that is to say, the Sabbath; and another thing to go beyond all time and to rest endlessly henceforth in the Artisan of time, which is signified by the eighth day." We find here again, in phrases of wonderful depth, the old millenarianism of Irenaeus. The blessedness which will be enjoyed in time is different from the blessedness which will be enjoyed beyond time. This is the extreme effort of Augustine to disengage

[32] P.G., XLIV, 404 A.

the religious significance of millenarianism. It appears to us as developing this significance in its most profound interpretation, as Origen had done for the mystery of the jubilee. These are the summits of the Christian theology of time. But Augustine was to come to realize that they represented a sacrilegious attempt to penetrate a secret which God had reserved for Himself.

Before approaching the text which gives witness to this evolution, we must remind ourselves again of its riches. Having mentioned millenarianism, Augustine goes back to the chronological symbolism of the eighth day. "In these days which have a certain figurative meaning, the first is found to be also the eighth. The Lord's Day indeed (*dominicus dies*) is called *prima sabbati,* but the first day gives way to the second which comes after. But in that day, on the contrary, which is signified by this, the first and the eighth, is found that first eternity that we left behind by the original sin of our first parents to descend into the mortality of here below, and the last octave-day that, after the last resurrection and the destruction of the enemy, Death, we shall regain, in such a way that that which is corruptible shall be clothed with incorruptibility, and that the returning prodigal son shall receive the first robe which, after the weariness of his long journeying and the food of pigs and the other cares of mortal life and the sevenfold circles of time, shall be given back to him, the very same, at the end, and as the eighth. It is not, then, without reason that Our Lord Himself, on this day of the Lord, at once the first and the eighth, was pleased to show in His mortal flesh also the type of the bodily resurrection" (184-185).[33]

In this passage, we meet the echo of the patristic interpretation of the parable of the prodigal son, to whom is restored his first robe of incorruptibility. Under the inspiration of St. Augustine, the scriptural figures, which sometimes appear, one might say, as somewhat withered, are reanimated and become the expression of spiritual reality.

But we must now return to the Augustinian conception of history, in the work which is its chief construction, the *City of God.* In approaching the whole unfolding of the religious history of mankind, St. Augustine could not help meeting the problem of

[33] See also an important passage in *Epist.,* LV, 13-23, in which the eighth day is represented as a revelation of the Resurrection.

millenarianism. We shall see that he rejected it under the material shape which it had been given by Irenaeus and Lactantius. He does not retain even the idea of a visible reign of Christ on earth, as he did in his sermons on the octave. Yet he could not detach himself completely from the symbolism of the week and of the octave, and, on the final page of his book, it is to this that he returns at last to express the essential mystery of sacred history. It is in the seventh chapter of Book XX of the *City of God* that St. Augustine definitely attacks the problem, in connection with the interpretation of the Apocalypse. He first gives a resume of the millenarianist position: "Those who, on the strength of this passage (XX, 1-6), have suspected that the first resurrection is future and bodily, have been moved among other things, especially by the number of a thousand years—as if it were a fit thing that the saints should thus enjoy a kind of Sabbath-rest during that period, a holy leisure after the labors of the six thousand years since man was created, and was on account of his great sin dismissed from the blessedness of paradise into the woes of this mortal life, so that thus, as it is written, 'One day is with the Lord as a thousand years, and a thousand years as one day', there should follow on the completion of six thousand years as of six days, a kind of seventh-day Sabbath in the succeeding thousand years; and that it is for this purpose that the saints rise, viz., to celebrate this Sabbath" (PL., XLI, 667, *The City of God*, Modern Library Ed., p. 719).

The judgment of St. Augustine on this teaching is interesting: "And this opinion would not be objectionable, if it were believed that the joys of the saints in that Sabbath shall be spiritual, and consequent on the presence of God; for I myself, too, once held this opinion. But as they assert that those who then rise again shall enjoy the leisure of immoderate carnal banquets, furnished with an amount of meat and drink such as not only to shock the feeling of the temperate, but even to surpass the measure of credulity itself, such assertions can be believed only by the carnal." This passage teaches us two things: first, that there is a millenarianism which Augustine condemns in every way: this is the temporal notion of a kind of human life in which all sorts of enjoyments are simply to be multiplied. This is the idea of carnal-minded men, and has nothing in common with the Christian idea. In the second place, there is a millenarianism which speaks of a spiritual reign of God on earth: this opinion was once held by St. Augustine himself, and this is what we have found in his sermons. But here, he seems to repudiate this idea. What happens, then, to the thousand years spoken of in the Apocalypse? St. Augustine proposes two interpretations: either it means the sixth millennium, thought of as the sixth day, of which the last hours are now passing by and which is to be followed by the Sabbath that has no evening, that is to say, the rest of the saints, which has no end. This presupposes the conception of the world as divided into millenia, and shows us that Augustine has not yet rejected it. What he rejects is only the intermediary millennium between the sixth and the world to come. The seventh day signifies this future world itself. The other idea sees in the thousand years of the Apocalypse the whole duration of the world. But Augustine leans towards the first interpretation. Furthermore, the thousand years coincide with the sixth millennium, inaugurated by Christ, that is to say, with the Church in which the reign of Christ is already effectively exercised (673) St. Augustine proposes the interpretation which modern exegesis has taken up once more with P. Allo and of which Cullmann has drawn the consequences.[34]

Although he rejects the idea of an earthly reign of Christ before the eternal octave-day, Augustine, on the last page of *The City of God*, the most beautiful that has been devoted to the subject of the spiritual Sabbath, still retains the theme of a seventh day which is already heavenly and which is fulfilled in an eternal eighth day, but his thought does not seek to penetrate further into this mystery. "There shall be fulfilled the words of the Psalm, 'Be still and know that I am God.' There shall be the great Sabbath which has no evening, which God celebrated among His first works, as it is written, 'And God rested on the seventh day from all His works which He had made. And God blessed the seventh day, and sanctified it; because that in it He had rested from all His work which God began to make.' For we shall ourselves be the seventh day, when we shall be filled and replenished with God's blessing and sanctification. There shall we be still, and know that He is God. . . . But when we are restored by Him, and perfected with greater grace, we shall have eternal leisure to see that He is God, for we shall be full of Him when He shall be all in all. . . . This Sabbath

[34] *Le Christ et le temps* (French translation), 1947, p. 107.

shall appear more clearly if we count the ages as days, in accordance with the period of time defined by Scripture, for that period will be found to be the seventh."

St. Augustine then goes through the division of history into five ages up to Christ: "The sixth is now passing, and cannot be measured by any number of generations, as it has been said, 'It is not for you to know the times which the Father hath put in His own power.' After this period, God shall rest as on the seventh day, when He shall give us (who shall be the seventh day) rest in Himself. But there is not now space to treat of these ages; suffice it to say that the seventh day shall be our Sabbath, which shall be brought to a close, not by an evening, but by the Lord's Day, as an eighth and eternal day, consecrated by the Resurrection of Christ, and prefiguring the eternal repose not only of the spirit, but also of the body. There we shall rest and see, see and love, love and praise" (803-804. Mod. Lib. Ed., p. 867).

Such was the final thought of Augustine on the mystery of the seventh and of the eighth day. He does away with all millenarianism. And, at the same time, this text answers two other questions. The first is that of Augustine's attitude concerning, not millenarianism, but the idea of human history as a week of millenia. For Hippolytus, this idea was to be taken in the strict literal sense, and and so serve as the basis for calculations with the purpose of fixing the date of the end of the world. But in this passage St. Augustine formally rejects such an idea. He keeps the conception of the millenia as giving a framework to history and as serving to distinguish periods that really differ from one another. And this is important, and constitutes a historical perspective; but he rejects entirely—at least for the last period,—the idea that the count of a thousand years is to be taken literally. It is only a symbol to stand for a whole epoch.[35] Augustine has already touched on this point in his *Enarrationes in Psalmos VI:* "It has seemed to certain men that (the number 8 in the title of the Psalm) means the day of Judgment, that is to say, the time of the coming of Our Lord. It is estimated, when we count the years since Adam, that this coming should be after seven thousand years, so that the seven millenia go

[35] See St. Ambrose: "We might understand the six days as meaning six millenia, but we prefer to take them in a symbolic sense" (*Exp. Luc.,* VII, 7; C.S.E.L., XXXII, p. 285).

by like seven days, and that this time comes afterwards like the eighth day. But as it is said by the Lord: *Non est nostrum scire tempora,* we can easily see that nobody should try to win for himself the knowledge of this time by calculations of years" (P.L., XXXVI, 90). So Augustine keeps—and yet without attaching any importance to it—the septenary idea of history, but he leaves out all concordism like that of Hippolytus.

The last question, finally, is that of the content of the Sabbath rest. As we have said, this theme, in Augustine, united both his ideas on history and his ideas on man, *The City of God* and his *Confessions*. If the theme of the first work is actually that of the progress of the whole world toward the eternal octave-day, that of the second is the search of the soul for its rest, of which the Sabbath is the figure. And St. Augustine has described this rest in marvellous phrases in this passage that we have just read: "We shall rest and we shall see; we shall see and we shall love; we shall love and we shall praise." The teaching here compressed into this succinct formula, expressing all the drive of St. Augustine's soul, is also to be found on each page of his work. One of the leitmotifs of his work is the idea of the Sabbath, thought of not in a historical perspective, but in its interior reality. This rest is, first of all, in this present life, the tranquility of the soul. And the tranquility of the soul comes from the peace of a good conscience. For "he who does not sin truly observes the Sabbath" (*Sermon* XXXVIII, P.L., 270, 1242). This is the same theme as we found in St. Justin,[36] but restated in a more interior way. This break with sin has its principle in Baptism which introduces us to the true Sabbath (*De Gen. ad litt.* IV, 13; P.L., XXXIV, 305).

But this rest is not enough for the soul of Augustine, for, inasmuch as we are in this life, it is imperfect. "There is a sacrament of the Sabbath, prescribed by God to the fathers of old, that we Christians observe spiritually by abstaining from all servile work, that is to say, from all sin, and in having rest in our heart, that is to say, spiritual tranquility. But even though we try to do this in this present time, we shall not arrive at this spiritual rest until we go out of this life" (*Co. Jo.* XX, 2; P.L., XXXV, 1556). And also St. Augustine aspires to that fullness in which his soul will be entirely free for contemplation, for love and for praise,

[36] *Dialogue,* XII, 3.

without being distracted by the things of the world. But it remains true that if the rest of the soul is the absence of sin, then exterior occupations cannot take it away. It is already peace, while awaiting a still greater peace. This is the final teaching of Augustine: "He whose conscience is good, is tranquil, and this peace is the Sabbath of the heart. For indeed it is turned toward the hope of Him Who promises, and although he is tried in the present, he aspires toward the hope of Him Who is to come, and then all clouds of sadness are scattered. This joy, in the peace of our hope, —this is our Sabbath" (*En. in Ps.,* XCI, 2; P.L., XXVII, 1172). Thus St. Augustine, master of interior experience, at the end of this long journey shows us in the mystery of the Sabbath the fundamental attitude of the Christian toward the mystery of time. This is neither a possession nor only a hope, but a waiting which is already peace because it rests wholly on the promise of the faithful God.

CHAPTER SEVENTEEN

Easter

THE paschal mystery is, in a sense, the whole Christian mystery. But this Christian mystery reveals its inexhaustible content by means of the different perspectives under which it is considered. And it is the Old Testament which shows these dimensions according to which the Christian mystery is to be thought about. The Pasch, in the most limited sense of the word, is one of these dimensions, including various aspects under which the mystery of Christ is shown to us. The whole of Christianity is the fulfillment of these paschal realities: in a sense, it is not the liturgical feast of Easter, it is the very mystery of the Redemption and its sacramental participation which are prefigured by the Pasch. But the liturgical feast of Easter emphasizes more especially the characteristics which make the Christian mystery a development of the Jewish Pasch. It is these characteristics which we are now to study. Our task is to see how patristic tradition understood the typological interpretation of the twelfth chapter of Exodus, which is the paschal text *par excellence.*

The history of Exodus begins by giving chronological directions: the month of the Pasch is to be considered as the first of months; the lamb is to be taken on the tenth day of the month and eaten on the fourteenth, towards evening. These directions constitute the specifying element of the Pasch: it is the time when it is to be celebrated which characterizes the liturgical feast of the Pasch in contrast to the Christian mystery taken as a whole. It is, therefore, the time itself whose symbolism is peculiar to the liturgical feast, as we have already seen to be true in relation to the Lord's Day. By the cycle of the year, the mystery of Christ is woven into the cosmic cycle, and the cosmic cycle becomes, as it were, a first prefiguring of it. The liturgical year thus introduces us into the symbolism of time.

The Pasch takes place in the first month of the year, which for the Jews was April. It thus came with the spring, and this fact was charged with meaning for the Fathers. But, to begin with, it is interesting to note that Christians were not the first to interpret the date of the Pasch in a spiritual way, for the Jews had done so before them. Here Christian exegesis is derived from the Jewish. We read in Philo of Alexandria: "The month of the azymes, which is the seventh, is the first in number, order and dignity according to the solar cycle. This is why it is the first in the holy Books. For truly it seems that the spring equinox is the figure and the image of the beginning in which the world was created. God, in order to remind us each year of the creation of the world, made the springtime in which everything is burgeoning and flowering. This is why it is not without cause that it is named as the first in the Law, being the image of the first beginning" (*Spec. Leg.* II, 150).[1]

In this passage, spring is seen, even in the natural order, as the yearly commemoration of creation. The Fathers of the Church used this idea and showed that springtime is the figure of the second creation by the resurrection of Christ. We should note that the first author to give this interpretation refers to Jewish tradition. Hippolytus writes: "It is said first of all: This month is the beginning of months. Why is the month of the Pasch the first month of the year? A secret teaching of the Jews says, that it is the time in which the shepherd draws out the shining milk, in which the bee gathers sweet honey and makes wax, in which the sailor dares to confront the sea" (17: Nautin, 145). This description recalls what we shall find later on in the Fourth Century. It might very well, however, not be a primitive idea, but one derived from the sophistry of the time.

But Hippolytus does not stop with this naturalistic explanation. Without rejecting it, he prefers the typical and prophetic one, in

[1] See above, p. 194.

which the spring is not the memorial of creation, but the figure of the Resurrection: "I do not refuse to believe in these things, but I think, or, better still, I believe, that it is because of the spiritual Pasch, principle, head and ruler of all times, that this month is that of the Pasch, in which this great mystery was consummated and celebrated, so that, as the Lord is the first-born of all creatures intelligible and invisible, since the beginning, so this month, which is honored by His holy sacrifice, is the first of the year and the beginning of all times" (17: Nautin, 149). Thus the primacy of spring comes from the fact that since the beginning it was to be the month in which He Who is the Prince of time offered His sacrifice.

Hippolytus contrasted the cosmic interpretation and the Christological. Eusebius brings them together in an important passage of his *Treatise on Easter*. Having shown why the other seasons would not be fitting for the Resurrection of Christ, he comes to the springtime: "There remains the shining springtime, which is in some way to the whole year what the head is to the body. Then the sun begins to run the first part of his course, and the moon at his side, in its full brilliance, transforms the whole course of the night into a luminous day. Ended are the furies of the storms of winter, ended the long nights, ended the floods. Henceforth, in the newness of a shining atmosphere, sailors find the sea calm. The fields with their ears filled with grain and trees loaded with fruit, adorned with the gifts of God, give to the laborers, in the giving of thanks, the reward for their work" (P. G., XXIII, 696 D).

But the reason for the choice of spring as the time of the Resurrection was not only its beauty. It is—and here Eusebius takes up the theme of Philo—because it is the anniversary of creation. It is because of this—and here Eusebius differs from Hippolytus,—that it is a fitting time for the Resurrection. "This time was that very one which appeared at the moment of the first creation of the world, when the earth brought forth shoots, and the stars appeared; it is at this time that the Lord of the whole world celebrated the mystery of His own feast and, like a great star, appeared to light up the whole world with the rays of religion and thus to bring back the anniversary of the cosmos" (697 A). Thus "the first sun on the first morning" awakens in the spirit of Eusebius the rising, on the morning of the second creation, of the Sun of Justice, which lights up the new cosmos of the Church. The theme of Christ the Sun, dear to Eusebius, is here brought together with that of the springtime.[2]

In the interval between creation and the Resurrection, furthermore, as Eusebius does not forget, the time was that of the Jewish Pasch which was first placed in the cycle of spring: "It is at the time of this feast that the Egyptians, friends of the demons, found their ruin, and the Jews, in celebrating the feast of God, their liberation." Thus the Resurrection of Christ is seen to be both the fulfillment of the cosmic feast of spring and of the Jewish feast of the Exodus: "It is at this time that the figure was realized, the ancient Pasch, which is called a passing-over: it contains also the symbol of the immolation of the lamb and the food of the unleavened bread." We shall return to the last points. What concerns us now is to see how Eusebius shows that the Christian Pasch subsumes the cosmic religion and the Jewish.

He continues: "All these things find their fulfillment in the feast of salvation. It is He, the Christ, Who was the Lamb whose Body was stretched out. But it was He also, the Sun of Justice, whose divine springtime and salvation-bearing change caused the life of men to pass from evil to good. The spirits who cause the peoples to go astray have ceased to be active with the evils of winter, and the abundance of new fruits crowns the Church with the charisms of the Holy Spirit. The fields which were cultivated by the Word with spiritual cultivation bear the lovely flowers of holiness and, freed from the scourge of darkness, we are made worthy of the light of the knowledge of the Day of the Lord" (697 B-C). We should note that, in this passage, Eusebius takes up again all the expressions used in his description of spring to show how they are figures fulfilled in Christianity. This subsumption of cosmic religion, as we have said before, is fully legitimate, since it certainly represents the first religion, the revelation of God through His providence in the world of nature.

Later tradition presents the same theme. Gregory Nazianzen in his sermon on Easter thus comments on Exodus XII: "The month to which he makes allusion is the first, or, better, the chief of months, whether it was so since the beginning among the Hebrews, or whether it became so later and received the honor of being the first from the Christian mystery" (XXXVI, 642 C). We find once

[2] See Hugo Rahner, *Griechische Mythen in christlicher Deutung,* p. 149 et seq.

more the hesitation of Hippolytus. As for the description of spring, it is not found in the *Sermon on Easter*, but in that on *The Octave of Easter*. Gregory Nazianzen takes up this subject at much greater length than any of the authors that we have quoted so far. And the influence of literary descriptions is much more evident than in previous works.[3]

Let us quote the beginning of this sermon: "Everything contributes to the beauty and the joy of the feast. The queen of the seasons makes a feast for the queen of days and offers her everything she has that is most beautiful and most pleasing. The sky is its most transparent, the sun at its highest and brightest, the course of the moon at its most brilliant, and the choir of the stars at its purest. The springs run at their clearest, the rivers are most abundant, freed from their fetters of ice. The fields are filled with sweet scents, green things spring up, the lambs bound in the green grass. Ships go out from their ports with all the sails filled, and the dolphins accompany them bounding and joyfully blowing. The shepherd and cow-herd tune their flutes and pipe a melody" (XXXVI, 620 A). We should notice that, although the development is more colorful, the themes remain the same: the sun, moon and stars: the sailor and the laborer. We have here a description whose rules were fixed by the laws of rhetoric and on which each writer could only embroider some few variations.

But Gregory Nazianzen does not show that the springtime is a figure of the Resurrection, as does Eusebius. It is the tradition of the latter which we find again in Cyril of Alexandria. We have thirty of his *Paschal Homilies* (P. G. LXXVII, 391-970). In many places we find the symbolism of spring, for example in the *Second Homily:* "The threats of winter have ceased, the winds of spring are blowing, the fields are covered with flowers, the trees bear their fruits. It is not without cause that the Law commanded us to observe the months of first-fruits. For human nature must rival the flowering fields and be seen, as it were, covered with the flowers of virtue" (LXXVII, 429 D). And Cyril describes a whole parallel between winter and sin, the spring winds and the Holy Spirit, the perfume of flowers and that of virtues.

Elsewhere, after another description of spring, Cyril continues:

[3] On the *ecphrasis* in the Fathers of the Church, see L. Meridier, *L'Influence de la Seconde Sophistique sur l'oeuvre de saint Grégoire de Nysse,* p. 139 et seq.

"But what is more wonderful than all this is that, together with the green things and the flowers, that nature is also renewed who rules over everything on earth. I mean man. Indeed, the season of spring brings us the Resurrection of the Lord, by which all are refashioned in newness of life, having escaped from the strange corruption of death. It would be truly unthinkable that all growing things should regain their first appearance by the power of God who gives life to everything, and that he for whose sake these things were invented should remain unquickened, with no help from on high" (LXXVII, 581 B-C. See also 752 A-D).

Until now, we have remained in the world of Greek thought; but we can find analogous developments in the Paschal preaching of the West. I shall quote only the beginning of the first Paschal Homily of Gaudentius of Brescia: "The Lord Jesus decreed that the blessed feast of the Pasch should be celebrated at a suitable time, after the fog of autumn, after the sadness of winter, and before the heat of summer. For, indeed, Christ, the Sun of Justice, was to scatter the darkness of Judaism and the ice of paganism before the heat of the future judgment by the peaceful light of His Resurrection, and bring back to the peaceful state of their origin all the things which had been covered with obscurity by the prince of darkness" (P. L., XX, 844-845).

And Gaudentius goes on in words directly derived from the common tradition: "It is indeed in the springtime that God created the world. And, indeed, it was in the month of March that God said to Moses: 'The month shall be for you the first of the months of the year.' Now the truthful God would not have called this the first month, if it had not been such in fact, as He would not have called the Sabbath the seventh day, if Sunday had not been the first. This is why the Son of God raised up the fallen world by His own resurrection at the very time in which He first created it out of nothing, so that all things might be refashioned in Him"[4] (845). Gaudentius disengages the most profound meaning of this symbol: he notes that it is the creative Word by Whom all things were made, Who is also He Who comes to remake everything at the end of time.

To the direction concerning the first month of the year for the celebration of the Pasch, Exodus adds other chronological details:

[4] See also Gregory of Elvira, *Tractatus,* ed. Batiffol. p. 100, 15 et seq.

the lamb is to be taken on the tenth day of the month and slain on the fourteenth. We should add that the fourteenth day of Nisan is the day of the spring equinox and the full moon. And, finally, the lambs should be slain toward evening. We have here one of the features commented on by the exegetes. Concerning the tenth and the fourteenth days, we have two different traditions. The first appears in the *Paschal Homily* of Hippolytus: "It is to be taken on the tenth day of the month: and this also is full of meaning. For the Law is separated from the Gospel. But the height of the teaching of the Law is the Decalogue. It is after the Ten Commandments of the Law that the mystical Lamb comes, He Who descends from Heaven. He is preserved for a space of some days: the Scripture prefigures by this interval of time that preceded the Passion, when the Lord, having been taken captive, was guarded at the house of the high-priest" (20-21; Nautin, 151).

Here we have an interpretation of the type of St. Matthew, one, that is to say, in which the figures of the Old Testament are connected with chronological details of the life of Christ: the ten days are a figure of the Old Testament; the five days of the time which separated the arrest of Christ from His immolation. We shall not find this kind of exegesis later on.[5] The only feature to appear again is that of the ten days as a figure of the Old Testament, and it is to be noticed that it reappears in Western tradition in Gaudentius of Brescia: "The choice of the lamb on the tenth day and its immolation on the fourteenth signify that the Jewish people were to crucify the Son of God, after He had been received in the Decalogue of the Law and had been born fourteen generations after the Babylonian captivity" (P. L. XX, 863 A).

But alongside this kind of interpretation, we meet another which sees in the choice of the lamb on the tenth day the pre-existence of the Lamb in the thought of God, and, in its immolation on the fourteenth, the accomplishment of His sacrifice at the end of time. This theme appears in Cyril of Alexandria. In the *De Adoratione*, he points out, "He is taken on the tenth day and immolated on the fourteenth towards the evening to show that the Mystery of Christ is not new, nor known for the first time, although it pleased

[5] It may possibly appear as early as the New Testament. St. John's Gospel, in which numbers are often symbolic, notes that the entrance of Jesus into Jerusalem before the Passion took place on the tenth day of Nisan (John XII, 1).

the Jews to turn it into derision. The knowledge of it existed long before the Passion, the saints proclaimed it in advance, the Law announced it, and Holy Scripture prefigured for us the mystery which is in Him" (P. G., LXVIII, 1068 B-D). The fact that the choice of the lamb comes before its immolation thus shows that the knowledge of the mystery preceded its realization. Nevertheless, he did not emphasize the actual number of days.

But this is what we find in the *Glapyhres* of the same author: Cyril connects the parable of the workers coming at the last hour with this text, and continues: "You can see, in a most evident way, that our world is divided into five epochs." The four first ages were inaugurated by Adam, Noe, Abraham and Moses: "Toward the eleventh hour, that is to say, at the fifth epoch, the day was already going by and the present world declining towards its ending, Christ called into His service the nations which up to that time had not been called to the knowledge of the truth. Thus, the lamb is taken in the first of the five days, which is the figure of the beginning of time, and, kept until the last, it is slain towards evening: you should understand by this that the mystery of Christ is not recent, nor unforeseen, but that it was kept in the foreknowledge of the Father since the creation of the world" (LXIX, 424 A-B).

Here we meet themes that we have found elsewhere: the parable of the years interpreted as the five ages of the world, the preexistence of the mystery showing that Christ is not new. And the source of these ideas is well known: they come from Origen, on whom Cyril depends in many ways. The originality of Cyril consists in having found in the five days which separated the choice of the lamb from its immolation, a symbol of the five ages of the world. And it is remarkable that we find the same theme in the *Paschal Homilies* of Pseudo-Chrysostom which came out of the same milieu as the writings of Cyril of Alexandria: "From the begining, the sacrifice of Christ was prefigured in the sufferings of the just—beginning with Abel—and Christ suffered in all of them. But Christ's sacrifice was not accomplished until the divine Lamb came Himself and suffered Himself. The lamb, chosen on the tenth day to be immolated and immolated on the fourteenth towards evening, is a figure of the fact that the design of the Passion existed from the beginning of the world, but was not realized until the end" (P. G., LIX, 735).

Here we have the general theme; a precise allusion to the five days is found in another passage: "This space of five days is a figure of the whole time of the world, divided into five periods, from Adam to Noe, from Noe to Abraham, from Abraham to Moses, from Moses to the coming of Christ, and from the coming of Christ until now. During all this time salvation by the holy Victim was presented to men, but the victim was not yet immolated. It is in the fifth epoch of history that the true Pasch was immolated and that the first man, saved by it, came out into the light of eternity" (P. G. LIX, 724). The similarity is complete between these homilies and the writings of St. Cyril; we are in the same theological milieu. The idea of Christ's coming as taking place in the fifth age of the world is found elsewhere at this period—the beginning of the fifth century. St. Augustine in particular uses it a great deal in his *De catechizandis rudibus*. The idea, therefore, belongs to the common catechesis. The originality of the writers we have been considering consists in the application they make of it to the Paschal lamb.[6]

But though the symbolism of the five ages certainly is of secondary importance, can we say the same of the symbolism of the distinction between the choice of the lamb and its immolation as a figure of the eternal pre-existence of Christ in the divine thought and its realization at the end of time. It is not impossible that this symbolism goes back to the New Testament itself. The First Epistle of St. Peter includes a whole figurative interpretation of the subject of this chapter: the dress of travellers, the journey from Egypt are interpreted as figures of Christian conversion (I Peter 1: 13, 18). And we read this: "You know that you were redeemed . . . with the precious blood of Christ, as of a lamb without blemish (*amomos*) and without spot. Foreknown, indeed, before the foundation of the world, He has been manifested in the last times for your sake" (I:20).

Clearly, this is the source of the developments in the homilies we have been discussing. The question presents itself whether, in the text of the First Epistle of St. Peter, the contrast between the pre-existing design and its eschatological manifestation is a symbolic commentary on the choice of the lamb on the tenth day and

[6] See also *The Detailed Contemplation of the Pasch,* in the *spuria* of St. Cyril (P.G., 1204 A-D).

its immolation on the fourteenth. We should realize that this text is a very close commentary on the twelfth chapter of Exodus. The word *amomos*, without blemish, applied by the Epistle to the Lamb, is an exact translation of the Hebrew word which the Septuagint rendered by *teleios*, perfect (XII, 5). The word is found elsewhere describing the paschal lamb in Lev. XXII: 17. The Epistle here avoided using the word *teleios* because of the *teleioi* in verse 13.[7] This being so, it is quite possible that the Epistle is giving a primary exegesis of the symbolism of the tenth and the fourteenth day, and that the interpretation of Cyril thus becomes the development of a primitive Christian exegesis.

We have not yet studied the precise indication of the time of the immolation of the lamb, which was to take place towards evening. Here we find two lines of interpretation, along the lines of St. Matthew and those of the Alexandrian school. The first sees here an announcement of the fact that it was on the evening of Good Friday that Christ was to be immolated. This is the interpretation given us by Hippolytus: "The lamb is immolated towards evening: and it was indeed at the setting of the sun that the holy Lamb was put to death" (23: Nautin, 151). Such also is the exegesis of Theodoret: "The lamb is slain in the evening: it was indeed toward evening that Christ was handed over to the Jews" (P. G. LXXX, 252 B). Hippolytus is thinking of the evening of Good Friday, while Theodoret of that of Thursday. Gregory Nazianzen follows the latter, while joining this historical interpretation to an eschatological one: "The lamb is immolated in the evening, for the Passion of Christ took place at the end of time." And this also may be an allusion to the hour of the institution of the Eucharist (XXXVI, 644 C).

The same conception is found again in Gaudentius of Brescia, with this new detail that the allusion to the immolation in the evening is related to the darkening of the sun, the *occasus solis*, of the evening of the Passion. This is what is prefigured by the evening of the immolation of the paschal lamb: "It is immolated in the evening, either the evening of the world, since He suffered in the last years of the age, or the evening of the setting sun, since the sun was darkened at the time of the crucifixion of Christ" (P. L., XX, 863 B). But we should remark that together with this

[7] See E. G. Selwyn, *The First Epistle of St. Peter*, pp. 145-146.

interpretation along the lines of St. Matthew, we see the appearance of another.

This second interpretation sees in the "evening" the last years of the world. It is this doubtless to which the First Epistle of St. Peter alludes in speaking of the Lamb manifested "in the last times" (I:22). We have seen it in Irenaeus (*Adv. haer.* IV, 10; P. G. VII, 1000 B). We find it again in Origen: "Since the paschal Law prescribes that the lamb should be eaten in the evening, the Saviour suffered in the evening of the world, so that you might always eat the flesh of the Word, you who live always in the evening until the morning shall come" (*Ho. Gen.* X, 3). This was, in Gregory Nazianzen and in Gaudentius of Brescia, harmonized with the other interpretation. Cyril of Alexandria also gives it: "It is eaten towards evening, for it is in the last times of the world and when it was coming near its time of setting, that the death of Christ was accomplished" (LXVIII, 1068 D). And the Homilies of Pseudo-Chrysostom are along the same lines: "The fact that it was not in the evening, but towards evening that the victim was immolated, shows that it was not at the very end of the present time, but towards that end that Christ was to suffer" (P. G. LIX, 724).[8]

The fourteenth day of the month of Nisan, on which the Pasch was celebrated, has the characteristic of being the day of the spring equinox, that of the full moon. And thus also the light of the moon follows directly on that of the sun so that this day and night are without darkness. This fact has also been the object of a symbolic interpretation which, perhaps, is the richest of those we have been studying.[9] It is remarkable that, as in the interpretation of the symbolism of springtime, so here also the Christians were preceded by the Jews. We find in Philo a symbolic interpretation of the paschal equinox: "the beginning of the feast is half-way through the month, the fourteenth day, when the moon is at its full, to show that there is no darkness on this day, but that it is full of light, the sun shining from the dawn to the evening, and the moon from the evening to the dawn" (*De spec. leg.*, 150).

[8] St. Cyprian joins the two interpretations, seeing in the very death of Christ in the evening a symbol of the 'evening of the world' (*Epist.*, LXIII, 16; C.S.E.L., 714).
[9] See H. Rahner, *Mysterium lunae,* Zeitsch. Kath. Theol. 1939, 311-349, 428-442; 1940, 61-80, 121-131.

This interpretation is taken up and developed by Christian authors. We meet it first of all in Eusebius who observes that at the time of the Pasch "the moon in its full splendor transforms into a luminous day the course of the night" (P. G., XXIII, 696 D). But he gives no other symbolism. It is in Gregory of Nyssa that again we find the interpretation of Philo applied to Christianity. In his first *Sermon on the Resurrection,* he proposes to refute the criticisms that the Jews make of the Christians, reproaching them for not celebrating the Pasch on the fourteenth Nisan. We know that after the Council of Nice, the custom of celebrating the feast on the Sunday after the fourteenth Nisan became general. Gregory answers that it is not the literal practice that matters: the law is abolished. But what is important is the spiritual significance.

This leads him to explain the spiritual meaning of the equinox: "He who, through the whole week of his life, keeps himself without any mixture of vice, separates himself from all darkness. Now this is what is signified by the fourteenth day of the lunar cycle. It is the day on which the moon is at the full. She does not permit it to be entirely night either in the evening nor in the morning. For, indeed, before the rays of the setting sun disappear, the moon rises at the other end of the sky and enlightens the earth with its light. This teaches us that we should celebrate the unique Pasch for the whole week of this life, by causing this time to be filled with light" (XLVI, 628 C-D). Because of the displacement of the date of Easter, the luminous night does not correspond to the actual day of the celebration. But Gregory, following Origen, interprets the rites of the Law as figures of all Christian existence. This is the day without darkness prefigured by the paschal equinox of Judaism.

Gregory came back to this subject in his *Fourth Letter.* He is dealing with a parallel between Christmas and Easter. Christmas, at the winter solstice, is the moment when the light begins to conquer the darkness, symbolizing the appearance of the Sun of Justice. Easter, on the other hand, at the spring equinox, signifies the triumph of Christ by His Resurrection: "The good does not have to struggle any longer with equal arms against a hostile army, but the luminous life now triumphs, having scattered the darkness of idolatry in the abundance of its light. This is why the course of the moon, on the fourteenth day, shows it as facing the rays of the sun. Having welcomed the sun when he is setting, she herself does not set before she has mingled her own rays with those of the sun, so that one only light endures without any lack of continuity, through the whole cycle of day and night, with no interval of darkness. Let your whole life, then, be one sole feast and one great day, pure of all darkness" (XLVI, 1028 C-D).

We can sense, in the background of this text, the incorporation into the Christian mystery of a whole solar mythology. The conflict of light with darkness is expressed by the myth of Ormuzd and Ahriman, of Apollo and Poseidon. But Christ is the sun of the new creation. He rose at the time of the Incarnation: His name is the Orient, the Dawn in the East, He attacked the power of darkness, and on the day of His Resurrection, He completely scattered the darkness of death and of sin. So Christianity disengages the cosmic symbols from the pagan myths in which they had become perverted, and incorporates them as figures of the mystery of truth. This line of thought shows that we are here in the Fourth Century, at the time of the decline of paganism, when Christianity began to clothe itself in its garments.

The same symbolism reappears in the *Homilies* of Pseudo-Chrysostom: "When the fifth day has come, he who is saved enjoys a perpetual light, the moon shining all night long and the sun following her: this happens indeed on the fifteenth day, which is that of the full moon. The fourteenth day is, therefore, to be understood symbolically" (LIX, 724). We should notice nevertheless that this symbolism does not correspond to the fact of the paschal night when it was no longer celebrated on the fourteenth Nisan. So we see that a different symbolism is given to it in the Fourth Century. The luminous night, the figure of the routing of darkness by the resurrection of Christ, is no longer symbolized by the shining of the moon following directly on that of the sun, but by the brightness of the candles of the Easter vigil, which light up the whole night and make it a luminous day.

This appears in the sermons of the Fourth Century. So Gregory of Nyssa: "Since this luminous night which mingles the brightness of the candles with the rays of the rising sun, becomes one whole continuous day, not interrupted by any darkness coming in between—let us understand by this, brethren, that it fulfills the prophecy which says: 'This is the day that the Lord has made' "

(XLVI, 681 C). It is the light of the candles which henceforth permits us to see in the Paschal night, the "night shining like the day" of Psalm CXXXVIII: "May God soon show you this night, this shining darkness, of which it is written: 'The night shall shine like the day" (XXXIII, 357 A). And St. Ambrose in the Exsultet echoes St. Cyril: "This is the night of which it is said: 'And the night shall shine like the day.' "[10]

This symbolism of the full moon is nevertheless not the only one. We find an entirely different one in Cyril of Alexandria, who sees in the moon the symbol of the forces of evil, which began to wane from the moment of the Resurrection. The contrast is no longer that between light and darkness, but between the sun and moon. Commenting on the twelfth Chapter of Exodus, Cyril writes in the *Glaphyres:* "Let us admire still another mystery in this passing-over. The lamb is immolated on the fourteenth day of the month when the orb of the moon is at its full and enlightens the earth with a bastard light, which begins to wane, little by little, forced to renounce its dignity."

What is the meaning of this symbolism: "Understand by this, letting yourself be guided by what is proposed to you as by an image and a shadow, toward the understanding of the realities, that the prince of the night was exalted in the whole universe. This prince is the devil, who is symbolically designated by the moon. For the moon, as we know, is set to rule the night. This prince, by placing in the hearts of men gone astray, like a bastard light, the wisdom of this world, arrogates to himself all glory. But Christ, the true Lamb Who takes away the sins of the world, died for us, and he destroyed the glory of the devil. And he [the devil] now must diminish and disappear little by little, the crowd of the nations hastening to mount toward the peace and love of God, in being converted to Him by faith" (LXX, 424 C-D).

This theme is taken up by Cyril in his *Paschal Homilies:* "Justice shall arise in His day, until the moon be taken away. For Justice to arise, it is necessary that the moon be abolished, that is today, the devil, prince of the night and of darkness, who is here symbolically called the moon" (LXXVII, 408 C). This interpretation is related to a whole mythological idea, according to

[10] See H. Capelle, *L'Exultet pascal oeuvre de saint Ambroise,* Mercati, I. p. 226 et seq.

which the moon, Hecate, is the queen of darkness and of the world of the dead.[11] We know that, for the ancients, the moon was the abode of the dead.[12] The Resurrection of Christ destroyed the power of death. This is why the waning phase of the moon following the fourteenth Nisan appeared to be the symbol of the victory of Christ, which made the power of death give way. We see again how the symbolism of the liturgy takes up and transposes mythological themes.

We find an analogous theme in St. Augustine. Treating of the symbolism of the Pasch in his *Letter to Januarius,* he writes: "We find here also another mystery (*sacramentum*). Do not be disturbed if you find it more obscure, for you are less initiated into these things" (P. L. XXXIII, 207 A). Augustine then remarks that the moon waxes only by going further from the sun and wanes when approaching it. It thus represents the illusory world of sin, according to the Scripture which says that: "the foolish man is as changeful as the moon" (*Eccles.* XXVII:11). "Who is this fool who changes like the moon but Adam, in whom we all have sinned? The human soul in going away from the sun of justice, that is to say, from the interior contemplation of the unchangeable truth, has turned all its forces without and is more and more darkened. But when she begins to come back to unchangeable wisdom, the nearer she approaches, the more the exterior man is dissolved, while the interior is renewed from day to day" (XXXIII, 208 B). It is no longer the prince of darkness, but the world of illusion which is symbolized by the moon, but the symbolism is the same. Its waning phase signifies the continuous retreat of evil at the rising of the sun of the Resurrection.

So we see the symbolism of the date of Easter in its various aspects. We should notice that from now on this has introduced us to the element which constitutes the proper interest of the symbolism of the liturgical year. In part it is the time itself which is symbolic. The content of the mystery is the same as that of Baptism, but what characterizes this aspect is the date of the year. The essential part, therefore, is the interpretation of the temporal cycle as a figure of Christian events. The temporal cycle is prop-

[11] M. Eliade, *Histoire des religions,* pp. 164-165.
[12] F. Cumont, *Le symbolisme funéraire chez les romains,* p. 181 et seq.

erly that of cosmic life. In consequence, then, beyond the figure taken from the religion of the Bible, it is natural realities that are symbolized. These are the realities that constitute the *hierophanies,* the visible signs through which the living God reveals Himself in natural religion. For "if He let all the nations follow their own ways: . . . yet He did not leave Himself without testimony, bestowing blessings, giving rains from heaven and fruitful seasons, filling your hearts with food and gladness" (Acts XIV:16). This revelation was everywhere perverted by the pagan religions "who changed the glory of the incorruptible God for an image made like to corruptible man" (Rom. I, 23), and who adored the signs instead of Him Whom they signified. But the Christian cult took up this cosmic religion, purified it from its errors, and made it the sign and prefiguration of the Christian mystery which fulfilled it.[13]

[13] See J. Daniélou, *The Problem of Symbolism,* Thought, 1950, p. 423 et seq.

CHAPTER EIGHTEEN

The Ascension

WE HAVE often had occasion to remark that the symbolism of the sacraments is connected with different biblical themes. So, in Baptism, the white garments send us back to the theology of Adam, the *sphragis* to that of the covenant, the anointing with oil to that of the messianic king. Thus the unique baptismal mystery, refracted in these different media, is seen from various angles in all the varied richness of its meanings. Something analogous is to be seen in the liturgical cycle of Easter which we are now studying. It shows us a diversity of theological aspects connected with different parts of the Old Testament by means of which the unique Paschal mystery is to be contemplated.

Thus, when seen in the perspective of the Exodus, it appears as the mystery of Christ dead and risen again. The essential theme is that of the passing over from the old life to a new life, prefigured by the Exodus from Egypt. Inasmuch as the Paschal mystery is a new creation, it is considered as the anniversary of the first creation and the prefiguration of the new. As we shall see, Pentecost also was at first considered as the entire Paschal mystery seen in a particular biblical perspective; and this is true also of the Ascension. Inasmuch as it is a feast celebrating dogma, it expresses the Paschal mystery in the perspective of the Messias. It is the feast of His royal enthronement, as this is prefigured in the liturgy of the Psalms; [1] and the Psalms are the chief biblical *loci* for this feast.[2]

We shall study successively the three chief Psalms of the Ascension. Justin writes in his *Apology:* "You see that He was to mount up to heaven according to the prophecies. It was said: 'Lift up the gates of heaven, let them open and the king of glory shall enter in' " (LI, 6-7). This is a quotation from Psalm XXIII:17. The most ancient witness we possess of the application of this Psalm to the Ascension is found in the *Apocalypse of Peter:* "The angels crowd around, so that the word of Scripture may be fulfilled: 'Open your gates, O princes' " (*Rev. Or. chrét.* 1910, p. 317). Here the princes are thought of as angels, guardians of the heavenly sphere into which at the Ascension of the Word of God introduced the humanity which He had united to Himself.

The application of these verses to the Ascension was very soon combined with a theological theme which had appeared at an ancient date, that of Christ descending into the world without the knowledge of the angelic powers of the intermediate heavens, who are then stupefied when they see Him coming back in His glory at His Ascension.[3] This theme appears first in the *Ascension of Isaias:* "When the Word came down into the third heaven and transformed Himself according to the form of the angels who were in the third heaven, those who guarded the gate of the heaven demanded that He give the password, and the Lord did so in order not to be recognized; and when they saw Him, they did not praise Him, for He looked like one of themselves" (X. 24-26). When on His return, Christ "mounted into the third heaven, He did not transform Himself, but all the angels who were at the right and the left, and the throne which is in the midst of them, adored Him and praised Him, and they said: 'How did Our Lord hide Himself from us when He descended, and we did not understand it?' " (XI, 25-26).

The theme of the Incarnation as being hidden from the angels is found again in an extraordinary passage of St. Ignatius of Antioch: "The prince of this world did not know of the virginity of Mary and of her child-bearing, nor of the death of the Lord,—

1 See B. Fischer, *Die Psalmen froemmigkeit der Maertyrkirche,* 1949.

2 As we have seen, there was also a connection with the Ascension of Elias, which takes us into another order of ideas. See above, p. 108.

3 See also Cyprian, *Testimonia,* II, 29; Athanasius, *Ad Marc.,* 8, 23, 26.

three resounding mysteries accomplished in the silence of God" (*Eph.* XIX, 1). This theme of the ignorance of the powers at the time of the Incarnation and the manifestation made to them at the time of the Ascension goes back to St. Paul: "But we speak the wisdom of God, mysterious, hidden, . . . a wisdom which none of the rulers of this world has known; for had they known it, they would never have crucified the Lord of glory" (I Cor. 2:7-8). And it is "in order that through the Church there be made known to the Principalities and the Powers in the heavens the manifold wisdom of God" (Eph. III:10). This theme of the hidden *descensus* and of the *ascensus* manifested to the angels, who guard the gates of heaven, admirably harmonizes with the application of Psalm XXIII to the Ascension.

We find them together in Justin: "O princes, lift up your gates; be raised, O eternal doors, and the king of glory shall come in. When Christ rose from among the dead and ascended to heaven, the princes established by God in the heavens were commanded to open the gates of the heavens, so that He who is the king of glory might enter in and ascend to sit at the right hand of the Father, until He has made His enemies His footstool. But when the princes of heaven saw Him without beauty, honor, or glory, they did not recognize Him and they said: 'Who is this king of glory?' " (XXXVI, 4-6). Here we see a new element appearing. At the time of the *ascensus,* the angels did not recognize Christ because of the human appearance with which He was clothed. The expression "without beauty" is an allusion to Isaias LIII:2, which was one of the texts most frequently quoted in the primitive Christian community.[4]

St. Irenaeus also commented on the Psalm in this sense, but without this last idea: "That He was to be lifted up to heaven, David said beforehand: 'Lift up your gates, O princes; be raised, eternal doors, and the king of glory shall enter in.' The eternal doors are heaven. As the Word came down to earth without being visible to creatures, He was not recognized by them in His descent. Rendered visible by His incarnation, He was raised to heaven. In seeing Him, the lower angels cried out to those above: 'Open your gates, be raised, eternal doors, and the King of glory

[4] Cerfaux, *La première communauté chrétienne à Jerusalem,* Eph., Lov., 1939, pp. 13 et seq.

will make His entrance.' And as the angels on high said in their astonishment: Who is he? those who saw Him, acclaimed Him again: 'It is the Lord strong and mighty, it is He, the King of glory' " (*Dem.* 84).

The theological viewpoint of Irenaeus is a slight modification of that of Justin: "When He, the Conqueror, came forward, with His Body risen from the dead, certain of the Powers said: 'Who is He, Who comes from Bosra, with His vestments dyed with red?' (*Is.* LXIII:1). But those who accompanied Him said to those set over the gates of heaven: 'Open, eternal doors' " (*Co. Jo.* VI, 56; Preuschen, 165). St. Athanasius gives this idea another shade of meaning: "The angels of the Lord who followed Him on earth, saw Him ascend and announced Him to the heavenly powers so that they would open their gates. The powers were in astonishment at seeing Him in the flesh. This is why they cried out: 'Who is He?' astounded by this amazing economy of God's providence. And the angels ascending with Christ answered them: 'The Lord of powers, He is the king of glory,' teaching this great mystery to those who were in the heavens, that is, that He Who had conquered the spiritual enemies, He is the King of glory." (*Exp. Psalm* 23: P. G. XXVII, 141 D). We perceive the influence of Origen in this theme of the angels who descended to earth with Jesus and ascended with Him.[5]

The theme is taken up by Gregory of Nyssa in a different way, in a text that is the more interesting to us since it is to be found in the Roman Breviary as a lesson for the Second Nocturne of the Wednesday in the Octave of the Ascension: "David, being gone out of himself so that he was no longer tied down by the weight of the body, and having mingled with the hypercosmic powers, describes their words to us while, accompanying the Lord in His descent, they command the angels who surround the earth and to whom human existence is entrusted, to raise their gates" (P. G. XLVI, 693). But the angels of the perigeum did not recognize the Lord because "He, always adapting Himself to the capacity of those who received Him, as He became a man with men, became an angel with the angels—They said therefore: 'Who is this king of glory?' " We find here once more the idea of the *Ascension of Isaias* that Christ took on in succession the forms of the

[5] Jean Daniélou, *Origène*, pp. 236-237.

angelic natures through which He passed in His descent to earth, made more profound by the Origen's idea that the Word adapts Himself to the capacity of those who receive Him.

Then comes the Ascension: "And now, it is just the opposite; it is our guardians who form His cortege and who command the hypercosmic doors to open so that He may once again be adored within them. But they do not recognize Him, since He is clothed with the poor tunic of our nature, since His garments are red from the wine-press of human evils. And it is they, this time, who cry out: 'Who is this King of glory?' " (693 B-C). The absence of beauty in Christ, resulting from His human nature and from His passion, and preventing His being recognized by the heavenly powers at the time of His Ascension, recalls Justin and Origen (the same quotation of Isaias 63:1).

And we recall, finally, that this theme appears in the *De Mysteriis* of St. Ambrose: "The angels themselves also doubted when Christ rose again, in seeing that His flesh ascended to heaven. They said then: 'Who is this king of glory?' and while some said: 'Lift up the gates, O princes, and the king of glory shall enter in,' others doubted and said: 'Who is he who ascends from Edom' (Is. LXIII:1)" (*De Myst.* 36. Botte 119).[6]

We have noted the fact that, in the passage from the Dialogue of Justin, (XXXVI:4) to the quotation from Psalm XXIII is added one from Psalm CIX: "The princes were commanded to open their gates so that He Who is the king of glory might enter and ascend to seat Himself at the right hand of His Father until He has made His enemies His footstool." In a passage such as this, we see how completely the theology of the primitive Christian community is saturated by the Old Testament. We might say that it was in the categories of the Old Testament that the First Fathers thought about the fact of Christ.[7] This is particularly noticeable in the case we are about to consider, where a Psalm has furnished a Christian dogma with definitive expression.

[6] See above, p. 198. We should note that Ambrose, in this passage, shows Baptism to be a conformation to the Ascension. Here again one can see how the sacramental spirit and the spirit of the feast coincide.

[7] For Justin, the *kerygma* is essentially the testimony given to Christ by the Old Testament, 'the Christological meaning of Scripture' (H. Holstein, *La tradition des Apôtres chez saint Irénée,* Rech. Sc. Relig., 1949, p. 248.

Psalm CIX is, in fact, an essential source for the theology of the Ascension, and the New Testament itself is the first to apply it in this way. As a description of the Ascension, this Psalm verse is found incorporated in the oldest profession of Christian faith, the discourse of St. Peter on the day of Pentecost: "Therefore since he (David) was a prophet and knew that God 'had sworn to him with an oath that of the fruit of his loins one should sit upon his throne,' he, foreseeing it, spoke of the Resurrection of the Christ. For neither was he abandoned to hell, nor did his flesh undergo decay. This Jesus God has raised up, and we are all witnesses of it. Therefore, exalted by the right hand of God, and receiving from the Father the promise of the Holy Spirit, he has poured forth this Spirit which you see and hear. For David himself did not ascend into heaven, but he himself said: 'The Lord said to my Lord: Sit thou at my right hand, until I make thy enemies thy footstool' " (Acts II:30-35).

This passage clearly describes the Ascension of Christ as being the mystery predicted by David in Psalm CIX. We should notice that here, as in all these texts, it is the Ascension in the theological sense which is being treated, that is to say, the exaltation of the humanity of Christ in the glory of the Father, which followed immediately on the Resurrection, and not the bodily Ascension which took place forty days later.[8] This is a characteristic of ancient theology. We should add a passage from the Epistle to the Ephesians: ". . . the working of His mighty power which he has wrought in Christ in raising him from the dead, and setting him at his right hand in heaven above every Principality and Power and Virtue and Dominion—in short, above every name that is named, not only in this world, but also in that which is to come. And all things he made subject under his feet" (Eph. 1:20-22). It is certain that Psalm CIX is to be found in the background of this passage. This appears first in the *sessio a dextris,* taken from the Psalm to describe the installation of the humanity of Christ in the glory of the Trinity, and then in the expression: "He has put all things under his feet," which is an allusion to the *scabellum pedum.*

The expression *sessio a dextris* expressing the exaltation of the humanity of Christ at the Ascension is found elsewhere in the

[8] See P. Benoit, *L'Ascension,* in Revue biblique, 1949, pp. 162 et seq.

New Testament (Rom. VIII:34),[9] and passed into the common catechesis. We find it in these words in the Symbol in which it expresses a special mystery, not the Ascension itself, but the state of the humanity of Christ in its glorification beside the Father during the time intervening between the Ascension and the Parousia: *Ascendit ad caelos, sedet ad dexteram Paris, unde venturus est.* We can see from this example how greatly the Old Testament and the Psalms in particular were used by the Christian community in building up its theology.

We shall not be astonished, then, to see that the Fathers always apply this Psalm to the Ascension. St. Justin comes back to it elsewhere: "God, the Father of the world, was to raise Christ to heaven after His resurrection, and He was to keep Him there until He had struck down the demons, His enemies, and until the number of the elect should be complete, for whose sake He has not yet consigned the universe to flames. Hear the prophet David predict these events: The Lord said to my Lord 'Sit at my right hand until I make Thy enemies thy footstool' " (*Apol.* XLV, 1-3). We should notice that here the victory over the powers of evil described by the *scabellum pedum* is understood of the Parousia, which is the term of the mystery of the *sessio a dextris,* as the Ascension is its beginning.

This interpretation of the Psalm as describing these three mysteries is found in St. Paul. The First Epistle to the Corinthians interprets the *scabellum pedum* in the eschatological sense: "For he must reign until 'he had put all his enemies under his feet.' And the last enemy to be destroyed will be death, for 'he has put all things under his feet' " (I Cor. XV:25-26). We see here clearly that the *scabellum pedum* is already a present reality as in Ephes. 1:22, and at the same time an eschatological one. We should further remark, as D. Mollat has well pointed out, that, having first understood the victory of Christ over these powers in the eschatological sense, later on, during the time of the Epistles of the captivity, St. Paul insisted more on its character of present actuality, of eschatology already realized.[10]

Still more explicit than the Epistle to the Corinthians is the

[9] I pass over the passages in which the Psalm is quoted as a proof of the divinity of Christ without reference to the Ascension.

[10] Donatien Mollat, *Jugement dans le Nouveau Testament,* dans S.D.B., IV (1949), col. 1350-1354.

Epistle to the Hebrews, in which we find again a commentary on these same verses. We know that the Epistle to the Hebrews expresses the theology of the Ascension in terms of the entrance of the high-priest into the Holy of Holies after the offering of the expiatory Sacrifice. It is in these terms that the Psalm is introduced: "but Jesus, having offered one sacrifice for sins, has taken his seat forever at the right hand of God, waiting henceforth until his enemies be made the footstool under his feet" (Heb. X; 12-13). Here we find the same contrast between the *sessio a dextris* as describing the present royalty of Christ, the definitive character of which the author of the Epistle elsewhere brings out, and the *scabellum pedum* which is still to be expected and which corresponds to the final victory of Christ over the power of evil.[11]

Later tradition continues to see in Psalm CIX the prophecy of the special mystery of the *sessio a dextris* which follows the Ascension. Thus Eusebius of Cesarea writes: "The throne means the royal dignity of Christ; the *sessio,* the immoveable stability of His royal state; the *a dextris* means His participation in the blessings at the right hand of the Father. The Son indeed receives from the Father all the good and salutary blessings of His right hand to distribute them" (*Co. Ps.* P. G., XXIII, 1341 B). In the same way, St. Athanasius distinguishes the prophecies of the Ascension properly speaking from that of the *sessio* (*kathisis*) which is our Psalm. All these witnesses show us that the mystery of the *sessio,* which is part of the Creed, found its whole formulation in Psalm CIX.

This is not the only aspect of the theology of the Ascension which is in harmony with this Psalm. If we go back to the text of Justin, we see that he continues: "The Lord will cause the sceptre of your power to go forth from Sion. This phrase announces the powerful word which the Apostles, going forth from Jerusalem, preached everywhere" (*Apol.* XLV, 5). Here a quotation of the following verse of Psalm CIX is applied to the preaching of the Gospel. The same interpretation is found in Eusebius: "I think that the sceptre of power in this passage means the preaching of the Gospel. This word, indeed, which announces the power of our Saviour and the economy of His work, is a sceptre symboliz-

[11] See A. M. Vitto, *L'Ascensione nella littera agli Ebrei,* S. Paolo, Rome, 1936, p. 156.

ing at the same time teaching and salvation" (P. G., XXIII, 1342 C).

The important point is that in these two passages the mystery of the evangelization of the world is directly connected with the mystery of the Ascension.[12] And if we read the Acts, we find this passage: "Therefore, exalted by the right hand of God, and receiving from the Father the promise of the Holy Spirit, he has poured forth this Spirit which you see and hear" (Acts II:33). If we look again at the Epistle to the Ephesians, we read: "And all things he made subject under his feet, and him he gave as head over all the Church" (1:22). And further on: "He who descended, he it is who ascended also above all the heavens, that he might fill all things. And he himself gave some men as apostles, and some as prophets . . ." (IV:10-11). In the same way, in St. Mark: "So then the Lord, after he had spoken to them, was taken up into heaven, and sits at the right hand of God. But they went forth and preached everywhere, while the Lord worked with them and confirmed the preaching by the signs that followed" (XVI:19).

Here we find again the same sequence: ascension, session, mission. And it is remarkable that in the three passages we have quoted allusion is made to Psalm CIX. Mark quotes the *sessio a dextris,* Ephesians the *scabellum pedum,* and the Acts quotes both. We can further ask ourselves whether the second part of these passages, that which concerns the mission, is not in harmony with the following verse of the Psalm. M. Cerfaux has shown that the passage from Phil. II:5-11, on the self-abasement and the exaltation of Christ, was built on Isaias LIII.[13] Here we have an analogous situation. We have ascertained that a *theologoumenon,* common to several passages in the New Testament, is built up on Psalm CIX; 1-2. Thus, we see once again that the New Testament expresses itself in the theological forms of ancient Scripture.

The third Psalm of the Ascension is Psalm LXVII. Here again it is the New Testament which first applies it to this mystery in a particularly significant passage: "But to each of us grace was given according to the measure of Christ's bestowal. Thus it says, 'As-

[12] See Jean Daniélou, *Le mystère de l'Avent,* pp. 160-176.

[13] *L'hymne au Christ serviteur de Dieu,* dans Miscellanea de Meyer, I, pp. 176 et seqq.

cending on high, he led away captives; he gave gifts to men.' Now this 'he ascended' what does it mean but that he also first descended into the lower parts of the earth? He who ascended, he it is who ascended also above all the heavens, that he might fill all things. And he himself gave some men as apostles, and some as prophets, . . ." (Eph. IV:7-11). We find again in this passage the contrast between the *descensus* and the *ascensus* as the *Ascension of Isaias* explained it to us. And also we find the connection between the Ascension and the Mission.

One characteristic of the translation of Psalm 67 used by St. Paul deserves our attention, for it is important for our thesis. While the Hebrew text speaks of gifts "received" by Yahweh, Paul speaks of gifts "given" by Christ. Here we have a modification of the text which is certainly intentional. And, as Balthasar Fischer has well observed, this is in harmony with the "christologization" of the Psalm.[14] What is said concerning Yahweh in the Old Testament is here applied to Christ, and this application is entirely legitimate. And the change in the text marks clearly the transition from the God of the Old Testament to that of the New. But what interests us here is that this change emphasizes the christological character of the interpretation of the Psalms in the primitive Church. What St. Paul sees here is not the expression of the transcendence of God, which is the literal sense of the passage, but that of the mercy of Christ, which is the typological sense. And it is this prophetic sense only that concerns him.[15]

St. Paul's interpretation of this Psalm is found again in tradition. Justin applies it to the Ascension (*Dial.* XXXIX, 1 and LXXXVII, 6). St. Irenaeus writes: "And, risen again from the dead, he must ascend into heaven, as David said: 'The chariot of God is thousands and thousands of angels; the Lord is among them, in Sinai, in the sanctuary. He mounts on high, leading the crowd of captives; he has given gifts to men.' The prophet calls captivity the destruction of the power of the rebel angels. And he has pointed out the place where He was to rise from earth to heaven, for the Lord, he says, is gone up from Sion, that is to say, from the mountain which faces Jerusalem and is called the

[14] *Die Psalmen froemmigkeit der Martyrkirche,* p. 15.

[15] B. Fischer shows that other modifications of the Psalms are the result of this intention: thus the addition, *a ligno,* to verse 1 of Psalm XCV: *Dominus regnavit,* the Christological and 'staurocentric' intention of which is evident.

Mount of Olives. After having risen from the dead, He assembled his disciples, and it was before their eyes that His ascension took place and they saw the heavens open to receive Him" (*Dem.* 83; P. O. XII, 793).

Origen, bringing this verse together with Matthew XII:29, sees in it the prophecy of the participation of the just in the Resurrection and the Ascension: "He began on the cross by chaining the demon, and, having entered into his house, that is to say, into Hell, and having ascended from there into the heights, He led away captives, that is to say, those who rose again and entered with Him into the heavenly Jerusalem" (*Co. Ro.* V, 10; P. G., XIV, 1052 A).

But these verses are not the only ones from this Psalm to be applied to the Ascension. Verse 34 speaks of Yahweh "Who ascends above the heaven of heavens to the East." This verse is most important in the history of liturgy. For it says that the Ascension of Christ took place to the East, and it is this verse which is quoted by the *Didascalia of the Apostles* (II:57, 5) as the foundation for the custom of praying toward the East,[16] and furthermore, it is from the East that Christ is expected to return. Now, as Erik Petersen believes, this is the primitive origin of the orientation of prayer. It is an awaiting of the return of Christ Who is to appear in the East [17] (Acts I:11). But, granting the antiquity of this usage, if it is connected with the application of Psalm 67 to the Ascension, it follows that the application of this verse of the Psalm to the Ascension is still more ancient, and dates from apostolic times.

Nevertheless we find a difficulty here in the exegesis of the Psalm. For if the Ascension took place to the East, what happens to the statement of verse 5: "Prepare the ways of Him Who ascends to the West." This difficulty has been resolved in various ways. Eusebius finds in it the same contrast as that brought out by the Epistle to the Ephesians between the *descensus* and the *ascensus:* The text adds: "It is He Who mounts on the heaven of heavens to the East, which corresponds exactly to what was written above: Prepare the way for Him Who ascends to the West. It

[16] F. J. Doelger, *Sol Salutis,* pp. 210-211.

[17] E. Petersen, *La croce a la preghiera verso l'Oriente,* in Eph. liturgicae, LIX (1945) pp. 52 et seq.

is fitting indeed that having been told of His descent, we should be instructed as to His return. His descent took place to the West by the obscuring of the rays of His divinity; His ascension took place on the heaven of heavens to the East by His glorious re-ascension (*apocatastasis*) into the heavens" (P. G., XXIII, 720).

This symbolism of the West and the East was, as we know, familiar to the ancient Christian community. In the rites of Baptism, the renunciation of Satan took place while the candidate faced the West; the consecration to Christ, facing the East.[18] Moreover, Eusebius explains this symbolism to us: "You understand what is meant by the comparison of the sun. In the same way as, at its setting, it accomplishes an invisible course, and, coming to the eastern horizon, it rises straight into heaven, illuminating all things and giving to the day its light, so in the same way the Lord is shown to us here, after He had carried out His setting, as it were, at the time of His Passion and Death, having crossed this region, He mounts on the heaven of heavens to the East" (P. G XXIII, 720 A). Athanasius gives the same interpretation: the *oc casus* is the descent into hell, the *oriens* the Ascension (P. G XVII, 294 B. 303 D).

But we encounter also another interpretation of the *ascensus super occasum;* it means the victory of Christ over death, of which the *occasus* is the symbol. This appears in Gregory of Nyssa: "The sin of man was the cause of his being sent away from paradise. He left the East (Gen. II:8) to live in the West. Because of this, it is in the East that He Who is the Orient (Zach. VI:12) appeared: 'Praise the Lord Who goes up to the West, so that the sun may enlighten the darkness' " (P. G., XLVI, 496 A). In this text, we should notice how the allusions to passages from the Old Testament in which are to be found the equation between Christ and the Orient are all in harmony with one another. The abandonment of the East for the West as the equivalent of the exile from paradise is a theme that goes back to Origen.[19]

The same idea is taken up by St. Hilary, doubtless in dependence on the same source. St. Hilary knows the two explanations (P. L., IX, 467 B), but he dwells on the second: "Everything that comes into existence knows a setting. And this destruction of

[18] See above, p. 30-33.
[19] Jean Daniélou, *Origène,* 226-229.

things that have a setting is death. We must then exalt and prepare the ways for Him Who mounts above the setting of death, that is to say, for Him Who has done away with all setting in triumphing over His own. He is mounting on the setting of our death, He Who has obtained for us life from among the dead by His Resurrection. This is the joy of the apostles when they saw and touched Him after His resurrection" (P. L. IX, 446 B). The victory over the *occasus* is, for St. Hilary therefore, the Resurrection which comes before the Ascension, while for Eusebius and Athanasius, it is the descent into Hell.[20]

Thus, these many witnesses prove to us that the Psalms we have studied were considered to be prophecies of the Ascension by the New Testament and the primitive Christian community, and that it is because of this fact that they have been incorporated into the liturgy of the Church. But this gives rise to another question: is this prophetic interpretation well founded? Does it not rest to some extent on arbitrary connections? Is it not in harmony with the preoccupations of the times in which the conflict between Judaism and Christianity brought the question of the prophetic sense of Scripture to the forefront? Is not this preoccupation secondary with us? And would there not be an advantage in disengaging the Psalms from the messianism and only retaining their lasting value as inspired prayers?

But the fact is this: the whole of ancient tradition concerning the liturgical use of the Psalms rests on their messianic significance. For one thing, it is this significance which constituted all their value for the primitive Christian community. It adopted the Psalms, not because of their religious value nor because of their inspired character, but only because it thought that they were concerned with Christ. Their whole use in the Church rests, therefore, on a messianic meaning. If this is no longer their real meaning, their liturgical use is based only on an accommodated symbolism and loses all dogmatic significance. This use is of value only to the extent to which the christological interpretation is not something added, but truly corresponds to their literal significance.

[20] I forbear to mention Psalm XLVI, which is important in the present Roman liturgy but is lacking in evidence which goes back to Apostolic times for its application in the present instance.

What about the Psalms that we have been studying? If we adopt the conception of prophecy beginning with Theodore of Mopsuestia, which retains as messianic only certain predictions whose application is always disputable, we should still admit that Psalm CIX is messianic and deny that the other two are. If, on the other hand, we consider, together with all the Fathers, that the persons, events, and institutions of the Old Testament are the figures of eschatological realities and that they are fulfilled in Jesus Christ, then the christological explanation of these psalms is seen to be entirely valid. And this interpretation has its foundation in the Old Testament itself. Psalm XXIII describes a procession entering into the Temple in Jerusalem.[21] But we know that, in the Old Testament, the Temple of Jerusalem was the figure of the Temple of the future Jerusalem, and that its cult had an eschatological meaning. The Epistle to the Hebrews, then, in applying this Psalm to the entrance of Christ into the heavenly Temple at the Ascension is only affirming the fulfillment in Christ of what the cult of the Temple had already proclaimed.

Psalm LXVII is also a processional: "The singers march before," writes Pedersen, "then the players on instruments in the midst of young girls dancing to the sound of tambourines" (P. 437). And the Apocalypse shows us that this earthly liturgy is a figure of the heavenly (XV:2).[22] But already, and even more clearly than in the preceding case, the text itself invites us to give an eschatological sense to the liturgy: "The Psalms," writes Gunkel, "when they speak of the past or the present of Yahweh, speak also of the future. The heart of the man who loves God beats fast with joy when he thinks of the future time in which the Lord will show Himself in His true grandeur and take possession of the Throne of the World. Such a glorious celebration of the future is obviously described in Psalm LXVII." [23] St. Paul, in Ephesians IV:8, then, did not give to Psalm LXVII an entirely new meaning. It certainly describes the eschatological entrance into the heavenly Temple. But Paul says that what was said of

[21] Pedersen, *Israel,* II, p. 437. M. Podechard (*Le Psautier,* I, 1949, p. 117), recognizes that the Psalm may even in Old Testament times "have borne an eschatological meaning."

[22] Erik Peterson, *Theologische Traktate,* pp. 330 et seq.

[23] *Einleitung in die Psalmen,* 1928, pp. 79-80.

Yahweh is fulfilled in Jesus. And this is one of the aspects in which the New Testament fulfills the Old.[24]

Psalm CIX shows us another aspect of the eschatological typology of the Old Testament. Here it is not the liturgy of the Temple which is the figure, but the king of the line of David. But he belongs to the same order of types, for the bonds were close between royalty and the Temple,[25] as is shown by this Psalm which associates the priesthood with the kingship. It is even possible that it alludes to a rite of kingly anointing that was part of the liturgy of the Temple.[26] This bond between the Temple and the King recalls the attribution of the Psalms to David. And the king of David's line was a figure of the Messias. And there is more: the king here is an eschatological personage.[27] Here, then, is a prophecy in the strict sense (Matt. XXII:44).

It is certainly true even so that we are still here to discuss any particular detailed interpretation given by ancient tradition. The Fathers used the text of the Septuagint, and this is the reason why they read "princes" (XXIII:7) where the Hebrew text says "lintels of the gates." There is no question of the "west" in Psalm LXVII:5, but only of "plains." [28] And there is no question of the "east" in LXVII:34, but only of the "ancient" heavens. And also the Fathers took liberties with the text, as we have seen that St. Paul replaced "receive" with "give" (LXVII:19). This allows us to question all such interpretations of details, which we can preserve inasmuch as they are part of the New Testament or of tradition, but for which we can find no foundation in the Old Testament itself.

But it is not these detailed interpretations which are important. They are taken from inadequate translations, or from rabbinical methods of interpretation which are no longer ours. We do not need to linger over them any further, for the essential point is elsewhere. It is, as we have just seen, in the fact that the eschatological explanation given to the Psalms by the Fathers clearly corresponds to their meaning, as that meaning springs

[24] Balthasar Fischer, loc. cit., p. 8. See also Werner Bieder, *Die Vorstellung von den Höllenfahrt J.C.* 1949, p. 82.
[25] Pedersen, *Israel,* II, pp. 430-431.
[26] Harald Riesenfeld, *Jésus transfiguré,* p. 142.
[27] Gunkel, *Einleitung in die Psalmen,* pp. 97-98.
[28] The New Psalter gives the translation: *per desertum.*

from the general typology of the Old Testament where it is most precisely prophetic. Thus the demonstration of the New Testament remains entirely valid for us. The Fathers, following the New Testament, had good reason to say that the Psalms had an eschatological meaning—since that indeed is their meaning—and to say that they had found their fulfillment in Jesus Christ, since He is indeed the *eschatos anthropos.*

CHAPTER NINETEEN

Pentecost

As WE saw at the beginning of the previous chapter, the Paschal Feast originally was the feast of the entire Christian mystery: the Incarnation, the Passion, the Resurrection, the Ascension, the Descent of the Holy Spirit. This is what we find in the oldest homilies, those of Melitos and of Hippolytus.[1] Gregory Nazianzen echoes this teaching in the Fourth Century: "Such is the Feast that you celebrate today: celebrate the birth of Him Who was born for you and weep for the death of Him Who died for you" (XXXVI, 652 D). And furthermore, this feast filled the whole Paschal season, which was one long feast-day. This is well brought out in the *Easter Letters* of St. Athanasius: "The holy Sunday extends by a continuous grace through all the seven weeks of the holy Pentecost, during which we celebrate the Paschal Feast" (XXVI, 1389 C). In this passage, Pentecost means the Paschal season, and its content is the Resurrection.[2]

But, beginning with the Fourth Century, a new tendency developed toward dividing the unique feast of the unique mystery into many feasts connected with particular episodes. Easter day is connected with the Resurrection, the fortieth day with the Ascension, the fiftieth with the outpouring of the Spirit. The historical aspect tends to overpower the theological, as Dom

[1] Ch. Martin, *Hippolyte de Rome et Proclus de Constantinople,* Rev. Hist. Eccles., 1937, p. 263.

[2] Athanasius denotes the whole of this time by the expression 'the great Sunday' (XXVI, 1366 A).

Odo Casel has well observed.[3] The evolution seems to have come about mainly under the influence of pilgrimages to Jerusalem, where the custom developed of commemorating the episodes of the historical life of Christ and the date and place where they happened, as we see in the *Pilgrimage of Etheria.*[4] To this cause was added at this same time the need for having more Christian feasts in order to replace the pagan ones, and also that of solemnizing the dogmas defined by the councils against the heretics.

And all this has a special importance for Pentecost. This word was used for two different realities. For the most primitive Christianity, Pentecost meant the seven weeks following Easter, and its content was the whole Paschal mystery seen under the aspects which were particularly brought out by the Jewish feast of the harvest, which corresponded with these seven weeks. Then, beginning with the fourth century, the word Pentecost began to mean more particularly the last day of this period, and the feast to have the Descent of the Holy Spirit only as its content. Among the symbolic themes we are about to study, the two first are especially connected with the first aspect of Pentecost, and the last with the second.

In his treatise *De specialibus legibus,* so valuable for our knowledge of the Jewish cult at the time of Christ, Philo of Alexandria deals with the different feast-days. Having spoken of the Pasch and the Azymes, the first taking place on the 14th Nisan and the second beginning on the 15th Nisan and ending seven days later, he continues: "There is a feast-day within the feast, which takes place on the day after the first day, which is called the feast of the Sheaves" (*De spec. leg.* II, 162). Then, having explained the meaning of this feast, he comes to the one following it: "The feast which takes place according to the number fifty (*pentekoston*) has been given the name: the Feast of first-fruits" (*Id* 179). These two feasts are actually to be taken together: they constitute the first and the last days of the seven weeks that make up the time of harvest. This is why the closing day is called, the *Feast of Weeks.*[5]

[3] *Art und Sinn des aelteste christlichen Osterfeier,* Jahr. Lit. Wiss., XIV, 1938, p. 58.
[4] Baumstack, *Liturgie comparée,* p. 168.
[5] Pedersen, *Israel,* II, pp. 415-418.

If we read Deuteronomy, we find the explanation of this feast: "You shall count seven weeks and you shall celebrate the Feast of the Weeks in honor of Yahweh, your God" (XVI:9). We see that the feast is inaugurated by the beginning of the harvest and ends at its completion. Elsewhere other texts fix more exactly this double solemnity and its dates: "When you come into the land which I am giving you and reap your harvest, you shall bring a sheaf of the first-fruits of your harvest to the priest, you shall wave the sheaf before the Lord that it may be acceptable for you. On the day after the Sabbath the priest shall do this. . . . Beginning with the day after the Sabbath, the day on which you bring the wave-offering sheaf, you shall count seven full weeks, and then, on the day after the seventh week, the fiftieth day, you shall present the new cereal offering to the Lord" (Lev. XXIII: 10-15). Here we have a very marked liturgical unit, that of the seven weeks of the harvest. Its beginning, which consists in the offering of the sheaf, is found to fall on the second day of the Azymes, the 16th Nisan, but it has nothing to do with the feast of Azymes. Its conclusion is the Feast of the Weeks, fifty days afterwards—hence its title of Pentecost.

The characteristic action of this liturgical unit is the offering of the first-fruits, whose fulfillment the Fathers show to be in the Christian Pentecost. But before them, Philo of Alexandria was searching for the religious significance of the liturgical action of offering the sheaves. And it is remarkable that he gives precisely the same symbolism to the feast of the sheaf on the 16th Nisan and to the feast of the first-fruits, fifty days later. Speaking of the first, he writes: "the sheaf is brought to the altar as the first-fruit (*aparche*) both of the land that the people had been given as a dwelling-place, and of the whole earth, as thanksgiving (*eucharistia*) for prosperity and abundance.

"The first-fruits bring both thought of God, Who is the most excellent good, and the rightful acknowledgment of Him as being the true cause of all prosperity" (*De spec. leg.* 162-171).

The commentary on the terminal feast of Pentecost, that of the first-fruits, takes up this same theme: "This feast is called the feast of the first-fruits either because before the year's grain is used by man, the first produce of the new harvest and the first fruit are to be presented as first-fruits—for indeed it is right and just, when we have received prosperity from God as the greatest gift, not to enjoy the most necessary food, which is at the same time the most useful and delightful, and not to appropriate it entirely to ourselves before having offered the first-fruits to Him Who has given it to us; not that we give Him anything, for all things, riches and gifts belong to Him—but because, by this humble sign, we show an attitude of thanksgiving and of piety towards Him Who is not sparing with His graces, but Who extends them continually and liberally—or because the sheaf of wheat is par excellence the first and best of produce" (*Id.* 179-181).

Philo gives us here a whole theology of first-fruits as the expression of thanksgiving, that is to say, as an acknowledgment of the total dependence of man on God. This theology is found again in the Fathers of the Church. Thus, Origen, in his *23rd Homily on the Book of Numbers,* treats of the symbolism of the Jewish feast, and interprets the feast of first-fruits (*nova*) as expressing the renewal of the interior man (*Ho. Num.* XXIII, 8; P. G. XII, 753 A). But although this interpretation gives us the spiritual realization in the Christian dispensation of the reality expressed ritually in the Jewish liturgy, it is not related to the liturgical reality of Pentecost.

The liturgical interpretation is developed especially by Cyril of Alexandria. It is in his work that we find a truly Christian symbolism of the Jewish feast of the harvest. In his *De Adoratione in spiritu et veritate,* he comments successively on two of the biblical texts concerning Pentecost. The first commentary is concerned with Numbers XXVIII:26-31: "On the day of the first-fruits (*nova*) you shall offer to Yahweh a new oblation on the Feast of the Weeks." Cyril thus comments on the texts: "We say that it is the mystery of the Resurrection of the Lord which is signified by the feast of the first-fruits. For inded it is in Christ that human nature first flowered anew, henceforth doing away with corruption and rejecting the old age of sin" (P. G. LXVIII, 1093 A). This passage clearly shows that for Cyril the content of the feast of Pentecost is the Resurrection.

And he explains himself further, in comparing the feast of Easter with that of Pentecost. The content of the Paschal feast is "the death of Emmanuel for us. But the feast immediately following it which is in no way inferior to it, is the resurrection from among the dead which shook off corruption and caused us to pass over to a new life. Indeed we have stripped off the old man and put on the new man, who is Christ. Then contemplate the first-fruits of renewed humanity, that is to say, Christ Himself, in the figure of the sheaf and in the first-fruits of the field and in the first ears of grain, offered in holy oblation to God the Father" (LXVIII, 1093 C). Thus, the feast of the harvest is seen to be the figure of the Resurrection of Christ under the double aspect which characterizes the content of the feast: first, it is an offering, and this is a figure of the offering of Christ to His Father, of the sacrificial character of the Resurrection; and secondly, it is an offering of first-fruits: and Christ is Himself the first-fruits of redeemed humanity.[6] And Cyril explains this further: "Therefore Christ is prefigured here in the symbol of the sheaf, considered as the first-fruit of the ears of grain and as the new fruit: He is indeed the first-born from among the dead, the way which opens to us the Resurrection, He Who makes all things new. The old things have passed away, now everything has become new, says Holy Scripture. The sheaf is presented before the face of the Lord: so Emmanuel, risen from the dead, the new and incorruptible fruit of the human race, ascended to heaven to present Himself henceforth for us before the face of the Father" 1096 A). We see clearly how Pentecost is for Cyril the Paschal mystery as a whole: the presentation of the sheaf on the altar is a figure of the Ascension, whereby Christ, the first-born of risen humanity, is forever present before the Father to intercede for us.

We should notice that, in these passages, Cyril refers sometimes to texts concerning the feast of the sheaves and sometimes to the feast of the first-fruits. For him the theme of the two feasts is, therefore, much the same, as it is for Philo. He only gives to it a different interpretation. As a result, the fulfillment in the Christian liturgy of the mystery prefigured in the Jewish Pentecost does not refer only to the last day of the holy fifty-day period, but to this time as a whole. This is why Cyril says expressly: "The text gives us an evident prefiguration of the Holy Pentecost when it says that we should count seven weeks after

[6] The first idea appears at an earlier date in a fragment of Hippolytus, quoted by Theodoret: "Pentecost is a symbol of the kingdom of heaven, Christ having gone up to his Father and offered his Humanity as a gift to God" (Achelis, 122, 10-11).

the offering of the sheaf. For indeed, after the Resurrection of the Savior, we wait for seven weeks to celebrate the feast" (1097 A).

This last text leads us directly into the liturgical reality. The day of Pentecost, at the end of the seven weeks, is seen to be a feast of the whole Paschal mystery. So Cyril distinguishes Easter from Pentecost not by its content, which is the same, but by the aspect under which it is considered. In the Feast of Easter, the mystery of Christ is seen under the form of the sacrifice of the lamb; in Pentecost, it is under the form of the offering of the first ears of grain. So we see the line of the theology of the two feasts, distinguishing them not by their reference to events in the history of Christ's life, but by the categories of the Old Testament in which the one mystery of Christ is expressed. This theological line is quite in conformity with ancient Christian thought, for which theology is the formulation of the fact of Christ in categories taken from the Old Testament. The liturgical feast is thus seen as the manifestation of this fact on the level of the life of the Christian community.

The first characteristic of the Jewish feast of Pentecost is the offering of the first-fruits. The second is that it lasts for fifty days, that is to say, seven times seven weeks and a day more. It is from this characteristic that the usual titles of the feast are derived—the Feast of Weeks, or Pentecost (fiftieth). The use of the number seven is obviously connected with the general symbolism of the Sabbath in the Old Testament. In his *Sermon on Pentecost,* Gregory Nazianzen recalled its different aspects (XXXVI, 429-433). We do not need to return to this symbolism, since we have already spoken of it in connection with the Sabbath. But here we have not only one week, but the week of weeks. This introduces two special kinds of symbolism which we shall find again the Fathers and which give us new perspectives on the theology of Pentecost.

A first interpretation is connected with a special symbolism given in Judaism to the week of weeks. We know that there was a custom in the Old Testament, according to which on all the seven weeks of years, that is to say, every fifty years, debts were remitted and slaves set free (Lev. XXV:10). The number 50, therefore, was thought of as the symbol of the remission (*aphesis*) of debts. Already in Philo we find this significance applied to the feast of Pentecost: "The feast of the sheaf is a kind of preparatory feast, if one may say so, for a still greater feast. Indeed, beginning from this day, we calculate the fiftieth day (*pentekoston*), at the end of seven weeks, the sacred number of the remission (*aphesis*) sealed by the monad, which is the image of the incorporeal God" (*De spec. leg,* 176).

This text shows, first of all, the relation of the feast of the sheaf and the feast of the first-fruits, the first being as it were the beginning of the second. And also we see the appearance of two important symbols. Let us set aside for the moment the symbol of the fiftieth day, the one added to the seven weeks, and consider the link established by Philo between the seven weeks of Pentecost and the idea of remission. For this symbolism will be found again in a whole Christian tradition, that of the School of Alexandria, which will apply this symbolism to the remission (*aphesis*) of sins, which is one aspect of the Redemption accomplished by Christ. Thus Pentecost is found to be a figure of the mystery of the Redemption under a new aspect, and it is the important biblical category of the idea of remission which brings out its symbolic value.

Clement of Alexandria, whose dependence on Philo is well-known, is the first Christian writer to see in the number 50 the symbol of the remission of sins. He is dealing with the dimensions of the Ark of Noe, which was fifty cubits broad. "Some men say that this number 50 is the symbol of hope and of the pardon which takes place by the Pentecost." [7] Clement presents his idea as representing an older tradition, but this might merely be Philo himself. Following Clement, Origen also interprets the dimensions of the Ark in a symbolic manner: "To the width, we attribute the number 50, which is the number sacred to foregiveness and remission. According to the Law, indeed, there was a time for forgiveness of debts every fifty years" (*Ho. Gen.* II, 5).

But Origen did not content himself with this statement. To begin with, in the following sentences of the text we have just quoted, he explicitly applies the symbolism of Pentecost to the redemption effected by Christ: "Now Christ, the spiritual Noe, in His ark, that is to say, the Church, in which He saves the human

[7] *Stromates,* VI, 11; Staehlin, p. 475.

race from destruction, has attributed this number of forgiveness to the width. For if He had not granted the forgiveness of sins to believers, the Church would not have spread across the world." We have here the application to Christ of the forgiveness symbolized by the number fifty, but no allusion is made to the liturgical Pentecost. This is found elsewhere: "The number 50 contains forgiveness according to the mystery of the Jubilee which takes place every fifty years, or of the feast which takes place at Pentecost" (*Ho. Matt,* XI 3; P.G., XIII, 908 A).

This symbolism of Pentecost as signifying forgiveness has a particular importance for Origen, for in the seven liturgical weeks he sees the figure of the age-long weeks of weeks through which is achieved the complete forgiveness of all sins and the restoration of all humanity in its perfection through successive existences: "We must examine whether the texts relative to the days, to the months, to the time and to the years, are not relative to the ages (*aiones*). For if the Law is the shadow of future blessings, it follows that the sabbaths are the shadow of other Sabbaths. And what should I say of the feast of the seven weeks of days" (*De Or.* XXVII, 14; Koetschau, 373, 14).[8]

It is interesting also to notice that Origen, in the *Homilies on the Book of Numbers,* sought to find in the Gospel the symbolism of Pentecost as the symbol of forgiveness: "The number fifty contains the mystery of forgiveness and pardon, as we have abundantly shown in many passages of Scripture. The fiftieth day after Easter is considered as a feast by the Law. And in the Gospel also, in teaching the parable of forgiveness and pardon, the Lord speaks of a debtor who had a debt of fifty denarii" (*Ho. Num.* V, 2; see also XXV, 2). It is not impossible that there is actually a relation between the use of the word fifty and the theme of forgiveness. Thus, the symbolism of Pentecost as a figure of the pardon given by Christ would have a foundation in the New Testament.[9]

After the time of Origen, this symbolism continued in the Alexandrian world on the level of the common teaching. It is as such that we find it in the *Paschal Letters* of St. Athanasius:

[8] See Jean Daniélou, *Origène,* pp. 279-281.

[9] What strikes the eye more readily is the allusion to the symbolism of the number fifty as meaning forgiveness in Christ's command to pardon "seventy times seven" (= 50 × 10 — 10) (Matt., XVIII, 22).

"Counting seven weeks from Easter, we shall celebrate the holy day of Pentecost, which formerly among the Jews was prefigured under the name of the Feast of the Weeks. At this time the freeing of slaves and the forgiveness of debts took place. And this day, finally, was in every way a day of liberty" (P.G., XXVI, 1366A). St. Anthanasius seems to connect with the yearly feast of Pentecost the forgiveness which took place only on the year of the Jubilee. But what is interesting in his text is that he unites, more directly than does Origen, the idea of forgiveness with the Christian liturgical feast of Pentecost. It is certainly this feast, then, whose content is for St. Athanasius the mystery of the forgiveness of sins signified by the number 50. Thus, Pentecost causes us to see the unique mystery of redemption under still another theological aspect.[10]

Having shown that Pentecost is a figure of forgiveness, Philo suggests a second interpretation of the number 50, drawn from Pythagorean symbolism of (*De spec. leg.*, 177). This introduces us to another aspect of the symbolism of Pentecost, drawn not from its relation to the Jubilee year of weeks, but from the properties of the number fifty itself, consisting of seven times seven plus one. It thus unites the perfection of the number seven multiplied by itself, and the perfection of the monad, at least this is what Philo says. The Fathers of the Church were inspired by this symbolism of numbers, but they preferred to show that the monad of Philo is also the Christian octave-day, the eighth day on which Christ rose again, which is the figure of the resurrection in the future life. So, from another approach, which is only a development of the symbolism of Sunday, Pentecost is found to be a sign of the Resurrection. It is in this sense the Sunday *par excellence,* the Great Sunday, as St. Athanasius calls it (XXVI, 1366 B).

It is, in fact, in this author that we first meet the symbolism according to which Pentecost is the figure of life everlasting: "As this time is the symbol of the future world, we shall celebrate the great Sunday, taking here and now the pledges of the life eternal to come. Indeed, it is when we depart from here that we shall fully celebrate this feast with the Lord" (Id., 1366 B). The theme of Pentecost as the figure of eternal life often returns in

[10] See also Gregory of Naziansen, *In Pent.*, 3: P.G., XXXVI, 432 A.

the works of St. Athanasius: "When a certain number of days have gone by, we shall celebrate the solemnity of holy Pentecost, whose cycle of days is a figure of the future world in which, living always with Christ, we shall praise the God of the universe" (*Id.* 1379 A). For Athanasius, the days of Pentecost are the figure of eternal life. But we do not see exactly whence this symbolism is derived.

This is given us by St. Basil. Explaining, in his Treatise on the Holy Spirit, that there are various customs in Christianity coming from apostolic tradition of which Christians no longer know the meaning, he goes on to speak about Pentecost; "The whole period of the fifty days (*pentekoste*) reminds us of the resurrection that we await in eternity. Indeed this day that is one and the first, seven times multiplied by seven, accomplishes the seven weeks of Pentecost, for it begins on the first day and is ended by it, unfolding itself fifty times in the time between in days that are like one another. So it has certain resemblances to eternity, since by a circular movement it comes to end where it began. On that day, the laws of the Church teach us to stand upright while we pray, to show that the superior part of our soul should travel from the present toward what is to come" (*De Spir. Sancto* 27; Pruche, p. 237).

For St. Basil, as for Athanasius, Pentecost is a figure of the Resurrection. And it is a figure of the Resurrection because it is the eighth day. According to Basil's reasoning, it consists in the repetition, during seven times seven days, of the first day which begins it, which is a Sunday, and is thus also the eighth day. Pentecost is thus seen to be made up of fifty Sundays.[11] It is indeed the Great Sunday of which Athanasius speaks. But Sunday is at the same time the memorial of Christ's Resurrection and the figure of the Resurrection to come. It is because it is inaugurated by a Sunday and ended by a Sunday that the whole Pentecost is thus seen as a figure of the Resurrection.

Gregory Nazianzen develops an analogous theme: "The weeks of days bring forth the Pentecost, the day considered holy among the Jews; the weeks of years bring forth the year of Jubilee, as they call it, the day of rest for the earth and of liberation for the

[11] Ambrose, *Exp. Luc.*: "During these fifty days, the Church knows no fasting, as on Sunday, and all these days are like Sundays" (VIII. 25).

slaves. For this nation consecrated to God the first-fruits, not only of the earth and of animals, but also of days and years. It is thus that the number 7, by the veneration of which it is the object, has communicated this honor to Pentecost. For indeed, when it is multiplied by itself it produces fifty, minus a day which we take in the age to come, the octave which is always the same and the first, or better, one and indestructible. There indeed, the present sabbath-keeping of our lives has an end, so that one part may be given to seven and one to eight, as certain of our predecessors have interpreted this passage of Solomon" (XXXVI, 432 A-B).

The perspective of this quotation is a little different from that of Basil. He understands the week of weeks to consist of so many Sundays. Gregory, on the other hand, sees in this week of weeks the figure of time, of the cosmic week representing the whole of history, and he sees in the fiftieth day which is added to make fifty, the figure of the eternity which is symbolized not by the eighth day, the symbol of the Resurrection, but by the monad, the figure of indivisible eternity. The symbolism is more Pythagorean, nearer to that of Philo than is St. Basil's. We have here simply a development of the symbolism of Sunday with the eschatological accent so dear to the Cappadocians.[12]

With St. Augustine we come nearer again to the line of St. Basil. "The day of Pentecost has a mysterious significance because seven times seven makes forty-nine, and in coming back to its point of departure, the eighth day which is also the first, it accomplishes the fiftieth: these fifty days are celebrated after the Resurrection of the Lord as a figure not of work but of rest and joy. This is why we also cease to fast, and why we stand when we pray, which is the sign of the Resurrection, and the Alleluia is sung, to show that our future work will consist only in praising God" (*Epist.* LV, 28; P.L. XXXIII, 218 A). The fifty days, begun and ended by the Sunday, figure of the future life, are as a whole the symbol of rest and of the joy of eternity.

We should notice that Augustine points out another feature of this time, that Christians stand when they pray. This was stated earlier in the passage from St. Basil quoted above. It is mentioned as early as in Tertullian (*De orat.* 25; P.L. I, 1193 A). Augustine sees in this absence of kneeling an allusion to the

[12] See above, p. 267.

Resurrection. Basil, still more precise, sees in it the sign that "we should journey toward the future life." Thus, this rite also refers to the Resurrection. This characteristic is valuable to notice, for it is the only rite properly speaking which characterizes the liturgical season of Pentecost, together with the Alleluia. The symbolism of these rites confirms the typology of the texts in showing in Pentecost the figure of the future life and of the Resurrection to come.

The themes that we have been considering so far are connected with Pentecost considered all together as the mystery of the Resurrection. But, as we said in the beginning of this chapter, from the Fourth Century on, a tendency arose to assign different days of the fifty to the different events of the Resurrection, the Ascension, the outpouring of the Spirit. This tendency led little by little to applying the name of Pentecost only to the fiftieth day of the Paschal season and to seeing in it, not the whole Paschal mystery under its aspect of oblation of the first-fruits, forgiveness of sins or anticipation of eternal life, but only the last event in the Paschal cycle, the outpouring of the Holy Spirit. We are now on the road leading to the modern idea of Pentecost.

This idea appears as early as the Homelies of the Fourth Century, together with passages which spring from the primitive notion. Thus Gregory Nazianzen, having commented on the symbolism of the number 50, writes: "We celebrate Pentecost and the coming of the Spirit, and the day fixed for the fulfillment of the realization of hope" (XXXVI, 436 B). In the same way, Gregory of Nyssa also says: 'Today, the days of Pentecost being accomplished, according to the yearly cycle of the times, at this very hour, that is to say, at the third hour, the inexpressible grace came down: the Spirit is newly united to men' " (XLVI, 697B). The exact allusion to the celebration of the event at the very hour in which it happened is directly in line with the liturgy of Jerusalem, in which, as Etheria tells us, they celebrated the descent of the Holy Spirit on Pentecost morning, by a reunion of the Church of Sion on the site of the Cenacle at the third hour, and read the text of the Acts of the Apostles concerning the descent of the Holy Spirit (43, 2-3; Pétré, p. 249).

We now have to deal with a new conception of Pentecost as

the coming of the Holy Spirit, fifty days after Easter. Under this new aspect, Pentecost comes to have a different symbolism. For up till now we have only been connecting the Jewish feast of the fiftieth day with the theme of the nature feast of the Harvest. This is the only symbolism of which there is any question in the Scriptures, or in Philo. But, in the same way as, in the case of the Pasch, the historical commemoration of the Exodus was joined to the seasonal feast of the azymes, so for Pentecost, to the seasonal feast of the first-fruits of the harvest was added the commemoration of a historical event of the cycle of the Exodus, that is, the promulgation of the Law on Mt. Sinai.[13]

When Pentecost became for the Christians a special feast of the fiftieth day, they began to look for its prefiguring in Judaism, and so they came to relate it to the promulgation of the Law on Sinai. This appears first of all in St. Augustine: previous Greek tradition is mute on this point. In his *Letter to Januarius,* St. Augustine looks for authorities on which to base the feast of the fiftieth day. These authorities are first of all the Gospel, "because it was at that time that the Holy Spirit came" (XXXIII, 218 C). But it is to be found also in the Old Testament: "Indeed there, after they had celebrated the Pasch by immolating the lamb, they counted fifty days until the day when the Law was given on Mount Sinai to Moses, the servant of God, written with the finger of God" (218 D). The specification of fifty days between the first Pasch and Mount Sinai is not explicitly expressed in Scripture, but corresponds in general to its indications.[14] We find it in the Book of Jubilees (I, 4).

We remarked that Augustine pointed out that "the Law was written with the finger of God." This is actually the characteristic by which the gift of the Law on Sinai became the figure of the coming of the Holy Spirit. "In fact," says Augustine, "It is very clearly stated in the books of the Gospels that the finger of God signifies the Holy Spirit. Indeed one of the evangelists has said: 'It is by the finger of God that I drive out demons' (Luke XI:20), another expresses the same thing, saying: 'It is by the Spirit of God that I drive out demons' " (Matt. XII:28) (XXXIII, 218 D).

[13] Foote-Moore, *Judaism,* II, p. 48 et seq; Bonsirven, *Le Judaisme au temps du Christ,* II, p. 123.
[14] See St. Augustine's proof, XXXIII, 219 C-D.

So the concordance between the Two Testaments is obvious: "The victim is immolated, the Pasch is celebrated, and, fifty days after, the Law of fear is given, written with the finger of God. Christ is immolated, Who was led like a lamb to the slaughter as Isaias witnesses, the true Pasch is celebrated, and, fifty days afterwards, the Holy Spirit, Who is the finger of God, is given in view of charity" (XXXIII, 219 A).[15]

This agreement of the two testaments arouses a burst of enthusiasm in the soul of St. Augustine: "Who would not prefer this joy of the divine mysteries, when they shine with the light of holy teaching, to all the empires of the world, even if they were made peaceful by an unaccustomed peace. Is it not as if, like the two seraphim, they answer one another in singing the praises of God: 'Holy, holy, holy is the Lord, the God of hosts! So the two Testaments in faithful harmony together sing the holy truth" (XXXIII, 218 D). And he continues the comparison: "The Law placed in the Ark is holiness in the body of the Lord. It is by His Resurrection that future rest is promised to us. And it is in view of participation in this Resurrection that charity is communicated to us by the Holy Spirit" (XXXIII 219 C).

With Pentecost, we have completed our study of the symbolism of the Paschal feasts. We see how two conceptions of the feast are opposed to one another. One defines it above all in connection with the events of the New Testament. The Feast thus becomes merely a commemoration, and has no other content than that of the event itself. But the other conception sees in it the mystery of Christ refracted through the categories of cosmic religion and of Mosaic religion. These categories representing the forms of revelation are like so many prefigurations. And they have their precise object to give us the forms in which to express the events of Christ. It is because of this that the conception of the Christian feast which is connected with the liturgy of the Old Testament is richer in dogmatic content.

[15] See also *The City of God,* XVI, 43; P.L. 522 A. "The Holy Ghost is called the finger of God in the Gospel in order to recall to our memory the foreshadowing event."

CHAPTER TWENTY

The Feast of Tabernacles

THE New Testament is not the destruction, but the fulfillment of the Old. There is no more remarkable example of this principle than that of liturgical feasts. The solemnities of Jewish religion, the Pasch and Pentecost, have remained those of Christianity, simply being charged with a new content. But there is one exception to this law—the third great feast of Judaism, that of Tabernacles, the *Scenopegia* of the Septuagint,[1] which took place from the 15th to the 22nd of September. Only a vestige of this feast is to be found in the Roman liturgy, consisting of the reading of the text of Leviticus concerning this feast (XXIII:29-43), on the Saturday of the September Ember-days. Nevertheless, although the Jewish feast of Tabernacles has not been carried on into the Christian liturgy of today, this feast was seen by the Fathers of the Church as a figure of Christian realities.

The origin of the Feast of Tabernacles is to be found in the cycle of seasonal feasts. It is the feast of the reaping, as Pentecost is that of the harvest. The very text of Leviticus which prescribes the celebration points this out (XXIII:39). And Philo also emphasizes this aspect (*Spec. leg.* II, 204).[2] It is with this seasonal aspect that the characteristic rites of the feast are connected: living for seven days, in huts made out of branches, libations of water signi-

[1] For the word σκηνοπηγία, see A. Deissman, Licht von Osten, 1909, p. 81.
[2] Pedersen, *Israel,* II, p. 418-425.

fying prayer for rain, the procession around the altar waving the bouquet (*lulab*) made from three kinds of trees: willow, myrtle and palm, and carrying a fruit of the lemon-tree (*etrog*).[3]

But, as in the case of the other feasts which have a similar origin, Jewish thought wove the memory of a great event of its history into the cyclical framework of the seasonal feast. So Easter, the feast of the first grain, of the azymes, became the feast of the first-born spared by the destroying angel. The transformation no doubt took place more slowly for the Feast of Tabernacles.[4] Nevertheless, it is already indicated in *Leviticus:* the feast of Tabernacles (*scenai*) is meant to recall to the Jews the memory of their dwelling in tents (*scenai*) during the crossing of the desert of the Exodus (Lev. XXIII:43). This purpose appears again in Philo (*Spec. leg.* II, 207).[5] And we find it again in the Fathers of the Church (Aug. *In Joan.* XXVIII, 7, 3; P.L. XXXV, 1623; Jerome, *In Zach.* 3, 14; P. L. XXV, 1536).

But during the age of the prophets, the past events of the history of Israel, and of the Exodus in particular, were recalled only to nourish the hope of the people in the future events in which the power of Yahweh would manifest itself in a still greater way in favor of His Own: the events of the Exodus became the figures of eschatological realities. Here is the origin of typology. We find, then, such an interpretation of the Feast of Tabernacles. The Prophets represent the life of the just man in the messianic kingdom as a dwelling in tabernacles, or tents, symbolized by the tents in which the Israelites dwelt in the desert. So we read in Isaias: "The people shall sit down in rest and peace, and they shall dwell in security in their tents" XXXII:18).[6] From this time on, the liturgy of the feast, while remaining a figure of the past, became also a symbol of the future. This is what we find in later Judaism. "The huts were thought of, not only as a remembrance of the protection of God in the desert, but also as a prefiguration of the *sukkoth* in which the just are to dwell in the age to come. Thus, it seems that a very exact eschatological sym-

[3] Strack-Billerbeck, II, pp. 774-812.

[4] All the same, Harald Riesenfeld is no doubt going too far when he speaks of a "secondary theological rationalization" (*Jésus transfiguré*, p. 147).

[5] And also in the rabbinical tradition. Strack-Billerbeck, II, 778.

[6] B. Zielinski, *De transfigurationis sensu,* Verbum Domini, 1948, p. 34.

bolism was attached to the most characteristic rite of the Feast of Tabernacles, as this was celebrated in Jewish times." [7]

We have perhaps a document of this symbolism in the paintings of the synagogue of Dura-Europos. The thirteenth picture represents the Jews in the tents of the Exodus. But these tents are conceived as being like the huts of the Feast of Tabernacles. And, like the other representations in Dura, they have an eschatological significance. Riesenfeld writes: "The huts of the Feast of the Tabernacles make concrete the connection between the tents of the biblical episode, represented in the picture, and the dwellings of the just of Israel in the age to come." [8] Rabbinical literature also presents the idea that the just will dwell in Paridise in such tents, and the feast of Tabernacles nourishes this hope. Around this central theme develop secondary ideas, such as that "the furnishing of the pavilions of the future will be in harmony with the the actions of the just during their earthly lives." [9]

Nevertheless, there is a question here. This eschatological significance of the memories of the Exodus is not peculiar to the Feast of Tabernacles; it is true also of the other feasts. Is there some reason why an eschatological meaning should be given especially to this feast? A basic reason is suggested by Philo: it is the feast which ends the agrarian cycle of the year (*teleiosis*) (*spec leg.* II, 204). This reason might have some value; we shall see it taken up later by the Fathers of the Church, in particular by Methodius: "We shall celebrate the great Feast of Tabernacles in the new creation and without sadness, the fruits of the earth being all gathered in" (*Conv.* IX, 1; 114, 8-9). But there is a reason more ancient and more profound, namely, that from New Testament times on, we find the Feast of Tabernacles connected with messianic hopes. The sources of this connection are obscure. It is well known that according to a whole school of thought, the origin of the Feast of Tabernacles was the annual feast of the royal installation, such as it existed in the ancient Syrian religions.[10] It is this feast of which we find the scattered

[7] Harald Riesenfeld, *Jésus transfiguré,* p. 189; Bonsirven, *Judaïsme palestinien,* 1, 522; Harald Sahlin, *Zur typologie des Johannes evangeliums,* p. 54.
[8] Loc. cit., p. 195.
[9] Loc. cit., p. 197.
[10] Mowinckel, *Psalmenstudien;* Engnell, *Studies in Divine Kingship.*

remnants in the three Jewish feasts of the beginning of September, Rosh-ha-shana, Kippur and Sukkoth. This feast might have taken on a messianic character in Judaism, that is to say, the adoration of the actual king of the time might have been transformed into the waiting for a king to come. This influence can not be excluded. Nevertheless, it does not seem as if we should look here, with Harald Riesenfeld, for the first origin of the feast, which seems rather to be connected with the cult of the seasons. There is question here rather of some transformation which this cult might have undergone during the age of the kings, and which would have brought into it new overtones.

What is certain in any case is that of the Feast of Tabernacles took on a special importance in post-exilian Judaism in connection with the messianic expectation. In a very messianic context, the Prophet Zacharias shows us, after the victory of the Messiah, that is in eschatological times, "all the nations going up to the future Jerusalem to celebrate there the Feast of Tabernacles" (XIV:16). Thus, the liturgical feast is seen as a prefiguration of messianic times. Furthermore, there is a Psalm belonging to the post-exilian liturgy of the Feast of Tabernacles the messianic character of which is very clear. This is Psalm CXVII sung during the solemn procession when, on the seventh day of the feast, the faithful went around the altar while waving the *lulab,* the bouquet made up of willow-branches, palm and myrtle. It is to this procession that the verse alludes: "Join in procession with leafy boughs up to the horns of the altar." Now, this Psalm calls the Messias "He who is to come": "Blessed is he who comes in the name of the Lord." And it heralds his coming with the cry Hosanna: "Save me" (verse 25). So this day of the feast is called "The Great Hosanna." [11]

Thus, in the same way as the expectation of the tabernacles of the New Exodus gave an eschatological significance to the huts made of branches used during the Feast of Tabernacles, so the expectation of the coming of the Messias gave a messianic significance to another feature of the ritual of the feast, the solemn procession around the altar. As a result, from Old Testament times, and in a very special way in the Judaism of Our Lord's own life-time, the ritual of the feast had taken on a typological

[11] Herkenne, *Das Buch der Psalmen,* pp. 378-380.

significance, and it had done so particularly by means of the emphasis placed on messianism, on eschatological significance. Thus, the New Testament and the Fathers did not need to invent a typology which was already in existence, but only to show in a more precise way how this typology had been fulfilled.

We can observe, finally, that this eschatological interpretation of the Feast of Tabernacles in the Old Testament continued to be made in Judaism. We find traces of these rabbinical speculations in the Fathers of the Church. Thus, Methodius writes in the *Banquet:* "Only those who have celebrated the Feast of Tabernacles will enter into the holy land. Leaving their tabernacles, they hasten to arrive in the Temple and the City of God, that is to say, to a joy more great and more heavenly, as it took place among the Jews in the figures of these things. In the same way, indeed, as, having come out of the borders of Egypt, they, by journeying, came to tabernacles and, from there, having advanced still further, they reached the Promised Land, so is it with us. I also, having started on the journey, I come out of the Egypt of this life, I come first to the Resurrection, to the true *Scenopegia.* There, having built my beautiful tent on the first day of the feast, that of the judgment, I celebrate the feast with Christ during the millennium of rest (*anapausis*), called the seven days, the true Sabbaths. Then, following Jesus Who has crossed the heavens, I start on my journey again, as they, after the rest of the Feast of Tabernacles, journeyed toward the land of promise, the heavens, not waiting any longer in tabernacles, that is to say, my tabernacle not remaining any longer the same, but, after the millennium, having passed from a corruptible human form to an angelic grandeur and beauty. Then, going out from the place of tabernacles, having celebrated the feast of the Resurrection, we shall go towards better things, ascending to the house that is above the heavens" (IX, 5:120).

It seems that here Methodius is in the direct tradition of the messianic interpretation of the Feast of Tabernacles given by the rabbis. For them, the festivities of the day in which each man ate and drank with his family in his tent adorned with various branches, were a prefiguration of the material joys of the just in the messianic kingdom. We find a valuable confirmation of this idea in St. Jerome, speaking for the patristic era. He writes about the Feast of Tabernacles: "The Jews also promise that these things shall take place in the kingdom of a thousand years, with a deceptive hope" (In Zach. III, 14). The millennium signifies the earthly reign of the Messias. Thus, there existed in Judaism a tradition which saw in the Feast of Tabernacles a figure of the millennium, and Methodius gives an echo of this tradition.

This earthly conception of the happiness of the just is not the only trait in which the influence of Jewish speculations concerning the Feast of Tabernacles are to be found in Methodius' works. We find also an interpretation of the *lulab* and of the *etrog,* designed to adorn the tabernacles, which were considered to be symbols of the good actions done in this life which merit the glory of the risen bodies.[12] "I solemnly celebrate the feast of God, having adorned the tabernacle of my body with good actions. Examined on the first day of the resurrection, I will carry what is prescribed, to see if I am adorned with the fruits of virtue. If the *Scenopegia* is the resurrection, what is prescribed for the adornment of the huts are the works of justice" (116, 23-27). And Methodius sees in the *etrog* the tree of life, figure of the faith,[13] with which we must present ourselves on the first day at the judgment-seat of Christ. The palms symbolize ascesis; the myrtles, charity; and the willows, purity.[14]

Now, all these ideas seem to be of rabbinical origin and to be related to the eschatological interpretation of the Feast of Tabernacles in ancient Judaism. The obligation for each man to present his own *lulab* composed according to the prescription appears in the *Mishna.*[15] More clearly still, "the idea that the decoration of the future pavilions will be in harmony with the actions of a man during his earthly life" is familiar to the *Midrashim.*[16] The relating of the *etrog,* whose beautiful fruit is to be carried in the hand during the feast, with the tree of life and its marvellous fruits, seems also to be connected with the customs of the

[12] Riesenfeld, *Jésus transfiguré,* p. 36.
[13] See also Didymus, *De Trin.,* 2; P.G., XXIX, 721 A.
[14] On the symbolism of the willow, see Hugo Rahner, *Grieshische Mythen in christlicher Deutung,* p. 370 et seq.
[15] Strack-Billerbeck, II, 9, 783.
[16] H. Riesenfeld, *Jésus transfiguré,* p. 197.

Jewish feast,[17] and with the speculations on the tree of life so frequently to be found in Judaism.[18]

It is a remarkable fact that the great events of the life of Christ took place within the framework of the great Feasts of Judaism: the Resurrection in the Paschal order, and the sending of the Holy Spirit in the Pentecostal. It is obvious that this is meant to show us that in Christ are fulfilled the figures of the Old Testament, of which these feasts are the memorials. At first glance, it does not seem as if this were true of the Feast of Tabernacles. Only one event in the life of Jesus is explicitly stated to have taken place during the celebration of this feast, and this is not one of the chief mysteries: it is the event, reported by St. John, of Christ's presenting Himself as the source of living waters (John VII:37). But a more precise study shows us that several episodes in the New Testament "signify that the eschatological and messianic hopes connected with the Feast of Tabernacles are in the course of being realized." [19]

The first of these events is that of the Transfiguration. Few texts of the New Testament are so filled with Old Testament overtones as is this one: the cloud, the voice from heaven, Moses and Elias. But it seems that we may go even further, and see in this scene an explicit allusion to the Feast of Tabernacles. A detailed study of the motifs of the Transfiguration in their connection with the Feast of Tabernacles has been made by Harald Riesenfeld. His work suggests many connections between these events, but we must distinguish in it nevertheless what is strictly concerned with the Feast of Tabernacles and alone engages us here, from what concerns the whole series of the feasts of autumn and implies the thesis of the unity of these feasts and of their connection with the feast of royal installation—a thesis which seems to be insufficiently established.

A first sign of the connection between the Transfiguration and the Feast of Tabernacles is found in one chronological detail at the beginning of the scene. Mark and Matthew say that the Transfiguration took place "six days later" (Matt. XVII:1; Mark

[17] H. Riesenfeld, loc. cit., p. 24; Volz, *Das Neujahrsfest Yahweh,* p. 35 et seqq.

[18] The *lulab* and the *etrog,* reproduced on certain Jewish memorials of the dead, no doubt symbolize the resurrection. Riesenfeld, loc. cit., p. 36.

[19] Riesenfeld, loc. cit., p. 277.

IX, 2): Luke says: "About eight days after" (IX:28). The difference itself indicates that there is question of a yearly event in which the interval of six to eight days has a special meaning. This would be particularly fitting for the Feast of Tabernacles which lasts for seven days and in which the eighth day has a particular importance. The cloud (Luke IX: 35-36) is connected with the worship in the Temple: its presence in the Tabernacle is the sign of the *shekina* of Yahweh. We know also that it has in Judaism an eschatological significance, and that its presence was considered to be the sign of the dwelling of Yahweh among the just in the world to come.

But the most important fact is that of the tents (*scenai*) that Peter proposes building for the Lord, for Moses and Elias. It seems certain that we should see in these tents an allusion to the Feast of Tabernacles.[20] After what has been said above, the meaning of the scene becomes clear. The manifestation of the glory of Jesus appears to Peter to be the sign that the times of the Messias have arrived. And one of the qualities of these messianic times was to be the dwelling of the just in the tents signified by the huts of the Feast of Tabernacles. This detail is explained still more clearly if the Transfiguration actually took place at the time of the Feast of Tabernacles. Then it would show that the realities prefigured by the Feast were accomplisehd: the Transfiguration represents the true Feast of Tabernacles. This eschatological significance is still clearer if we admit with Riesenfeld that the exclamation of St. Peter: "It is good for us to be here" is the expression of the rest, of the eschatological *anapausis*.[21] The Feast of Tabernacles prefigures in this way the rest of the life to come.

We should further notice that the conception according to which the just are to dwell in tabernacles or tents in the future life, an idea which as we have seen was conceived in Judaism, appears also in the New Testament. We meet in Matthew the expression "eternal tabernacles" (*aionai scenai*) to designate the dwellings of the just in the future life. In the same way, the expression *scenoun*, meaning the dwelling in heaven of the just, is frequent in the Apocalypse (VII: 15; XII: 12; XIII: 6; XXI: 3). It is not a ques-

[20] Zielinski, *De Transfigurationis sensu*, Verbum Domini, 1948, p. 34. The link between the mountain and the transfiguration is pointed out by Nehemias (VIII, 15): "Go forth to the mountain and fetch branches to make tabernacles."
[21] Loc. cit., p. 258.

tion, then, in this event of Christ's life, of one isolated text, but of a continuous theme the messianic significance of which was commonly realized.[22] Thus, the scene of the Transfiguration marks the fact that the messianic times have come.

The motif of the tents in the Feast of Tabernacles is thus seen as fulfilled in the coming of Christ. But there is also another aspect in the liturgy of the feast which gives its significance to another event in the life of Christ, the entrance into Jerusalem on Palm Sunday. We have said that the procession around the altar on the seventh day of the Feast, when all the participants waved their *lulab* to the song of Hosanna and the Benedictus of Psalm CXVII, had a messianic character. And it is obvious that these liturgical actions are described in the scene of Palm Sunday. We see here the crowd accompanying the entrance of Jesus, as He rode on the ass, just as Zachary describes the messianic king (IX:9), the crowd holding palm-branches in their hands (John XII:13) and singing the two verses of Psalm CXVII: "Hosanna . . . Blessed is He Who comes in the name of the Lord" (XII:15). The meaning of the scene is clear. It signifies that the coming of the Messias, prefigured by the solemn procession of the seventh day of the Feast of Tabernacles, is fulfilled in the person of Jesus.

We should add one remark: as in the case of the Transfiguration, we have here only a preliminary realization of the Feast of Tabernacles; the mystery of the glorious Parousia was glimpsed, but it disappeared once more, for its manifestation is reserved for the end of time. It is certainly in this way that Jesus Himself understood it when He reminded us that the true Feast of Tabernacles, in which we will sing Psalm CXVII, is reserved for later on: "You shall not see me henceforth until you shall sing: 'Blessed is He Who comes in the name of the Lord' " (Matt. XXIII: 39). Thus, as Methodius profoundly remarks concerning the Feast of Tabernacles: "The Law is the figure and the shadow of the image, that is to say, of the Gospel; the Gospel is this of the reality" (*Conv.* 115: 26-27). The scene of Palm Sunday, signified by the Feast of Tabernacles, itself prefigures the glorious Parousia. And the verse *Benedictus* accompanies each of these Parousiai.

And, further, it is not only Psalm CXVII of which the New Tes-

[22] The connection between the Transfiguration and the Parousia is clearly marked by II Peter, I, 18.

tament gives us an eschatological interpretation. The whole liturgy of the Feast of Tabernacles serves St. John in the Apocalypse to describe the procession of the elect around the heavenly altar. It is, in fact, the liturgy of this Feast which we are to recognize in the passage of the Apocalypse (VII: 9-17) describing the "great crowd" which stands before the throne of the Lamb. Many details are connected with the Feast: the palm-branches (*phoiniches*) in their hands,[23] the white robes, which recall the garments of Christ at the Transfiguration (VII:9), the tabernacle in which the Lord dwells in the midst of the elect (*scenosei*) (VII:15), the springs of living water where they quench their thirst (VII:17). We have here, on the second level of eschatology, the projection of the first fulfillment which was, on the level of the Gospel, the episode of Palm Sunday.

We have just said that in the scene from the Apocalypse, the springs of living water are also an allusion to the Feast of Tabernacles. In fact, as we said earlier, the waters drawn from the cistern of Siloe used for the ablutions in the Temple during the seven days of the feast, were one of its characteristic rites. And there is a third episode of the Gospel in which the Feast of Tabernacles is recalled, and precisely on the occasion of this rite, as St. John tells us: "Now on the last, the great day of the feast, Jesus stood and cried out, saying: 'If anyone thirst, let him come to me and drink.' He who believes in me, as the Scripture says, 'From within him (his bosom) there shall flow rivers of living water' " (VII: 37-38).[24] Most of the commentators agree in seeing in this image used by Christ our Lord an allusion to the ablutions of water on the last day of the Feast of Tabernacles.

In their primitive form, these ablutions were connected with seasonal rites intended to draw down the rain. But, in the historical transposition of the feast which took place in Judaism, they recalled the spring of living water which Yahweh caused to flow out of the rock in the desert at the time of the Exodus when the Jews dwelt in tents. And also the rite of the feast, in recalling this past event, announces a new outpouring of this water at the end

[23] We may note that only St. John had noticed, in the scene of the strewing of branches before our Lord, that the branches were palm-branches and that they were held in the hand (XII, 13).

[24] On the various interpretations of this verse, see Hugo Rahner, *Flumina de ventre Christi,* Biblica, 1941, 269, et seq.

of time. In showing that it is He from whom living water is to come, Christ also shows that it is in Him that the reality prefigured by the Feast of Tabernacles is fulfilled. And more precisely still, the Evangelist shows us in the living water the figure of the eschatological outpouring of the Holy Spirit which was to take place "when Christ should be glorified" (VII:39).[25]

We have now arrived at a second stage. We have seen first that three of the rites of the Feast of Tabernacles had taken on an eschatological meaning in Judaism: the huts built of branches, the procession accompanied by the *lulab* and the hosanna, and the ablutions with living water. And we have seen that three events in the New Testament shows us that this eschatological significance of the rites is fulfilled in the person of Christ. It remains for us to see how the Fathers show us in the liturgy of the Church the continuation of this typology.

We have already remarked that the New Testament, in the question which now concerns us, is content with affirming that the eschatological realities prefigured by the Feast of Tabernacles are now fulfilled in Christ. In the case of the Pasch and of Pentecost, the Fathers have shown us that this realization is continued in the Church by means of the liturgical cycle. Now we come to the special problem of the Feast of Tabernacles: there is no strict equivalent for this feast in the Christian liturgical year. Is this to say that we can find no trace of it? This is the last question that we have now to consider.

We have the first indication of this problem in the work of Didymus the Blind. The Feast of Tabernacles is considered to be the figure of the liturgical year as a whole: "The Jews, by the grace of the *Scenopegia*, announced in figure (*mystichos*) in advance the synaxes of the Holy Churches and *Martyria* which, by faith and good works, lead us to the heavenly tabernacles. It is concerning these that He Who has built them says: 'Make friends with the riches of iniquity, so that they may receive you into everlasting tabernacles)' " (P. G., XXXIX, 721 A). The Feast of Tabernacles is connected here with the whole series of Sundays, and especially

[25] This is taken up by Cyril of Alexandria: "The source of water in the feast of Tabernacles is the spiritual and heavenly Christ who waters with the fountains on high those who receive him" (*De Ad.;* LXVIII, 1109 A).

with the time after Pentecost, which is precisely that during which the feast took place, and in which allusion is still made to it on the Saturday of the September Ember-days. Commemorating the time of the crossing of the desert, between the Exodus from Egypt and the entrance into the Promised Land, it is a wonderful figure of the life of the Church between Baptism and heaven, which corresponds liturgically to the time after Pentecost.

Can we go further and establish a relationship between the Feast of Tabernacles and any one Christian feast? We find an attempt to do so in a Sermon, "The Nativity of Christ," by Gregory Nazianzen (P. G., XLVI, 1129-1130). At first, this idea seems astonishing, and we see no obvious connection between the Feast of Tabernacles and the Nativity. But we should remember that, for the fourth century, the feast of the 25th of December was essentially the feast of an idea, that is to say, it was not connected with an event of the life of Christ, but with an aspect of Christology. And this aspect was that of the manifestation of the Messias, who is, in fact, according to Psalm CXVII, the essential object prefigured by the Feast of Tabernacles. What is peculiar to Gregory is the attempt to connect the third great feast of the Christian liturgical cycle, that of the 25th of December (or the 6th of January) with the third great feast of the Jewish liturgical cycle which up till then had seemed to have no counterpart. This was an interesting effort, but it was not followed up, and the liturgy has retained no trace of it.

The first feature of the interpretation of Gregory of Nyssa is that of messianism. As we have said, this feature characterizes the Feast of Tabernacles as described in Psalm CXVII. The feast is seen as the expression of the expectation of the Messias and the figure of His coming: "The prophet David tells us that the God of the universe, the Lord of the world has appeared (*epephanen*) to us to constitute the solemn Feast in the thick branches of foliage" (*pychnazomena,* Ps. CXVII, 27). He means by the term "thick branches of foliage," the Feast of Tabernacles which had been established for a long time, according to the tradition of Moses.[26] But, although it has been announced for a long time, it had not yet been fulfilled. Indeed the reality was prefigured by the symbolic events, but the true builder of tabernacles had not yet come. It is

[26] It will be noticed that Gregory knows that Psalm CXVII is connected with the Feast of Tabernacles.

to fulfill this feast, in conformity with the prophetic word, that the God and Lord of all has manifested (*epephanen*) Himself to us" (*De anima;* P. G., XLV, 132 B). Gregory's point of departure is the expression "He has appeared" (*epephanen*). The Psalm of the Tabernacles announced this Epiphany, and this is what is fulfilled in the person of Jesus. And it is precisely the Feast of the Epiphany on the 25th of December or the 6th of January, which commemorates this manifestation. It is this point which is emphasized by the *Sermon on the Nativity*, connecting this manifestation with the Incarnation: "The subject of today's feast (25th December) is the true Feast of Tabernacles. Indeed, in this feast, the human tabernacle was built up by Him who put on human nature because of us. Our tabernacles, which were struck down by death, are raised up again by Him Who built our dwelling from the beginning. Therefore, harmonizing our voices with that of David, let us also sing the Psalm: 'Blessed is He Who comes in the name of the Lord.' How does He come? Not in a boat or in a chariot. But he comes into human existence by the immaculate Virgin. It is He, Our Lord, who has appeared (*epephanen*) to make the solemn feast day in thick branches of foliage up to the horns of the altar" (P. C., XLVI, 1129 B-C).

The coming of Christ, His birth, thus is seen to be the inauguration of the true Feast of Tabernacles. Here appears a new harmony: the *scenai*, the human dwellings built at the beginning, have been struck down by sin. This interpretation comes from Methodius, who follows Gregory.[27] Christ comes to raise them up, to restore human nature, to inaugurate the true feast of Tabernacles prefigured in the Jewish liturgy. And the beginning of this *Scenopegia* is the Incarnation itself in which, according to St. John, Christ built the tabernacles of His own Body (*escenosen*) (John I: 14). It does indeed seem as if it were this term ot St. John's which makes the connection between the feast of the *scenai* and the feast of the Birth of Christ.[28] By this a new theme, foreign to the biblical

[27] 'The prescriptions of the levitical law concerning the Feast of Tabernacles foreshadow the resurrection of the body' (*Conv.*, 113, 24). The comparison of bodies to tabernacles (= tents) seems to come from Plato (*Axiochos*, 365 E). It passed into the Greek *Wisdom* (IX, 15), from which St. Paul may have borrowed it (II Cor., V, 2-8).

[28] Eusebius (Dem. Ev. 9; P.G. XXVII, 1173 D) speaks of the body of Christ as a σκήνωμα.

theme of the Feast of Tabernacles and connected with another line of thought, comes to unite with the symbolism of this Feast.

We should notice that Gregory founds his interpretation of the feast not only on the expression "apparuit nobis," as in the *De Anima*, but also on the verse: "Blessed is He Who comes in the name of the Lord." It is in fact this verse which properly expresses messianic salvation. We have seen that the Gospel applies it to the triumphant entrance of Our Lord on Palm Sunday and to the final Parousia. Gregory of Nyssa also applies it to the first Parousia, that of Christ in the flesh. If we remember that it is this verse which the liturgy uses to salute Christ in His eucharistic coming, it is seen to be the messianic verse *par excellence*, the song which spans the successive parousias in the successive ages of the history of salvation.

But Gregory of Nyssa does not emphasize only the prefiguring of the coming of the Messias by the building of the tabernacles, but also another eschatological figure: the rebuilding of the unity of spiritual creation destroyed by sin. Both an element in the liturgy of the feast and a verse from Psalm CXVII are its figures: the solemn procession around the altar, and the verse: "Celebrate the solemn feast day with leafy branches even to the horns of the altar." This procession, accompanied by the song of psalms around the altar appears to him as the figure of the restored choir of all creation, men henceforth uniting once more their voices with those of the angels.[29]

The Sermon on the Nativity thus expresses it: We are not ignorant, dear brothers, of the mystery contained in this verse of the Psalm, that is that all creation is one great sanctuary of the God of creation. But when sin appeared, the mouths of those who were touched by it were closed, and the choir of those who celebrated the feast was broken up, and human nature no longer took part in it with angelic nature. But the words of life have sounded in the ears that were shut, so that one feast of harmony is made by the reunion in one cluster (*pychnazomenon*) in the feast of Tabernacles, of the creation below with the sublime powers around the heavenly altar. Indeed, the horns of the altar are the sublime and eminent powers of spiritual nature, the Principalities, the Powers, the Thrones and the Dominations to which human nature is reunited by the *Scenopegia* in a common feast (XLVI, 1129-1130).

[29] See Hilary, *In Psalm.* CXXXVI, P.L., IX, 780 B.

This theme of the reconstitution of the completeness (the *pleroma*) of spiritual creation is dear to Gregory of Nyssa, who comes back to it several times.[30] Its special relation to the Feast of Tabernacles might have been suggested by the heavenly liturgy of the Apocalypse, in which the angels and saints are seen as united around the heavenly altar. More directly, we see with which features of Psalm CXVII Gregory connects it. The angelic creation appears to him as symbolized by the horns of the altar. This is an exegesis of verse 27 of this Psalm which we find elsewhere (Athanasius(?) Sel. Psalm; P. G. XXVII, 480 B). And the union of men with angels is connected especially with the circular procession going around the altar, which is a figure of the restoration of the heavenly choir. Secondarily, Gregory connects it with the *lulab*, the bouquet made of different branches, named in the Psalms by the expression *condensa* (*pychazomena*), which is a sign of the various spiritual creatures.

This attempt of Gregory of Nyssa was not followed up. We see, however, that the Gradual of the Second Mass of Christmas contains three verses from Psalm CXVII—and precisely those which our author applies to the Nativity: 28, 29 and 23. It is indeed at Christmas that the eschatological tabernacle was built for the first time, when the Word "established His dwelling amongst us," and the unity of men and angels was restored when the angels visited the shepherds. But the Feast of Tabernacles is still not entirely connected with any mystery of the life of Christ. This is perhaps why, more than any other feast, it is connected with that mystery which is not yet fulfilled, that of the last Parousia. If ever this mystery, which is that of the ruling power of Christ over history, comes to be celebrated liturgically, the texts of Leviticus and of the Gospel, the verses of Psalm CXVII, the readings from Gregory of Nyssa and Cyril of Alexandria could compose for it a most wonderful Office.

30 Jean Daniélou, *Trois textes eschatologiques de saint Grégoire de Nysse,* Rech. Sc. Relig., 1940, pp. 348 et seq.

Bibliography

Allo, P., *Le Christ et le temps,* French translation, 1947, of Cullman, Oscar, *Christus und die Zeit,* Zollikon-Zurich, Evangelischer Verlag, 1946

Amann, E., *L'ange du baptême chez Tertullien,* Rev. Sc. Rel., 1921, p. 208 ff.

Ambrose, St., *De mysteriis,* text and trans. B. Botte; Sources chrétiennes, Les éditions du Cerf, 1949, Paris

Ambrose, St., *De Noe et arca*

Ambrose, St., *Desacramentis,* text and trans. B. Botte; Sources chrétiennes, Les éditions du Cerf, 1949, Paris

Ambrose, St., *Exp. Luc. II, ii;* LV; 66

Ambrose, St., *Exp. Psalm* CXVIII, XIV, 2; CSEL, LXII, 299

Aphraates, *Dem., XIII, 3;* P.S., 1, 547; XIII, 9, 563

Athanasius, St., *Life of St. Antony,* trans. by R. T. Meyer, Westminster, Md., Newman Press, 1950

Augustine, St., *Contra Faustum,* XII, 15 and 19

Augustine, St., *De catechizandis rudibus* P.L. XL, 313

Augustine, St., *De catechizandis rudibus* 7, P.L. XL, 317 C

Bacher, *Agada der Jannaiten*

Bardy, G., *Melchisédech dans la tradition patristique,* Rev. Bibl., 1926; 1927

Barret, C. K., *The Holy Spirit and the Gospel Tradition,* London, 1945

Basil, St., *De Spiritu Sancto,* 14

Basil, St., *Treatise on the Holy Spirit,* text and trans. Pruche; Sources chrétiennes, Les éditions du Cerf, 1947, Paris

Baumstarlk, A., *Liturgie comparée*

Behm, *Artos,* Theol. Woert., I, p. 476; Editor: Gerhard Kittel, W. Kahlhammer Verl. Stuttgart, 1932–56

Benoit, P., *L'Ascension,* Rev. Biblique, 1949, p. 161 ff.

Bettencourt, A., *Doctrina ascetica Origenis,* Studia Anselmiana, fasc. 16 Libreria Vaticana, 1945

Bieder, W., *Die Vorstellung von der Hollenfahrt J.-C.,* 1949

Bonsirven, Joseph, *Exégèse rabbinique et exégèse paulinienne,* Paris, Beauchesne et ses fils, 1939

Bonsirven, Joseph, *Le Judaisme palestinien au temps du Christ,* 11, p. 123; Paris, Beauchesne et ses fils, 1934/5

Bouyer, Louis, *La première eucharistie dans la dernière Cene,* La Maison-Dieu, LVIII, p. 34-7

Boyance, Pierre, *Études sur le songe de Scipion*

Boyance, Pierre, *Le culte des Muses,* 1939
Braun, F. M., *L'eau et l'esprit,* Rev. Thomiste, 1949, 1-30
Braun, F. M., *Le baptême d'après le IVe, Évangile,* Rev. Thomiste, 1948, pp. 364-5
Cabasilas, Nicholas, *Explication de la Sainte Liturgie;* trad. Salaville, p. 137; Sources chrétiennes, Les éditions du Cerf, Paris, 1943
Capelle, B., *L'Exultet pascal oeuvre de saint Ambroise,* Misc. Mercati I, p. 226 ff.
Casel, Dom, *Art und Sinn des aelteste Osterfier,* Jahr, L.t. Wiss., XIV, 1938
Casel, Dom, *Le bain nuptial de l'Eglise,* Dieu vivant, IV, p. 43-4
Cerfaux, *L'hymne au Christ serviteur de Dieu,* Miscellanea de Meyer, I, p. 176 ff.
Cerfaux, *La première communauté chrétienne à Jérusalem,* Eph. lov., 1939, p. 13 ff.
Chrysostom, *De resurrectione,* 3, P.G., L, 439 D
Chrysostom, *De sacerdotio* VI, 4
Chrysostom, *Ho. I Cor.*
Chrysostom, *Ho. Laz.* 6
Chrysostom, *Ho. Res.;* P.G., L, 441 A
Chrysostom, *In Ep. ad Hebr.,* IV, 8; P.G., LXIII, 55-58
Chrysostom, *On the Incomprehensible,* P.G., XLVIII, 707 B
Clement of Alexandria, *Eclog. proph.* 5-6
Clement of Alexandria, *Pedag.* II, 8
Clement of Alexandria, *Stromata,* VI, 16
Clement of Rome, St., *Epistles*
Connolly, R. B., *The De Sacramentis Work of S. Ambrosius,* Oxford, 1942
Conybeare, F. C., *Rituale Armenorum*
Coppens, Joseph, *Les Harmonies des deux Testaments*
Coppens, Joseph, *L'imposition des mains et les rites connexes,* Louvain, 1923
Correll, A., *Consummatum est,* Upsala, 1950
Courtonne, Y., *Saint Basile et l'hellénisme,* p. 35-6, Paris, Firmin-Didat, 1934
Crehan, S. H., *Early Christian Baptism and the Creed,* London, 1948
Cullman, Oscar, *Die Tauflehre der Neuen Testaments,* Zurich, Zwingli Verlag 1948
Cullman, Oscar, *Les premières confessions de foi chrétienne*
Cullman, Oscar, *La signification de la sainte Cène dâns le Christianisme primitif,* Rev. Hist. Phil., Rel. 1936, p. 1-22
Cullman, Oscar, *Ürchristentum und Gottesdienst,* second ed.
Cumont, Franz, *La fin du monde selon les mages occidentaux,* Rev. Hist., Rel., 1931, p. 55
Cumont, Franz, *Recherches sur le symbolisme funéraire chez les Anciens,* 1942
Cumont, Franz, *Le symbolisme funéraire chez les romains*
Cyprian, *Epist. LXIII,* 16; CSEL 714
Cyprian, *Epist. LXVIII,* 14; CSEL 763
Cyprian, *Epist. LXXIII*
Cyprian, *Tertiom.,* I, 12; CSEL 47
Cyprian, *Test.* I, 12; CSEL 47
Cyril of Alexandria, *The Detailed Study of the Pasch* (among his spuria), P.G., LXXVII, 1204 A-D
Cyril of Alexandria, *Glaphyres,* P.G., LXIX, 428 A

Cyril of Alexandria, *Ho. Pasch.*, XIX; P.G., LXXVII, 825 A
Cyril of Alexandria, *Ho. Pasch.*, 14; P.G., LXXVII, 712 B
Cyril of Jerusalem, *Mystagogic Catecheses,* P.G. XXXIII, Eng. trans.
Dabeck, P., *Siehe, es erschienen Moses und Elias,* Biblica, 1942
Dahl, N.-A., *La terre où coulent le lait et le miel,* Mélanges Goguel, 1950
Danielou, Jean, *L'incompréhensibilité de Dieu d'après saint Jean Chrysostome,* Rech. Sc. Relig. 1950, pp. 190-5
Danielou, Jean, *Le mystère de l'Avent*
Danielou, Jean, *Le mystére du culte dans les Homélies liturgiques de saint Grégoire de Nysse,* Festgabe Casel, (Vom christlichen Dusseldorf, Patmos Verlez) Mysterium 1951
Danielou, Jean, *Origen,* Sheed & Ward, 1955
Danielou, Jean, *Platonisme et théologie mystique,* Paris, Aulirer, 1944
Danielou, Jean, *The Problem of Symbolism,* Thought, 1950, p. 423 ff.
Danielou, Jean, *Les repas de la Bible et leur signification,* La Maison-Dieu, XVIII, p. 133
Danielou, Jean, *Sacramentum futuri,* Lex Orandi Series, Paris, 1950
Danielou, Jean, *Trois textes eschatologiques de saint Grégoire de Nysse,* Rech. Sc. Relig., 1940, p. 348 ff.
Danielou, Jean, *La typologie millénariste de la Semaine dans le christianisme primitif,* Vigiliae christianae, 1948, I, p. 1-16
de Bruyne, L., *La décoration des baptistères paléochrétiens,* Mel. Mohlberg, 1948
Deissmann, A., *Licht von Osten,* 1909
Delatte, A., *Études sur la littérature pythagoricienne,* 232-245
de Montcheuil, *La signification eschatologique du repas eucharistique,* R.S.R., 1936, p. 5 ff.
Denzinger, *Ritus Orientalium,* 1863
de Ghellinck, *Recherches sur le symbole des Apôtres,* Patristique et Moyen Age, I
Didymus the Blind, *De Trinitate;* P.G., *XXXIX,* 672 C
Dix, Gregory, *The Seal in the Second Century. Theology,* Jan. 1948
Dix, Gregory, *The Shape of the Liturgy,* Westminster, 1946
Doelger, F.-J., *Die achtzahl in der altchristlichen Symbolik,* Antike und Christentum, Munster/Westfalen Verl. Aschendorff
Doelger, F.-J., *Der Durchzug durch das Rote Meer als Sinnbild des Christlichen Taufe,* Ant. und Christ., 1930, pp. 63-9
Doelger, F.-J., *Der Exorcismus im altchristlichen Taufritual,* Paderborn, 1909
Doelger, F.-J., *Die Heiligkeit des Altars und ihre Begrundung,* Ant. Christ. II, 3
Doelger, F.-J., *Das Martyrium als Kampf die Daemonen,* Ant. und Christ. III
Doelger, F.-J., *Die Sonne der Gerechtigkeit und die Schwarze,* Munster, 1919
Doelger, F.-J., *Sphragis,* Paderborn, 1911
Doelger, F.-J., *Zur Symbolik des altchristlichen Taufhauses,* Ant. und Christ. IV
Dondeyne, A., *La discipline des scrutins,* Rev. Hist. Eccl. 1932, p. 20-1
Dondeyne, A., *La discipline des scrutins dans l'Église latine avant Charlemagne,* Rev. Hist. Eccl. 1932
Dupont-Sommer, A., *La doctrine gnostique de la lettre Waw*
Dubarle, A.-M., *Pascal et l'interprétation de l'Écriture,* R.S.P.T., 1941, p. 346 ff.
Edsman, C.-M., *Le baptême de feu*

Ehade, M., *Histoire des religions*
Engrell, *Studies in Divine Kingship*
Etheriae, *Peregrinatio*, trans. by Pétré, Sources Chretiennes
Études sur une série de discours d'un évêque de Naples au VIe siecle, Rev., Bened. 1894, p. 385 ff.
Eusebius of Caesarea, *Dem. Ev. IV*, 15; P.G., XXII, 289 D
Eusebius of Caesarea, *De Pascha;* P.G., XXIII, 697 A
Eusebius of Caesarea, *Prep. Ev.*, XIII, 12, pp. 9-12
Eusebius of Caesarea, *Vit. Const.*, IV, 18; P.G., XX, 1165, B-C
Eusebius of Emesa, *On Sunday*, P.G., LXXXVI, 1413 ff.
Faller, O., *Ambrosius, der Verfasser von de Sacramentis*, Z.K.T. 1940
Feret, P., *La messe et sa catéchèse*
Festugiere, A. S., *Le monde gréco-romain au temps de Notre Seigneur*
Feuillet, A., *Le messianisme du Livre d'Isaie*, Rech. Sc. Rel., 1949
Feuillet, A., *Les ouvriers de la vigne et la théologie de l'alliance*, Rech. Sc. Rel. 1947, p. 320 ff.
Fischer, Balthasar, *Die Psalmen froemmigkeit der Martyrkirche*, Frieburg, 1949
Flemington, W. F., *The New Testament Doctrine of Baptism*, London, 1948
Foote-Moore, G., *Judaism*
Gaudemet, Jean, *La législation religieuse de Constantin*, Rev. Hist. Egl. Fr., XXXIII, janvier 1947, pp. 43 ff.
Gaudentius of Brescia, *Sermo 2;* P.L. XX, 855 B
Geschwind, *Die Niederfahrt Christi in der Unterwelt*
Grebaut, *Sacramentaire éthiopien*
Gregory of Elvira, *Tractatus*, ed. Batiffol
Gregory of Nazianzen, *In Pent.*, 3; P.G. XXXVI, 432 A
Gregory of Nyssa, *De Cain et Abel*, I, 20-21; CSEL, 356-357
Gregory of Nyssa, *Ho. Bapt.*
Gregory of Nyssa, *Sermon against those who put off their Baptism*, P.G. XLVI, 417 B
Guillet, *Thêmes bibliques*, 1951, pp. 22-25
Gunkel, *Einleitung in die Psalmen*, 1928
Gunkel, *Schöpfung und Chaos*
Harris, Rendel, *Testimonies*
Hebert, A. G., *The Authority of the Old Testament*
Hebert, A. G., *The Throne of David*
Herkenne, *Das Buch der Psalmen*
Hilary, *In Psalm. CXXXVI;* P.L. IX, 780 B
Hippolytus, *Co. Dan.* IV, 23-24
Hippolytus, *Sermo in Theophania*, (Achelis, p. 261)
Hippolytus, *Traditio Apostolica*, trans. Bernard Botte, Sources chretiennes
Holstein, H., *La tradition des Apôtres chez saint Irénée*, Rech. Sc. Rel., 1949, p. 248
Holzmeister, A., *Jesus lebte mit den wilden tieren, vom Wort des Lebens*, Festschrift Meinertz, 1951
Hoskyns, E. C., *The Fourth Gospel*, London, Faher & Faher, 1947
Humbert, Paul, *Emplois et portée du verbe bara dans l'Ancien Testament*, Theol. Zeitschr. Nov. 1947
Ignatius of Antioch, *Magne.*, IX, 1
Irenaeus, *Adv. Haer.*, IV, 17 and 18; P.G. 1025 A

Justin, *Dial.* XXIV, 1; CXI, 13
Justin, *Dial. XXVIII, 5; XXIX, I; XLI, 2; CXVI, 3*
Jungmann, J. A., *Missarum solemnia,* Wien, Herder, 1948/9
Kelly, J. N. D., *Early Christian Creeds,* London-New York, Longmans, Green, 1950
Koch, Hugo, *Psuedo-Dionysios in seinen Beziehungen zum Neuplatonismus und Mysterien weisen,* Mainz, 1900
Kruse, H., *Da partem septem necnon et octo,* Verbum Domini, 1949, p. 164-9
Lactantius, *Div. Inst.* IV, 26; P.L. VI, 531
Leenhardt, F. J., *Le sacrement de la Sainte Cène*
Leeuyer, J., *Le sacerdoce chrétien et le sacrifice eucharistique selon Théodore de Mopsuestia,* Rech. Sc. Rel., 1949
Leo the Great, St., *Homilies on the liturgical year,* text and trans. Dom Dolle, Sources chretiennes, 1949
Lewy, Hans, *Sobria ebrietas*
Lods, A., *Israel des origines aux Prophètes*
Lohmeyer, *Vom urchristlichen Abendmahl,* Theologische Rundschau, 1937
Lohmeyer, *Von Gottlichen Wohlgeruch,* 1919
Lot-Borodine, Mme., *La grace déifiante des sacrements d'après Nicolas Cabasilas, Rev. Sc. Theol.* 1937, p. 698
Lundberg, Per, *La typologie baptismale dans l'Ancienne Église,* Lund, 1941
Manson, T. W., ΙΛΑΣΤΗΡΙΟΝ J.T.S. 1945, p. 20 ff.
Marmorstein, A., *Quelques problèmes d'anciènne apol. juive,* Rev. Et. Jui., 1914, p. 161
Marrou, H.-I., *Saint Augustin et la fin de la culture antique,* Paris, E. de Boccard, 1938
Martin, Ch., *Hippolyte de Rome et Proclus de Constantinople,* Rev. Hist., Eccl., 1937, p. 263
Martin, Charles, *Un peri tou Pascha de St. Hippolyte retrouvé,* Rech. Sc. Rel., 1926
The Meaning of Time in the Ancient World, New Scholasticism, Jan. 1947, p. 1 ff.
Melito of Sardis, *Homily on the Passion, the,* ed. Campbell Bonner, 1940
Méridier, L., *L'influence de la Seconde Sophistique sur l'oeuvre de saint Gregoire de Nysse,* p. 139 ff.
Mollat, D., *Jugement dans le Nouveau Testament,* S.D.B., IV (1949) col. 1350-4
Morgenstein, J., *The Despoiling of the Egyptians,* Journ. Bibl. Litt., 1949, 25-6
Morin, G., *Pour l'authenticité du De sacramentis et le l'explanatio fidei de saint Ambroise,* Jahr. Lit. Wiss. VIII, 1928
Mowinckel, *Psalmen studien*
Oesterley, W. O. E., *The Jewish Background of the Christian Liturgy*
Oppenheim, P., *Symbolik und religiose Wertung des Monchskleides im Christ. Altertum,* Munster, 1932
Origen, *Co. Cant.,* 2; P.G., XIII, 121 B
Origen, *Co. Matt. XV, 32*
Origen, *Co. Rom.,* P.G. XIV, 900
Origen, *Ho. Jos.* VI, 4-6
Origen, *Ho. Jud.* IV, 2

Origen, *Ho. Lev.* XIII, 5
Origen, *In Johannem,* VI, 48
Passion of Ss. Perpetua and Felicity, trans. W. H. Shewring, Sheed & Ward, 1931
Peterson, Erik, *La croce e la preghiera verso l'oriente,* Eph. liturgicae, LIX (1945) p. 52 ff.
Peterson, Erik, *Christianos,* Miscell. Mercati. I
Peterson, Erik, *Die geschichtliche Bedeutung der judischen Gebetsrichtung,* Theol. Zeitsch. 1947
Peterson Erik, *Pour un théologie du vêtement,* Lym, 1943
Peterson, Erik, *Religion et vêtement, Rhythmes du monde,* 1946
Peterson, Erik, *Theologische Traktate*
Philo, *De dec.,* 106
Philo, *De opif.*
Philolaos ap. Lydus, *De mensibus,* II, 12
Pira, Fr., *Dénys le Mystique et la theomachia,* R.S.P.T. 1936
Plumpe, *Mater Ecclesia,* Wash. Cath. Univ. of Am. Press 1943
Pedechard, M., *Le Psautier,* 1, 1949
Pseudo-Cyprian, *Ad Novatianum,* C.S.E.L. 55, 22-27
Pseudo-Dionysius, *The Ecclesiastical Hierarchy,* P.G. I, 585 A-1120 A; French trans. and int. Maurice de Gandillac, Paris, 1943
Puech, H. Ch., *La symbolique du cerf et du serpent,* Cahiers Archéologiques IV, 1949
Quasten, J., *Das Bild des Guten Hirten in den altchristlichen Baptisterien,* Pisciculi, 1939, pp. 220-244
Quasten, J., *Der Gute Hirte in fruhchristlicher Totenliturgie und Grabenkunst,* Misc. Mercati, 1, p. 373 ff.
Quasten, J., *Sobria ebrietas in Ambrosius De Sacramentis,* Mel. Mohlberg
Quasten, J., *Théodore of Mopsuestia on the exorcism of cilicium,* Harvard Theological Review, 1942
Quodvultdeus, *De symbolo ad Catech.,* P.L. XL, 637
Rahner, Hugo, *Griechische Mythen in Christlicher Deutung,* pp. 141-9, Zurich, Rheim-Verlag, 1945
Rahner, Hugo, *Mysterium lunae,* Zeitsch. Kath. Theol., 1939
Rahner, Hugo, *Pompa diaboli,* Zeitsch. Kath. Theol., 1931
Rahner, Karl, *Esquisse d'une doctrine des sens spirituels chez Origène,* R.A.M., 1932
Rahner, Karl, *Flumina de Ventre Christi,* Biblica, 1941
Reicke, Bo, *The Disobedient Spirits and Christian Baptism,* Lund, 1948
Reine, Francis J., *The Eucharistic Doctrine and Liturgy of the Mystical Catecheses of T. of U.,* Washington, 1942
Reitzenstein, *Die Vorgeschichte der Christlichen Taufe*
Reisenfeld, Harald, *Jésus transfiguré*
Reisenfeld, Harald, *The Resurrection in Ezechiel XXXVII and in the Dura-Europos paintings*
Reisenfeld, Harald, *La signification sacramentaire du baptême johannique,* Dieu vivant, XIII, p. 31 ff.
Robert, A., *Les attaches littéraires de Prov. I-IX,* Rev. Bibl., 1934, p. 374 ff.
Robert, A., *Le genre littéraire du Cantique des Cantiques,* Vivre et penser, (Rev. Bibl.), III, 1944, p. 192 ff.

Rowley, H. H., *The Relevance of Apocalyptic,* p. 95, London, Lutterworth Press, 2 ed. 1944
Rusch, A., *Death and Burial in Christian Antiquity,* C.V. Press, Washington, 1941
Sagnard, F.-M., *La gnose valentinienne et le témoignage de saint Irenée*
Sahlis, Harald, *Zur typologie des Johannes évangeliums,* Upsala, 1950
Schmidt, Carl, *Gespraeche Jesu mit seinen Jüngern,* p. 279
Schnackenburg, Rudolf, *Das Heilsgeschen bei der Taufe nach dem Apostel Paulus,* Munich, 1950
Schoeps, J.-H., *Theologie und Geschichte des Judenchristentums*
Schuerer, *Die siebentaetige Woche in Gebrauche der christlichen Kirche der ersten Jahr.,* Zeit. Neu. Test. Wiss., 1905
Selwyn, E. G., *The First Epistle of Saint Peter*
Steinmann, J., *L'Exode dans l'Ancien Testament,* La vie spirituelle, Mar. 1951 p. 240
Stiglmayr, Fr., *Der sogennante D. Areopagiticus und Severus von Antiochen,* Scholastik, 1928
Strack-Bitterbeck, II, 774-812
Swaans, W. J., *Á propos des Catechèses mystagogiques attribués a saint Cyrille de Jerusalem,* Museon, 1942
Tertullian, *Adv. jud.,* 5
Tertullian, *De Anima,* ed. J. H. Waszink
Tertulliam, *Apol.* XLII, 2-4
Tertullian, *De baptismo*
Tertullian, *De Corona*
Tertullian, *De orig.,* 23
Tertullian, *De Spectaculis*
Theodore of Mopsuestia, *Commentary of T. of U. on the Sacraments of Baptism and the Eucharist,* trans. A. Mingana, Woodbrooke Studies VI, Cambridge, 1933; *Les Homélies catechétique de T. de U.,* Syrian text, trans. P. Tonneau, int. Msgr. Devreese, Cité du Vatican, 1949
Theodoret, *Quaest. Ex. XII,* P.G. LXXX, 252 D
Theophilus of Antioch, *Ad Autolycum,* Ante-Nicene Christian Lit., V, 3; Edinburgh, Clark 1880 or Sources Chrétiennes, no. 20
Urs von Balthasar, *Présence et pensée,* Paris, Beauchesne et fils, 1942
Van Imschoot, *Baptême de feu et baptême d'eau, Ephemerides Lov.,* 1936 pp. 653 ff.
Vincent, Abel, *Jérusalem, Recherches de topographie, d'archéologie et d'histoire*
Vischer, W., *Les livres de Moise,* fr. trans.
Vitti, A. M., *L'Ascensione nella littera agli Ebrei,* S. Paolo, Rome, 1936
Volz, *Das Neujahrfest Iahweh*
von Ivanka, E., *Vom Platonismus zur Theorie der Mystik,* Scholastik, 1936, p. 185 ff.
Vorwahl, H., Ευωσία Χριστοῦ, Archiv. f. Relig. Wiss. 1934
Waszink, J. H., *Pompa Diaboli,* Vigiliae christianee, 1947
Waszink, J. H., *Tertullien, De anima*
Waszink, J. H., *Tertullians eschatologische Deutung der Siebenzahl,* Pisciculi, p. 276 ff.
Widengren, George, *The Ascension of the Apostle and the Heavenly Book,* Upsala, 1950

Winzen, Dom Damasus, *Pathways in Holy Scripture*, 1952, Mount Saviour Monastery, Elmira, N.Y.
Ziegler, J., *Dulcedo Dei*, 1937
Zielinski, B., *De transfigurationis sensu*, Verbum Domini, 1948, p. 38

Index

CPSIA information can be obtained
at www.ICGtesting.com
Printed in the USA
LVHW031834171219
640781LV00002B/103/P